nd Parsonage

The Early Writings of
Charlotte Brontë

DRAWN BY
CHARLOTTE BRONTË

1 *Pencil drawing reminiscent of Charlotte Brontë's description of her favourite early heroine Mary Henrietta Percy*

The Early Writings of Charlotte Brontë

Christine Alexander

Prometheus Books

700 East Amherst St. Buffalo, New York 14215

Published 1983 by Prometheus Books
700 E. Amherst Street, Buffalo, New York 14215
Printed in the United States of America

©Christine Anne Alexander 1983
First published 1983
Basil Blackwell Publisher Limited
108 Crowley Road, Oxford OX4 1JF, England

ISBN: 0-87975-226-2
Library of Congress Catalogue Card No.: 83-62190

Contents

List of Illustrations		vii
Acknowledgements		x
Abbreviations		xiii
Introduction		1

PART I
The Glass Town Saga *(1826—1831)*

1	Childhood Influences	11
2	The Young Men's Play	27
3	The Young Men's Magazine	36
4	Our Fellows' Play	40
5	The Islanders' Play	42
6	The Fusion of the Plays	53
7	The Great Glass Town	57
8	The Young Author	62
9	Glass Town Eclipsed	71

PART II
Romance and the Rise of Angria *(1832—1835)*

10	Sunlight on Africa Again	79
11	Something about Arthur	87
12	A New Albion	91
13	Alexander Percy	97
14	Arthuriana	103
15	Mary Percy	111
16	High Life in Verdopolis	115
17	Angria Arise!	122
18	Political Rivalry	131

PART III
The Angrian Legend (*1836—1839)*

19 The 'Roe Head Journal'   139
20 War-torn Angria   146
21 Charlotte Restores Peace   156
22 Mina Laury   165
23 High Life in Angria   169
24 William Percy and Elizabeth Hastings   180
25 Farewell to Angria   192

PART IV
The Juvenilia and the Later Writings

26 Ashworth and Angria   203
27 Branwell's Influence   210
28 The Search after Love   213
29 Two Rival Brothers   219
30 The Authorial Voice   225
31 A Visual Imagination   234
    Conclusion   244

Appendix A   A List of Other Principal Characters in the
               Juvenilia   247
Appendix B   A Chronological List of Charlotte Brontë's Early
               Prose Manuscripts   250

Notes   258
Select Bibliography   298
Index   305

Illustrations

The endpapers show Haworth Church and Parsonage.
By courtesy N. K. Howarth, Keighley.

1   Pencil drawing reminiscent of Charlotte Brontë's   frontispiece
    description of her favourite early heroine Mary
    Henrietta Percy.
    Diagram of the relationships between the principal
    characters in the juvenilia.   7
2   Charlotte Brontë's earliest extant manuscript, written
    for her youngest sister Anne, c. 1826 — 1828.   12
3   One of Charlotte Brontë's many early drawings for her
    sister Anne, 2 September 1828.   13
4   The Reverend Patrick Brontë, 1809.   14
5   Title page to *The Cottage In The Wood,* by the
    Reverend Patrick Brontë.   15
6   Haworth Parsonage in the time of the Brontës.   16
7   The final page and inside back cover of Branwell
    Brontë's copy of *The Works of Virgil,* by John Dryden.   23
8   Map of the Glass Town Confederacy, drawn by Branwell
    Brontë as a frontispiece to *The History Of The Young
    Men,* December 1830—May 1831. By permission
    of the British Library.   33
9   'The origin of the Islanders', 12 March 1829. A rare
    example of Charlotte Brontë's early cursive writing. By
    courtesy of the Berg Collection, New York Public
    Library.   44
10 The final page of *Tales of the Islanders,* Volume IV, 30
    July 1830, written in the typical miniature script of
    Charlotte Brontë's earliest manuscripts. By courtesy of
    the Berg Collection, New York Public Library.   45

11   Arthur Wellesley, Marquis of Douro and Duke of
      Zamorna. Undated pencil drawing attributed to
      Charlotte Brontë.   60
12   Miss Wooler's school at Roe Head, drawn by Charlotte
      Brontë.   73
13   'English Lady', pencil drawing by Charlotte Brontë after
      W. Finden's engraving of the Countess of Jersey, 15
      October 1834, suggestive of Marian Hume.   82
14   The 'Gun' portrait of Branwell Brontë and his sisters
      Emily, Charlotte and Anne, painted by Branwell
      c. 1833.   84
15   The Great Bay of Glass Town. Watercolour by
      Charlotte Brontë after John Martin.   94
16   Title page and Preface to *The Green Dwarf*, 2
      September 1833, typical of the size and script of
      Charlotte Brontë's manuscripts during the years
      1832—1835. By courtesy of the Humanities Research
      Center, University of Texas at Austin.   98
17   Watercolour by Charlotte Brontë reminiscent of scenes
      in the early juvenilia, 6 July 1833.   99
18   Alexander Percy, later Lord Ellrington and Duke of
      Northangerland. Pen and ink sketch by Branwell
      Brontë in Mary Pearson's commonplace book, 1846. By
      courtesy of the Humanities Research Center, University
      of Texas at Austin   100
19   Watercolour portrait by Charlotte Brontë, 14 August
      1833, suggestive of Lily Hart.   109
20   Charlotte Brontë's copy of W. Finden's engraving
      'Geneva', 23 August 1834, evocative of the Angrian
      landscape in the province of Zamorna.   126
21   The Duke of Zamorna. Pen and ink drawing by
      Branwell Brontë, 1835.   152
22   Alexander Percy at the death-bed of his daughter Mary.
      Watercolour attributed to Charlotte Brontë.   154
23   Watercolour by Charlotte Brontë after W. Finden's
      engraving of 'The Maid of Saragoza', representing Mina
      Laury.   168
24   The first page of Charlotte Brontë's unpublished
      manuscript known as *Stancliffe's Hotel*, 28 June 1838,
      typical of her later juvenile manuscripts.   172
25   'Sonnet' and pen and ink profile of Northangerland by
      Branwell Brontë, written in a commonplace book
      belonging to Mary Pearson, 'at Ovenden Cross in the

Autumn of 1846'. By courtesy of the Humanities
Research Center, University of Texas at Austin. 194
26 'The Cross of Rivaulx' by Charlotte Brontë after Gilpin,
23 December 1834. 235
27 Manuscript page of an early draft of Charlotte Brontë's
poem 'The moon dawned slow in the dusky gloaming',
January 1834. 236
28 The Duchess of Zamorna at Alnwick. Pencil drawing by
Charlotte Brontë, *c.*1836. 239

All illustrations are reproduced by courtesy of the Brontë Society, unless otherwise stated.

Acknowledgements

Since nearly a third of Charlotte Brontë's manuscripts remain unpublished and many of the remainder have appeared only in unreadable facsimiles, it was necessary to transcribe the unpublished manuscripts in order to provide myself with a text from which to work. Because of the minuscule script she used throughout her juvenile writings, it proved impossible to rely on photographic copies of the manuscripts for an accurate transcription: a full stop in a microfilm, for example, would often prove to be a speck of dust. It was therefore necessary to work on the original manuscripts, which are distributed almost equally between Britain and the USA. What was frequently a tedious and lonely task was at all times made bearable by the courtesy and assistance of the staff of the various libraries where I worked.

This is especially true of the Brontë Parsonage Museum where for four years my frequent visits were welcomed with the warmest hospitality. In particular I should like to thank the following people who made my research at Haworth so enjoyable and rewarding: Mr N. Raistrick, former curator; Miss Amy Foster, former archivist; Miss S. Stonehouse, present librarian; and Mr W. T. Oliver and Mrs E. M. Wier for their encouragement of my American research. Mr Donald Hopewell, Mr Charles Lemon, Mr Albert H. Preston and Mr Mark R. D. Seaward also kindly helped me at various times. To the members of the Brontë Society Council all Brontë researchers owe a great debt, and I should like to express my sincere gratitude and respect for their careful preservation of Brontë manuscripts and their unfailing willingness to assist Brontë scholarship.

My thanks are due to the following institutions and in particular to those staff members mentioned in brackets, who courteously assisted me while I was working on the original manuscripts and who have patiently answered my queries over the last eight years: the British Library (Miss L. Graham and Mr T. A. J. Burnett); The Brotherton Library (Mr David I. Masson and Mr C. D. W. Sheppard); the Ellis Library, University of Missouri-Columbia; Harvard College Library (Dr W. H. Bond and Miss Martha Eliza Shaw); the Humanities Research Center, University of Texas at Austin (Mr David Farmer and Mrs Ellen S. Dunlap); the Huntington Library (Miss Jean F. Preston, Mrs Virginia Rust, Mr William Ingoldsby and Miss Sara S. Hodson); The King's School, Canterbury (Mr D. S. Goodes); the Manchester Public Libraries; the Newberry Library; New York Public Library (Mrs Lola L. Szladits and Mr David Pankow); the Carl H. Pforzheimer Library (Mr Mihai H. Handrea); the Pierpont Morgan Library (Mr Herbert Cahoon, Mrs George H. Semler, Jr, and Mr Verlyn Klinkenborg); Princeton University Library (Mr Alexander P. Clark, Mr Alexander Wainwright and Mrs Nancy N. Coffin); Rutgers University Library; the John Rylands University Library of Manchester (Miss Glenise A. Matheson); the Library of the State University of New York at Buffalo; The Victoria and Albert Museum; Wellesley College Library (Miss Eleanor L. Nicholes); and Yale University Library (Miss Marjorie G. Wynne). Tribute is also due to the staff of the Cambridge University Library and of the Social Sciences and Humanities Library of the University of New South Wales for their assistance in tracing secondary material.

The following private collectors have generously given me photocopies and detailed descriptions of manuscripts in their possession: Mr Roger W. Barrett, Mr Arthur A. Houghton, Jr, Mr William Self, Mr James W. Symington, and Mr Robert H. Taylor.

Others who have provided information and assistance include Professor T. V. Buttrey, Professor Mildred G. Christian, Dr Enid L. Duthie, Mr John F. Fleming, Mr Joseph R. Geer, Mrs Winifred Gérin, Mrs Hazel Hedge, Mr and Mrs J. M. A. Hickson, Mr and Mrs D. Hindmarsh, Mr William Holtz, Dr Melodie Monahan, Professor Herbert Rosengarten, Mr Richard R. Seidel, Mr George Watson, and Dr Tom Winnifrith. I would like to thank the Master of Adams House, Harvard University, for accommodation in his college and Miss Gail Boose for arranging this. I am especially grateful for the generous hospitality of my friends Dr Kate Frost of the University of Texas at Austin and Mr and Mrs S. Edwards of Canaby House, Haworth.

I wish to thank the family of the late Mr C. K. Shorter for permission to quote from the unpublished juvenile manuscripts of Charlotte and Patrick Branwell Brontë. I am grateful to the libraries listed above for permission to quote from manuscripts in their possession, and to the Brontë Society in particular for allowing me to reproduce so many of their drawings and paintings. I would also like to acknowledge the industry of a previous scholar of the Brontë juvenilia, Mr C. W. Hatfield, whose transcriptions of many manuscripts since lost are invaluable to Brontë research.

For my knowledge of Charlotte Brontë's published juvenile works I have relied on the Shakespeare Head editions of *The Poems of Charlotte Brontë and Patrick Branwell Brontë* and the *Miscellaneous and Unpublished Writings of Charlotte and Patrick Branwell Brontë*. This study would have been severely handicapped without them, despite the inaccuracies in their transcriptions. I am grateful to Basil Blackwell for permission to quote from these editions which in several cases preserve the only record we have of manuscripts now lost. I would also like to thank the Folio Press for permission to quote from *Five Novelettes* edited by Winifred Gérin, and the Yale University Press for permission to quote from *Legends of Angria* edited by Fannie E. Ratchford and William Clyde DeVane.

A New Zealand Postgraduate Scholarship and a New Zealand University Women's Fellowship gave me the opportunity to carry out the initial research for this book and to write the first draft. I have been greatly helped in the gathering of material by generous financial help from The Brontë Society; Clare Hall, Cambridge; and the Sir Ernest Cassel Trust. A grant from the University of New South Wales helped with the cost of typing the final manuscript.

I would like to acknowledge the early encouragement of two New Zealand colleagues, Professor J.C. Garrett and Professor Roger Robinson, who helped me at a time when I needed direction. My college, Clare Hall, has always been a loyal supporter of my work, and in particular Mrs Leslie Barnett provided unfailing encouragement. Dr Philip Gaskell of Trinity College, Cambridge, willingly assisted me in bibliographical matters.

I am especially grateful to Professor Ian Jack of Pembroke College, Cambridge, for his constant advice and enthusiasm for my work on the Brontë juvenilia. Without his valuable guidance this study would never have been attempted.

I owe a special debt of gratitude to my parents for their years of encouragement and support. Finally, unquestionably my greatest debt is to my husband, who has provided unfailing help at all times.

Abbreviations

B	Brotherton Library: Brotherton Collection
BL	British Library
BPM	Brontë Parsonage Museum
BST	*Brontë Society Transactions,* 1895–1982. References are keyed to the date and number of the volume, followed by the number of the part and then the page number.
HCL	Harvard College Library
HL	Huntington Library
HRC	Humanities Research Center, University of Texas at Austin
NYPL	New York Public Library: Berg Collection
PML	Pierpont Morgan Library
PMLA	Publications of the Modern Languages Association of America
PUL	Princeton University Library
SHCBM	*The Miscellaneous and Unpublished Writings of Charlotte and Patrick Branwell Brontë* (The Shakespeare Head Brontë), ed. Thomas James Wise and John Alexander Symington, 2 vols., 1936 and 1938
SHCBP	*The Poems of Charlotte Brontë and Patrick Branwell Brontë* (The Shakespeare Head Brontë), ed. Thomas James Wise and John Alexander Symington, 1934
SHLL	*The Brontës: Their Lives, Friendships and Correspondence* (The Shakespeare Head Brontë), ed. Thomas James Wise and John Alexander Symington, 4 vols., 1932
SUNY	University Libraries, State University of New York at Buffalo

All references to the novels of the Brontës are keyed to The Shakespeare Head Brontë, except for *Jane Eyre, Shirley* and *Wuthering Heights,* where the new Clarendon Edition is used.

To Peter

Introduction

Charlotte Brontë wrote in her preface to *The Professor*: 'A first attempt it certainly was not, as the pen which wrote it had been previously worn a good deal in a practice of some years.' Her novels stand at the end of a long apprenticeship. Through a close study of her juvenile manuscripts, it is possible to follow the course of Charlotte's early work and to relate it to her later development as a writer. In her case, the meaning of the term 'juvenile' must be extended: until the age of twenty-three she wrote stories and poems about the imaginary African kingdom which she and her brothers and sisters had created.

The Brontë juvenilia began as the result of childhood play, woven around a set of twelve wooden toy soldiers given to Charlotte's younger brother Branwell on 5 June 1826. Three years later the children began writing miniature books for the toy soldiers. Gradually the plays took on an exclusively literary nature as the children chronicled the events and stories of their imaginary characters. Little evidence survives of the roles which Emily and Anne played in this early imaginary world; after 1831 they withdrew to form their own legend of Gondal. But for another eight years Charlotte and Branwell continued to write their 'Glass Town Saga', which later came to concentrate on the imaginary kingdom of 'Angria'.

It is important to have a clear idea of the development of the saga, since its immense complexity of detail can be overwhelming. Because stories and poems were not always conceived in chronological order, some manuscripts describe the past of certain characters while others concentrate on the fictional present, and one manuscript, 'A Leaf from an Unopened Volume', looks forward to the destruction of Angria. This book follows the development of the juvenilia as the manuscripts were

composed. The writings fall naturally into three periods, divided by the
years when Charlotte went to boarding school at Roe Head; she wrote
very little when she was away from the security and companionship of her
home. The following diagram plots the basic outline of the juvenilia:

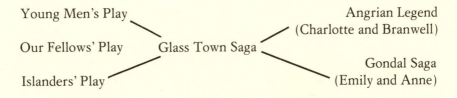

Young Men's Play   Angrian Legend
                                                        (Charlotte and Branwell)
Our Fellows' Play   Glass Town Saga
                                                               Gondal Saga
Islanders' Play   (Emily and Anne)

Charlotte and Branwell developed an elaborate world of aristocratic
intrigue based on the rival factions of their favourite characters: the Duke
of Wellington and Alexander Percy. Charlotte gradually replaced the
Duke by his sons — the eldest (Arthur, Marquis of Douro) became the
fascinatingly wicked Byronic hero the Duke of Zamorna and King of
Angria; and the younger, Lord Charles Wellesley, Charlotte's early *nom
de plume,* degenerated into little more than a mouthpiece, becoming the
cynical narrator Charles Townshend.

The central drama of Angria turns upon the Duke of Zamorna and his
ambivalent relationship with Alexander Percy, who gains the titles first of
Lord Ellrington and then Duke of Northangerland. Zamorna (after various
affaires and several wives) marries Percy's daughter Mary and when he
becomes King of Angria he appoints Percy as his prime minister. But
Percy's evil nature is stronger than his loyalty to his son-in-law; Percy
raises rebellion and the only way to punish him is to hurt his beloved
daughter Mary. But Mary is Zamorna's beloved wife, so by deserting her
and punishing Percy, Zamorna is also punishing himself. And Mary is
caught between the two men she loves.

This is the situation which fascinated Charlotte. While Branwell directed
a background of wars, parliamentary debates and business deals, Charlotte
became the purveyor of bedroom dramas. Influenced more and more by
Byron and especially by the newspaper gossip of his *affaires,* she became
intimately involved in the predicament of her heroines and their fascination
for her hero Zamorna.

As the plot grew in complexity, characters proliferated. Political rivalries
and illicit love affairs added to the confusing relationships between
characters. Even Charlotte and Branwell themselves occasionally
confounded the identities of their minor characters. A diagram of the
relationships between the principal characters has been provided at the
end of this Introduction to help the reader find his or her way through the

web of imaginary characters, and a supplementary list of other principal characters can be found in Appendix A.

To understand why there is no previous study of Charlotte Brontë's juvenilia based on knowledge of all her existing works, we must bear in mind the nature and history of the early manuscripts. In quantity, they amount to more than all her later novels, yet only half of them have been published. Their tiny size and Charlotte's minuscule script make transcription extremely slow and difficult. The aid of a magnifying glass, and occasionally a microscope, is necessary to decipher the earliest manuscripts which were little bigger than postage stamps, written to match the size of the children's toy soldiers. Gradually these tiny, hand-sewn booklets gave way to the quarto pages of an increasingly self-conscious narrator; but still Charlotte's script remained microscopic.

The first reference to this early writing was made by Mrs Gaskell in a letter to George Smith (Charlotte's publisher) on 25 July 1856. Mrs Gaskell had just made a visit to the Rev. Patrick Brontë in Haworth to collect material for her biography of Charlotte Brontë, who had died the previous year. Although it was Patrick Brontë who had asked her to undertake the biography, Mrs Gaskell had never felt easy with him. Her nervousness was increased by the reticence and the unhelpful attitude of the Rev. Arthur Bell Nicholls, who had inherited almost all the manuscripts, and who, understandably enough, had no wish to expose his painfully brief married life to the world. Had it not been for Sir James Kay-Shuttleworth, the philanthropist and would-be friend of Charlotte, who unexpectedly accompanied Mrs Gaskell on her visit to Haworth Parsonage, we might not have known so much about the juvenilia. She tells how he 'coolly took actual possession of many things while Mr Nicholls was saying he could not possibly part with them'. Mrs Gaskell, somewhat embarrassed, 'came away with the "Professor", the beginning of her new tale "Emma" — about 10 pages written in the finest pencil writing, — & by far the most extraordinary of all, a packet about the size of a lady's travelling writing case, full of paper books of different sizes . . . all in this indescribably fine writing'.[1]

Before Mrs Gaskell returned these 'quantities of fragments', as she called them, to Mr Nicholls, she had had to rewrite about forty pages of the biography. In chapter 5 of *The Life of Charlotte Brontë* (I, 88) she explains:

> I have had a curious packet confided to me, containing an immense amount of manuscript, in an inconceivably small space; tales, dramas, poems, romances, written principally by Charlotte, in a hand which it is almost impossible to decipher without the aid of a magnifying glass.

Although she was not able to read all the manuscripts and so was unaware of their interconnection and their significance in relation to Charlotte's later novels, Mrs Gaskell was certainly the first to recognize Charlotte's juvenilia as evidence of her literary apprenticeship.

We hear no more of the juvenilia until March 1895, when Clement Shorter visited Mr Nicholls at his home in Banagher, Ireland. Mr Nicholls had returned to Ireland after Mr Brontë's death, taking with him the parcel of early manuscripts lent to Mrs Gaskell. There they had lain 'in the bottom of a cupboard tied up in a newspaper' for nearly thirty years.[2] Shorter purchased this parcel, with many other manuscripts, for Thomas James Wise and took them to England.

Their subsequent fate is well known. Many of the manuscripts were published privately — heavily abridged and inaccurately transcribed — in expensive limited editions. Wise compiled a bibliography of his collection, and he regrouped the manuscripts and had them handsomely bound in red, green and blue morocco. Then, after retaining some for his own library, he disposed of the rest in private sales amongst collectors and friends. Pages of stories were detached and lost. Some manuscripts found their way abroad and became widely dispersed: for example, one fragment written by Charlotte in 1832 and now in the Brontë Parsonage in Haworth, was originally part of a manuscript which is in the Pierpont Morgan Library in New York.[3]

Biographers and editors of Charlotte Brontë's novels have had to rely for information about her juvenilia on the valuable pioneering work of Fannie Elizabeth Ratchford whose book *The Brontës' Web of Childhood* was written in 1941. It has been described as the 'best available conspectus'.[4] Unfortunately Fannie Ratchford's work is based on only a small fraction of the manuscripts we now know to exist; many of her references are inaccurate and, in her fervour to stress the importance of the early writings, her claims for their influence on Charlotte's novels are extravagant. She maintains, for example, that after the age of twenty-three Charlotte 'created nothing', that she merely reshaped her early imaginative world to conform with her adult experiences. Although my disagreement with such statements is implicit in the following pages, her work remains a landmark in Brontë studies, to which I am deeply indebted.

More recent work has been done on the juvenilia by Winifred Gérin in her search for new biographical information about the Brontës; but she too relies heavily on Fannie Ratchford's work. In her book, *Charlotte Brontë: The Evolution of Genius,* several references to the early manuscripts are inaccurate, many statements cannot be checked and, on one occasion, she reproduces an incorrect transcription by Mrs Gaskell instead of consulting the original manuscript.[5] I have been guided, however, by Winifred Gérin's many valuable references to sources in the juvenilia and her handsome edition, *Five Novelettes,* has been of constant use.

Apart from the work of these two scholars little consideration has been given to the juvenilia. The attention they have received has been hampered by inadequate knowledge of original material, by reliance on inaccurate and fragmented publication, and by a tendency to study individual stories in isolation. Claims for a direct relationship between Charlotte's early and later writings have been largely speculative. It has been claimed that the juvenilia are evidence of the evolution of a writer but no detailed work has been done to substantiate this claim. There is even uncertainty about what constitutes Charlotte's juvenilia since so few of her manuscripts have been published and those which are available in facsimile are virtually impossible to read. Various myths, such as the supposed absence of religious reference in Charlotte's early writings,[6] are perpetuated by serious scholars who do not have the time necessary to sift through the mass of unpublished material in order to obtain a balanced view of her work. This uncertainty, the unreliability of secondary sources, and the obvious extravagance of previous claims for the juvenilia, have led many recent scholars (such as Tom Winnifrith in *The Brontës and their Background,* p. 18) to regard any attempt to study the Brontë juvenilia as unprofitable.

Thus I felt there was a need to reassert the value of working on the writer's early manuscripts, irrespective of their literary merit, and to provide Brontë scholarship with an accurate basic survey of Charlotte's early work.

The first three sections of this book trace in detail the three periods of Charlotte's early writing. Special emphasis has been laid on the nature and location of the manuscripts (many of which have previously been incorrectly described), the development of characters who recur throughout the manuscripts, and the sequence of the stories and their relationship to each other. It is hoped that in these sections the development of Charlotte's technique as a writer will be seen to emerge: for example, her use of various male pseudonyms; her transposition of real characters and the political events of the post-Napoleonic era into her early stories; her later concentration on scene and character at the expense of plot; her recurrent use of certain themes; her keen visual imagination, which is closely related to her ability to draw; and above all, the gradual movement in attitude and material from childhood and adolescent fantasy towards greater realism.

The final section seeks to relate this development to Charlotte's later writing. An attempt has been made to take account not only of the novels but of the later fragmentary manuscripts which have received little critical attention, but this book makes no pretence to be an exhaustive study of the relationships between the juvenilia and the novels: this alone would be material for another book. I wish to stress in this study, however, the cautionary advice of Brian Southam against arguing speculatively that there is a direct and visible relationship between an author's early and later writing.[7] This is not to deny that Charlotte's early stories contributed to the later novels: however naive and crude they often are, they constitute her apprenticeship in writing. But in the final section, instead of concentrating on an attempt to 'identify' Angrian characters and plot in the novels, I have tried to indicate the more general trends of her development, as studied in the three previous sections, which persist in her published novels and help to give them their distinctive features.

Although I have concentrated on Charlotte's manuscripts, it is impossible to ignore the enormous body of Branwell's early writing, which is approximately equal to Charlotte's in quantity. Although pages of his writing have been badly scattered, it is possible to piece together enough manuscripts to confirm much of what Fannie Ratchford has said about Branwell and to identify some important periods in which Charlotte rebelled against his influence. An effort has been made to indicate both the positive and negative effects of their early collaboration. Between the years 1834—5, Charlotte's writing was particularly influenced by his ideas and stories: brother and sister were partners, pursuing their own interests in their respective writings but drawing their inspiration from the same imaginary world. His impact on her later writings, however, was largely negative.

Further influences on Charlotte's early writing, such as her environment and childhood reading, have been indicated where possible; but the book makes no claim to be a study of the sources of the juvenilia. It is, however, the first attempt at a scholarly survey of the early manuscripts in their entirety.

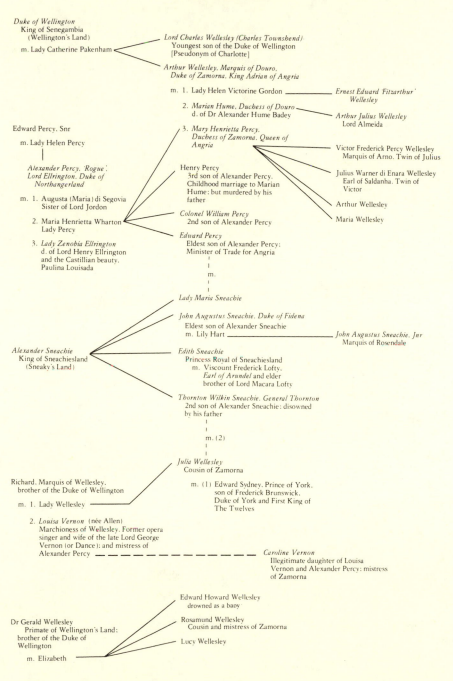

Duke of Wellington
King of Senegambia
(Wellington's Land)
m. Lady Catherine Pakenham

Lord Charles Wellesley *(Charles Townshend)*
Youngest son of the Duke of Wellington
[Pseudonym of Charlotte]

Arthur Wellesley, Marquis of Douro,
Duke of Zamorna, King Adrian of Angria

m. 1. Lady Helen Victorine Gordon ——— Ernest Edward 'Fitzarthur'
Wellesley

2. Marian Hume, Duchess of Douro
d. of Dr Alexander Hume Badey

Arthur Julius Wellesley
Lord Almeida

3. Mary Henrietta Percy,
Duchess of Zamorna, Queen of
Angria

Victor Frederick Percy Wellesley
Marquis of Arno. Twin of Julius

Edward Percy, Snr
m. Lady Helen Percy

Julius Warner di Enara Wellesley
Earl of Saldanha. Twin of
Victor

Alexander Percy, 'Rogue',
Lord Ellrington, Duke of
Northangerland

Henry Percy
3rd son of Alexander Percy.
Childhood marriage to Marian
Hume: but murdered by his
father

Arthur Wellesley

Maria Wellesley

m. 1. Augusta (Maria) di Segovia
Sister of Lord Jordon

Colonel William Percy
2nd son of Alexander Percy

2. Maria Henrietta Wharton
Lady Percy

Edward Percy
Eldest son of Alexander Percy:
Minister of Trade for Angria

3. Lady Zenobia Ellrington
d. of Lord Henry Ellrington
and the Castillian beauty.
Paulina Louisada

m.

Lady Maria Sneachie

John Augustus Sneachie, Duke of Fidena
Eldest son of Alexander Sneachie
m. Lily Hart ——— John Augustus Sneachie, Jnr
Marquis of Rosendale

Alexander Sneachie
King of Sneachiesland
(Sneaky's Land)

Edith Sneachie
Princess Royal of Sneachiesland
m. Viscount Frederick Lofty,
Earl of Arundel and elder
brother of Lord Macara Lofty

Thornton Wilkin Sneachie, General Thornton
2nd son of Alexander Sneachie: disowned
by his father

m. (2)

Julia Wellesley
Cousin of Zamorna

Richard, Marquis of Wellesley,
brother of the Duke of Wellington

m. 1. Lady Wellesley

m. (1) Edward Sydney, Prince of York,
son of Frederick Brunswick,
Duke of York and First King of
The Twelves

2. Louisa Vernon (née Allen)
Marchioness of Wellesley. Former opera
singer and wife of the late Lord George
Vernon (or Dance): and mistress of
Alexander Percy — — — — — — — — Caroline Vernon
Illegitimate daughter of Louisa
Vernon and Alexander Percy: mistress
of Zamorna

Edward Howard Wellesley
drowned as a baby

Dr Gerald Wellesley
Primate of Wellington's Land:
brother of the Duke of
Wellington

Rosamund Wellesley
Cousin and mistress of Zamorna

Lucy Wellesley

m. Elizabeth

*Diagram of the relationships between the principal characters in the juvenilia
(other principal characters are listed in Appendix A)*

PART I

The Glass Town Saga
(1826—1831)

1

Childhood Influences

'There was once a little girl and her name was Ane.'[1] These are the earliest surviving words written by Charlotte Brontë at about ten years old for her youngest sister Anne. Like all good story-tellers, she used the well-worn formula of fairy tale to arouse her little sister's interest. In bold, childish writing she tells how Anne was born in the small village of Thornton, not far from where the Brontës lived in bleak, windswept Haworth. With a mixture of fact and fiction, Charlotte emphasizes her little sister's importance: 'Ane' is the only child of rich parents, a good girl and 'not too much indulged'. Ane and her mother visit a fine castle ten miles from London, but when she travels with her parents in a ship her mother becomes very ill and Ane attends her 'with so much care', administering the required medicine. One suspects that Anne herself had been ill and that Charlotte was attempting to cheer her up.

It is not unusual for siblings to recite stories to each other; it is less common to record them on scraps of paper and to take such care with their execution. Charlotte lovingly illustrated her story for Anne with tiny coloured paintings of the castle, a rowing boat, a sailing ship, a lady walking a dog and the mother's sick room. Then she sewed the small pages (3.6 × 5.6 cm) together to form a booklet. As a cover she used an old scrap of patterned wallpaper, and we can only imagine with what pride she presented it to her sister.

The children had no mother. Mr Brontë had been a widower since soon after Anne's birth and he had cared for his six children, five girls and one boy, with the help of his wife's maiden sister, 'Aunt Branwell'. Practical, stern and religious, Miss Branwell disciplined the children as best she could and brought a semblance of order into their chaotic early lives; but

2   *Charlotte Brontë's earliest extant manuscript, written for her youngest
sister Anne, c. 1826—1828*

she was no substitute for a loving mother. Mrs Gaskell tells how the little
Brontës huddled together for emotional security.[2] Strangers who met
them later in life remarked on their clinging love for each other in the face
of a hostile world. This need for emotional security may help to account
for the intense passion with which the young Brontës pursued their joint
creative adventures. Their physical isolation, too, as children of the local
priest in a remote country village encouraged them to form what their
father called 'a little society amongst themselves'.[3]

   Legend informs us that Mr Brontë was an irascible, neglectful father,
preoccupied by his loneliness and increasing hypochondria. Eccentric he
may have been, but Mrs Gaskell's caricature of him is now accepted as
unfounded and nowhere is his beneficial influence over his children more
marked than in the records of their childhood games. His enthusiasm for
the military and literary heroes of the day, for politics and military
campaigns, for poetry and the classics, and his early love of writing are all
reflected in his children's juvenilia. The early manuscripts present a
picture of contentment, confidence and fun that belies legend, and it
seems that the father was central to the happiness of the four surviving
children.

3 *One of Charlotte Brontë's many early drawings for her sister Anne*
2 September 1828

Mr Brontë was born in Ireland in a crofter's cottage. With the assistance of local benefactors and with a burning ambition to succeed in life, he took various teaching jobs and eventually made his way to Cambridge in October 1802, entering St John's College as a sizar eleven years after Wordsworth, whom he admired. On obtaining his BA he took orders in the Anglican Church in July 1806 and after several curacies in the south of England was appointed to successive livings in the West Riding of Yorkshire: at Hartshead (1811—15), Thornton (1815—20) and Haworth (1820 until his death in 1861). His career embodied the fairy-tale story of rags to riches and bespoke a character of intelligence and determination.

Mr Brontë had a passion for literature. As a boy, working for a blacksmith, he had learnt Milton by heart. Until his wife's death, he gained 'indescribable pleasure' from writing. In the Preface to his first volume of verse, *Cottage Poems* (1811), he tells how he wrote 'from morning till noon, and from noon till night' as a relief from his clerical duties. His works are chiefly didactic, stressing his love of nature and his interest in religion and politics: *The Rural Minstrel: A Miscellany of Descriptive Poems* (1813), *The Cottage in the Wood; or the Art of becoming Rich and Happy* (1815) and *The Maid of Killarney; or, Albion and Flora* (1818). He published several sermons and often contributed verses to magazines and newspapers. His children were used to seeing their father's name in print or reading his letters to the editor of the *Leeds Mercury* or the *Leeds Intelligencer*. A Bradford printer later remembered one of the young Brontës helping to correct the father's proofs.[4]

4   *The Reverend Patrick Brontë, 1809*

Mr Brontë's publications, regardless of their literary merit, were early incentives in making his children writers. The similarity in wording and format between the title pages of his works (see plate 5) and those of his children's earliest booklets is striking.[5] Charlotte's mother, too, had once written an article entitled 'The Advantages of Poverty in Religious Concerns',[6] possibly for publication in the *Methodist Magazine* which she and her sister, 'Aunt Branwell', subscribed to. Charlotte's first books had

THE

COTTAGE

IN THE WOOD;

OR THE

Art of becoming Rich and Happy.

———

BY THE REV. P. BRONTË, A.B.

MINISTER OF THORNTON, BRADFORD, YORKSHIRE.

———

" Happy is the man that findeth wisdom, and the man that getteth
understanding. For the merchandise of it is better than the merchandise of silver, and the gain thereof than fine gold."---Prov. iii. 13, 14

Bradford:

Printed and Sold by T. Inkersley;

SOLD ALSO BY SHERWOOD AND CO. LONDON; ROBINSON
AND CO. LEEDS; HOLDEN, HALIFAX; J. HURST,
WAKEFIELD; AND ALL OTHER BOOKSELLERS.
1815.

5   *Title page to* The Cottage In The Wood, *by the
Reverend Patrick Brontë*

6   *Haworth Parsonage in the time of the Brontës*

belonged to her mother[7] and were chiefly of a religious nature. Had she lived, it seems likely that the children would have had a more orthodox Christian upbringing.

Despite his profession, Mr Brontë appears to have had a particularly liberal view of education. He subscribed to Wordsworth's view that the beauties of nature were a beneficent force, and he allowed his children to roam freely on the moors accompanied by a servant and later by the family dog. Apart from the fresh air and exercise (denied to many Victorian children) they gained a sensitivity and an allegiance to natural landscape that reveals itself in their earliest writings. In one early tale, Charlotte prescribes a system of education which may reflect her father's views. She writes:

> I will nerve his frame in very childhood by bearing him to wild and distant mountains, I will humble his soul by constant and familiar intercourse with the lowest of mankind . . .as to learning, he shall not till he is twelve years old at least be overburdened with that. Men and manners till that time shall form the subjects of his study.[8]

Mr Brontë fostered his children's natural inclinations. When Branwell showed a talent for painting and an enthusiasm for music, he hired teachers not only for Branwell but for the girls as well. Charlotte's early stories show a keen interest in art and an eye trained to seek out detail in a scene. She also shows a lively awareness of the ridiculous in her brother. She satirizes Branwell as Patrick Benjamin Wiggins, who, on the arrival of a noted musician in the neighbourhood of Howard (Haworth), describes how he stands on his head for fifteen minutes in sheer delight:

'Then' said I [Wiggins], 'this is a God and not a Man.' As long as the music sounded in my ears, I dared neither speak, breathe, nor even look up. When it ceased I glanced furtively at the performer, my heart had previously been ravished by the mere knowledge of his fame and skill: but how resistlessly was it captivated, when I saw in Mr Greenwood a tall man dressed in black, with a pair of shoulders, light complexion and hair inclining to red — my very beau ideal of personal beauty, carrying even some slight and dim resemblance to the notion I had formed of ROGUE. Instantly I assumed that inverted position which with me is always a mark of the highest astonishment, delight, and admiration. In other words I clapt my plate to the ground and let my heels fly up with a spring. They happened to hit Mr Sudbury Figgs' chin, as he stood in his usual way, picking his teeth and projecting his under-jaw a yard beyond the rest of his countenance. He exclaimed so loud as to attract Mr Greenwood's attention. He turned round and saw me. 'What's that fellow playing his mountebank tricks here for?' I heard them say. Before anybody could answer I was at his feet licking the dust under them and crying aloud, 'O Greenwood! the greatest, the mightiest, the most famous of men, doubtless you are ignorant of a nit the foal of a louse like me, but I have learnt to know you through the medium of your wonderful works. Suffer the basest of creatures to devote himself utterly to your service, as a shoe-black, a rosiner of fiddlesticks, a great-coat carrier — a Port-music, in short a thorough going toadie.'[9]

Such descriptions show that Charlotte early possessed that sense of humour often denied to the Brontës by those familiar only with their later works. Unlike Branwell, she has the ability to mock herself and to see herself and her sisters from her brother's 'superior' point of view:

'I've some people who call themselves akin to me in the shape of three girls, not that they are honoured by possessing me as a brother, but I deny that they're my sisters. Robert Patrick SDEATH, Esqr., is partly my uncle, but he's the only relative I'll acknowledge.'
'What are your sisters' names?'
'CHARLOTTE Wiggins, JANE Wiggins, and ANNE Wiggins.'
'Are they as queer as you?'
'Oh, they are miserable silly creatures not worth talking about. CHARLOTTE's eighteen years old, a broad dumpy thing, whose head does not come higher than my elbow. Emily's sixteen, lean and scant, with a face about the size of a penny, and Anne is nothing, absolutely nothing.'
'What! Is she an idiot?'
'Next door to it.'[10]

Her humour extends too to the subject of religion, to the comic features of her father's clerical associates or the excesses of the evangelical preacher of the day. The intolerance of her aunt's strict Calvinism is censured in the figure of Warner Howard Warner, and the bigotry of the Roman Catholic Church in Ireland is the subject of her earliest allegory.[11]

Mr Brontë made few efforts to impose a religious creed on his children but he believed that a thorough grounding in the Bible was essential. On page 103 of his copy of Hannah More's *Moral Sketches* he underlined the following sentence: 'Human learning will only teach him the knowledge of others, the Bible that of himself.'[12] When Charlotte went to Miss Wooler's school at Roe Head in 1831 she surpassed her fellow pupils in her knowledge of scripture, as in everything else.[13]

The Bible was certainly a major source of inspiration for her juvenilia. Previous writers have stressed the constant allusions to Bunyan, Milton, Scott, the *Arabian Nights' Entertainments* and *Blackwood's Magazine,* but the most obvious source of all has been ignored and even denied.[14] In her earliest writing Charlotte included not only biblical allusions but references to controversial religious issues.[15] More significantly, however, the Bible was a basic source of inspiration, revered for its religious teachings and valued as the supreme example of literature and historical narrative. Like Ernest Edward 'Fitzarthur', whose character she described in 1834, Charlotte had derived her first lessons from that 'certain old-fashioned book':[16] 'the sublime Poetry — the simple Historical Narrative of the Bible fascinated him at the very first and with strange eagerness did the small, delicate child, seize and devour what food the book of life had to give.'[17] At seven years old, she had thought it the best book in the world.[18]

The fabulous nature of the early Glass Town can be traced not only to the *Arabian Nights* and Sir Charles Morell's *Tales of the Genii,*[19] but to the Bible, especially the Book of the Revelation. Here, like the chief genii in Charlotte's stories, God appears with clouds, a trumpet-like voice and lightning and thunder. There are numerous incidents in the early juvenilia of mortals being blinded and falling 'as dead' before the splendour of princely halls and thrones of precious stones. The capital of Glass Town is the Babylon of Africa, the Tower of All Nations is Charlotte's African equivalent of the Tower of Babel, and the famous 'Twelves', founders of the African Kingdom, may even owe their name to the twelve apostles. Several of Charlotte's early poems were directly inspired by biblical heroes while others have patently Christian themes.[20] Even Charlotte's fascination with possible supernatural occurrences is a legacy of her early religious training. Jane Eyre's sensitivity to Rochester's voice had its origins in a similar incident in an early story, and such occurrences of mental prescience in the juvenilia are usually associated with divine inspiration.[21]

Reading was the 'very delight'[22] of Charlotte's existence and her chief source of early inspiration. At six years old, fired by the descriptions of the

celestial city in *Pilgrim's Progress,* she apparently set off for Bradford in
the hope of reaching her dream city.[23] In her descriptions of the magical
Glass Town she recalls that childhood dream. A volume entitled *A
Description of London,* given to the ten-year-old Branwell in 1828,[24]
contains plates of famous public buildings such as St Paul's Cathedral, the
Bank of England, Whitehall and the Horse Guards, plates which helped to
suggest the classical-styled palaces of the juvenilia; and the early geography
books owned by the children provided such exotic names as Fezan,
Kashna, Ashantee, Dahomey, Coomassie, Sofala, the Niger, the Gambia,
the Senegal, St Helena and the Mountains of the Moon which occur
throughout the early stories. Goldsmith's *Grammar of General Geography,*
heavily used by all the children if one can judge from marginal notes and
scribblings,[25] includes illustrations and information on such places as
Isphahan, the Caucasus, Paris and Switzerland, which form the background
of Charlotte's articles for her magazine.

Mr Brontë's Celtic heritage is often seen as a contributing factor to his
children's creative imagination. Certainly they were reared on 'strange
stories' told to Mr Brontë by ancients of his parish — 'of the extraordinary
lives and doings of people who resided in far-off, out-of-the-way places . . .
stories which made one shiver and shrink from hearing; but they were full
of grim humour and interest for Mr Brontë and his children'.[26] No doubt
he also entertained them with stories of Ireland. An early geography book,
originally belonging to Mr Brontë and his brothers and published in
Dublin, contains a note written in a childish hand that accords with
Charlotte's many descriptions of her 'Western' heroes and heroines, which
she occasionally refers to as 'Irish':

> of what temper are the irish the[y] are bolde and
> cuorageous haughty quick witted ingeneouous hospitale
> credelious bould at glory full of resentment and
> violent in all their affections[27]

One of the best-used books in the Brontë Parsonage today is James
MacPherson's *Poems of Ossian,* annotated by all the children and having
numerous passages marked. One of Branwell's earliest magazines carries
first a commentary on 'Ossian's Poems' and then a review of the
commentary, complete with footnotes; it is not surprising when he
concludes: 'This is one of the most long-winded Books that have ever been
printed. We must now conclude for we are dreadfully tired.'[28]

Charlotte's earliest autobiographical fragment shows that reading and
writing were an accepted part of the busy parsonage household. In large
handwriting, full of spelling errors and with little sense of punctuation
she writes:

Once papa lent my Sister Maria A Book it was an old Geography [?one] and she wrote on its Blank leaf papa lent me this Book. the Book is an hundred and twenty years old it is at this moment lying Before me while I write this I am in the kitchin of the parsonage house Haworth Taby the servent is washing up after Breakfast and Anne my youngest Sister (Maria was my eldest) is kneeling on a chair looking at some cakes whiche Tabby has been Baking for us. Emily is in the parlour brushing it papa and Branwell are gone to Keighly Aunt is up stairs in her Room and I am sitting by the table writing this in the kitchin.[29]

Books, magazines and newspapers were scarce luxuries in a parsimonious house. Mr Brontë's stipend was small, but each week he and Branwell collected two newspapers, the *Leeds Intelligencer* and the *Leeds Mercury,*[30] from the neighbouring town of Keighley. We are told that when Maria and Elizabeth were alive, Mr Brontë used to read the latest news to his children in the parlour and discuss the current political events with them, treating them as adult companions.[31]

From 1825 on their knowledge of current affairs was supplemented by *Blackwood's Magazine,* lent to Mr Brontë by the local doctor for several years. It became the prototype for their earliest literary productions and there is evidence that they were still reading it in July 1841.[32] Branwell later recalled the excitement with which he and his sisters read and re-read the pages of *Blackwood's.* In 1835 he addressed the editor, hoping to become a contributor himself:

I cannot express, though you can understand, the heavenliness of associations connected with such articles as Professor Wilson's, read and re-read while a little child, with all their poetry of language and divine flights into that visionary region of imagination which one very young would believe reality, and which one entering into manhood would look back upon as a glorious dream. I speak so, sir, because as a child 'Blackwood' formed my chief delight, and I feel certain that no child before enjoyed reading as I did, because none ever had such works as 'The Noctes', 'Christmas Dreams', 'Christopher in his Sporting Jacket', to read.[33]

The children's tiny magazines mirror the pages of *Blackwood's*: they include book reviews, topical poems, discussions of paintings, tales inspired by articles on Hoffmann and references to current affairs such as the Bill for the suppression of the Faction Du Mange, the American wool trade,[34] the Arctic and African explorations of Mungo Park, Parry and Ross, and the effects of the recent Peninsular War.

The range of reading matter available to the children was wide. Every effort was made to acquire books for them. Mr Brontë joined the Keighley Mechanics' Institute soon after it was founded in 1825 so that his children might borrow books from the library. The list of its early holdings[35] includes possible sources for many of Charlotte's early references left unexplained by the pages of *Blackwood's* or by the books on her father's shelves. In 1831 Aunt Branwell subscribed to *Fraser's Magazine,* a new periodical launched that year, and Charlotte had access to various *Annuals,* such as *Friendship's Offering* whose engravings served as a springboard for her criticisms of art.

It is also possible that the young Brontës occasionally used the famous library of the nearby Heaton family of Ponden House, who were prominent Haworth parishioners. Mr Brontë was on good terms with them and the children would have passed Ponden House on their many rambles over the moors. The library of some 1,400 books included a First Folio of Shakespeare and was particularly strong in sixteenth- and seventeenth-century literature. Charlotte's extensive knowledge of Elizabethan and Jacobean dramatists[36] and classical French authors may be derived from this source although it is impossible to prove that she had access to it. It is difficult, however, to explain Branwell's early imitation of Chateaubriand, the author of *Travels in Greece and the Holy Land* which he had read, or Charlotte's translation of the *Henriad* without recourse to the Ponden House library. Foreign books were rare in rural Yorkshire. The children's attitude to France and especially to Paris, as a 'world in miniature, full of wickedness, rioting, idleness and grandeur' with 'little dirty narrow lanes' and 'low villains'[37] was probably formed by biased English newspapers written in the aftermath of the Napoleonic Wars. Certainly the legend of French cruelty to children, echoed in the early manuscripts, was current at that time.

Only once was Mr Brontë known to have censored his children's reading. Charlotte tells how she was particularly fond of some old issues of the *Ladies' Magazine* which had belonged to either her mother or her aunt:

> they had crossed the sea, had suffered shipwreck and were discoloured with brine — I read them as a treat on holiday afternoons or by stealth when I should have been minding my lessons — I shall never see anything which will interest me so much again — One black day my father burnt them because they contained foolish love stories.[38]

But Mr Brontë placed no such veto on the romantic poets[39] or on the novels of Scott. His library contained the complete works of Byron and Charlotte quotes freely from *Childe Harold, Manfred* and *Cain* throughout her juvenilia. At twelve Branwell was writing poetic dramas in imitation of Byron[40] and in *Caroline Vernon* Charlotte describes how reading Lord Byron can 'half-turn' the head of a romantic young girl. Her early penchant for love stories was fostered by such popular works as *Evelina* and *Clarissa*[41] and by romantic tales narrated by the servant

Tabbitha Ackroyd. Like Jane Eyre's nurse, Tabby fed the imaginations of her charges with 'passages of love and adventure taken from old fairy tales and older ballads; or (as at a later period I discovered) from the pages of *Pamela* and *Henry, Earl of Moreland*.'[42]

In 1834 Charlotte drew up a reading list for her schoolfriend Ellen Nussey, recommending the poetry of 'Milton, Shakespeare, Thomson, Goldsmith, Pope (if you will though I don't admire him) Scott, Byron, Campbell, Wordsworth and Southey' but hesitating over Shakespeare and Byron. She was now aware that her early reading had been unorthodox. Quotation from Shakespeare is as much a part of the texture of her early prose as is biblical allusion. She appears to have been especially fond of *Othello, Macbeth* and *A Midsummer Night's Dream.* Her advice to Ellen is a clear statement of much of what she has read:

> Omit the Comedies of Shakespeare and the Don Juan, perhaps the Cain of Byron though the latter is a magnificent Poem and read the rest fearlessly. That must indeed be a depraved mind which can gather evil from Henry the 8th from Richard 3rd from Macbeth and Hamlet and Julius Cesar, Scott's sweet, wild, romantic Poetry can do you no harm nor can Wordsworth nor Campbell's nor Southey's, the greater part at least of his, some is certainly exceptionable. For History read Hume, Rollin, and the Universal History if you can — I never did. For fiction — read Scott alone; all novels after his are worthless. For biography, read Johnson's Lives of the Poets, Boswell's Life of Johnson, Southey's Life of Nelson, Lockhart's Life of Burns, Moore's Life of Sheridan, Moore's Life of Byron, Wolfe's Remains, For Natural History, read Bewick, and Audubon, and Goldsmith and White — of Selborne.[43]

Charlotte seldom refers to the classics or ancient history in her letters yet her juvenilia shows that she was familiar with such figures as Homer, Sophocles, Euripides, Aeschylus, Tasso and Virgil, probably in translation by Dryden or Pope. At the age of fourteen she sings their praises and laments that 'Athens and Spata are no more'.[44] Branwell's copy of *The Works of Virgil,* translated by Dryden, is heavily annotated with Angrian names and Charlotte's signature appears at the end of Book X of the *Aeneid.*[45] The marked titles of books advertised on the back pages of this volume (see plate 7) give further evidence of the young Brontës' reading and the sketches of faces such as that of Wellington (inverted) are the typical embellishments of favourite books.

According to Mr Brontë, most of Charlotte's early heroes were gleaned from ancient history, but this is not substantiated by a study of the juvenilia. Certainly Branwell's bloodthirsty battles draw on descriptions of the Battle of Marathon and the struggle at the Pass of Thermopylae;[46] and the whole historical conception of the kingdoms of Glass Town and Angria is founded on the idea of the rise and fall of empires.[47] But both

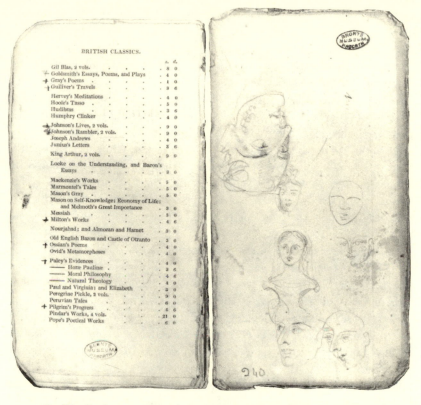

7   *The final page and inside back cover of Branwell Brontë's copy of*
The Works of Virgil, *by John Dryden*

Branwell's and Charlotte's early heroes are firmly based on political, military and literary figures of the day. The single exception is Charlotte's heroine Zenobia, 'the very Empress of Women' with 'a masculine soul in a femine casket'.[48] She bears a remarkable resemblance to Edward Gibbon's description of the historical Zenobia in *The History of the Decline and Fall of the Roman Empire,* which Charlotte may have borrowed from the Keighley Mechanics' Library.[49] Gibbon records that Zenobia was the celebrated queen of Palmyra and the East, equal in beauty to her ancestor Cleopatra and 'the most heroic of her sex'. He speaks of her superior genius breaking through the 'servile indolence' imposed on the females of her race. Like that of Charlotte's heroine, her complexion was dark, 'her large black eyes sparkled with uncommon fire' and her 'manly understanding was strengthened and adorned by study.'[50] She was proficient in Latin, Greek, Syrian and Egyptian, skilled in oriental history and familiar with Homer and Plato, having studied under 'the sublime Longinus'. Charlotte compares her heroine to Cleopatra and Madame de

Staël and describes her reading Herodotus and Aeschylus in the original Greek, studying the Persian language and teaching astronomy to a Glass Town 'blue-stocking'.[51]

In general, though, current affairs rather than ancient history contributed to the original conceptions of Charlotte's central characters. In particular, the career and family of Arthur Wellesley, 1st Duke of Wellington (1769–1852), were of supreme importance. His many titles (including Marquis of Douro) and the names of towns and fortresses he captured during the Peninsular Wars (for example, Almeida) become the names of characters in the juvenilia. His opponents in life become his enemies in the saga. Even his colleagues in parliament are depicted in her earliest manuscripts with an awareness that borders on cynicism. Castlereagh, for example, is portrayed as a faithful lap-dog curled at the Duke's feet.[52]

Charlotte's enthusiasm for Wellington was inspired by her father, whose interest extended beyond politics to military affairs. Ellen Nussey remarked that Mr Brontë's tastes 'led him to delight in the perusal of battle-scenes, and in following the artifice of war; had he entered on military service instead of ecclesiastical he would probably have had a distinguished career.'[53] Wellington embodied Mr Brontë's unfulfilled dream of an heroic army career, and both were Tories and Irishmen. As a Cambridge student Mr Brontë had followed Wellington's career and hailed him as Europe's greatest military genius and the country's finest patriot. Later, he even sent a letter to Wellington suggesting a novel sighting device for army muskets which he had tried out on a flying bird; but he received a crushing reply from the 'Iron' Duke, reminiscent of Charlotte's own imaginary letter from the Duke in her *Tales of the Islanders*.[54]

The Duke is accorded every honour in the saga and his word is law. Mr Brontë recalled that as soon as his children could read and write 'Charlotte and her brother and sisters used to invent and act little plays of their own, in which the Duke of Wellington, my daughter Charlotte's hero, was sure to come off the conquering hero'.[55] From 8 July to 2 October 1829, Charlotte carefully noted various *Anectdotes of the duke of Wellington* as she called them, which she had collected from Malcolm's *Tales of Flood and Field,* the *United Service Journal* and Scott's *History of the Emperor Napoleon*.[56] In another fragment she prophesies that the grave of the Duke will be eternally illumined by a supernatural light.[57]

The disparate natures of Wellington's two sons may even be the source for Charlotte's favourite theme of two rival brothers. In reality the youngest, Charles, displayed a 'breezy indolence' and was 'a wild, rattling, high spirited boy, full of tricks and not the least afraid of his father'.[58]

Douro was an entirely different character, withdrawn and promising at first, but later a disappointment to his father. After a thwarted love affair with Elizabeth Hume, the daughter of Wellington's surgeon and the prototype of Marian Hume in the juvenilia, he was continually falling in and out of love. When he finally married his wife was childless and unloved. Here, with later additions from the characters of Wellington himself and Byron, we have the germ of Charlotte's persona Arthur, Marquis of Douro, Duke of Zamorna and King of Angria.

Composing and acting little dramas inspired by their reading were perhaps the only games the Brontë children knew. They had few toys and no acquaintance with organized play. Mrs Chadwick tells of their painful shyness at a birthday party given by the trustees of Haworth church: they had 'no idea of ordinary games that any village child could play, such as "hunt the slipper" and "here we go round the gooseberry bush".'[59] Instead, they had formulated their own childhood games. Maria, the eldest, had been a little mother to them since Mrs Brontë's death in 1821. She had taught them to 'play': to pretend they were other characters and to 'make out' their actions.[60] Fairy stories, local legend, adult conversation, books and newspapers would supply the outline of a character; their imaginations could do the rest. Mrs Gaskell speaks of them 'reading, or whispering low, in the "children's study"',[61] a room of only nine by five feet, whose walls today still bear witness to the characters the children created there.

But Maria and Elizabeth had both died of consumption in 1825. Charlotte had since assumed the role of leader with Branwell as a close rival. Nowhere is this joint leadership more evident than in the games they now created.

The Glass Town Saga was established in 1826. Three years later the thirteen-year-old Charlotte began to chronicle the events and characters of the 'plays' on tiny scraps of paper. The acting of the children's material world gave way to a new world of make-believe, which promised excitement, fictional power and escape from reality. It was a world that would eventually be rejected by the mature writer. But to the girl of thirteen this 'dream world' had all the lustre and fascination of a secret Aladdin's lamp.

From March 1829 to December 1830 Charlotte wrote constantly. Her second earliest surviving manuscript explains exactly how the 'plays' were formed. On 12 March 1829, she wrote in *The History of the Year:*

Our plays were established: *Young Men,* June 1826; *Our Fellows,* July 1827; *Islanders,* December 1827. These are our three great plays that are not kept secret. Emily's and my bed plays were established December 1, 1827; the others March 1828. Bed plays mean secret plays; they are very nice ones. All our plays are very strange ones. Their nature I need not write on paper, for I think I shall always remember them.[62]

To us the bed plays remain a secret. Charlotte never again refers to them, but since Charlotte and Emily shared the same small bedroom, their 'bed plays' were probably the result of conversations before they went to sleep. We can suppose that these bed plays were not unlike the 'three great plays' which are similar to each other in content. Initially, however, the three main plays arose from quite different sources and must be examined separately: 'The *Young Men's* play took its rise from some wooden soldiers Branwell had; *Our Fellows* from *Aesop's Fables;* and the *Islanders* from several events which happened'.[63]

2

The Young Men's Play

The Young Men's Play began in June 1826. The story of its formation has been told many times. On 5 June Mr Brontë attended a Clerical Conference in Leeds, returning home that evening laden with gifts for his children. He brought a set of ninepins for Charlotte, a toy village for Emily, a dancing doll for Anne and a set of toy soldiers for Branwell. None of the children appears to have been very interested in the ninepins, the toy village or the dancing doll, but the twelve toy soldiers produced an immediate reaction. Both Charlotte and Branwell record this famous event, and we can see from Charlotte's account, in *The History of the Year,* that she began this game with enthusiasm:

> When papa came home it was night and we were in bed, so next morning Branwell came to our door with a box of soldiers. Emily and I jumped out of bed and I snatched up one and exclaimed, 'this is the Duke of Wellington! it shall be mine!' When I said this Emily likewise took one and said it should be hers. When Anne came down she took one also. Mine was the prettiest of the whole and perfect in every part. Emily's was a grave-looking fellow: we called him Gravey. Anne's was a queer little thing very much like herself. He was called Waiting Boy. Branwell chose Bonaparte.[1]

The choice of characters by the children is significant. Charlotte and Branwell chose the two greatest historical antagonists of the age. Their heroes had dominated events from before the turn of the century and had finally met in 1815 at the Battle of Waterloo, a year before Charlotte's birth. Wellington was still alive, a leading political figure in England; Napoleon had recently died in May 1827, a restive prisoner on St Helena. By comparison 'Gravey' and 'Waiting Boy' did not stand a chance in the glamour of a heroic fairy-tale world. Their feeble names were soon exchanged for those of Parry and Ross, two famous explorers and more suitable companions for Wellington and Bonaparte. The children had probably found their names in the pages of *Blackwood's Magazine:* the November issue for 1820 had included an article on Captain Parry's latest expedition and a map of his discoveries made in the Polar Sea, as surveyed by Captain Ross, and the issue for June the following year had carried a further article on Captain Parry.

But in all Charlotte's and Branwell's stories Parry and Ross are relegated to secondary roles. It is not surprising that the two younger sisters eventually broke away from this and the Islanders' Play to form their own world of Gondal. Unfortunately there are no surviving records of these early plays by Emily or Anne. Charlotte and Branwell have left many manuscripts and since the children worked closely together at this stage, it is probable that Emily and Anne also wrote stories about the Young Men which have not survived. The earliest reference made by them to any 'play' is in a diary note by Emily dated 24 November 1834, referring to the world of Gondal. Anne's list of Gondal names in Goldsmith's *Grammar of General Geography* is possibly earlier but undated.[2] From the participation of their favourite characters in Charlotte's manuscripts, however, we can be sure that until 1831 Emily and Anne followed the lead of their older brother and sister.

Branwell appears to have been the dominant force in the Young Men's Play. After all, the soldiers were initially his, as he makes clear in the swaggering tone that was to become the hallmark of this favoured only son:

> I carried them to Emily, Charlotte and Anne. They each took up a soldier, gave them names, which I consented to, and I gave Charlotte, Twemy (i.e. Wellington) to Emily, Pare (Parry) to Anne, Trott (Ross) to take care of them, though they were to be mine and I to have the disposal of them as I would.[3]

His account of these events was written a year and a half later than Charlotte's in *The History Of The Young Men From Their First Settlement To The present time* (15 December 1830—7 May 1831). Although it is more detailed than Charlotte's account, it is less immediate and less dramatic.

Branwell explains that he had had many sets of toy soldiers. The first set of twelve, 'the best I ever have had', were bought for him by his father from Bradford in the summer of 1824. Charlotte had been sent to join her two elder sisters at the Clergy Daughters' School at Cowan Bridge in the August of that year. Emily followed in November. Anne was only four years old and too young to play with the seven-year-old Branwell. The

soldiers were obviously intended to help compensate for the vacuum left
by his older sisters. A second set of soldiers soon followed. These Branwell
purchased himself from Keighley and kept for about a year 'until either
maimed, lost, burnt or destroyed by various casualties they "departed and
left not a wreck behind!"'[4] Not satisfied with these, the lonely boy spent
his pocket money on yet another set: a band of Turkish musicians, which
he kept until Charlotte and Emily returned from school in the autumn of
1825. Maria and Elizabeth had just died. The house was grave and busy.
No one was interested in toy soldiers or games. Indeed, Charlotte seems to
have shown no interest in Branwell's early sets of soldiers at all. She may
not even have known about them. As we have already seen, it was not
until ten months later that the purchase of yet another set of soldiers was
to fire the imaginations of the four surviving Brontë children. Branwell's
account of this important event must also be related:

> on June the 5th A.D. 1826 papa procured me from Leeds another set
> (these were the 12s) which I kept for 2 years, though 2 or 3 of them are
> in being at the time of my writing this (Dec. 15 A.D. 1830). Sometime
> in 1827 I bought another set of Turkish Musicians at Halifax, and in
> 1828 I purchased the Last Box, a band of Indians, at Haworth. Both
> these I still keep. Here now ends the catalogue of soldiers bought by or
> for me. And I must now conclude this Introduction already too long
> with saying, that what is contained in this History is a statement of what
> Myself, Charlotte, Emily and Anne really pretended did happen among
> the 'Young Men' (that being the name we gave them) during the period
> of nearly 6 years.[5]

Branwell describes the Young Men's settlement on the African coast in
great detail. But because he was writing a year later than Charlotte, many
of the characters are different and the events more elaborate. His is
essentially an imaginative history of the children's characters as they
existed at the end of 1830. Written by Branwell as Captain John Bud, 'the
greatest prose writer' among the Young Men, it provides a valuable
indication of how the African saga developed in the course of a year and a
half; but it is to Charlotte's manuscript that we must go for the first
record of 'The Twelve Adventurers'.

A Romantic Tale, written on 15 April 1829 and listed in Charlotte's
Catalogue of my Books (3 August 1830) as 'The Twelve Adventurers', is
Charlotte's first story about the Young Men. It describes their voyage
from England to the east coast of Africa and, after many struggles with
the Ashantee natives, their eventual settlement and the building of the
'Glass Town'.

The idea of an African colony would not have been unusual in 1829:
from newspapers and local gossip, the Brontë children would have been

aware that many people from Yorkshire, and the United Kingdom generally, emigrated during the 1820s—1840s to such places as New Zealand (where Charlotte's own friend Mary Taylor eventually settled) and to Natal and the Western Cape in South Africa. The actual site of the Glass Town may well have been inspired by the article in *Blackwood's Magazine* of June 1826, entitled 'Geography of Central Africa. Denham and Clapperton's Journals'. Here the author regrets the failure of British attempts to 'civilize' Africa and suggests that they should move their base to 'a place like Fernando Po, where health and safety dwell, and where, commanding the outlets of the Niger, Great Britain would command the trade, the improvement, and the civilization of all North Central Africa'. A detailed map accompanies this article and shows Fernando Po to be exactly where the young Brontës founded Glass Town, a centre of commerce and civilization.

A knowledge of *A Romantic Tale* is essential to an understanding of the background of the children's African 'saga'. In chapter I Charlotte quotes an extract from a book she has read entitled *The Travels of Captain Parnell.* Caught in a hurricane in the desert, a traveller discovers an immense skeleton, possibly 'one of those ancient Britons who, tradition tells us, came from their own country to this evil land, and here miserably perished'. Charlotte concludes that 'these skeletons are evil genii chained in these deserts by the fairy Maimoune', the daughter of Damriel, king of a legion of genii in *The Arabian Nights' Entertainments.*[6] Thus she establishes the presence of a supernatural power in that 'wild, barren land, the evil desert'. This evil desert remains a distinct geographical feature of the African kingdom in all Charlotte's early stories. The presence of a larger supernatural force controlling the destiny of this land and its people manifests itself in the form of genii.

There are four Chief Genii. They are the Brontë children themselves, who control the course of events and the movements of their particular characters, originally the wooden soldiers but now, in 1829, imaginary people whose world has been committed to paper. As Branwell explains:

> I am the chief Genius Brannii, with me there are 3 others; she, Wellesly, who protects you is named Tallii, she who protects Parry is named Emmii; she who protects Ross is called Annii. Those lesser ones whom ye saw are Genii and Fairies, our slaves and minions. We are the Guardians of this land, we are the guardians of you all.[7]

Charlotte appears to be the first to introduce the concept of the 'Genii' into the children's early writing. There is no mention of Genii in Branwell's three manuscripts which predate *A Romantic Tale,*[8] but from June 1829 on he makes abundant use of this new material. Unlike the earlier January issue, his 'editions' of *Branwell's Blackwood's Magazine* for June and July each carry an elaborate colophon on the title page bearing the signature 'PB Chief Genius'.[9] His poems and stories are full of the conflict between the Young Men and the authority of the Genii. Charlotte, however, makes no mention of this conflict. In *A Romantic Tale* the role of the Chief Genius is that of protector and prophet.

As an unnamed member of the crew, Charlotte relates (in chapter 2) how in the year 1793 twelve young men set out in the *Invincible* on a voyage of discovery. After being driven off course by innumerable storms, they eventually land in what seems to be part of an immense continent. The twelve adventurers travel inland but their progress is soon halted by the native Ashantee tribes, originally Charlotte's small ninepins, which were brought from Leeds by Mr Brontë at the same time as the twelve toy soldiers and were used as native tribesmen in the early physical game of the children. After capturing the Ashantee chief however the 'Twelves' make a peace settlement and in true colonial style set about building a city: 'The situation was in the middle of a large plain, bounded on the north by high mountains, on the south by the sea, on the east by gloomy forests, and on the west by evil deserts'.[10] With the help of the Genii the Hall of Justice, the Grand Inn, the Great Tower of All Nations and the fortifications of the new city are completed in a few months.

Such prosperity is viewed with envy by 'the King of the Blacks'. In chapter 3, Arthur Wellesley, one of the Twelves and 'a common trumpeter', speaks of the necessity of an army for defence against the Ashantees. The Genii have helped them to build a city; they might also help them to cross the sea to Britain again to recruit an army. Suddenly a voice commands the Twelves to go to the evil desert. With Frederick Brunswick, Duke of York, at their head they are led towards a brilliant light which emanates from the Palaces of the Genii. The description which follows is the first of many similar scenes which Charlotte evokes throughout her manuscripts of 1829 and 1830:

> Out of the barren desert arose a palace of diamond, the pillars of which were ruby and emerald illuminated with lamps too bright to look upon. The Genius led us into a hall of sapphire in which were thrones of gold. On the thrones sat the Princes of the Genii. In the midst of the hall hung a lamp like the sun. Around it stood genii and fairies without whose robes were of beaten gold sparkling with diamonds. As soon as their chiefs saw us they sprang up from their thrones, and one of them seizing A. W. and exclaimed: 'This is the Duke of Wellington!'[11]

Here Charlotte dramatizes in fairy-tale form her earlier account of the naming of her favourite toy soldier. In the guise of a genius she foretells the struggle between Arthur Wellesley and 'the desolator of Europe', the prophecy ending in Wellesley's glory and renown.

Next morning the Ashantees attack; but as a result of Arthur Wellesley's quickwittedness and confidence in the Genii they are defeated. A ship then arrives from England. It is refitted by the genii and returns home with Arthur Wellesley on board. Twenty years pass. Wellesley returns to Africa at the head of a huge army, and to the amazement of his old comrades he is now 'our most Noble General . . . the conqueror of Bonaparte and the deliverer of Europe'.[12] The Duke of York, formerly leader of the Twelves, decides to return to England. On 14 June 1827, 'a council of the whole nation' elects Arthur Wellesley, now Duke of Wellington, as King — to rule over their city of 15,000 men: a city soon to be called the 'Great Glass Town'.

This is the background to the Young Men's Play. Branwell corroborates Charlotte's account, elaborates on it and expands the various wars with the Ashantee into detailed battle scenes in *The History Of The Young Men.* He ostentatiously quotes 'the Author of the *Romantic Tale'* as an authority for his own history and illustrates his work with a detailed folding map (see plate 8), plotting major cities, roads, rivers and mountain ranges. His map is coloured and labelled according to the various kingdoms founded by the children's four chief characters: Wellington's Land, Parry's Land, Ross's Land and Sneaky's Land.[13] The Great Glass Town is the centre of this confederation of states. Each state has its own particular Glass Town modelled on the capital which is controlled by all four Chief Genii. Two islands to the south west of the African coast were given to Stumps and Monkey, two of the twelve adventurers, and a third island was settled by the French with its capital modelled on Paris.

There is an even earlier map associated with the Young Men's Play. It is to be found at the back of Charlotte's first little booklet written for Anne in *c.*1826 and its significance has previously been ignored. This crudely coloured map indicates four small countries distinguished by the names 'Taley', 'Brany', 'Vittoria' and 'Waiting', which represent the four Brontë children and show that Chief Genius Taley and Chief Genius Brany (later spelt 'Tallii' and 'Brannii') existed in the early stages of the Young Men's Play although no mention is made of them until *A Romantic Tale.* 'Waiting', spelt 'Wating' on the map, is the early name of Anne's soldier and 'Vittoria' is a heroine later associated with Emily in the Islanders' Play.[14] Charlotte tells us that the Islanders' Play was formed in December 1827, so this little map was probably not drawn until after this date, possibly early in 1828.[15] Moreover, the map is followed by two pages of geographical notes about Wellington's and Parry's lands. The geographical notes consist of a list of places taken from an atlas or geography book and ranged under the protection of Wellington and Parry. No doubt there were others listed for Sneaky (Bonaparte) and Ross. From its earliest

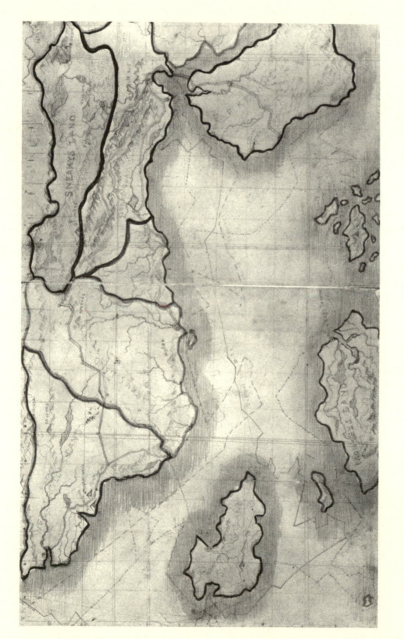

8   Map of the Glass Town Confederacy, drawn by Branwell Brontë as a frontispiece to The History Of The Young Men, December 1830—May 1831

stages, then, the children's imaginative world had a solid geographical setting.

There are about three years between Charlotte's and Branwell's maps. They are obviously different but the basic idea of four kingdoms controlled ultimately by the four Brontë children themselves remains the same. The names of Branwell's twelve adventurers also differ from those of Charlotte who was writing an imaginative tale and not an elaborate history. This is the essential difference between the two young literary partners in their early manuscripts. Their subject matter is the same; but whereas Branwell closely documents the moves of his soldiers, Charlotte can create stories sometimes only vaguely related to the Young Men's world. This makes Charlotte's manuscripts more interesting to read: her stories show a more fertile imagination. Branwell's rather pedantic history, however, is rich in details about the Young Men's Play.

Branwell tells us that thirteen men originally set sail in the *Invincible* bound for Ashantee or the coast of Guinea:

BUTTER CRASHEY	Captain	aged 140 years	
ALEXANDER CHEEKY	Surgeon	20	
ARTHUR WELLESLY	Trumpeter	12	
WILLIAM EDWARD PARRY	Trumpeter	aged 15 years	
ALEXANDER SNEAKY	Sailor	17	
JOHN ROSS	Lieutenant	16	
WILLIAM BRAVEY	Sailor	27	
EDWARD GRAVEY	Sailor	17	
FREDERICK GUELPH	Sailor	27	
STUMPS	12 Middy		
MONKEY	11 Middy		
TRACKY	10 Middy		
CRACKY	5 Middy[16]		

The names of only two of Charlotte's twelve adventurers are duplicated here by Branwell, Arthur Wellesley and Frederick Guelph (Frederick Brunswick, Duke of York). It is Branwell's adventurers and not Charlotte's who survive throughout the Young Men's Play. In his version of the play, only twelve of the original thirteen men survived to become the 'founders' of the new land: Stumps is killed by the Dutch on Ascension Island. Others are killed too but 'soon *made alive* by the usual means',[17] namely the intervention of the Genii. Stumps also reappears later to become King of the Twelves, after the 'death' of the Duke of York, but eventually abdicates in favour of Arthur Wellesley. Such resuscitation was necessary in the face of Branwell's overriding desire for frequent battles with limited forces.

In his enthusiasm Branwell invented a language for the Young Men:

'the old young men tongue'. *Branwell's Blackwood's Magazine* for January 1829 carries a letter to the editor in this bizarre language:

> Bany do ought not to —
> Punit de Doung [?manot]
> For having rebelled against
> do _____
> For dhey did deir Duty
>   — Goody — [18]

This speech has been described as 'Yorkshire dialect spoken by holding [the] nose between finger and thumb'.[19] There is some evidence for this in Branwell's *Letters From An Englishman,* volume I, which was written in September 1830. Dr Hume Bady (often spelt 'Badey') speaks in the 'old young men tongue', and when Lord Charles Wellesley addresses Bady he also speaks with 'his fingers applied to his nose'.[20] If we look at a later rendering of Branwell's Young Men's language, it appears that this may indeed be the earliest attempt by any of the Brontë children to reproduce the local dialect: '"Hellow! Dear! Oi tee troy bowts cawming oup tow us" (i.e., Hello there! I see 3 boats coming up to us).'[21] Charlotte, however, makes no mention of the language in any of her manuscripts. She was obviously unimpressed by such embellishments to their play.

In fact, Charlotte's earliest manuscripts show little interest in the Young Men's Play. After the geographical notes and map, the account of the origin of the play and *A Romantic Tale,* Charlotte is content to leave the Young Men's Play to Branwell. She probably became tired of his tyranny and repetitive battles. In June 1829 she turned instead to the Islanders' Play and its exciting associations with the politics of the day. It was not until the middle of August when Charlotte replaced Branwell as editor of *Blackwood's Young Men's Magazine* that her interest in the Young Men revived.

3

The Young Men's Magazine

The idea of a magazine for the Young Men came from Branwell, who was obviously fascinated by the pages of his father's *Blackwood's Magazine.* In January 1829 he produced the first issue of *Branwell's Blackwood's Magazine,* as it was then called. Later, Charlotte changed the name, first to *Blackwood's Young Men's Magazine* in August 1829, and then to *Young Men's Magazine* in August 1830 when she began the Second Series.

Branwell's first issue is a crude little handmade booklet of four leaves, each 5.4 × 3.5 cm. The cover is made from a printed pamphlet advertising *The Life of the Rev. John Wesley* by J. Kershaw for 1s 6d. Paper must have been both scarce and expensive, and it was four miles to the nearest stationers in Keighley. There is no title-page to this magazine but subsequent surviving issues all have both a title-page with an elaborate colophon and a page of contents. Only three of Branwell's miniature magazines survive: those for January, June and July 1829. It is very likely that he also produced issues for the intervening months, for we know for certain that there was a *Branwell's Blackwood's Magazine* for May, as a character in the July issue (Young Soult) says that 'the one for May had two or three pieces of poetry in it'.[1] Moreover, Part 2 of *The Enfant*[2] by Charlotte is featured in *Branwell's Blackwood's Magazine* for June which implies that Part 1 existed in an earlier issue, now lost.

The Young Men were now furnished with a literature proportionate to their size; and while some of them made news, others recorded it in prose and verse. At the end of the July issue of his magazine, Branwell 'published' a Concluding Address to his readers:

We have hitherto conducted this Magazine & we hope to the satisfaction of most. (No one can please all) but as we are conducting a Newspaper which requires all the time and attention we can spare from other employments we have found it expedient to relenquish the editorship of this Magazine, but we recommend our readers to be to the new Editor as they were to me. The new one is the chief Genius Charlotte. She will conduct it in future tho [we] shall write now and then for it. ΔΘH

July 1829 P B Brontë[3]

Branwell's attention may have been diverted to one of the many Glass Town newspapers that he lists in his *Magazine* for June 1829 as Young Mans Intelligencer, The Opposition, The Greybottle, The Glasstown Intelligencer, The Courier Du Francois, and The Quatre Deinne.[4] The addition of Greek letters to the signature of his Concluding Address may indicate that he was also busy with Greek, a new subject that Mr Brontë had added to his son's lessons at home at this time.[5] But it is even more likely that Branwell had become tired of the venture and of Charlotte's constant opposition to its subject matter.

Two poems written in November for the first December issue of Charlotte's *Blackwood's Young Men's Magazine* reveal the rivalry between Charlotte and Branwell for control not only of the magazine but of the whole direction of the Young Men's Play. Branwell, as Sergeant Bud, a Glass Town lawyer, laments the transfer of the magazine to Charlotte:

> All soberness is past and gone
> the reign of gravity is done
> Frivolity comes in its place
> light smiling sits on every face.[6]

Charlotte's writing is 'a flimsy torch glare' compared to the 'grave and gorgeous light' of Branwell's work. But to Charlotte, author of the following poem, the transfer heralds the cessation of a Popian Dullness: 'let thy music rise, lute no more Dullness reigns.'[7] She brings to the magazine 'Foolish romances' and rich descriptions of the 'splendid cloud halls' of 'princely Geni'.

Branwell seems to have disliked the role of the Genii and tried to dispose of them by provoking a Young Men's rebellion against their tyranny. Charlotte, however, sees them as an integral part of her creative world. They provide her with a rich source of description and her magazines are full of articles describing the magical environment of the Genii:

> no longer hid your name is
> ye spirits of the air
> for now your mighty fame is
> set forth in colours fair.[8]

The only time Charlotte mentions the tyranny of the Genii is in the following declamatory fragment, probably intended as a letter, with allegorical significance, to the editor of the *Young Men's Magazine.*

> Sir,—it is well known that the Genii have declared that unless they perform certain arduous duties every year, of a mysterious nature, all the worlds in the firmament will be burnt up, and gathered together in one mighty globe, which will roll in solitary grandeur through the vast wilderness of space, inhabited only by the four high princes of the Genii, till time shall be succeeded by Eternity; and the impudence of this is only to be paralleled by another of their assertions, namely, 'that by their magic might they can reduce the world to a desert, the purest waters to streams of livid poison, and the clearest lakes to stagnant waters, the pestilential vapours of which shall slay all living creatures, except the blood-thirsty beast of the forest, and the ravenous bird of the rock. But that in the midst of this desolation the palace of the Chief Geni shall rise sparkling in the wilderness, and the horrible howl of their warcry shall spread over the land at morning, at noontide and night; but that they shall have their annual feast over the bones of the dead, and shall yearly rejoice with the joy of victors. I think, sir, that the horrible wickedness of this needs no remark, and therefore I haste to subscribe myself, etc.[9]

The high-flown tone of the writing, however, is that of Branwell and although the manuscript is in Charlotte's hand, the signature has been erased and replaced by 'UT' ('us two'), implying that Branwell contributed to its composition.

Many poems throughout *Blackwood's Young Men's Magazine* are signed either 'UT' or 'WT' ('we two'). It seems likely that these initials stand for collaborative efforts by Charlotte and Branwell, since Branwell said he would contribute 'now and then' to the magazines. Yet *Military Conversations,* a contribution to *Blackwood's Young Men's Magazine* for August 1829, suggests a further interpretation for 'UT': here a crusty old General says that he admired a speech by the Marquis of Douro and Lord Charles Wellesley on the subject of the Genii. If this speech refers to the preceding poem in the magazine, which is signed 'UT', then the initials may stand for the Marquis of Douro and Lord Charles, both Charlotte's favourite characters and pseudonyms she used in her early writing. The poem, 'O when shall our brave land be free', rails against the tyranny of the Genii and is more polished than Branwell's 'Dirge of the Geni' written a couple of months earlier: both subject and style are closer to those of Charlotte, so it is possible that she may be the author of almost all the juvenile works signed 'UT' or 'WT'. There are only eleven such manuscripts, however, and since all are in Charlotte's script there is no question but that she had some hand in their composition.[10] It seems that problems of authorship of the early Brontë manuscripts have been greatly exaggerated.

In August 1829, therefore, Charlotte 'edited' her first *Blackwood's Young Men's Magazine.* This was followed by five more monthly issues including a double number for December which ended the first series of the magazine. By gaining control of what was now the central feature of the Young Men's Play, Charlotte was able to develop it according to her own taste. She still worked closely with Branwell, who occasionally contributed to her magazine; but increasingly the magazine became a vehicle for the expression of her own interests and for her apprenticeship in story-telling. With renewed enthusiasm, Charlotte wrote reviews, dialogues, poems and stories for and about the developing Glass Town society. Sometimes she wrote as editor, sometimes as Captain Tree. Glass Town rapidly produced authors, artists, poets and critics whose voices the young author could assume. These she described in detail on 17 December 1829.[11] By the time Charlotte wrote these *Characters of the Celebrated Men of the Present Time* she was fully committed to the Young Men's Play.

4

Our Fellows' Play

The story of Our Fellows' Play is a very different one. Apart from Charlotte's reference to it in *The History of the Year*, there are only two manuscripts that relate directly to Our Fellows' Play, one of them by Branwell and one by Charlotte. The latter is an untitled fragment dated 12 March 1829, and known as 'The origin of the O'Deans.¹' Written on the same day and on paper of the same size, this single page appears to be a continuation of *The History of the Year*. In the latter manuscript Charlotte says, 'I will sketch out the origin of our plays more explicitly if I can. 1 Young men's . . .', and then she proceeds to describe the origins of the Young Men, as we have already seen; but here the manuscript ends abruptly. The fragmentary 'origin of the O'Deans' appears to continue Charlotte's explanation of the second of 'our plays'.

Our Fellows' Play was short-lived. It was established in July 1827 but replaced in December of the same year by the Islanders' Play. With so little evidence its nature is difficult to reconstruct. The following short manuscript is the only surviving description of the origins of Our Fellows:

> The origin of the O'Deans was as follows: we pretended we had each a large island inhabited by people 6 miles high. The people we took out of Esops fables. Hay Man was my chief Man, Boaster Branwell's, Hunter Anne's and Clown Emily's. Our Chief Men were 10 miles high except Emily's who was only 4.
>
> March 12 1829²

The names of the characters were taken from Aesop's *Fables*³ but this tells us little about them. Boaster is the only character to feature in a manuscript other than 'The origin of the O'Deans': he appears as a leading character in Branwell's *History of the Rebellion In My Fellows*, 1828.⁴

Here, in very immature writing and spelling, Branwell describes a series of battles which took place (presumably amongst the wooden soldiers) because Goodman, a rascal, 'did want to Raise A Rebellion'. With '02000 FOOT And 5000 Horse', Goodman marches into Lorraine and sends the following challenge:

Sept. 1827 I will go to war with you little Branwell.
Sept[e]mber 1827 to little -Branwell-
signed good
man.[5]

Branwell orders Boaster to raise more troops and, after losing Lorraine, he successfully besieges Loo, Goodman's capital. Heavy taxes, however, anger the people, so Branwell is obliged to send an embassy to 'Charlotte's country' for more troops. The Battle of Pariment on 1 December 1827, ends the war in Branwell's favour: Goodman agrees to pay him homage, Boaster is created Duke of Bamo, and Branwell, being at peace, begins to build 'churches, castles and other public Buildings, in abundance'.

The dates of the various battles and the presence of Boaster in this manuscript suggest that Branwell is describing an event in Our Fellows' Play of the previous year.[6] As we saw earlier, a character named Goody, possibly this same Goodman, sends a letter to the editor of *Branwell's Blackwood's Magazine* for January 1829. It is written in the 'old young men tongue' invented by Branwell, which may well have originated with Our Fellows.

Our Fellows' Play, then, seems to have been very similar to the early stages of the Young Men's Play. Branwell and his chief man Boaster were in control, and battles were the order of the day. The three girls appear to have taken little interest in Our Fellows. The concept of chief men echoes the Young Men's Play and the idea of islands looks forward to the Islanders' Play. In volume 4 of Charlotte's *Tales of the Islanders* (30 July 1830) we find huge bird-like creatures 'seven feet in height',[7] reminiscent of the giants in Our Fellows' Play. The character of 'Pigtail', a mad Frenchman in *The Enfant* (13 July 1829) and in several of Branwell's manuscripts, is also '7 feet high'.[8] Apart from these minor similarities, however, Our Fellows' Play left little mark on the developing Glass Town Saga.

5

The Islanders' Play

It was the third and last of the Brontë children's 'plays' which had the greatest influence on Charlotte's early creative writing. This was the Islanders' Play, established in December 1827. On 12 March 1829, Charlotte described how it was begun in 'The origin of the Islanders' (see plate 9) which, like 'The origin of the O'Deans', appears to be a continuation of *The History of the Year* since it was written on the same date (12 March 1829), on the same size and type of paper, and its content (a description of the origins of the third 'play') follows naturally after 'The origin of the O'Deans'.[1] The following June, while Branwell was still occupied with *Branwell's Blackwood's Magazine* for the Young Men, Charlotte wrote volume 1 of *Tales of the Islanders,* her first extended attempt at story-telling, involving both political allegory and fairy tale.

In chapter 1 Charlotte gives 'An Account of their Origin'.[2] Here she rewrites her earlier account of 12 March giving a more dramatic description of the scene:

> The play of the Islanders was formed in December 1827 in the following manner. One night about the time when the cold sleet and dreary fogs of November are succeeded by the snow storms and high piercing night winds of confirmed winter, we were all sitting round the warm blazing kitchen fire having just concluded a quarrel with Tabby concerning the propriety of lighting a candle from which she came off victorious, no candle having been produced. a long pause succeeded which was at last broken by B saying, in a lazy manner, 'I don't know what to do.' This was re-echoed by E and A.
>
> T: Wha ya may go t'bed.
> B: I'd rather do anything [than] that.
> & C: You're so glum tonight T. [?Well] suppose we had each an Island.

B: If we had I would choose the Island of Man.
C: And I would choose Isle of Wight.
E: The Isle of Aran for me.
A: And mine should be Guernsey.
C: The Duke of Wellington should be my chief man.
B: [?Heries] should be mine.
E: Walter Scott should be mine.
A: I should have Bentinck.

Here our conversation was interrupted by [the], to us, dismal sound of the clock striking 7 and we were summoned off to bed. The next day we added several others to our list of names till we had got almost all the chief men in the kingdom.[3]

The other chief men referred to are listed in the earlier version. Branwell chose John Bull, Astley Cooper and Leigh Hunt; to Sir Walter Scott, Emily added his son-in-law and grandson, Mr Lockhart and Johnny Lockhart; Anne chose Michael Sadler and Henry Halford to accompany Lord Bentinck; and Charlotte chose, as she put it, 'Duke of Wellington & son, North & Co., 30 officers, Mr Abernethy, & &'.

Tales of the Islanders, however, deals almost exclusively with the adventures of Charlotte's characters. Branwell, Emily and Anne all participate in the Islanders' Play, but Charlotte describes and develops it from her own point of view. In volume I and volume II (chapters 1 and 2 only), Charlotte is describing past events: she traces the setting and early adventures of the Islanders from December 1827 until October 1829. From here on the partnership of the four children seems to lapse, and the continuing tales become Charlotte's own creation.

Free from Branwell's 'Genii tyranny' and the materialism of toy soldiers, the Islanders' Play gave the three girls an opportunity to create a purely fairy-tale world. The Isles of Wight, Aran, Man and Guernsey were soon forgotten. In their place appeared 'a beautiful fiction': Vision Island, which was 'rightly named a dream, for never but in the visions of the night has the eye of man beheld such gorgeous beauty, such wild magnificence, as is in this fairy land.'[4] The island was fifty miles in circumference. Its scenery displayed its debt to the world of enchantment. In parts the island was made 'terribly sublime by mighty rocks rushing streams and roaring cataracts'; in other parts there were glittering fountains, flowery meadows and pleasant woods 'where fairys were said to dwell'. Clear lakes appeared like 'the crystal emerald, framed mirrors of some huge Giant'.[5]

In June 1828 the Palace School was erected on Vision Island. It was to contain a thousand children, all of whom were to be young nobles 'except such as J L' (Johnny Lockhart).[6] Charlotte's description shows that the school was an equally magical construction: 'from a beautiful grove of

9 'The origin of the Islanders', 12 March 1829. A rare example of
Charlotte Brontë's early cursive writing

[?winter] roses and twining woodbine towers a magnificent palace of pure white marble, whose elegant and finely wrought pillars and majestic turrets seem the work of mighty Geni and not of feeble men.' But fairy land is not all beautiful. Behind a statue in the 'Hall of the fountain' a small door leads to a subterranean dungeon. Here the naughty school children are punished and locked in cells,

> so far down in the earth that the loudest shriek could not be heard by any inhabitant of the upper world; and in these, as well as the dungeons, the most unjust torturing might go on without any fear of detection, if it was not that I keep the key of the dungeon and Emily keeps the key of the cells, and the huge strong iron entrance will brave any assault except with the lawful instruments.[7]

As in the Young Men's Play, the children perform an active role in controlling events. Indeed, 'Branwell has a large black club with which he thumps the children upon occasion and that most unmercifully' and, when Branwell can be restrained, the Brontës employed special guards 'for threshing the children'. The Brontës are no longer 'Chief Genii' but 'Little King and Queens'. They form the highest authority on Vision Island. The chief Governor under them is the Duke of Wellington; but this is only an honorary distinction as they realized he was really too busy to run a school for four Yorkshire children in a remote village parsonage. Indeed, from January 1828 the real Duke of Wellington had been Prime Minister of England. They composed an imaginary answer to their request:

> Little King and Queens (these are our titles),
>   I am sorry to say my avocations of Soldier and Statesman will not allow me to comply with your requests that I would be Governer of some 100reds, not [to say] any 1000ds, of children, unless the title be merely honorary and I am to have a few scores of subordinates under me. With the request that it may be,
>   I remain your obedient Subject,
>   W.[8]

His duties are delegated to his two sons, the Marquis of Douro and Lord Charles Wellesley. This is the first time that the Duke's sons are mentioned by name in the juvenilia and their replacement of the Duke is significant. In Charlotte's manuscripts of both the Young Men's Play and the Islanders' Play, 'MD' and 'LCW' gradually become the protagonists at the expense of their father who plays an increasingly minor role. The Duke, his friends and his recent role in political events, however, are still the main concern of this manuscript. Even the school doctors, Sir A. Hume, Sir A. Cooper and Sir H. Halford, have namesakes who are connected with Charlotte's favourite hero: Dr John Robert Hume was the Duke's surgeon from the time of the Peninsular Wars (1808); Sir Astley Cooper was a noted surgeon to George IV and the Duke's neurologist; and Sir Henry Halford was a well-known doctor to Mrs Charles Arbuthnot, a close friend of the Duke.

It is no surprise, then, to find that after the first two chapters of volume I, in which Charlotte sets the scene for the Islanders' Play, chapters 3 and 4 contain adventure stories centred on the Duke of Wellington and his sons. Both chapters are based on political events. The first involves an attempt by Ratten (son of the Whig editor of the *Leeds Mercury*) to poison the Duke who had 'obscured the bright dawn of Whigish intellect!' A 'Giant of Clouds', however, intervenes to save him and after a reverent touch 'new life seemed to be given him'. This incident is a reference to Whig criticism of Wellington in the *Leeds Mercury*. Charlotte is now writing political allegory and, as elsewhere in *Tales of the Islanders,* references to the Duke are couched in biblical phrases. In chapter 4, Charlotte and Emily witness the kidnapping of the Marquis of Douro and Lord Charles by Prince Leopold and Sir George Hill, probably modelled on Prince Leopold of Saxe-Coburg (later King of the Belgians) and General Sir Roland Hill,[9] whom the Duke of Wellington served with in Copenhagen (1807) and again in the Peninsular Wars, and who was Commander-in-Chief of the British Army while Wellington was Prime Minister. This time it is the Duke himself who comes to the rescue with his great bloodhounds; again, with probable political significance, Prince Leopold cringes before him.

The last adventure of volume I involves Charlotte and Emily alone, and may have arisen from one of their earlier 'bed plays'. The landscape, like that of Emily's Parry's Land in the Young Men's Play, is reminiscent of Haworth: here 'the wind sweeps with more fearful blast over this wild bleak moor', mountain sheep graze on the heath and find shelter among the rocks, and the lark springs from his mossy bed when the young authors approach. Later, in volume II of *Tales of the Islanders,* it is Emily's characters who are the main instigators of the School Rebellion. She seems to have played a major role in the formation of the Islanders' Play, which in turn may have influenced her creation of Gondal with its island setting and story of rebellion.[10]

Having recorded the formation of the Islanders' Play in volume I, Charlotte now returned with renewed enthusiasm to the Young Men's Play to take over the 'editorship' of *Blackwood's Young Men's Magazine.* Her attention was also diverted by the exciting political events of 1829. As Charlotte admits, 'For sometime we heard not a word about the school and never took the trouble to inquire.'[11] The centre of interest was the Catholic Emancipation Act which, after much debate, was passed in April 1829. By it, Wellington and Peel had averted the danger of civil war in

Ireland (between Protestant and Roman Catholic) but they had also alienated much of their Tory support, a move which eventually led to their downfall in November 1830. The young Brontës' breathless response to these events has often been quoted. It is recorded in *Tales of the Islanders,* volume II, chapter 1:

> Parliament was opened and the Great Catholic question was brought forward and the Duke's measures were disclosed and all was slander violence party spirit and confusion. O those 3 months from the time of the King's speech to the end! Nobody could think, speak or write on anything but the catholic question and the Duke of Wellington or Mr. Peel. I remember the day when the Intelligence extraordinary came with Mr. Peel's speech in it containing the terms on which the Catholics were to be let in. With what eagerness papa tore off the cover and how we all gathered round him, and with what breathless anxiety we listened as one by one they were disclosed and explained and argued upon so ably and so well; and then, when it was all out, how aunt said she thought it was excellent and that the catholics [could] do no harm with such good security. I remember also the doubts as to whether it would pass into the house of Lords and the prophecies that it would not. And when the paper came which was to decide the question, the anxiety was almost dreadful with which we listened to the whole affair: the opening of the doors, the hush, the Royal Dukes in their robes and the Great Duke in green sash and waistcoat, the rising of all the peeresses when he rose, the reading of his speech, papa saying that his words were like precious gold and, lastly, the majority one to 4 in favour of the bill.

Political discussion, reading the newspapers, a visit to Uncle Fennell at Crosstone, twelve miles from Haworth,[12] and writing articles for *Blackwood's Young Men's Magazine,* kept Charlotte occupied until the end of 1829. At intervals, however, from 6 October until 2 December, she found time to write a second volume of *Tales of the Islanders.* She turned her neglect of the play into subject material: lack of interest in the Palace School leads to 'The School Rebellion'.

Because of the 'catholic question' the Duke of Wellington and Mr Peel were obliged to remain in London. Little King and Queens went there too. The guards, O'Shaugnesy and his nephew Fogharty, were away on a shooting trip and the management of the school was left to the Marquis of Douro and Lord Charles Wellesley. The pupils, who were 'becoming something like civilised beings', suddenly degenerate. They rebel and spilt into four factions headed by Prince Polignes, Prince George, Johnny Lockhart and Princess Vittoria. Sometimes they quarrel amongst themselves, sometimes they unite against the Duke's sons. Eventually the Duke arrives in a balloon from Strathfieldsaye, his country estate,[13] to quell the rebellion with a single autocratic threat. This rebellion is possibly a reference to the various alliances and factions preceding Catholic Emancipation. George IV vacillated between his brother Cumberland, who opposed the bill, and Wellington. Polignes is probably Prince Jules de Polignac, French ambassador in London and later the chief minister of Charles X, whose reactionary policies helped to precipitate the 1830 French Revolution of the 'July Days' after which the French king and his family took refuge in England. The European monarchs were inclined to club together and Polignac, a leader of the so-called 'Cottage Clique' of foreign ambassadors and thought to be the natural son of Charles X, had often caused difficulties for Wellington in his relationship with George IV. Such political intrigue obviously fascinated Charlotte, especially if her hero was involved.

The School Rebellion, however, seems to be symbolic: its denouement is all too simple. The Brontë children had become tired of the Palace School and the Islanders' Play. They 'sent the children off, to their own homes and now only fairies dwell in the Island of a Dream'.[14] Charlotte is now left exclusively in charge. Alone, she pursues her favourite interests: the Duke of Wellington, his two sons, and politics.

The second half of volume II (chapters 3, 4 and 5) and the whole of volumes III and IV contain separate adventure stories centring on these three interests. Vision Island has gone; the scene is set solidly in England at Strathfieldsaye, the Horse Guards and No.10 Downing Street. But fairy land is not entirely dismissed: it plays a necessary part in Charlotte's political allegory.

In volume II, chapter 4 (21 November 1829), Lord Charles Wellesley asks his father for a story of one of his adventures in India or Spain. The Duke then describes a Vision of the Future presented to him after the Battle of Salamanca during the Peninsular Wars. He tells how, having written his despatches, he went for a walk in the coolness of a Spanish evening. He followed the River Tormes far from the city into an enchanted forest. There he was confronted with a huge mirror with the word 'Futurity' flashing in letters of lightning among the dark clouds reflected from some unknown source. When the storm in the mirror cleared, a beautiful island appeared linked by a golden chain to a smaller island:

> In the middle of the largest of these 2 islands was a tall and majestic female seated on a throne of ruby, crowned with roses, bearing in one hand a wreath of oak-leaves and in the other a sword, while over her the tree of liberty flourished spreading its branches far and wide and casting the perfume of its flowers to the uttermost parts of the earth. [In] the midst of the other island there was likewise a female who sat on an emerald throne. Her crown was formed of shamrocks. In her right hand she held a harp and her robes were of a crimson hue, as if they had been

dyed in blood. She was as majestic as the other but in her countenance was something very sad and sorrowful, as if a terrible evil hung upon her.

Here, Charlotte is recalling the many illustrations of England and Ireland personified which she must have seen in the newspapers and magazines of the time. While the Duke watches the mirror, a tremendous monster branded with the word 'bigotry' bursts from the sea and begins to desolate the smaller island:

> He seemed to pursue with inveterate fury a horrible old man who a voice whispered in my ear was called the Romish Religion. At first he seemed weak and impotent, but as he ran he gathered strength and the more he was persecuted the stronger he became, till at length he began with a terrible voice to defy his persecutor and at the same time strove to break the golden chain which united the two islands.

A warrior, whose brow was already crowned with many wreaths, enters the scene and, protected by a mighty shield in the sky, slays the monster with the dart of Justice. The desolate land again becomes green, the tree of liberty flourishes, and the spirits of both islands honour their saviour. Wellington has become St George and the political events which Charlotte described so enthusiastically in volume II, chapter 1, have become allegory.

The following chapter, written on 2 December 1829, is also related to the question of Catholic Emancipation. A traveller tells how he discovered the wickedness of Roman Catholicism in Southern Ireland and its association with necromancy. A servant shows him the value of searching the Bible for himself and thus he is converted to the Church of England, whose doctrines 'most closely assimilated with the word of God'.

Volume III, chapter 1 (5 May 1830), opens with an amusing scene at No. 10 Downing Street. The Duke of Wellington, who was Prime Minister at the time Charlotte wrote this, is surrounded by his cabinet: Eldon, 'one-armed Hardinge', 'coxcomical Rosslyn', Castlereagh and 'Mr. Secretary Peel . . . whispering and wheedling in the Duke's ear'. The Duke is unravelling 'a confused mass of exchequer-like figures left by poor Vesey in a sad state of disorder when he was seized with the sickness which superannuated him', namely, the loss of his seat in County Clare to the 'illegal' Catholic candidate Daniel O'Connell.[15] Political cynicism is curiously blended here with fairy-tale naivety; for while the Duke is busy working, one of the Little Queens enters disguised as a shrunken old woman. She presents the Duke with a letter written in blood and sealed with a seal bearing the motto 'le message d'un revenant'. The Marquis of Douro is in danger and the Duke rushes immediately to Strathfieldsaye. There he enlists the help of Seringapatan,[16] an old veteran who lives on his estate, and with Lord Charles Wellesley, they go in search of the Marquis. After a long journey through the romantic scenery of precipices and cataracts, the Duke finds his son in a vast cavern, and they are all miraculously assisted home by a supernatural power.

This episode is typical of Charlotte's early stories. The introductory scene is described with care, then an unrelated incident occurs to remove the story to another scene. Seringapatan's cottage is vividly realized, as is the countryside surrounding Strathfieldsaye. The journey in search of the Marquis moves rapidly and with a certain amount of anticipation, but the denouement is an anti-climax. Whether because Charlotte lost interest or because her inventive power was flagging, the ending is huddled into one of the eight manuscript pages. The Duke and the Genii together fulfil the role of *deus ex machina* and a rather feeble apology is appended: 'To all the questions put to the marquis respecting his sufferings while in that cave, his invariable answer has been that they were indescribable.' Charlotte is more concerned with the description of political characters and natural scenery than with the form of her adventure stories, although the following story in volume II, chapter 2, is more balanced: it begins and ends at Downing Street after a visit made by the Duke and Little King and Queens to the Horseguards.

Throughout *Tales of the Islanders,* the role of Little King and Queens becomes increasingly important. It culminates in their disguise as the '3 Old Washerwomen of Strathfieldsaye' in volume IV, chapter 1 (14 July 1830), which includes an amusing self-portrait of Charlotte and her brother and sisters:

> The path brought [the Duke] in sight of the figures of 3 old women seated on a green bank under a holly, knitting with the utmost rapidity and keeping their tongues in constant motion all the while. Stretched in a lounging posture beside them lay Little King, languidly gathering the violets and cuckoo-meat which grew around. At the Duke's approach he started up, as likewise did the old women. They courtesied and he bowed, much after the fashion of a Dip-Tail on a stone.

Little King acts as spokesman and requests employment for the old washerwomen since they have recently been dismissed by the new Sir Robert Peel 'to make room for the modern trash of foppish varlets that now constitute every gentleman's establishment'.[17] The Duke refers them to his housekeeper Mrs Laura Dovelike, a possible portrait of Aunt Branwell with her 'old fashioned bustling black silk gown with cap and ruff starched to the consistence of buckram'. They are employed at Strathfieldsaye but their stay is fraught with quarrels incited by Little King, who does no work but has a 'constant disposition to all kinds of mischief'. Charlotte's sketch of Branwell is an early criticism of his privileged position in the

Brontë household, for he acts more like 'an evil brownie than a legitimate fairy'.

In volume IV, chapter 2 (30 June 1830), Charlotte used the framework of a tale-within-a-tale for her story about Mirza, a Moslem woodcutter in the Caucasus. A conversation about astrology, the Marquis of Douro's favourite subject, prompts Lord Charles to relate a story to his brother about Mirza's adventures on the moon. These are a combination of 'Sinbad the Sailor', from the *Arabian Nights,* and *Gulliver's Travels:* first Mirza is borne into the air by a dragon and rescued from a landscape of earthquake and lava by strange birds who nurse him in their tree-top nests; and then he is rescued by an eagle, only to be dropped into another strange land and surrounded by huge female forms. The giants, thirty to forty feet tall, anoint Mirza and sacrifice him to their mountain god. As in so many of Charlotte's early tales, however, the conclusion is 'clad in a veil of mystery'. Lord Charles tells how Mirza miraculously survived the sacrificial flame to awake at the door of his hut.

The framework of this last tale of the Islanders' Play is particularly significant. Before Lord Charles tells his story he and his brother watch Marian Hume, a character from the Young Men's Play, in the garden of her home which is situated near the Duke of Wellington's country palace. Yet at the end of the tale the Duke appears to fetch his sons home to Strathfieldsaye — his English estate of the Islanders' Play. Already, Strathfieldsaye has merged into a 'Glass Town' setting.

6

The Fusion of the Plays

For a year and a half the Young Men's Play and the Islanders' Play continued to develop side by side. The little Brontës did not simply turn from the Islanders back to the toy soldiers and the Young Men.[1] The sequence of Charlotte's manuscripts shows that the creative process is not as simple as this. Elements of both plays, especially the principal characters, overlapped; gradually they merged into a single imaginary vision.

The fusion of the two plays in Charlotte's mind was inevitable. Little King and Queens of the Islanders' Play were the four Chief Genii of the Young Men's Play. Both were part of a supernatural world: all-powerful, they could direct events and cure 'instantaneously by the application of some fairy remedy'.[2] The Duke of Wellington, Charlotte's chief man, was the main character in both plays. It was political interest which kept him in England for so long in the Islanders' Play; but it was only a matter of time till he joined his 'African' counterpart of the Young Men's Play.

As early as 7 August 1829, we find Charlotte writing a fragment of 300 words in which both worlds are combined.[3] With excited anticipation the Wellesley family await Arthur's return from England. They have not seen him since he was a small boy and was 'conveyed on board the ship which was to take [him] to Eton College', the school of the real Duke of Wellington and his two sons. The young Arthur of this fragment could refer to the Duke of Wellington himself, but Arthur is more likely to be his son, since the adult children of the Marquis and Marchioness of Wellesley (Wellington's parents) all feature in this manuscript. In an untitled poem of February 1830 (often called 'Homesickness') Charlotte also writes of the Duke's younger son, Lord Charles Wellesley, pining at Eton for his West African home:

> Of College I am tired; I wish to be at home,
> Far from the pompous tutor's voice, and the hated school-boy's groan.
>
> I wish that I had freedom to walk about at will;
> That I no more was troubled with my Greek and slate and quill.
>
> I wish to see my kitten, to hear my ape rejoice,
> To listen to my nightingale's or parrot's lovely voice.
>
> And England does not suit me: it's cold and full of snow;
> So different from black Africa's warm, sunny, genial glow.[4]

The Search after Happiness, written in the same month as the first fragment above, is set in Glass Town; but again the Chief of the City and his sons are in every way similar to the Duke and his sons of the Islanders' Play. Although they are not referred to by name in the story, these characters are identified in the Preface, and the African setting is clearly referred to in the description of sunrise over the city. Sunrise and sunset were favourite subjects for the young author and the following passage is typical of her early writing:

> All along the eastern horizon there was a rich glowing light which as it rose gradually melted into the pale blue of the sky in which just over the light there was still visible the silver crescent of the moon. In a short time the sun began to rise in golden glory casting his splendid radiance over all the face of nature and illuminating the magnificent city in the midst of which towering in silent grandeur there appeared the Palace where dwelt the mighty Prince of that great and beautiful city all around the brazen gates and massive walls of which there flowed the majestic stream of the Guadima whose Banks were bordered by splendid palaces and magnificent gardens. Behind these stretching for many a league were fruitful plains and forests whose shade seemed almost impenetrable to a single ray of light while in the distance blue mountains were seen raising their heads to the sky and forming a misty girdle to the plains of Dahomey.[5]

Henry O'Donell is discontented with his life in this new city. In a manner reminiscent of Johnson's *Rasselas,* he sets out in pursuit of happiness and is soon joined by Alexander De Lancy, a Frenchman on a similar quest. After passing through a subterranean tunnel they emerge in a fantasy land of liquid mountains, black forests and vivid skies streaked by lightning. They dwell here contented until the voice of memory reminds O'Donell of old friends. A chance meeting with an old man reinforces his longing for home: he hears how the old man's experiences with 'dreadful scenes of magic' have left him lonely and apprehensive of the future. Several years pass until one day De Lancy disappears. Again O'Donell thinks of his old friends, the 'mighty Warrior King' and the two young princes. In desperation, he promises a lifetime of servitude to a Genius in return for a visit to Glass Town. Once there, he no sooner relates his experiences to the Duke than a loud voice absolves him of his promise and he is free to dwell in his native city for the rest of his life. Even Alexander De Lancy, he soon learns, is safe at home in the city of Paris, now a rich merchant and favourite with the Emperor Napoleon. Happiness, the young Charlotte implies, lies with loved ones at home.

The main difference between the two plays of the Islanders and the Young Men is in the setting and the minor characters. Apart from visions of fairyland, the realistic English scene forms the background of the Islanders' Play, whereas the Young Men are firmly established in an imaginary African setting. Unlike the Young Men, minor characters in the Islanders' Play are more closely associated with real people who figure in the political events of the day. But gradually even these differences between the plays are resolved. After *Tales of the Islanders,* volume IV, such colourful creations as Seringapatan, Old Man Cockney and Game-Keeper (veterans residing at Strathfieldsaye) disappear from the juvenilia. The Duke's cabinet colleagues are also disposed of, although Castlereagh is eventually revived and a Prime Minister of the later juvenilia, Warner Howard Warner, bears a close resemblance to Peel. Several of the Duke's military friends survive the Islanders' Play: Hill and Murray[6] were, after all, original members of the Young Men's Play and feature in *A Romantic Tale.* Dr Hume, his daughter and Lady Wellington, also part of the Young Men's Play, continue to appear in the manuscripts of 1830.

The discrepancy in setting is not resolved until the end of the year when, in *Albion and Marina* (12 October 1830), Charlotte tells how the Duke and his sons were transported to Africa. After living in England for many years, his time divided between his country estate and other 'important avocations', the Duke determines to visit 'that wonder of the world, the great city of Africa: the Glass Town, of whose splendour, magnificence, and extent, strength and riches, occasional tidings came from afar, wafted by breezes of the ocean to Merry England.'[7] To most Englishmen, including the young Brontës themselves, Glass Town bore 'the character of a dream or gorgeous fiction'. Here we have an obvious echo from *Tales of the Islanders,* relating Vision Island to the Glass Town. The creations of both plays had for Charlotte the same dream-like quality. Englishmen visiting Glass Town could not believe that 'mere human beings could construct fabrics of such marvellous size and grandeur as many of the public buildings were represented to be'. The Duke wished to establish the truth of 'the exaggerating page of history', Charlotte's own effusive descriptions of her African kingdom. The Duke also possessed vast dominions near the African coast (Wellington's Land) which he had never seen. His fame had spread to that new land, and Glass Townians had often invited him to stay. He and his family are therefore warmly welcomed when they arrive in Africa. After visiting his kingdom the Duke returns to the 'chief metropolis' and establishes what proves to be a permanent residence, Waterloo Palace. Marian Hume, the Marquis of Douro's childhood sweetheart of the Islanders' Play, also becomes part of the Glass Town world although Charlotte continues to write poems on the separation of the two lovers.[8] The landscape of the English Strathfieldsaye is left behind; it reappears later in Wellington's Land. By the end of October, then, the main elements of the Islanders' Play had merged completely into the 'Glass Town Saga'.

7

The Great Glass Town

The manuscripts of 1830 show a preoccupation with the Glass Town scene.[1] Charlotte begins the year with a poem 'Written upon the occasion of the dinner given to the literati of the Glass Town'.[2] The dinner indicates how much prestige literature has in this new society. Increasingly Charlotte writes under the names of her Glass Town authors. On 16 January in the guise of 'Captain Tree', the only pseudonym she had used in 1829, Charlotte describes the Duke of Wellington's country palace situated far to the north-west of Glass Town. She invokes again the original scenery of the Young Men's Play: the Jibbel Kumri (or Mountains of the Moon) to the north of Glass Town and the great Sahara Desert where beings of a supernatural nature transform 'barren and dreary sand into blooming and fragrant paradises'. As Captain Tree travels through this desert an oasis appears, where a mixture of English and African vegetation surround a palace of the Classical style so popular with the Glass Town aristocracy:

> The whole horizon was bounded by gentle hills covered with groves of plantains and palmettos intermixed with long slopes of green and pleasant verdure. In the middle of the island was a palace of the purest white marble, whose simple and most beautiful and noble style of architecture forcibly reminded [me] of many of the great palaces of the Glass Town. Around it lay a wide garden stretched over all the country as far as the range of hills. Here the tufted olive, the fragrant myrtle, the stately palm-tree, the graceful almond, the rich vine and the queenly rose mingled in sweet and odorous shadiness, and bordered the high banks of a clear and murmuring river over whose waters a fresh breeze swept which cooled delightfully the burning air of the desert which surrounded [it].[3]

At the end of the manuscript Captain Tree draws an intimate picture of the Wellesley family, introducing for the first time Lord Charles Wellesley's pet animals: Tringia the monkey, Trill the kitten and Philomel the nightingale. An unnamed parrot is also referred to in the poem 'Homesickness' and features later in *Tales of the Islanders*, volume IV. The young Lord Charles, like the Brontë children themselves, is always surrounded by his pets — often to the exclusion of other people.

Almost every subsequent manuscript of the early period is written not by Captain Tree but either by Lord Charles himself or by his elder brother, often referred to as either 'LCW' or 'MD'. The Marquis writes poetry while Lord Charles writes prose and drama. Occasionally Captain Tree contributes an article to the *Young Men's Magazine* which is revived in August 1830.

On 22 February Lord Charles Wellesley writes *The Adventures of Mon Edouard de Crack*.[4] Edouard de Crack is an orphan who decides to seek his fortune in Paris, the capital of Frenchy Land. When he arrives in the city, however, his money is stolen and he is forced to work for a Tavern Master of dubious reputation, probably the notorious 'Pigtail' whose history is told by Branwell.[5] After five years a black giant whirls him away to fairy land where Eugene Beauchamp, a 'Pan-like' figure, directs him to Glass Town. He is awed by the sight of the fortified city which stands in the midst of a beautiful valley.

Glass Town has changed since its early formation in *A Romantic Tale*. It is still a fairy-tale creation:

> the architecture was the soul of nobleness, grandeur, magnificence and elegance combined. . . . The public buildings were resplendent with grace, symmetry, majesty and proportion; and an immense bridge which gloriously spanned the . . . river was a perfect model of bold, light, simple architecture. In short De Crack would have been in doubt as to whether this city was the abode of mortal if it was not for observing certain narrow black lines winding among the splendid palaces and squares.

But the city is now also a hive of commercial activity. The Industrial Age has reached Glass Town. All along the river bank there are

> lofty mills and warehouses piled up story above [story] to the very clouds, surmounted by high, tower-like chimneys vomiting forth huge columns of thick, black smoke, while from their walls the clanking, mighty din of machinery sounded and resounded till all that quarter of the city rang again with the tumult.

At the mouth of the river lie huge steam boats and merchant ships blackened by the pollution. The inhabitants, hurrying to and fro, smell of 'rancid train oil'. Each has 'a bold independent look and step, which told that they descended from the Dukes of York and Lanca[s]ter.'⁶ Stumps, after a long absence from Glass Town, also notices the alteration in 'the old lady'.⁷ So sophisticated does the city become by the end of 1830 that even its name must be changed to a more elevated form: Verreopolis, 'being compounded of a Greek and French word to that effect';⁸ although the new name is soon corrupted into Verdopolis.

Glass Town society has also changed. Many of its leading men are those of the Young Men's Play but their characters have altered. Others are newcomers, drawn by the brilliance and patronage which the new city offers. The Duke has slipped into the background. The Marquis of Douro is now an elegant young nobleman, a Captain in the Royal Regiment of the Horse Guards, who 'delights to dwell among pensive thoughts and ideas'.⁹ He gathers around him painters (De Lisle, Le Brun and Dundee) and poets such as Young Soult the Rhymer.¹⁰ The title-page of the Marquis's poems proclaims his varied interests:

MARQUIS OF
DOURO
MEMBER OF THE SOCIETY OF ANTI-
QUARIANS: PRESIDENT FOR 1830 OF
THE LITERARY CLUB; HONORARY
MEMBER OF THE ACADEMY OF ARTISTS
& TREASURER TO THE SOCIETY FOR
THE SPREAD OF CLASSICAL KNOW-
LEDGE; CHIEF SECRETARY OF THE
CONFEDERATE HUNDRED FOR PRO-
MOTING GYMNASTIC EXERCISES
&C. &C. &C.¹¹

One of his distinctive traits is his adherence to a medieval code of honour. In the early juvenilia his conduct is dictated by 'the stern Goddess of Honour'. In 1833 he is still under her 'iron Thraldom'¹² and continues to pay her lip service in later manuscripts. His powers of conversation are also notable: they are described in ecstatic terms by the unnamed author of a fragment written in 1881.¹³ The Marquis entertains his companion with a lively variety of subjects ranging from archery to astronomy, and with a command of language that leaves his listener wondering whether a mere human being could be endowed with such rare beauty and genius.

Unlike his elder brother, Lord Charles Wellesley is lively and gay. His songs are 'airy visions' compared to the 'shrouded cloudy ghosts' of the Marquis. But his wit is sharp and piercing: 'he often lets it play harmlessly round his opponent, then strikes him fiercely to the heart.'¹⁴ This sharpness of tongue gradually becomes more pronounced, as does his love of scandal.

11   *Arthur Wellesley, Marquis of Douro and Duke of Zamorna. Undated pencil
drawing attributed to Charlotte Brontë*

*An Interesting Passage in the Lives of Some eminent men of the Present
time* by Lord Charles Wellesley (18 June 1830)[15] clearly reveals his
nature. He is proud of his hypocrisy and deceit. The *valet de chambre* to
Captain Tree furnishes Lord Charles with a story which he delights in
repeating to his reader. We learn that there has been a robbery at the Glass
Town Public Library. Prominent members of Glass Town's literary society
are involved, including Lieutenant Brock (the Chief Librarian), Captain
Tree (prose writer), Sergeant Tree (bookseller and publisher), Captain

John Bud ('the ablest political writer'), and Sergeant Bud ('a clever lawyer' and 'dusty book-worm'). They secrete the stolen books in a coffin and lodge it in a large vault in the cemetery. Tree is surprised next day at the cemetery by Dr Hume Badey and two of Glass Town's villains, Young Man Naughty and Ned Laury, notorious body-snatchers eager for fresh material for the doctor's medical research. Hume promises not to inform on Tree if he undertakes to provide him with a living subject each week, but when Tree threatens to tell of Hume's illegal activities Hume kills him and then resuscitates him later in his 'macerating tub'. It would seem from this incident that Charlotte was aware of the famous case the previous year of the murderers Hare and Burke, who sold bodies to the surgeon, Dr Knox, for dissection.[16] The remainder of her story may also be based on current events, among them theft at the local Keighley Mechanics' Institute Library to which Mr Brontë belonged.

Lord Charles is 'at his dirty work again' in *The Poetaster A Drama In Two Volumes* (6—12 July 1830), where he ridicules Young Soult in the figure of Henry Rhymer. This would-be poet subscribes to the view that poetry should 'come spontaneously', yet his hackneyed language, pedestrian rhyme and fondness for pathetic fallacy all belie his pretension to inspirational genius. Captain Tree, Lord Charles's constant literary rival, is also treated disparagingly. He is mocked for his pompous attitude to poets as 'choice spirits' and is seen labouring in his study 'to bring some exquisite passage neatly to a close'.[17] After unsuccessful attempts to seek patronage, Rhymer murders Captain Tree in a fit of passion but is saved from the hangman's noose by the magnanimity of Lord Charles and the timely resuscitation of Tree. Rhymer must promise to take up a useful occupation and to write no more.

In *Visits in Verreopolis,* volume I (7—11 December 1830) Lord Charles torments his brother and mocks his love affairs. Captain Bud, one of Lord Charles's few friends, contributes to his scandalmongering with a verse drama on the rivals for the Marquis of Douro's love, namely Marian Hume and the Glass Town blue-stocking, Lady Zenobia Ellrington, renowned alike for her reading of Herodotus in the original and for her rage: as Lord Charles warns, 'it is no very pleasant thing to fall under the hatred of a learned lady.'[18] He has often been assisted from the room by her dextrous foot and usually retaliates by circulating some malicious rumour about her. With such practice, Lord Charles Wellesley is an accomplished reporter of Glass Town gossip by the end of 1830; he is the ideal vehicle for the young author eager to submerge her identity in her imaginary world.

8

The Young Author

In August 1830 Charlotte began a second series of the *Young Men's Magazine*. For two months she concentrated solely on its production, writing in rapid succession enough numbers to last until the end of the year (including two issues for December, as in 1829).[1] The chief contributors were the most prominent Glass Town authors: 'LCW', 'MD' and 'Captain Tree' (Charlotte's three pseudonyms). The magazine was 'Edited by Charlotte Brontë herself and sold by Sergeant Tree, Captain Tree's son, and all other booksellers in the Chief Glass Town. Its circulation reached all sectors of the African kingdoms: Duke of Wellington's Glass Town, Ross's Glass Town, Parry's Glass Town and Paris, in Branwell's Frenchy Land. Like the first series, the magazine contained poetry, prose, reviews, dialogues and letters. It provided the Glass Town inhabitants with the opportunity to advertise their latest books or inventions. Thus we find such whimsical announcements as 'THE ART OF BLOWING One's Nose' taught by Monsieur Pretty-foot of No. 105 Blue Rose Street or Young Man Naughty's offer to kill 'Rare lads' at Ned Laury's Inn.[2] 'Rare lads' or 'rare apes' are terms of approbation used loosely by the Glass Town 'heavies' to refer both to themselves and to others, usually those destined to be the victims of their body-snatching raids.

The magazine articles for 1830 provide us with valuable hints about the amount of co-operation between the four Brontë children at this stage. They had all contributed to the establishment of the various 'plays'. These had now merged into a single Glass Town world. There is evidence that, under Charlotte's directing hand, all four children were still in close partnership in July 1830 when Charlotte wrote the last volume of *Tales of the Islanders.* We have seen that this was very definitely Charlotte's version of the Islanders' Play, but she concluded the fourth volume with a significant farewell:

> 4 volume of the Plays of Islands,
> That is Emily's Branwell's Ann's and my lands;
> And now I bid a kind and glad good-bye
> To those who o'er my book cast indulgent eye.

It would appear that in the latter half of 1830 these lands, now part of the Glass Town Confederacy, were developing with very different characteristics. They reflect the changing interests and self-assertion of their controlling 'Genii'. Emily was now twelve years old; Anne was two years younger. They were no longer content to play a subordinate role in the Glass Town scene and seem to have reacted against Charlotte's romantic world. Their characters Parry and Ross are blunt, unpolished Yorkshiremen whose lands and capitals form a real contrast to the brilliance of Glass Town.

The *Young Men's Magazine* for October 1830 carries an article entitled *A Day at Parry's Palace,* by Lord Charles Wellesley. Charles, 'positively dying of ennui' in the city, decides to pay a visit to William Edward's Country (Sir Edward Parry's land, watched over by the protective gaze of 'Genius Emily'). He is immediately 'struck with the changed aspect of everything.' He and his creator Charlotte are scornful of the unromantic scenery: 'No proud castle or splendid palace towers insultingly over the cottages around. No high-born noble claimed allegiance of his vassals or surveyed his broad lands with hereditary pride.' This is not the dream-like vision Charlotte had created. All is eminently practical and mundane: 'rivers rushed not with foam and thunder . . . but glided canal-like along, walled on each side that no sportive child might therein find a watery grave.' Emily's land has the realism of Yorkshire with its stone walls and factories 'breathing thick columns of almost tangible smoke'. Parry's Palace is the antithesis of Waterloo Palace. It is a square stone building with a blue slate roof. Their 'majesties' are equally anti-heroic: shy and retiring except in the company of their great friend Captain John Ross (Anne's Chief Man). Lord Charles Wellesley is quite out of place. He understands little of their heavy northern dialect, finds their table manners uncouth and their diet of roast beef, Yorkshire pudding, mashed potatoes, apple pie and preserved cucumbers plain and unvaried. He concludes that although his visit was 'intolerably dull' it did give him 'some notion of things as they are'. This was the world of realism, to which Emily and Anne were to become increasingly committed. Charlotte and Branwell were moving steadily in the opposite direction.

The close partnership between Charlotte and her brother in their early writing has always been stressed by biographers. This is supported by constant references throughout Charlotte's manuscripts of 1830 to the developing friendship of the Marquis of Douro and Young Soult.[3] The origin of their intimacy is traced by Charlotte in *A Frenchmans Journal Concluded By Tree* (4 September 1830). Young Soult The Rhymer, son of the great French Marshal, has fallen upon hard times and is forced to work as a servant in a tavern. Such degradation causes him to waste away until he is found in a delirium by the Marquis of Douro and Lord Charles Wellesley who seek shelter for the night in the tavern. They rescue Soult from neglect and scorn France's abuse of her poet.

Young Alexander Soult is Branwell's favourite early pseudonym. Whereas Charlotte chose to write of Wellington's two sons, Branwell's preference had always been for France and her heroes. His chief man in the Young Men's Play had originally been Napoleon (since replaced by 'Sneaky'). He had been the founder of Frenchy Land and the creator of Young Napoleon and his friends Young Murat, Young Ney and Young Soult, imaginary sons of Napoleon's famous marshals. Now, with little regard for history, Young Soult is transported to Glass Town to join Wellington's family in Waterloo Palace: the Marquis of Douro and Young Soult are firm friends and fellow poets.

Lord Charles Wellesley is envious of this friendship and takes every opportunity to mock Young Soult whom he terms 'The Poetaster'. In chapter 4 of *Visits in Verreopolis,* volume I, Lord Charles describes Young Soult's penchant for romantic settings. Alexander Soult has left the bustle of Waterloo Palace for a secluded little Gothic hall, overgrown by climbing jasmine and roses. Lord Charles finds him posed against the sill of an open lattice window contemplating a fast-disappearing rainbow:

> 'Well, Alexander, how are you after the rain?'
> 'Why, how can I be otherwise than refreshed while the influence of that sweet spring shower is diffusing balm and peace over the earth.'
> 'It will help to bring forward the crops I hope.'
> 'Aye. I hear the flowers and grass growing! The sound is like the faint sigh of rising zephyrs.'
> 'Your ears are more acute than mine then, Alexander.'
> 'It may be so. Poetry refines all the senses in a marvellous degree.'

Young Soult has no sense of humour. Like Branwell, he is deadly serious about his poetry and Lord Charles may well be reflecting his creator's attitude to her brother's writing.

From the end of July 1829, when Branwell ceased to 'edit' the Glass Town magazine, he concentrated on writing poetry. As 'Young Soult the Rhymer' he produced *A Collection of Poems . . . Illustrated with Notes And Commentarys by Monsieur De La Chate[a]ubriand,* 30 September

1829.[4] The following December he wrote *Laussane: A Dramatic Poem,* again by Young Soult the Rhymer,[5] and throughout 1830 he continued to write poetry, in particular *Caractacus. A Dramatic Poem* and *The Revenge A Tragedy in 3 Acts.*[6] These little works show that the young Branwell had considerable knowledge of ancient history, the classics, seventeenth-, eighteenth- and early nineteenth-century literature (especially Shakespeare, Jonson, Pope and Goethe) and recent French history. They are also remarkable for the seriousness and pretension with which the thirteen-year-old boy sets about his task of producing 'great' literature. On the title-pages of *Caractacus* and *The Revenge* he quotes the imaginary Captain Bud's 'Synopis of Dramatic writing Vol.I p 130': 'In Dramatic Poetry the passions are the cheif thing and in Proportion as exelence in the depicting of these is obtained so the writer of the poem takes his class among dramatic authors.' And he concludes his preface on the following page with a direct challenge to Charlotte's good-humoured criticism: 'Let them who are impartial judge me and my work, not the base and sneering critics who having no excellence of their own employ themselves in underrating those of others.'[7]

From the first hint of discord when Charlotte took over the *Young Men's Magazine,* the children's manuscripts are full of rivalry. Their characters are constantly carping at each other or being misrepresented by their rival creators. *The Liar Unmasked* (19 June 1830), written by Captain Bud, Branwell's pseudonym when writing prose, begins:

> It has always been the fortune of eminent men in all ages and every country to have their lives, their actions and their works traduced by asses of unprincipled wretches who having no character of their own to support and being too indolent to work, vilely employ their days in spitting their venom on every author of reputation within their reach. Homer has his Zoilus, Virgil his Mearius and Captain Tree his Wellesley.[8]

Bud then gives his version of Lord Charles Wellesley's life, refuting his latest story of the library theft,[9] in which Lord Charles 'vomited forth a dose of scandal and self-importance in the shape of an octave volume'. It is fit, Bud says, only for Charlotte's 'Miss M. Hume, or any of her hysterical and delicate crew'. Even Charlotte's recent poem 'The Vision'[10] is censured as a mere repetition of earlier trifling works which have little to redeem them from oblivion.

When Lord Charles satirizes Young Soult a month later, then, in the guise of the poetaster Henry Rhymer, Charlotte is answering her brother's pompous prose and mocking his poetical efforts: in an onslaught of romantic cliché, Rhymer rails against the 'insatiate depths of [his] dark, unfathomable soul'. Branwell's 'extraneous effusions' are also ridiculed in an article in the *Young Men's Magazine*[11] written soon after *The Poetaster*. As usual Young Soult gets carried away by his own eloquence when he describes a recent jaunt in the country. He tells how he experienced 'a delightful kind of insanity' amidst the supernatural loveliness of Nature, and then swoons at the beauty of his poetic vision. Lord Charles mockingly cries, 'Ring the bell, be quick, bring Hartshorn, cold water, vinegar, salvolatic, [?salzaikaling] and sal everything else, the Poet has fallen into an inspiration dream! Haste, haste if you mean to save his life!' The Marquis calmly advises his friend Soult not to allow his genius to gain ascendancy over his reason, since it exposes him more to ridicule than to admiration. Is this the young Charlotte's advice to her brother? Certainly she is mocking the excesses of the Romantic imagination and the cultivation of wildness in Nature. As Sergeant Bud concludes, such poets are probably mad. Charlotte constantly reaffirms in her juvenile manuscripts that a writer cannot rely on inspiration alone:

> How much people in general are deceived in their ideas of great authors. Every sentence is by them thought the outpourings of a mind overflowing with the sublime and beautiful. Alas, did they but know the trouble it often costs me for me to bring some exquisite passage neatly to a close, to avoid the too frequent repetition of the same word, to polish and round the period and to do many other things. They would soon lower the high standard at which our reputation is fixed. But still the true poet and proser have many moments of unalloyed delight while preparing their lucubrations for the press and the public.[12]

Charlotte had drawn an even earlier sketch of her brother in her *Characters of the Celebrated Men of the Present Time* (December 1829). Here Young Soult is attributed with a fine imagination but his versification is not good. His disposition is reminiscent of the later caricature of Branwell in volume IV of *Tales of the Islanders.* Young Soult is 'devilish but humane and good natured'.[13] His hair is frizzed in such a manner 'as to make one suppose he had come out of a furze bush'; he is careless in his dress and twitches about the mouth. With a certain prescience not uncommon in the juvenilia, Charlotte describes Young Soult's fondness for drinking and gambling, which causes[5] him to be unnaturally excitable.

Branwell was not just a butt for Charlotte's developing sense of humour however. His preoccupation with poetry and his fascination with France had a distinct influence on her, as we see especially in her manuscripts of 1830. In this year she wrote three times as many poems as she did in 1829, and her stories increasingly include poems as part of the text. All Charlotte's early poems relate to the Glass Town Saga. The only exception to this is *A Translation into English Verse of the First Book of Voltaire's Henriade From the French* on 11 August 1830. The *Henriade* was popular in early nineteenth-century England. Charlotte possessed her own copy of it which she inscribed 'May, 1830'.[14] A later school-friend recorded that Charlotte had taught herself 'a little French' before going to Roe Head school in 1831; others maintain that she probably gained some knowledge of French from her aunt, Miss Branwell, who may have had a French governess in her home in Penzance.[15] There is no evidence that Mr Brontë, proud of his Greek and Latin, knew any French. But however she acquired the elements of the language, Charlotte's translation has been judged 'remarkably accurate' with 'no need to ask for any special indulgence for its author on the grounds of her youth'.[16] In the *Henriade* she infused an already dramatic subject with her own romanticism.

Charlotte's new interest in French and Branwell's enthusiasm are reflected especially in *A Frenchmans Journal,* a serial which ran through five numbers of the Second Series of the *Young Men's Magazine,*[17] and which provided the young author with an excuse to describe recent French history and the Parisian scene. Late the previous year she had written another French serial in two parts,[18] describing the good fortune a young Swiss artist experiences in Paris under the patronage of the Comte de Lausanne, a name obviously influenced by the central character in Branwell's dramatic poem *Laussane,* composed at the same time. Both these serials express Charlotte's childhood ambition to visit Paris, to experience the splendour of the Louvre in particular and to learn French: an ambition which was to be thwarted when she later had to accept a more economical school in Brussels as second best to learning French in Paris.

The close co-operation between Charlotte and Branwell at this stage can be clearly seen in one manuscript in particular: Branwell's first volume of *Letters From An Englishman,* by Captain Flower, 6 September 1830.[19] This consists of two letters written on 2 September from Glass Town by James Bellingham, an English banker, to his relative in London.[20] Bellingham has recently arrived in Africa to supervise his firm's business there. He extols the beauties of the Glass Town with 'that wonderful structure the Tower of Nations' and then describes at length an adventure which occurred two weeks after his arrival. Having been escorted round the city by Lord Charles Wellesley, he dines at Dr Hume Badey's house where he stays for the night. Next morning he finds himself in the doctor's dissecting room, at the mercy of his host and villainous associates: Ned Laury, Young Man Naughty and a tall, supercilious, merciless-looking Frenchman (probably 'Pigtail' who features in volume II and elsewhere in the juvenilia). The Duke of Wellington and Lord Charles Wellesley arrive on the scene just in time to rescue him and Bellingham returns to his hotel 'filled with wonder and admiration at the disposition of the Grandees of this city'.

Branwell's subject is as bloodthirsty as usual. Glass Town's villains play a prominent role and Dr Hume Badey still uses the 'old young men tongue'; but it is interesting to find Branwell writing about Charlotte's favourite characters and describing them in her terms. Lord Charles Wellesley is 'a young lad apparently 19 years of age, most gaily dressed and his manners, from what I could see of him were most light and giddy'. The Marquis, on the contrary, is 'a tall young man, very handsome, and with an air of melancholy in his countenance, which, however, did not detract from, but rather heightened the expression of his features'. Branwell might have written these sketches with Charlotte's *Characters of the Celebrated Men of the Present Time* in his hand. The role of the Duke as rescuer is also reminiscent of Charlotte's *Tales of the Islanders.* Branwell, although preferring to write about the shadier side of Glass Town society, was obviously well acquainted with Charlotte's manuscripts. While the younger sisters were moving away from the Glass Town saga, Charlotte and Branwell were being drawn closer together by their wish to preserve the same imaginary world.

But Charlotte still had interests very different from those of Branwell. Their basic concept of Glass Town might coincide yet they chose to develop different sides of it. The Marquis of Douro and Young Soult are both poets and therefore friends; but although the Marquis of Douro's actions can be said to represent the trend in Charlotte's own feelings, there is another dimension to her literary personality: that represented by Lord Charles Wellesley. The leading articles for the two December numbers of the *Young Men's Magazine* 1830 are written by Lord Charles. Both concern 'supernatural appearances or warnings', a topic often alluded to in *Blackwood's Magazine* as in the issue for June 1826 which includes a letter to the editor on the truth of a dream. In *Strange Events* (29 August 1830) and *An Extraordinary Dream* (2 September 1830), Lord Charles describes several dream sequences inspired by books from his father's library. Both have an uncanny relationship with reality; they confirm his faith in 'the truth of supernatural interference with the affairs of men', a belief held by all the protagonists of Charlotte's later novels.

Lord Charles's 'ghostly propensities' are again the topic of conversation at Bravey's Inn, the meeting place for the Glass Town coterie whose discussions are regularly reported in the *Young Men's Magazine.* He uses his recent articles to convince the more credulous patrons of his incorporeal nature, mischievously declaring to one that his 'spirit has been permitted to revisit Earth from that bourne whence, Shakespeare falsely says, no traveller returns'.[21] Charlotte had always been fascinated by the possibility of an 'other' world and a strange coincidence in her own family was always important enough to be written down. At 6 pm on 22 June 1830, for example, she recorded an incident that occurred early that morning: an old man appeared at the door of the parsonage with a message from the Lord, intimating the coming of Christ and the necessity to prepare for him. Her father was then very ill and the timely visit of the religious fanatic made a deep impression on Charlotte: 'I could not forbear weeping at his words, spoken so unexpectedly at that particular period.'[22] The desire for a closer acquaintance with the supernatural is latent in the concept of the 'Genii'. Magic in all its forms appealed to her. The land of elves and fairies was her favourite subject, whereas Branwell rarely mentioned such insubstantial beings.

Charlotte's few manuscripts of the early period unrelated to the Glass Town saga are fairy stories.[23] The subject of *An Adventure in Ireland* (28 April 1829), which Clement Shorter thought the only juvenile manuscript 'worth anything' because of its absence of 'Wellington enthusiasm', is a nightmare caused by the Ghost of O'Callaghan Castle and Dennis Mulready's Irish goodnight: 'may the saints keep you from all fairies and brownies'.[24] On 13 July 1829, Charlotte wrote a tiny illustrated story of enchantment entitled *The Keep of the Bridge*.[25] Written in the first person, it tells how the author is led at night by curiosity towards the abode of the fairy Ebon and becomes imprisoned in the dungeon of the keep.

Almost a year later, Charlotte wrote *The Adventures of Ernenst Alembert* (25 May 1830). This is a story of magic *par excellence*. It is inspired by 'Dim, dreamlike reminiscences . . . concerning tales of spirits who, in various shapes, had appeared to men shortly before their deaths, as if to prepare them for the ghostly society with which they would soon have to mingle'.[26] One autumn evening while Ernest is sitting by the fire a fairy called Rufus Warner[27] appears before him. Like all mortals in Charlotte's juvenilia, Ernest longs to visit the land 'where the trees bear without ceasing, and the earth casts up flowers which sparkle like jewels, the sun shines for ever, and the moon and stars are not quenched even at noonday'.[28] Next day he is led by Rufus to the Land of Faery. Here he witnesses the wonders of the supernatural world: fairies mounted on winged steads, a chariot drawn across the sky by swans, a city with streets of precious stones, a paradisal garden, and splendid palaces of lapis lazuli and liquid diamond too brilliant for mortals to behold. But after many years in this land, Ernest wishes to return home. He is given a magic drink which transports him to a beautiful green valley where he meets an old man who had also been captured by fairies. After hearing the old man's tale of ghastly wonders experienced at the bottom of the ocean, Ernest decides to stay with him in the lovely glen, far from the pinching frosts and snows of winter. We are told that they dwelt in perfect harmony for many years.

One would expect the fairy-tale element in Charlotte's writing to diminish as she grew older but it does not. She was fourteen years old on 21 April 1830; yet in her last manuscript for the year Captain Bud relates a story called 'The Fairy Gift' to Lord Charles Wellesley. Like the narrator, Charlotte is still amusing herself 'with wild and extravagant imaginations'.[29] Branwell's bloodthirsty poems by Young Soult are equally extravagant, but they are still closely related to the material world of the toy soldiers.[30] Charlotte, however, is beginning to build 'castles in the air'.[31]

9

Glass Town Eclipsed

The theme of romantic love is a significant new element in Charlotte's last manuscript for 1830. It gives impetus to the 'land of Faery' as we see in *Albion and Marina* (12 October), her first love story. The characters are those of Glass Town disguised by the 'thin veil' of altered names. The heroine Marina (Marian Hume) is a fairy-tale princess who resides in a glade in a thick forest with her father, the Scots physician to the Duke of Strathelleraye (Strathfieldsaye). Dressed always in 'pure white or vernal green',[1] she is compared to flowers and is often seen playing a harp, a description of Marian continually echoed in later juvenilia. Like many of Charlotte's other characters, she has an original associated with the real Duke of Wellington, in this case Elizabeth Hume, eldest daughter of Dr John Robert Hume, the Duke's surgeon. Charlotte had probably heard of the secret romance between the Duke's fourteen-year-old son Douro and Elizabeth, a romance supported for several years by Lady Wellington until the Duke ended the affair.

Despite her humble origins, Albion (the Marquis of Douro), eldest son of the Duke, falls in love with her; but they are young and a period of trial must intervene. The Duke of Strathelleraye then removes his family from the south of England to the African Glass Town, promising that his son may marry when they return. Here Albion eventually meets the accomplished Lady Zelzia (Zenobia) Ellrington, who impresses him with her eloquence and sophistication. But that evening Marina appears to him as an apparition warning him not to foresake her. With his father's consent he returns to England, only to find that she had died at the exact moment of his vision of her. Until now, Charlotte's enlightened hero had rejected the 'ancient creed' of superstition but this extraordinary incident forces him to acknowledge, as Charlotte herself does in later novels, the significance of the supernatural.

It is interesting to note that Charlotte's first love story has a cynical narrator, Lord Charles Wellesley. His tale expresses not only his current interest in the supernatural but his jealousy of his brother and his delight in mocking his brother's love affairs. Lord Charles makes clear in his preface that the conclusion of his story is entirely fictitious and that he disposed of the lovers 'out of revenge'. His ironical tone undercuts the overblown description of the handsome Albion and the fairy-tale Marina whose ringlets are more elegant than the tendrils of a vine. There is an early vein of anti-romanticism in Charlotte's writing which develops as a sober undercurrent to her newly awakened interest in romantic love.

The Marquis of Douro's adolescent love affair first appears in the juvenilia in *The Poetaster,* volume I (6 July 1830). Lord Charles Wellesley has been spying on his brother. We learn that the Marquis has given Miss Hume, the daughter of his father's doctor, a book 'wrapped in the finest silk paper . . . then in blue embossed, hot pressed satin paper sealed in green sealing wax, with the motto, "L'amour jamais."'[2] Later in the same month, Charlotte again refers to the Marquis's secret passion in *Tales of the Islanders,* volume IV, chapter 2. One sweet July evening,[3] the Marquis of Douro and Lord Charles Wellesley watch the unknowing Marian Hume watering 'the very rose-tree that Arthur gave her from the greenhouse and planted there with his own hands kind youth that he was', as the cynical Lord Charles puts it. In *Conversations* (1 September 1830), Lord Charles and De Lisle discuss the recent arrival in town of Dr Hume's daughter and the effect De Lisle's portrait of her as 'Hebè' had on the Marquis.[4] Douro's love for Marian Hume is again the subject of two poems written in November[5] and it is continued the following month in *Visits in Verreopolis.* It is this theme of romance which is to preclude any resolution to abandon the Glass Town Saga.

In January 1831 Charlotte went away to boarding school at Roe Head. For the first time the children's play was interrupted. But the effect of Charlotte's departure on the Glass Town Saga was not as dramatic as has been assumed.[6] We have already seen how Emily and Anne were becoming discontented with the development of the 'play'. They preferred to imagine their characters in a more realistic world. The partnership between Branwell and Charlotte was still close: both wrote about Glass Town, but their interests and their attitude to their subject were very different. Branwell had never shared Charlotte's enthusiasm for Wellington, now transferred to his son Douro. Northangerland, Branwell's future foil to the Marquis of Douro, who was to draw brother and sister closer together in a single creative fiction, was still undeveloped. It seems certain that some split would have occurred among the four children. Charlotte's departure for Roe Head hastened the inevitable.

It is unlikely that Charlotte made a dramatic resolution at this stage to destroy her imaginary world. School merely brought a break in her intense writing of the years 1829 and 1830: throughout her juvenilia the periods during which she was at school were periods when no extant manuscripts were written. The immediate concerns of the classroom — its lessons and playfellows — left her little time for writing stories. Her sense of responsibility precluded any self-indulgence. 'She always seemed to feel . . . that she was an object of expense to those at home.'[7] The atmosphere at school was different from that at Haworth. She missed her brother and sisters and she was homesick. Her writing ceased, but not her interest in the imaginary world, for she found relief in day-dreams. Mary Taylor told Mrs Gaskell that during play hours Charlotte would sit or stand still, often with a book, under the trees in the playground. She preferred this to games with the other girls. Her 'habit of "making out" interests' for herself, 'that most children get who have none in actual life, was very strong in her'.[8] Charlotte must have thought often about Glass Town. On the inside front cover of a French text book she wrote in pencil: 'like a vision came those sunny hours to me. Where are they now? They have

12   *Miss Wooler's school at Roe Head, drawn by Charlotte Brontë*

long since joined the past eternity.'[9] It was at this time that she confided to Mary Taylor the reason for her habit of writing in tiny characters:

> [She] said she had learnt it by writing in their magazine. They brought out a 'magazine' once a month, and wished it to look as like print as possible. She told us a tale out of it. No one wrote in it, and no one read it, but herself, her brother, and two sisters. She promised to show me some of these magazines, but retracted it afterwards, and would never be persuaded to do so.[10]

In early May Branwell visited Charlotte at Roe Head. She expresses 'the totally unexpected pleasure' of seeing him in a letter written to him from school on 17 May 1831.[11] She remembers 'many questions and subjects of conversation' which she had intended to mention to him. No doubt Branwell had talked about *The History Of The Young Men* which he had just finished on 7 May. He had written over half of the history before Charlotte had left home.[12] With her departure his writing ceased, to be resumed while she was away only to complete this earlier manuscript and to continue work on another just before she finally returned home.

It has previously been assumed that *Letters From An Englishman* 'begun in September before his sister went away, was continued through the eighteen months of her absence'.[13] A close examination of the dates throughout this manuscript, however, will show that this is not so. Branwell dates Bellingham's letters several months earlier than he, Branwell, is actually writing them. For example, the two letters of volume II are dated 16 and 18 March, but the signature at the end leaves us in no doubt of when Branwell wrote them: 'real date, P. B. Brontë, June 8th, 1831'.[14] From the 'real date[s]' we can establish when Branwell actually wrote the different volumes and these dates do not correspond to Charlotte's 'absence' from Haworth. On the contrary, it seems that Branwell wrote almost all of his *Letters From An Englishman* when Charlotte was at home: that is, before she went to school (6 September 1830), during her first summer holidays (8 and 11 June 1831), and just before and after she had left school (19 April, 16 June and 2 August 1832).[15] It would appear that her literary enthusiasm acted as a spur to Branwell's writing at this time.[16]

The first summer holidays show no change in Charlotte's attitude to the Glass Town. On her return home she immediately resumed her writing and appears to have been preoccupied with the romantic element in her saga. On 11 July 1831, she wrote *A Fragment* of poetry and prose describing a vision of Marian Hume 'in lands afar'.[17] Lord Charles Wellesley is the author. 'Overcome with that delightful sensation of lassitude' he lies on his back, watches the sky and lets his boat drift. As if 'soul-taught' it floats into 'a little willow fringed fairy bay'. Lord Charles disembarks and wanders through a shady wood. When he emerges the moon has risen and he is in a wild, rugged glen. Suddenly there is a burst of sweet, sad music and he sees a figure sitting on a precipice, clad in white and playing a harp. This is Marian Hume. She sings of a 'stately noble' (the Marquis of Douro) under supernatural protection, dwelling in a desert land far away from her lonely glen. She knows she is unworthy of his attention:

> No being of this low earth born
> Is worthy of his love
> Doth the royal rider of the storm
> e're look upon the dove.

The 'long chain of memory' leads her to 'other hours' when she was happy in his love; but then her rival's hated form salutes her 'mental eye'. Her lover and her rival are spirits 'of kindred mould'. She pictures them together in the orange grove by the River Gambia. Once this happiness was hers.

With her 'sorrowful strain' ended the maiden vanishes. Lord Charles Wellesley concludes his fragment on a cryptic note. He leaves the reader to determine who this maiden is, but cannot refrain from observing

> that about 5 years since, when a certain young Marquis of D. was married to the fair Lady Julia [?W], Marian H — disappeared & no tidings of her fate have ever been received save a vague rumour that overcome by despair she had left Africa for ever & returned to her native highlands of Scotland.

Charlotte's romance story has progressed a long way since *Albion and Marina.* Marian has been married and forsaken. The Marquis of Douro has remarried. *A Fragment* shows that Charlotte must have thought a great deal about Marian's fate during her first term at school, yet the manuscript has been ignored in the past by those who seek to prove that Charlotte's departure for school coincided immediately with the destruction of Glass Town. It is not until the following Christmas holidays that the trumpet sounds.

At Roe Head, Charlotte must have gradually realized for the first time the incompatibility between the real world and her dream-land. Mary Taylor had told her that she and her brother and sisters 'were like growing potatoes in a cellar'. Charlotte had answered sadly 'Yes! I know we are.'[18] Perhaps it was this realization which prompted her to follow Byron's example in 'The Destruction of Sennacherib', for during her first Christmas holidays she wrote a poem called 'The trumpet hath sounded' (11 December 1831).[19] Fannie Ratchford states that this is 'a characteristic account' of an event which happened a year earlier;[20] but this was the first time that

Charlotte had contemplated the destruction of Glass Town.

There is no particular evidence in the poem that the four children made this decision together. Emily and Anne would no doubt have agreed to the plan. A trumpet is sounded and the armies of the Genii gather in 'the heart of the sky':

> 'Twas the Ruler of Spirits that sent forth the sound
> To call his dread legions in myriads around.

They come from the ocean, from 'the chill and ice-bound North', from the forests and the woodland. Once gathered, they vanish — sweeping before them all life in the city below:

> The secrets of Genii my tongue may not tell,
> But hoarsely they murmured: 'Bright city, farewell!'
> Then melted away like a dream of the night,
> While their palace evanished in oceans of light.
> Far beneath them the city lay silent and calm;
> The breath of the night-wind was softer than balm . . .
>
> Mute, mute are the mighty, and chilled is their breath,
> For at midnight passed o'er them the Angel of Death!
> The King and the peasant, the lord and the slave,
> Lie entombed in the depth of one wide solemn grave.

If Charlotte did mean to abandon the Glass Town Saga, then her urge to write was stronger than her will. Two weeks later she describes the desolate African scene she has just created:

> The bright sun in vain to this far land is given,
> And the planets look forth from the windows of heaven;
> The birds sing unheeded in woods fresh and green,
> And the flowers grow unscented, ungathered, unseen.[21]

As in *The Adventures of Ernenst Alembert,* the land is as bright as 'Elysian dreams'. Here flowers bloom eternally but their blooms are not seen: mankind has vanished from the Glass Town. Charlotte returned to school for her final term.

PART II

Romance and the Rise of Angria
(1832—1835)

10

Sunlight on Africa Again

> O clouds come o'er that vision bright
> and soft it fades away
> The witchery of memory's might
> Inviting still it's stay.[1]

Charlotte had written this quatrain in July 1831 during her summer holidays from school. The following December the trumpet had sounded the destruction of the Glass Town Saga. Yet even before the destruction we see in this verse Charlotte's awareness of the power of remembrance — 'The long, long chain of memory which leads to other hours' — an image she was to evoke as late as 1839. While she was at school, the will of this conscientious young girl could hold her imaginative dream world in abeyance. But once she was at home again, free from the discipline of regular lessons and in the security of her family, the urge to create was too strong to be resisted. Nor was there any need to resist when those around her were pursuing a similar purpose. Indeed, Branwell had just begun writing again after a silence of almost a year, possibly in anticipation of his sister's return.

Charlotte left Roe Head in May 1832. At home she found Branwell resurrecting the old games of wars and toy soldiers. He had just completed volume IV of *Letters From An Englishman* (19 April) and was to begin volume V on 16 June, soon after her return. We have seen how his writing over the last fifteen months broadly coincided with Charlotte's school holidays. Her presence had acted as a catalyst to his writing but his manuscripts show that she had little other influence. His subject is still the same as in his first childish booklets of 1827 and 1828. The Rebellion in 'My Fellows' is now the Rebellion in the Great Glass Town or

Verdopolis (March 1831), followed by the Rebellion in Sneaky's Land (March 1832). Throughout volumes III—VI of *Letters From An Englishman* James Bellingham reports in tiresome detail on the leaders of the various factions, their movements and the bloody battles which take place.

One significant factor, however, does emerge from Branwell's chronicles of this time, namely, the appearance of 'Rogue', soon to be the master villain and 'vile demagogue' of the later juvenilia. As early as 18 June 1830, in *An Interesting Passage in the Lives of Some eminent men of the Present time,* Charlotte had made a passing reference to 'Old Rogue's youngest son, a promising youth';[2] but he appears to have remained in the background of the Glass Town Saga until Branwell adopted him as his hero in the later volumes of *Letters From An Englishman.* During the Great Rebellion of March 1831, Rogue leads the insurrection in Verdopolis and sets up a provisional government on the French model of 1789. Crashey, however, intervenes to stop this reign of terror and in a style reminiscent of the 'Chief Genii' restores peace by a single command.[3] Almost a year intervenes (while Charlotte is at school) before Rogue again appears as the leader of a Rebellion in Sneaky's Land, in the north of the Glass Town Confederacy. Rogue captures and burns the city of Fidena but is eventually defeated by Alexander Sneaky, King of Sneaky's Land, and his son John (later Duke of Fidena), helped by the forces of Parry, Stumps and the Duke of Wellington.[4] Although Rogue is shot, he is resurrected by Branwell in the manuscripts of 1833, and later that year Charlotte begins to take an interest in him. Under the suuccessive titles of Alexander Percy, Lord Ellrington and Duke of Northangerland, Rogue increasingly becomes Branwell's hero and an important foil to Charlotte's Marquis of Douro.

On her return home, Charlotte's initial reaction to Branwell's writing appears to have been unenthusiastic. Apart from a passing reference to Rogue and the unrest in Verdopolis, her only prose manuscript for 1832, *The Bridal,* ignores Branwell's constant tributes to Bellona. Charlotte returns to the theme of love and romance which was emerging so strongly in her stories at the end of 1830. Ignoring the melancholy fate she had planned for Marian Hume in *A Fragment* (11 July 1831), Charlotte recalls first in a poem, then in a prose story, the courtship and marriage of Marian and the Marquis of Douro, eldest son of the Duke of Wellington, here called 'Marina' and 'Albion'. As in *A Fragment,* the poem is in the form of a dream sequence. In an atmosphere of fairy-tale medieval romance, the author sees first a young knight pledging his faith to his lady and then the scene changes to that of a wedding feast:

I knew 'twas a bridal; for under a bower
Of the rose and the myrtle and fair lily flower
Stood that stately noble in plumèd pride,
And that sweet, fair lady, his plighted bride.

With the mystic ring on her finger fair,
And the nuptial wreath in her radiant hair,
They are joined — and forever the mingled name
Of Marina and Albion is hallowed to fame.[5]

Thus Charlotte describes the conclusion anticipated in the events of *Albion and Marina* two years before.

The following prose story again recalls the parting of Albion and Marina, but whereas Lord Charles Wellesley had caused Marina to die of a broken heart 'out of malignity' for his brother, the author of *The Bridal* (probably Captain Tree) gives a different account of the lovers' parting: Marian's attitude was one of hope rather than despair. In *The Bridal* we also learn the 'true' account of Bud's drama in chapter 3 of *Visits in Verreopolis,* volume I, entitled 'The Rivals' by writers on the Brontës.[6] Here Lady Zenobia Ellrington, Marian's 'Frenchified rival' of *Albion and Marina,* is driven mad by her jealous love for the Marquis of Douro. She tramps from Verdopolis to Wellington's Land and there in a dishevelled state accosts and humiliates Marian in front of Douro. *The Bridal* again describes this scene, with variations, and provides a sequel: during the Great Rebellion, Zenobia, roused by the Marquis of Douro's eloquent denunciation in parliament of Alexander Rogue — that 'Beelzebub of black iniquity' — again tries to persuade the Marquis not to marry Marian. Zenobia enlists the help of Danash, 'the evil genius' of the *Arabian Nights' Entertainments,* but is outwitted by the voice of a 'friendly spirit' in the Marquis's ear.

The above story of *The Bridal* would appear to be a strange medley of earlier manuscripts, but it is basically a picture of the happy relationship existing between the newly married Marquis and his bride. Gone is the cynical attitude towards the lovers in *Albion and Marina.* Charlotte attempts to recapture the events of her last three manuscripts for 1830 in order to bridge the gap in the Glass Town Saga caused by her absence at school. This seems to be the main purpose of *The Bridal* which, although written in August 1832, is set a year earlier in Autumn 1831. The author visits the Marquis of Douro's country palace for two months, so he is well situated to describe his host and hostess and their surroundings. The Marquis is still a noble youth, well-versed in literature and science, a champion sportsman and a connoisseur of art. Marian remains the green and white fairy princess of *Albion and Marina,* 'infinitely too beautiful for this earth'. She is described in terms reminiscent of Charlotte's copy of

13   *'English Lady', pencil drawing by Charlotte Brontë after W. Finden's engraving of the Countess of Jersey, 15 October 1834, suggestive of Marian Hume*

Finden's engraving of Lady Jersey (see plate 13), first published in Moore's *Life of Byron* (1830), to which Charlotte may have been recently introduced at school. It is also possible that her father may have owned a copy, since the sale catalogue of his effects, after his death, mentions 'Books Byrons'.[7] Like Haidee, Marian has auburn hair, arranged in soft waving ringlets. Her features are delicate and her hazel eyes brilliant and clear. As in earlier manuscripts, she wears no ornaments except a long chain of emeralds and gold that hangs below her waist and a gold ring which, 'together with a small crescent of pearls glistening on her forehead (which is always worn by the noble matrons of Verdopolis), betokened that she had entered the path of wedded life'.[8]

Charlotte is also aware of the events in her brother's *Letters From An Englishman*. In yet another effort to bridge the time gap in her writing, she makes an attempt to incorporate the Great Rebellion in her bridal story. The marriage of Douro and Marian is delayed while Douro joins the fight against Rogue. Despite its incongruity with her plot, Charlotte's handling of the disorder in Verdopolis is altogether more sophisticated than Branwell's. It is prophetic of the difference between their manuscripts of the following year. Unlike her brother, Charlotte has a fund of new knowledge and experience to draw on in her writing. To her, dissatisfaction among the lower orders in Verdopolis manifests itself as a conflict between the mill-owners and their workers, reminiscent of the recent stories of the Luddite Riots which she would have heard from Miss Wooler at Roe Head. In nearby Liversedge on 11 April 1812, there had been an attack on Rawfolds Mill by desperate cloth-workers armed with pistols, hatchets and bludgeons. Mrs Gaskell tells how the owner, Mr Cartwright, successfully defended the mill, but how, soon after, another manufacturer was shot.[9] Charlotte would also have heard Mr Brontë's own memories of the Luddite Riots. These well-established sources for the mill attack in *Shirley* are probably also the source of Charlotte's new attitude to the Glass Town insurrections. In *Something about Arthur,* written not long after *The Bridal,* there is an attack on a mill; and the silent march of the workers with their crude weapons towards one of 'those vile rumbling mills', their attitude to the 'incessant crash of its internal machinery' and to its master, all recall those perilous times.

The Bridal, then, is an excellent introduction to what can be seen as the second period of Charlotte's juvenilia. It sets the tone for her manuscripts of 1833 and early 1834 when she evokes a glittering picture of Verdopolitan society, the intrigues and love affairs of its characters and their often complicated past. Strongly influenced first by Scott and then increasingly by Byron, her stories now show a preoccupation with romantic love and adventure. Charlotte returned from Roe Head with renewed enthusiasm and an extended awareness of literature, history and human nature. She was obviously familiar with Branwell's wars and political machinations but apart from her adoption of the character 'Rogue', his manuscripts provided little more than background scenery for her plots at this stage. It is not until early 1834, with the creation of a daughter for

14   *The 'Gun' portrait of Branwell Brontë and his sisters Emily, Charlotte and Anne, painted by Branwell c. 1833*

Rogue and a kingdom for Douro, that brother and sister become united in a single 'Angrian' vision.

The trumpet sound of 1831 heralded not the destruction of Glass Town but the end of the Four Chief Genii. For Branwell, Charlotte's return home meant a reinstatement of the Glass Town Saga and, he thought, of the Chief Genii, In his 'Ode on the Celebration of the Great African Games' (26 June 1832) he enthusiastically reverses the situation created in 'The trumpet hath sounded':

> Once again bright Summer now
> Shines on Afric's scorched brow;
> Once again the vales appear
> In the new glories of the year.
> Once again! yet once again!
> Sunlight towering o'er the plain,
> Rises in light the immense Olympian Hall,
> Back casting from its front grey twilight's dusky pall.[10]

With buoyant hopes he recreates the avenging genii: 'Awful Brannii' leads 'Dread Tallii' into conflict with the Young Men, now referred to as the 'Twelves'. Emmii and Annii (Emily and Anne) bring up the rear, coming 'last with boding cry': their position presumably expresses hope by Branwell that they might reassume their former subservient role in the Glass Town Saga. He soon realizes, however, that his efforts are in vain and complains somewhat bitterly at the beginning of *The Monthly Intelligencer* (27 March — 26 April 1833) of the neglect of the former Chief Genii:

A FEW WORDS TO THE CHEIF GENII.

When a parent leaves his children, young and inexperienced, and without a cause absconds, never more troubling himself about them, those children, according to received notions among men, if they by good fortune should happen to survive this neglect and become of repute in society, are by no means bound to believe that he has done his duty to them as a parent merely because they have risen, nor are they indeed required to own or treat him as a parent. This is all very plain and we believe that four of our readers will understand our aim in thus speaking.

A Child of the G . . . ii.[11]

Again, at the end of this journal in a song by Young Soult, The Rhymer, he attempts to resurrect the old threat of war for those 'Long mindless of the Genii'.[12]

Emily and Anne were probably involved by this time in establishing their own world of Gondal, 'a large Island in the north Pacific', based on the example of discovery and exploration of the early Glass Town Saga in which they had participated. On 24 November 1834, in a diary note of Emily's, we find that the already established Gondal is expanding: 'The Gondals are discovering the interior of Gaaldine', 'a large Island newly discovered in the south Pacific'.[13] As Ellen Nussey recalls in her 'Reminiscences of Charlotte Brontë', Emily and Anne were 'like twins — inseparable companions, and in the very closest sympathy, which never had any interruption'.[14] From now on they ceased to have any significant influence on Charlotte's juvenilia. Their old characters of Parry and Ross make a fleeting appearance in two of Charlotte's manuscripts of early |1833 (*Something about Arthur* and *The Foundling*) before retiring into oblivion. Their old kingdoms, however, still part of the Glass Town Confederation, are often mentioned, and Parry's son Arthur becomes the 'Marquis of Ardrah', 'the scoundrelly Scott' who is Commander of the Verdopolitan Navy and opposed to the new kingdom of Angria.[15]

Branwell's 'A Few Words to the Cheif Genii' also apply to Charlotte, still his partner in the Glass Town Saga. Until May she had written very little, and we are soon to see that she becomes absorbed with her romances of 1833, probably to the resentment of her brother. She had no intention of contributing to his political journal and largely ignored all the political innovations of his 1833 manuscripts, in particular *The Monthly Intelligencer* and *The Politics of Verdopolis* (23 October — 15 November 1833).[16] Branwell's attempt to revive his old interest in France with Talleyrand and the Emperor Napoleon featuring in *The Pirate* (30 January — 8 February 1833),[17] a tale of Rogue's infamous past, had little appeal to Charlotte. Nor did she show much enthusiasm for the old concept of the Genii. Apart from a passing reference to 'old Brannii' in

Arthuriana (20 November 1833),[18] 'Those high and unseen spirits' the four Chief Genii appear in only two of Charlotte's manuscripts of this period: *The Foundling* (31 May—27 June 1833) and *The Green Dwarf* (2 September 1833). In the former the Genii play a very minor role and in the latter they are recalled as part of the 'olden days' of the Glass Town. They become the remote gods of Verdopolitan society, occasionally appealed to by a character in distress; gradually they degenerate into an expletive: 'By the Genii!' Only the fiery-haired scoundrel S'Death, an incarnation of 'old Brannii' and sometime alter- ego of Rogue, remains in Charlotte's manuscripts to remind us of Branwell's reluctance to relinquish his role of the Chief Genius, 'Brannii Lightening'.[19]

11

Something about Arthur

The 'halcyon period' of Charlotte's early writing, as the years 1832—35 are often called, did not begin immediately on her return home from Roe Head. For the first twelve months, until May 1833, there is a relative lack of manuscripts. Three poems,[1] one fragment in which prose and poetry are mingled (*The African Queen's Lament,* 12 February 1833), and one prose story (*The Bridal,* 20 August 1833) are Charlotte's only manuscripts belonging to these months. Apart from her visit to Ellen Nussey's home Rydings, near Birstall, in September 1832 there is little to explain her rather hesitant return to a world she was so fascinated by, as we see in *The Bridal.* A possible answer may lie in her preoccupation with the idea of self-improvement at this time.

Mary Taylor recalls in a letter to Mrs Gaskell how Charlotte always said that 'the thing most needed was to soften and refine our minds'. At school, she had 'picked up every scrap of information concerning painting, sculpture, poetry, music, etc., as if it were gold'.[2] Once home again, we know that much of Charlotte's time was occupied in imparting this new information to her sisters, in improving her drawing, and in reading.[3] She had complained to Mary Taylor 'that her supply of books was very small in proportion to her wants' at this time.[4] On 21 July 1831, Charlotte wrote to Ellen Nussey exhorting her to strive earnestly for personal improvement.[5] She tried to initiate a regular French correspondence with Ellen and on 1 January 1833, took stock of her own self-improvement of the past year:

> The first day of January always presents to my mind a train of very
> solemn and important reflections, and a question more easily asked than

answered, frequently occurs, viz.: How have I improved the past year, and with what good intentions do I view the dawn of its successor?[6]

Charlotte continued this letter to Ellen by discussing *Kenilworth,* 'one of the most interesting works that ever emanated from the great Sir Walter's pen'. To this period of self-improvement we may well ascribe the reading of many of the books recommended a year later by Charlotte for Ellen's perusal.[7] They include such authors as Milton, Shakespeare, Scott, Byron and Wordsworth, whose works — although she had been introduced to them earlier — now show an increasing influence on her writing of 1833 and 1834.

On 1 May Charlotte completed her first story for the year 1833: *Something about Arthur.* It is written by Lord Charles Albert Florian Wellesley, now Charlotte's established pseudonym.[8] Following the example of Scott, the tale begins with a 'moral maxim' from a volume by Captain Bud, the historian of the early Glass Town, admonishing those who associate with the lower orders of society. Lord Charles, who for the last six months has wandered from one low haunt to another, a voluntary exile from the elegant delights of cultivated society, is pricked with regret on reading Bud's maxim. Besides, he reasons, a kerbstone for one's bed, an empty stomach, a rag-covered back and bare bleeding feet are 'as so many powerful casuists each bringing forward unanswerable arguments to prove that it was my duty to reform & return like the Repentant Prodigal to my father's house'.[9] Safely ensconced in Waterloo Palace again, Lord Charles is provoked by the hostile attitude of his tutor, Mr Rundell, into recalling a similar occasion of truancy in his brother's life. Thus in chapter 2 he begins the relation of past events: 'a little anecdote of Arthur's earlier years'.

Always eager to expose his elder brother's vices, Lord Charles takes us back to the time when the fifteen-year-old Marquis of Douro's 'admiration of horse-flesh' led him to associate with a certain Verdopolitan libertine, Colonel George Frederick, Baron of Caversham.[10] The Marquis has just acquired a fiery black stallion named Thunderbolt. Caversham persuades Douro to enter Thunderbolt in the grand Verdopolitan horse-race, but secretly bribes Jerry Sneak, Thunderbolt's jockey, to guarantee he does not win. The Marquis is mortified by Thunderbolt's comic behaviour and his loss of honour before the whole of Verdopolis, including Crashey and the four sovereigns of the Glass Town Federation. In a fit of pride he shoots the unfortunate stallion and justifies his barbarous act by recourse to his usual exaggerated code of honour: 'a life stained by dishonour is but a protracted species of death.' Ned Laury, still a self-confessed 'rare lad' but now portrayed as a loyal retainer of the Duke of Wellington, offers to prove Caversham's guilt in the affair. He plans to extract the truth from his cousin, Jerry Sneak, by plying him with drink till he vomits 'all up like a soda sick sucking-pig'. Having obtained his proof by this picturesque method, the Marquis challenges Caversham to a duel. Caversham refuses to fight and a dramatic chase ensues through the streets of Verdopolis ending in the injury of the Marquis of Douro. In chapter 3 the young Marquis seeks yet another means of revenge. With the help of Ned Laury, he leads a band of forty 'rare lads' on a silent march to burn Caversham's mill. But Lord Caversham is avenged by Captain Tree and the chapter ends abruptly with the shooting of Douro.

Pleading a 'Shakespearian licence', the author moves the scene to the mountains of Wellington's Land, nearly 2,000 miles away. The Marquis is nursed back to health in a humble cabin by Mina, the daughter of Ned Laury. Romantic love now intrudes and the two final chapters of *Something about Arthur* describe in detail the growing devotion of 'the proud, Aristocratic, high-minded, refined, elegant Marquis of Douro' for 'a poor low-born Peasant's Daughter!' Only the intervention of the Duke of Wellington, in his usual role of *deus ex machina,* prevents an early marriage for his son.

Something about Arthur has only recently been made available to scholars.[11] Its importance in the sequence of Glass Town events justifies the detailed description of its plot. Apart from a description in *The Bridal* this is the first view we have had of Charlotte's hero in action since the manuscripts of 1830. From now on he is to become the focus of her writing. Individual manuscripts may centre on other characters but they are always his friends, enemies or lovers. Here, in *Something about Arthur,* Charlotte recalls her hero of the early period, but she now adds to his past two complicating factors: a petulant stubbornness and an early love affair. From her reading and from her experience at Roe Head, her knowledge of human nature has been enlarged. As we are soon to see, the once perfect hero is perfect no longer. He remains the darling of cultured society, surrounded by an adoring circle of females, but he becomes callous in his attitude to women and ruthless in his pursuit of ambition. In *Something about Arthur* we see the adolescent Douro and witness the first of his many *affaires.*

Mina Laury is to be the oldest and most faithful of Douro's mistresses. Her peasant background is often referred to in the later juvenilia, but her early relationship with the Marquis of Douro has previously been a mystery. Here in *Something about Arthur* she appears for the first time and we are able to understand the often cryptic references to her in later manuscripts. Whenever Mina and the Marquis are mistakenly thought to be married, for example, as in *High Life In Verdopolis* (20 February — 20 March 1834),[12] there is a knowing look between these two characters which Charlotte always leaves unexplained. Again, at the beginning of *The Spell* (21 June — 21 July 1834), we learn of the death of the Marquis of Douro's son despite the efforts of his nurse Mina Laury, 'whose tenderness once raised the father but could not raise the son to life'.[13] In *Something about Arthur* we see Mina's care of 'the father' and how close she and Douro were to marriage. At the end of the manuscript, when the narrator recalls us to the present time, the recent betrothal of the Marquis to Marian Hume is introduced and we learn that the memory of 'simple Mina Laury' — 'that wild little daisy' — is effaced before 'a flower so fair, so elegant & so highly cultured'. But there is a final hint that Mina's affection does not fade so easily. Here Charlotte has provided herself with material for a future illicit relationship: in her manuscripts she was to explore many aspects of romantic love.

12

A New Albion

Charlotte again returned to the past in *The Foundling* (31 May—27 June 1833) to create a character soon to be a close associate of the Marquis of Douro. In view of the growing influence of Rogue and his coterie, an influence only too obvious in Branwell's *The Monthly Intelligencer,* Charlotte felt the need to muster some opposition. The Marquis is now in search of rising talent for the government and chances upon Edward Sydney, newly arrived from England to seek his fortune in the 'Utopian Colony' in Africa. Douro imprisons Sydney in Waterloo Palace until he agrees, with little persuasion, to become a Member of Parliament in return for his staunch opposition to the 'vile demagogue Alexander Rogue'.[1] *The Foundling* traces the story of Sydney's rise in status from the time he was first found in England by the cottager John Cartwright and his wife Margaret, then raised and educated at Eton and Oxford as the son of Mr Hasleden of Oakwood Hall, to the time when he discovers his true identity as Prince Edward of York, son of Frederick the Great, Duke of York and King of the Twelves who (as we learnt in the early manuscripts) was slain at the Battle of Rosendale Hill. Thus Edward Sydney qualifies for association with the Verdopolitan elite and Lady Julia Wellesley, already betrothed to another, is bestowed on him.

The relationship between Julia and Sydney, a secondary plot of *The Foundling,* is an interesting one. Unlike that of Douro and Marian theirs is no true reciprocal love, only the infatuation of a suitor and the whim of 'a foolish petted little girl'. The Marquis of Douro, eager to satisfy his new ally, persuades his cousin Julia to accept Sydney; while Julia herself, originally opposed to him, sees her lover in the new light of romantic intrigue when her father forbids the match:

> The slovenliness of his outward man became elegant negligence, what she had before called jaundiced squalor was now designated as interesting paleness, and the good points he really possessed, his eloquence, his high principles and his profound scholarship shone out with unshadowed lustre.[2]

Thus the marriage of Julia and Edward Sydney is an unsuitable one, pregnant with material for comic marital strife which Charlotte exploits in later manuscripts.[3] Finally, in *My Angria and the Angrians* (14 October 1834) Julia escapes from her husband to the new city of Adrianopolis, and *A Late Occurrence* (*c.* January 1835) records their divorce.[4]

The plot of *The Foundling* is more intricate than anything Charlotte has yet handled. Its story is complicated, or rather confused, by copious references to the Old Glass Town scene which are grafted on to new elements in the developing saga. It is as if Charlotte is taking stock of her material, deciding what she will retain of the old world and what she will appropriate from Branwell's latest manuscripts. Pigtail, Skeleton and other villains of Branwell's *Letters From An Englishman* appear in *The Foundling.* Charlotte introduces a new element of violent hostility into the recent marriage between Lady Zenobia Ellrington and Rogue, which Branwell described in *The Pirate.*[5] She makes certain that Zenobia's infatuation with her own hero, the Marquis of Douro, does not suffer by Branwell's appropriation of her 'Verdopolitan de Staël' for Rogue. In keeping with Zenobia's 'masculine' spirit and Branwell's intentions to raise the status of his new hero, Rogue assumes Zenobia's title and becomes Lord Ellrington.[6]

The Foundling reintroduces us to many of 'the glorious Twelves', including Bravey, now the corpulent landlord of Bravey's Hotel, the fashionable successor of Bravey's Inn in the *Young Men's Magazine.* Gravey, deserted by Emily in the early Glass Town Saga, remained one of the venerable Twelves who first discovered Africa. In *The Foundling* he makes a fleeting appearance only, but we learn later in *Lily Hart* (7 November 1833) that he has become the Metropolitan archbishop — 'a clergyman of a remarkably grave and venerable aspect.'[7] The Duke of Wellington and Crashey are again instrumental in the plot, and the college on Philosopher's Island for the instruction of the noble youth of Verdopolis is reminiscent of the school for nobles on Vision Island in *Tales of the Islanders,* volume II. The early years of the peaceful Kashna, King of the Ashantees, and of his warlike son Sai-Too-Too are recalled. Even the magical formation of the early Glass Town is not forgotten. While he is imprisoned in Waterloo Palace, Sydney's food appears and disappears as if by magic. He is 'almost tempted to think himself in the hands of magicians or Genii who, he had heard, yet retained their influence over the inhabitants of Africa'.[8] In fact, his elusive servant is Finic, the 'hideous sprite' who appeared in two earlier manuscripts and who is soon to contribute to the Marquis of Douro's increasingly complicated early love affairs.[9] The Duke of Wellington recalls the fairy Maimoune who first protected the Twelves when they landed in Africa. He explains to Sydney how she assisted his father (Duke of York) to rescue and marry the Spanish lady Zorayda, despite the evil genius Danash.[10] When his parents died, Sydney was stolen by Danash, but Maimoune protected him in England and has now returned him safely to 'his fatherland'.

Sydney's arrival in the Glass Town provides Charlotte with an opportunity to describe Verdopolis as she now sees it. In *The Bridal* Verdopolis is a commercial centre, a 'gigantic emporium of commerce, of arts, of God-like wisdom, of boundless learning, and of superhuman knowledge'.[11] The old aura of magic and splendour still hovers about it, though the four Chief Genii have virtually gone. The city sits 'like a queen upon the waters'. Now in *The Foundling* we catch Edward Sydney's enthusiasm (and surely Charlotte's too) as he views for the first time this 'Queen of Nations': 'And that is Verdopolis! that splendid city rising with such graceful haughtiness from the green realm of Neptune.'[12] Sydney's eye rests first on the vast outline of the Tower of All Nations. He pauses on the quay and views the scene before him. In the foreground lies the harbour, with over 'a thousand vessels of war and merchandise, resting in safe anchorage on its long, rolling waves':

> Far about him the city walls and ramparts rose to a tremendous height frowning terribly on the foam-white waves which rushed roaring to their feet. A mingled noise of bypassing multitudes, rolling chariots and tramping horses soared dull and deep over the black battlements. Bells were at this instant announcing the hour of noon, and high above the rest the great Cathedral bell sent forth its solemn toll, sonorous as a trumpet's voice heard amongst lutes and harps

— surely a vestige of the Genii trumpets and fairy music of the early manuscripts. Charlotte completes her 'gorgeous picture' by describing the middle distance and then throwing over the background a Claude-like haze:

> Verdopolis lay at the mouth of a wide valley which was embosomed in long low hills, rich in hanging groves and gardens, vineyards, cornfields, meadows, &c. &c. The background was closed by lofty peaked mountains whose azure tint almost melted into the serene horizon, and all was faintly seen through a mellowing veil of mist which enhanced instead of depreciating the charms of this earthly paradise.

15 *The Great Bay of Glass Town. Watercolour by Charlotte Brontë*
after John Martin

With Sydney we explore the town and its people. We see the Houses of
Parliament displaying that pure classic taste which is the 'distinguishing
characteristic of all the public edifices of Verdopolis'. In the Rotunda, first
introduced in *Tales of the Islanders,* volume III, as a public apartment for
officers, the Marquis of Douro systematically introduces Sydney (and us)
to the illustrious men of Verdopolis, in particular Colonel Grenville,
Sergeant Bud, Captain Arbor, Captain Bud, John Gifford, Alexander
Rogue and Hector Matthias Montmorency. A fortnight later, the ballroom
offers him acquaintance with such Verdopolitan belles as Lady Zenobia
Ellrington, Lady Julia Sydney and the Marquis's wife, Marian.

Verdopolis has grown larger and even more magnificent, but essentially
it has not changed from the Great Glass Town. The streets of Verdopolis
are filled with 'rare lads', 'smart jaunty personages, attired in military
costume', cavalry officers and, in particular, 'some odd little specimens of
humanity'. In depicting the latter, Charlotte glances back with amusement
to the toy soldiers and Branwell's description of them in *The History Of
The Young Men.* The men are dressed in

> black three cornered hats, blue coats, red waistcoats, ornamented with
> large white buttons, black breeches, white stockings, and one great
> round wooden shoe on which they shuffled about with marvellous
> rapidity. The women wore blue gowns, red jackets, white aprons and
> little white caps without border or any other decoration other than a
> narrow red ribbon. Their shoes were similar in construction to the
> men's.[13]

This is an exact description of the two figures in a pencil and watercolour
sketch by Branwell entitled 'Mon & Wamon'. It occurs on the final page of
his first tiny magazine for January 1829, which also features examples of
the 'young men tongue'. Perhaps Charlotte had been browsing through
this early magazine for she also allows these odd little inhabitants from
Stumps and Monkey's Islands to sing some 'exquisite stanzas' in their
bizarre dialect.

It has been suggested that this little song, 'Eamala is a gurt bellaring
bull', is uncharacteristic of Charlotte and that *The Foundling* may therefore
have been written by Branwell. The clumsy, large signature on the title-
page was also thought to be a possible forgery by Thomas James Wise,
who was not above attributing a manuscript of Branwell's to Charlotte.[14]
Certainly a close examination of all Charlotte's signatures for the years
1832—35 shows that this one is markedly different, but it is not much
larger than that of *The Green Dwarf,* written soon after *The Foundling.*
The florid capital 'C' of Charlotte and the variant capital 'B' of Brontë,
however, are so unusual that it seems unlikely that a forger would have
written them. Moreover, the remainder of the writing on the title-page,

and that of the following story, is certainly Charlotte's and not Branwell's; and one may doubt that Wise or anyone else would bother to forge such a quantity of microscopic script. Charlotte was not incapable of writing a song in the 'young men tongue': such 'coarse stanzas', whether they be from the pen of brother or sister, are a familiar feature of the early Young Men's Play. Moreover the violence described in this song and elsewhere in *The Foundling* is not unusual in Charlotte's early writing. The gory fights between the Marquis and his enemies in *Something about Arthur,* for example, rival even the most violent scenes in Branwell's *Letters From An Englishman.*

   This is not to ignore, however, a close co-operation between Charlotte and Branwell in composing *The Foundling.* The content indicates that they had recently been either discussing or reading their early stories together. Certainly the revival of both good and bad characters from the dead in chapter 9 is a joint decision, for it is 'the mighty Branii's will to revivify both the murderers also'. This is the last instance in Charlotte's juvenilia of the Genii playing an active role. It is interesting that for a manuscript which recalls so much of the old Glass Town, Charlotte reverts to her original pseudonym of 'Captain Tree', which she had not used since September 1830.[15] This is the last time Charlotte writes as Captain Tree and it is perhaps significant that in a year's time in *A Peep Into A Picture Book* (30 May 1834), Lord Charles Wellesley will denounce *The Foundling* as a 'farrago of bombast, fustian and lies': that 'long since exploded catch-penny of Captain Tree's'.[16] Certainly, Charlotte never again returns in such profuse detail to the original Glass Town Saga.

13

Alexander Percy

Two months now intervened before Charlotte made another excursion
into the past with *The Green Dwarf. A Tale Of The Perfect Tense* (2
September 1833). This is a more overt attempt to imitate the novels of
Scott: it is a mock-romance. A beautiful maiden, Lady Emily Charlesworth,
is abducted by the villain Alexander Percy. She is carried through a dark
forest and imprisoned in a lofty and ruined tower. Eventually Lady Emily's
lover, the noble Earl St Clair, triumphs over his rival in both love and war.

The narrator of this story is Captain John Bud, who was a handsome
young ensign in these early Glass Town days. He recalls the Verdopolis of
twenty years ago for his eager young listener Lord Charles Wellesley who,
as the author of *The Green Dwarf,* repeats his 'Tale Of The Perfect
Tense' to us 'the reading public'. Lord Charles has just recovered from an
illness caused by the Marquis of Douro's savagely whipping him;
antagonism between the two brothers is a common theme in the
manuscripts of this period. Illness is Lord Charles's excuse for his long
silence though he fears his readers may think he has also been 'exspiflicated
by the literary captain's lash'. In *The Foundling* Captain Tree had taken
great delight in scotching 'one small reptile', namely, Lord Charles
Wellesley, for his 'malignant . . . insinuations' about Tree in *Something
about Arthur.* The rivalry between Charlotte's two pseudonyms is an
amusing result of the young author's attempts to write in the idiom of her
characters.

Captain Bud says 'our business is with the past, not the present day'. He
re-creates the Glass Town of June 1814, with its Turkish merchants,
sunburnt Spaniards, 'sallow, bilious Englishmen' and 'withered monsieurs'.

16 *Title page and Preface to* The Green Dwarf, *2 September 1833, typical of the size and script of Charlotte Brontë's manuscripts during the years 1832–35. The manuscript measures 11.5 cm × 9.2 cm*

17 *Watercolour by Charlotte Brontë reminiscent of scenes in the early juvenilia,*
6 July 1833

These were the days of 'the Genii's Inn', hosted by Tallii, Brannii, Emmii and Annii, where tales of 'Napoleon and The Spectre' are freely circulated by garrulous Frenchmen.[1] Ensign Bud persuades his antiquarian friend John Gifford to attend the first African Olympic Games celebrated in Branwell's 'Ode on the Celebration of the Great African Games'. Originally inspired by the Greek games, these were probably a product of Branwell's lessons with his father. Charlotte now grafts on to them all the paraphernalia of a medieval tournament. The 'rewarder of victors' is Lady Emily Charlesworth and the two chief opponents are Alexander Percy and the Earl St Clair, the latter disguised as an ancient chieftain.

Alexander Percy is Branwell's 'Rogue' of early days. Charlotte, having adopted him in her writing, makes an effort to mould Branwell's somewhat wooden villain into a plausible character. She gives him a past. The contradiction between the inner and the outer man, so constantly explored in succeeding manuscripts and later applied to Douro, can be seen in embryo in *The Green Dwarf* in the description of Alexander Percy:

> The countenance of this gentleman was, as I have said, handsome. His features were regularly formed. His forehead was lofty, though not very open. But there was in the expression of his blue, sparkling, but sinister, eyes and of the smile that ever played round his deceitful looking mouth,

ALEXANDER. PERCY. ESQ^R M.P.

18   *Alexander Percy, later Lord Ellrington and Duke of Northangerland. Pen and ink sketch by Branwell Brontë in Mary Pearson's commonplace book, 1846*

a spirit of deep, restless villainy which warned the penetrating observer that all was not as fair within as without, while his pallid cheek and somewhat haggard air bespoke at once the profligate, the gambler, and perhaps the drunkard.[2]

As we shall see later, Charlotte has already become aware of the idea that facial features are an indication of character. Although the Marquis of Douro does not appear in this manuscript, Charlotte underlines the contrast between him and Percy. They are soon to be the central antagonists of her saga. Unlike Douro, Percy renounces honour: 'Eavesdroppers, spies, or false-witnesses are all equally acceptable to me when there is a great end in view which can be more easily attained by their assistance.' He is above all a confirmed atheist, hardened by the way of the world: 'My conscience, if I ever had any, has been long seared.'

Immortality finds no place in my creed, and death is with me but an abbreviated term for lasting sleep.'

True to his word, Percy allies himself with Quashia in order to slander St Clair. Quashia Quamina, son of the great King Sai-Too-Too who died at the Battle of Coomassie won by the original Twelves, incites the Ashantee tribes to rebellion and makes a claim to his ancestral throne. We have been prepared for this by Charlotte's earlier manuscript fragment: *The African Queen's Lament* (12 February 1833). Here the Duke of Wellington, who had raised Quashia as his own son, expresses to Lord Charles his fears that Quashia, although too young to heed her words, may yet fulfil the prophecy of his dying mother:

> Look child where Hyle's waters lie.
> I hear a deep tone breathing thence
> A voice, a sound of prophecy,
> Which speaks a bloody recompense.[3]

The Green Dwarf describes the first of many attacks which Quashia leads against the Glass Town Federation. His name was possibly suggested by a character from *Blackwood's Magazine*[4] named Quashee, a 'silly blackamoor boy' and 'little black majesty', who having died on board ship continues to haunt the vessel as an agent of evil. True to his prototype, Quashia is to prove a major threat to the new kingdom of Angria.

Percy is exiled for his crimes against St Clair. For sixteen years he wanders the world, 'sometimes a pirate, sometimes a leader of banditti, and ever the companion of the most dissolute and profligate of mankind.'[5] Thus Charlotte creates a certain logic to his role in *The Pirate* and *Letters From An Englishman*. Nor can Lord Charles resist his own explanation of the scoundrelly boy known as 'the Green Dwarf'. A traitor to his master St Clair, he is sentenced to ten years' labour in the galleys, after which he becomes first a 'printer's devil', then a compositor. 'Being of a saving and pilfering disposition', he is next able to purchase a commission in the army, before taking up the trade of author. This composer of 'drivelling rhymes' and 'snivelling tales' turns out to be no other than Lord Charles's rival, Captain Tree!

Alexander Percy's early life is difficult to reconstruct from the Brontë juvenilia. He appears to have had three wives, although the frequent appearance of various mistresses (notably Harriet O'Connor and Louisa Vernon) confuses the issue. First he married the wicked Maria di Segovia (later called Augusta di Segovia), an Italian who dies a violent death;[6] and his second wife was Lady Maria Henrietta Percy with whom he is idyllically happy, living at Percy Hall in Wellington's Land. During the latter's short life three sons are born (Edward, William and Henry Percy) and a daughter (Mary Henrietta) just before Maria dies of consumption.[7] The first Maria has often been thought to be Percy's mistress rather than his first wife, but the separate graves of the two Marias, wives of Percy, are described in Branwell's unpublished manuscript *The Politics of Verdopolis*.[8] Another unpublished fragment by Branwell[9] also reveals that it is after the second Maria's death that Percy joins the army under Wellington to fight the Ashantees and is disgraced because of his conspiracy against St Clair. As we have just seen, sixteen years of exile follow, during which Percy becomes a pirate. He then abandons this life for a stormy third marriage to Zenobia Ellrington.

Apart from celebrating his hero's love for rebellion, Branwell was haunted by Percy's remorse for his second wife and often returns to this theme.[10] Charlotte seems to have been more concerned about Percy's unnatural hatred for his sons and his banishment of them as soon as they were born, which contributed to his ailing wife's death; and in later manuscripts she is fascinated by the love/hate relationship between Percy and the younger Marquis of Douro, a situation complicated by her hero's marriage to Percy's beloved daughter Mary. As with all characters in the juvenilia, the facts about Percy's life are not described in a single manuscript: they emerge gradually over the years in various fragments, poems and stories as both Charlotte and Branwell rewrite and refine their characters' pasts to accord with new developments in the present.

14

Arthuriana

After such a long manuscript devoted to Percy, Charlotte felt it was time to return to her own hero, the Marquis of Douro. This she does in a series of sketches entitled *Arthuriana Or Odds & Ends* by Lord Charles Wellesley. It appears that she had intended to write another long story centred on Arthur Augustus Wellesley, Marquis of Douro, but was unable to decide on a suitable subject. Consequently we have 'A Miscellaneous Collection of Pieces In Prose & Verse', as the sub-title announces. Charlotte gathered these pieces together on 20 November 1833, but the dates of the individual works show that she began writing them soon after she finished *The Green Dwarf,* on 27 September. There are six prose tales (one incomplete) and three poems. These Charlotte carefully bound together in a handsewn booklet with brown paper wrappers, measuring 9.3 × 11.5 cm.[1] All Charlotte's prose manuscripts for 1833 are identical to this in size and appearance, except the two earliest booklets containing *The Bridal* and *Something about Arthur,* which are smaller (9.2 × 5.6 cm).

That Charlotte originally intended to write a long story about the Marquis of Douro can be seen from the first two items in *Arthuriana: The Post Office* and *Brushwood Hall.* She began writing *The Post Office* on 27 September and finished *Brushwood Hall* on 1 October 1833. They are labelled chapter 1 and chapter 2 of a story which was intended to be called 'Brushwood Hall'. This title and the word 'Introduction' have been erased from the heading of Chapter 1 and 'The Post Office' inserted.[2] Charlotte must have realized that her story was not 'making out' and decided to include the chapters in *Arthuriana* as two separate pieces.

The Post Office is typical of Lord Charles Wellesley's 'Introductions'. A meeting with another character leads to a story which he can then relate to his audience. In this case, a letter wrested from the hands of the Post Master of Verdopolis rouses Lord Charles's curiosity to visit Brushwood Hall, the newly acquired residence of Mr Samuel Smith, a wealthy English merchant. The first half of the manuscript, however, is devoted to the Marquis of Douro's degenerating character — a subject which probably justifies its inclusion in *Arthuriana*. Lord Charles, in his usual urbane and patronizing tone, favours Mr Freeling, 'the smug official gentleman' who presides in the Post Office, with his opinion of Captain Flower's recent novel: *Real Life in Verdopolis*. Captain Flower was Branwell's pseudonym from 1831 to mid-1834 and this is more than likely a reference to a lost manuscript by Branwell. The title was listed in a bibliography in 1908[3] and there is certainly a gap in Branwell's existing manuscripts about this time (August—September, 1833). It is not inconceivable that Branwell would have written this tale about Douro while Charlotte was occupied with his hero in *The Green Dwarf*.

The Post Office gives us an idea of the contents of this lost manuscript. Lord Charles admires the fearless way in which Captain Flower 'exposes the iniquities of those proud ones who sit in high places', in particular the Marquis of Douro. Allowing for Lord Charles's resentment of his brother, we learn that he was 'ignorant to what a hopeless depth [Douro] had sunk in the black gulfs of sin and dissipation'.[4] Lord Charles affirms the truth of Flower's book and the Marquis's unblushing reception of it. Branwell appears to have been tired of Charlotte's spotless hero and determined to alter him, although we have already seen hints of his changing character in *Something about Arthur*. When Lord Charles unscrupulously opens Mr Smith's letter to his English associate in London we learn of the Marquis of Douro's callous, unsympathetic attitude to the barbaric treatment still accorded to Englishmen in Verdopolis. In the postscript, Mr Smith refers to Lord Ellrington's connection with a robbery and his flight from the hands of justice, possibly another indication of the content of *Real Life in Verdopolis*.

In *Brushwood Hall,* we learn where Lord Ellrington (Alexander Percy or Rogue as we have known him) is hiding. On leaving Verdopolis he was compelled by illness to take refuge in the deserted Brushwood Hall. The help of Marian, now living at nearby Douro Villa, is enlisted by Zenobia and they try to prevent Mr Smith taking up residence at the Hall by pretending to be ghosts. But Mr Smith, 'with a presence of mind unusual to an Englishman', shoots Lord Ellrington in the arm. The Marquis of Douro returns unexpectedly from a sojourn in Stumps and Monkey's Islands and discovers his wife's involvement with his enemy. A melo-dramatic scene ensues in which Zenobia appeals to Douro's honour. He gives Ellrington a week to escape from the Government and Mr Smith is able to return in peace to Brushwood Hall. Later that month, when Branwell begins *The Politics of Verdopolis* (23 October 1833), Rogue is still on the run, 'flying his country for ban of the law'.[5]

The Tragedy and The Essay (6 October 1833) shows the Marquis of Douro as the leader of literary society whose patronage is sought by aspiring authors. Edwin Hamilton, a young architect and one of Douro's numerous protégés', writes a tragedy entitled 'Petrus and Aria'. After initial scorn — 'that cool, keen, composed aspect of contempt which he sometimes assumed in order to torture the wretches dependent on his favour'[6] — Douro recommends the tragedy to Mr Price of the Theatre Royal. Unfortunately its reception is ruined by Lord Lofty and a 'bevy of puppies like himself'. Soon after, however, Lofty receives his just deserts. To gain admittance to the Verdopolitan 'bel-espirits' it is necessary to have 'written a book, painted a picture, or moulded a statue'. Thus, when Lofty seeks advice from the Marquis, he is gulled into writing an essay on 'the unjustly condemned art of the laundress' which makes him the laughing stock of Verdopolis.

Charlotte had always been fascinated by the theatre. The early juvenilia contain many descriptions of it and the young authoress made several attempts to write her own dramas.[7] Such references to Mrs Siddons, Mr Price,[8] and the Theatre Royal in *The Tragedy and The Essay* demonstrate her familiarity with the contemporary London theatre, probably gained from the pages of newspapers and magazines. Such information had an enriching effect on the Verdopolitan scene:

> Certainly there are few sights more animated and inspiring than a crowded theatre. The brilliant lights, the ceaseless hum of voices, the busy and visionary stage, all conspire to raise indescribable feelings in the soul. This evening there appeared no fewer than four monarchs in the royal box and what was more attractive because more rare — their queens graced it by their presence.* More than a thousand of the loveliest women on earth sparkled in the dress circle, where the waving of plumes, the rustling of robes, the glitter of diamonds and the light-bright eyes were perfectly dazzling.[9]

In Charlotte's manuscripts the aristocrats of Verdopolis form an intellectual elite. The descriptions of their meetings seem inspired by tales of the French salons of the late eighteenth century. Here, Lord Lofty marvels at the 'very flower of Africa's geniuses' who are entertained at Waterloo Palace:

> While he listened to the noble sentiment, the brilliant wit, the exhaustless knowledge, and the varied information which, clothed in the purest language and uttered in the soft subdued tones which perfect refinement dictates, formed a conversazione of such fascinating brilliancy as he had

never heard before, undefined longings arose in his heart to become a more immediate partaker of the feast of reason and the flow of soul he witnessed.

Sometimes the literati meet in the Rotunda of Bravey's Hotel, where the Marquis of Douro recently presented a 'poetic effusion' entitled 'The Red Cross Knight' (2 October 1833), satirizing the worthy antiquarian Mr John Gifford.[10] The latter was probably inspired by William Gifford, first editor of the *Quarterly Review,* who despised radical poets and rigorously adhered in his literary criticism to the 'old school' in literature. Byron laments the perversion of Gifford's talents in *English Bards and Scotch Reviewers,* which Charlotte would have read by 1833.

Alexander Soult, the 'rank and ragged poetaster' of the early juvenilia, is now a member of this exclusive society. He appeared with the Marquis of Douro in Branwell's *Letters From An Englishman,* volume II, and contributed a song to *The Monthly Intelligencer.* Now, in *Arthuriana* we hear that he has become 'a glorious poet' and has been elevated to the ranks of the aristocracy as Alphonse Soult, son of the Duke of Dalmatia. Later, with the advent of Angria, he becomes the Marquis of Marseilles, Angrian Ambassador to Verdopolis,[11] his French associations reflecting Branwell's continued interest in France. An untitled and incomplete story in *Arthuriana,* beginning 'Every-body knows how fond Arthur is of patronizing rising talent' (*c.* 9 October 1833) recalls an earlier discussion between Soult and Douro in the *Young Men's Magazine* for November 1830.[12] Being bored with society and familiar with the Persian language, Douro and Soult decide to travel to Persia using the magic carpet of Prince Houssain from the *Arabian Nights.* Once there, they enter a scene reminiscent of the Persian tale told by the Marquis in the earlier manuscript, where Houssain chooses an heir to his vast wealth from among three young candidates who are shown a vision of paradise. Crashey, the divine arbitrator and 'great progenitor' of the early Glass Town, wins the contest by displaying the wisdom of silence. In this later article in *Arthuriana* Douro is about to enter a debate to prove that Persia is not the only country ever to produce a good poet, when the manuscript stops abruptly in the middle of a sentence. Charlotte's writing had obviously been interrupted and the following one and a half blank pages suggest that she had intended to return to her story.

The remaining two prose manuscripts of *Arthuriana* relate to the Marquis of Douro's domestic life. *The Fresh Arrival* (7 October 1833) announces the birth of a son to Marian and Douro. His name is Arthur Gerald, Lord Rosendale, but in succeeding manuscripts he is referred to as Arthur Julius Wellesley, Lord Almeida. The title of 'Lord Rosendale' becomes that of John Augustus Sneaky, Jnr, young son of the Duke of

Fidena and Lily Hart.[13] Lord Charles Wellesley's unusually tender response to the 'wee bairnee' leads him to reflect on the future destiny of the child. He recalls the Marquis's own youth and spoilt childhood. Seven years at school on Philosophers' Island had hardened the effeminate form of Arthur but had failed to remove from his spirit 'the fatal seeds' of pride and 'bad passions'. Lord Charles amusingly forgets his own tender years, and recommends a Rousseauian education to prevent the child becoming like his father.

Soon after the new baby is christened, Marian invites Lord Charles to *The Tea Party* (9 October 1833). She is already becoming the victim of her husband's deception and while he neglects her she is subject to the drunken advances of Lord Ellrington and Thornton Sneaky who intrude on the otherwise sedate gathering. The scene degenerates into a boisterous romp — an amusing but rather juvenile production from the pen of a girl who was now seventeen.

The Secret (7 November 1833),[14] the first of two tales in another little handsewn booklet written immediately after *Arthuriana,* continues Charlotte's interest in the domestic life of her hero. Again we see Marian suffering. She is the victim not only of her autocratic husband but of her own past. Miss Foxley, the embittered governess who through jealousy tried to prevent Marian's marriage to Douro, appears again to plague her. She convinces Marian that Henry Percy, her husband by a former adolescent marriage, is still alive and that she is not the daughter of Sir Alexander Hume of Badey Hall in Wellington's Land, but the daughter of Lord Ellrington (alias Alexander Percy), her former husband's father and her new husband's most hated rival. Poor Marian, who is fated always to suffer, must brave the terrors of Ellrington's 'sanctum sanctorum' to destroy evidence of the latter secret: a pact between her mother and the late Lady Percy, Ellrington's second wife, to exchange children in order to preserve Lady Percy's sons from Ellrington's unnatural aversion to male offspring. Through the intervention of the Duke of Wellington, however, Miss Foxley and her accomplice Edward Percy, 'the well known scamp and oldest brother' of Henry, are made to confess the truth; the pact was never fulfilled and Henry Percy was drowned at sea soon after his marriage to Marian, the victim of his father's perverse hatred for his sons. Later, in 'Stanzas On The Fate Of Henry Percy' (15 June 1834),[15] we learn that he was murdered in his sleep while on a voyage to the South Sea Islands by the Commander of the *Mermaid,* Captain Steighton — a minion of Ellrington and later steward of his estates.

The Secret is an excellent example of the interrelation of Charlotte's writings. Its pages are full of characters, incidents, relationships and descriptions which are echoed in other manuscripts, especially *Arthuriana.*

Almost every manuscript of Charlotte is based on or written in reaction to events of a previous story. We learnt in *Something about Arthur,* for example, that the Duchess of Wellington employed Mina Laury after her adolescent affair with Douro. In *Brushwood Hall,* since the Duchess's death, Mina has been Marian's favourite waiting-maid. *The Secret* demonstrates the confidence Marian places in Mina and in her father Ned Laury, who came to her rescue in *The Tea Party.* Ellrington's insidious provocation of Marian in *Brushwood Hall* and *The Tea Party* helps to heighten the drama of Marian's visit to his private sanctuary in *The Secret.* In *Arthuriana*[16] we learnt of Douro's fluency in the Persian language which he is teaching to Zenobia, and in *The Secret* we see Zenobia studying 'one of the greatest poets Persia ever produced'. Chapter 1 of *The Secret* shows that the marriage of Julia and Sydney in *The Foundling* has degenerated into domestic comedy. In *The Post Office* Douro taunts Sydney with Julia's possible infidelity and as Sydney realizes the extent of the Marquis's influence over his wife he becomes less inclined to support him. Their relationship declines and later in *Arthuriana* we find that the Marquis has stolen Sydney's 'Lines written beside a fountain in the grounds of York Villa' and labelled them 'a piece of cursed cant'.[17] As Sydney moves from the circle of Douro's admirers, the presentation of his character suffers a corresponding decline and he becomes an 'incorrigible milk-sop' whose 'mind and body are a continual prey to all the heaviest cares of public and private life'.[18] His stinginess to his wife and the clerks at the Colonial Office is contrasted in *The Secret* with Douro's liberality. Later, in *A Late Occurrence,* Sydney finally breaks with 'the Young Autocrat'. While Douro and the army are away fighting the French in December 1833,[19] he sides with the government against the army. Parliament, however, is soon dispersed in true Cromwellian fashion and the ministers, including Sydney, are taken prisoner. Douro's revenge is to shatter Sydney's already fragile marriage.[20]

The Marquis of Douro's relationship with the Duke of Fidena, a friendship of much longer standing, is very different. It also suffers strains as Douro's ambition increases, but the mutual regard of boyhood is never completely destroyed.[21] We see this regard at its highest point in *Lily Hart* (7 November 1833), where the Marquis plays a prominent role in promoting the welfare of his friend. *Lily Hart* is essentially a fairy-tale love story set at the time of the Great Insurrection of 16 March 1831, first described in Branwell's *Letters From An Englishman.* The fighting is merely a background for the courtship and clandestine marriage of John Sneaky, Duke of Fidena, and Lily Hart, probably inspired by 'Emily Hart', the early assumed name of Emma Lyon (later Lady Hamilton). By 4 July 1834, Charlotte had read Southey's *Life of Nelson*[22] and although the

19   *Watercolour portrait by Charlotte Brontë, 14 August 1833,*
suggestive of Lily Hart

name 'Emily Hart' is not mentioned in this book, the Brontë family
interest in Nelson, Duke of Bronté, would have led her to read other
accounts of his life and his relationship with Lady Hamilton.

Lily Hart is the last of Charlotte's prose manuscripts for the year 1833.
She returns again to the past and spans the Glass Town events of the last
year. The wounded Fidena, disguised as Mr Seymour, is cared for by Lily
Hart's mother. An attachment grows between him and Lily, but it is
interrupted when Fidena disappears for a year (to defend his country
against Ellrington, or Rogue as he was then, in the Battle of Fidena). Lily,

now an orphan, is rescued from poverty by Fidena, who like a fairy godmother bestows on the little seamstress a life of riches and rank. For three years Lily dwells in the 'peaceful little paradise' of Elm Grove Villa. A son is born, but their marriage is still a secret to all but Douro. Finally, in a melodramatic revelation scene Maria and Edith Sneaky persuade their father, King Alexander Sneaky of Sneaky's Land, to accept his son's wife. Thus Lily takes her place in Verdopolitan society as the Marchioness of Fidena.

The time structure of *Lily Hart* is based firmly on events related in *Letters From An Englishman.* They are hardly referred to, but a knowledge of them is assumed. Although the theme of romance and a preoccupation with her aristocratic characters and their lives dominate her manuscripts of 1833, Charlotte is continually aware of the new changes in the Glass Town plot which Branwell is constantly initiating. Brother and sister are firm partners at this time, sharing intimately the same source of inspiration. Branwell began *The Politics of Verdopolis* on 23 October before Charlotte wrote *The Secret* and *Lily Hart,* and yet the last pages of his story, completed on 15 November show that he had read these most recent of her manuscripts. Conversely, Charlotte's poem at the end of *Arthuriana,* dated 20 November 1833, was actually inspired by an incident in 'Captain Flower's Last [? Novel],'[23] namely *The Politics of Verdopolis.* Charlotte uses a quotation from Branwell's manuscript as the introduction to her poem. Again, this same scene is re-created by Charlotte in *High Life In Verdopolis.*[24] She describes 'Flower's lovely heroine' and the wicket-gate of that churchyard 'so sweetly described' at the beginning of *The Politics of Verdopolis.* The very titles of the manuscripts are themselves indicative of their joint efforts to describe the Verdopolitan scene while at the same time preserving their own particular interests. Branwell's *The Politics of Verdopolis* traces in detail Ellrington's preparation for an election campaign, with special emphasis on the two seats of Wellington's Glass Town. *An Historical Narrative of the 'War of Encroachment'* (18 November – 17 December 1833)[25] preserves both his French and military interests of the early period; whereas Charlotte's absorbing concern at this time is well illustrated in *High Life In Verdopolis,* written early in 1834.

15

Mary Percy

Charlotte's manuscripts of early 1834 indicate a change of direction in the Glass Town Saga. The main cause of this change is Branwell's latest innovation: the introduction of Mary Percy, daughter of his hero Lord Ellrington (alias Rogue and Alexander Percy). There is always a time lag between Branwell's innovations and Charlotte's acceptance of them in her manuscripts. Mary Percy was introduced as early as 23 October 1833, in *The Politics of Verdopolis,* but she does not appear in Charlotte's manuscripts until January of the following year.[1] We do see in the stories of late 1833, however, a possible preparation for the advent of Mary Percy. *Arthuriana* shows that the Marquis of Douro's nature has changed. The pure, fairy-tale princess is no longer subtle enough to maintain the interest of this increasingly complicated hero. Marian becomes 'a delicate flower planted in a stormy situation'.[2] In *The Secret* she is made to suffer for her innocent credulity. Later, in retrospect, 'Stanzas On the Fate Of Henry Percy' warn of an 'untimely death' for Marian. Her first husband's unreturned love shall be 'avenged':

> The reaper's sickle shall cut down the sheaf
> While the young corn is budding fresh and green;
>   She shall be gathered like a springing leaf;
> One year, and that fair plant is no more seen;
> Few e'en shall know where once its sunny place has been.[3]

By the end of 1833, Charlotte has decided to part with her early heroine.

On 5 January she wrote the *Last Will And Testament Of Florence Marian Wellesley Marchioness Of Douro Duchess Of Zamorna And Princess Of The Blood Of The Twelves.* This is a replica of a legal document signed at the end by two witnesses: John Sneachi (or Sneaky) and Dr Henry Alford.[4] Marian is in 'feeble health' and dies soon after, aged only seventeen. She is buried, as she requests in her will, in the royal vault of St Michael's Cathedral, Verdopolis. Prince John Sneachi (Duke of Fidena), Marian's trusted friend and executor, watched over her last lingering illness. She was neglected by her husband, and in *A Peep Into A Picture Book* (30 May 1834) we gain the impression that Marian died of a broken heart:

> all the kindness, all the tenderness in the world were insufficient to raise that blighted lily so long as the sunshine of those eyes which had been her idolatry was withered; and so long as the music of that voice she had loved so fondly and truly sounded too far off to be heard.[5]

Zamorna himself later explains: 'For, if I had permitted her to remain an impediment to my inclinations, I should have hated her, lovely, devoted and innocent as she was, and my blood was cold at the bare imagination of that'.[6]

There are constant references in *High Life In Verdopolis* to the Marquis of Douro's causing death by heartbreak, but in *The Spell* (21 June—21 July 1834) we learn yet another cause of Marian's death: consumption. She had become ill and as her beauty wasted so her husband's interest in her declined. Her son Arthur Julius, Lord Almeida, dies of the same fatal disease soon after.[7] It seems that the presence of death was very real to Charlotte at this time. On 11 February 1834, she wrote to Ellen Nussey: 'with us an unusual number of deaths have lately taken place.' The winter had been a particularly harsh one. Mrs Gaskell paints a vivid picture of the frequent tolling of the funeral bells and the 'chip, chip' of the mason, as he cut the grave-stones in a shed close by.[8] No doubt with thoughts of her older sisters in mind, Charlotte told Ellen: 'I have seen enough of Consumption, to dread it as one of the most insidious, and fatal diseases incident to humanity.'[9]

Marian is replaced in the Glass Town Saga by Mary Percy. Branwell describes her first as a carefree young girl of seventeen or eighteen whose favourite occupation is to walk through the 'English-like' countryside of Wellington's Land, dreaming of Byron or his Verdopolitan equivalent the Marquis of Douro. She meets and falls in love with a rising young English politician, Sir Robert Weaver Pelham. The final chapter of *The Politics of Verdopolis* describes Mary's entrance into Verdopolitan society and her first meeting with the Marquis of Douro. There is no hint, however, of a change of allegiance from Pelham to Douro. The manuscript ends with a description of the vast preparations being made for her marriage to Sir Robert.

It would seem from Branwell's note at the end of the manuscript that Charlotte immediately accepted Mary as a heroine: 'N B. Highly important:

Lord Charles Wellesley has condescended to say, "She is one [of] whom I can say I am pleased."[10] It is difficult to say, however, who decided Marian should die and be replaced in Douro's affections by Mary. If it was Branwell's decision then Charlotte was quick to agree. Mary is well established in her manuscripts by 17 January 1834, when she takes a future glance at her characters in *A Leaf from an Unopened Volume*. But Marian is not abandoned: her death is recalled throughout the 1834 manuscripts with morbid regularity. The dead Marian holds an interest for Charlotte that almost rivals her fascination when alive.

Yet Charlotte also seizes upon her new heroine with vigour. There is an unprecedented delight in her description of Mary leading the royal progress in true Elizabethan style from Verdopolis to Percy Hall in Wellington's Land:

> Never have I seen any thing so fascinating as the sweet yet noble condescension of her manner. She would descend from her carriage and advance unattended into a throng of bold and hardy peasantry, gliding through their stern rough ranks like a sunbeam and answering their hoarse thunders of congratulation that shook the very welkin, in tones so sweet, so soft, in words so prompt and appropriate and in a manner so totally unembarrassed, so queenly yet so feminine and gentle, that her rude auditors unable to resist the charm of her speech and appearance would frequently burst into a simultaneous prayer for all the blessings of heaven above and of the deep that lieth under to be showered on the lovely angel who was imparadised in such sweet flesh.[11]

Mary is now the Duchess of Zamorna and Queen of Angria. Marian also held the former title shortly before her death. For their exploits in the recent 'War of Encroachment' against the French and Ashantee, the Marquis of Douro and Lord Ellrington both won new titles from the land they defended.[12] They are now referred to in the juvenilia as the Duke of Zamorna and the Earl of Northangerland respectively. Zamorna and Northangerland are provinces to the east of the Glass Town Federation and are incorporated into a new kingdom called Angria. The name 'Zamorna' is derived from the Spanish town and province of Zamora, situated on the River Duero ('Douro' in Portugese): the town and river are both associated with Wellington's Peninsular Campaign, as are other Spanish names in the juvenilia, such as (Maria di) Segovia. 'Northangerland' was suggested by the county of Northumberland, home of the 'ancient family of the Percys in the North of England' as we learn from the title page of *The Life of feild Marshal the Right Honourable Alexander Percy*, by Branwell.[13] The origins of the name Angria are less obvious. It is possible that the Brontë children had heard of the notorious mid-eighteenth-century pirate 'Angria', who was a particular threat to ships of the East India Company, and that they named their new kingdom after him.[14] The title of 'Queen of Angria', however, has little place in Charlotte's manuscripts of early 1834. Angria, which Branwell is rapidly establishing as the fruit of his recent wars, provides as yet only a colourful background to her study of Lords and Ladies of high degree.

16

High Life in Verdopolis

High Life In Verdopolis (20 February—20 March 1834) begins with an extract from Tree's 'Verdopolitan Magazine', a 'Tory' production which rivals Branwell's 'Verdopolitan Intelligencer'. The author is apparently Zamorna, as the Marquis of Douro is now called, but we suspect his views are closely shared by his eighteen-year-old creator:

> I like high life, I like its manners, its splendors, its luxuries, the beings which move in its enchanted sphere. I like to consider the habits of those beings, their way of thinking, speaking, acting. Let fools talk about the artificial, voluptuous, idle existences spun out by Dukes, Lords, Ladies, Knights and Squires of high degree. Such cant is not for me, I despise it. What is there of artificial [in] the lives of our Verdopolitan Aristocracy? What is there of idle? Voluptuous they are to a proverb, splendidly, magnificently voluptuous but not inactive, not unnatural.[1]

Descriptions of this voluptuousness fill the pages of Charlotte's manuscripts. She loved to describe not only the dress of her regal characters but also their splendid possessions, which in themselves became indications of character. The list of various items apportioned to Marian's friends in her *Last Will And Testament* has been drawn up with care. Lily, Marchioness of Fidena, for example, receives Marian's 'ruby clasped Bible, prayer-book and Psalter'; Alexander Soult, her 'uniform Edition of the French classics bound in watered satin, gilt and lettered'; and Julia, her music and 'Gold chain three yards in length, which is braided with seed pearl and forms a part of the bird of Paradise head-dress':[2] gifts suitable to the tastes of the recipients. It was, after all, Julia's fondness for jewels that had caused her quarrel with Sydney in *The Secret*.

The interiors of Charlotte's African aristocrats' palaces are no less splendid than their personal possessions. As Wellesley House prepares to receive 'all the grace, elegance, fashion and haut-ton of Verdopolis' at a ball, we accompany the critical housekeeper on her last surveillance of those vast 'lordly halls':

> With a slow tread and a critical eye the Stately Dame moved on, through all the vista of proud saloons glowing with brilliant fires and dazzling chandeliers, whose warm ruddy beams slept on rich carpets, silken sofas, cushions, ottomans, gleaming groups of statuary, sideboards where the flash of plate and glass almost blinded the eye that gazed on them, ample tables covered with splendid engravings, portfolios, magnificently bound volumes, gold musical boxes, enamelled miniature vases, guitars of elaborate and beautiful workmanship, clocks and lamps of alabaster and ormolu &c. &c. &c.[3]

Charlotte's enthusiasm for the aristocracy and its palaces helps us to understand her surprise, or rather dismay, at her friend Ellen's reaction to London, where she was staying with her brother at this time. Like Verdopolis, London is to Charlotte 'almost apocryphal as Babylon or Nineveh, or ancient Rome'. On the same day as she wrote the above descriptions in *High Life In Verdopolis,* Charlotte wrote to Ellen:

> did you not feel awed while gazing at St Paul's and Westminster Abbey? had you no feeling of intense, and ardent interest, when in St James's you saw the Palace where so many of England's Kings had held their courts, and beheld the representations of their persons on the walls. You should not be too much afraid of appearing *country-bred,* the magnificence of London has drawn exclamations of astonishment from travelled men, experienced in the World, its wonders, and beauties. Have you yet seen any of the Great Personages whom the sitting of Parliament now detains in London? The Duke of Wellington, Sir Robert Peel, Earl Grey, Mr Stanley, Mr O'Connell &c.?[4]

In Charlotte's mind, the great men in London are as splendid as their Verdopolitan counterparts.

The hero of *High Life In Verdopolis* is Warner Howard Warner, head of the oldest and most influential house in Angria and a necessary ally for Zamorna. The relationship between Zamorna and Warner, in fact, is not unlike that between the real Duke of Wellington and Peel: it is founded on expediency rather than personal liking. Warner becomes Zamorna's Home Secretary, 'the trust and stay' of his Empire.[5] Here, however, we view Warner's domestic life and his businesslike search for a bride. After systematically rejecting Lady Flora Roslyn for her lack of dowry, Maria and Edith Sneachi for their haughtiness and Louisa, Marchioness of Wellesley, for being Zamorna's aunt, he decides to pursue Ellen Grenville, only daughter of General Grenville. A 'youthful blue' and the protégée of

Zenobia, Ellen greets Warner in a tone of satire. She is disappointed by his rather slight feminine appearance, which makes him the butt of enemies who term him 'hermaphrodite'. But as she soon realizes, she underestimates this 'brisk gallant little cock' with 'eyes like living diamonds' and the gift of second sight. As we see in *A Day Abroad* (15 June 1834) he rules his extensive family with a rod of iron and 'a tongue that would outring a woman's and that's saying a great deal'.[6] With such singular attributes on both sides, the courtship of Warner and Ellen begins with 'not a particle of romance' but in a repartee reminiscent of Shakespeare's Beatrice and Benedick. Warner is eventually triumphant and General Grenville's objections to the match are removed when Lord Macara Lofty, Ellen's favoured suitor, is discredited.

Charlotte now seems less concerned with her plots. They form a very thin framework for the development of character. *A Peep Into A Picture Book* is a series of sketches of her favourite characters, linked merely by the author, Lord Charles Wellesley, as he turns the pages of an album and comments on the portraits he sees. *A Day Abroad* is simply a series of visits made by Lord Charles in the course of a day: an excuse to describe the inmates of Warner Hotel, Wellesley House and Ellrington Hall. Here we meet the comic characters of what is now an Angrian society still resident in Verdopolis: the Reverend Henry Warner and Arthur O'Connor, Maurice Flanigan of pugilistic fame and Patrick Benjamin Wiggins — that 'quizzical little personage' with an 'insane devotion' to all the celebrated persons in Verdopolis. Charlotte was aware that her stories were little more than a medley of character sketches and scenes at this stage: she labels the handsewn volume containing these two manuscripts *Corner Dishes* and subtitles it 'A Small Collection of Mixed and Unsubstantial Trifles in Prose and Verse'. Even in *High Life In Verdopolis* the plot is thin and melodramatic. The courtship of Ellen and Warner is huddled into the first and last chapters while in between Charlotte lingers over Zamorna and his favourites, the leaders of the rising 'Angrian Faction'.

High Life In Verdopolis has been described as an 'orgy of Byronism'.[7] Certainly Zamorna is now a Byronic hero. His changing, ever-darkening, vengeful moods, his cynicism, pride and defiance of conventional morality are now described in almost every manuscript. For women he has 'the basilisk's fascination': 'there is a charm, a talisman about him which wins all hearts and rivets chains round them which can never be undone.'[8] We see the feeble efforts of the coquettish Ellen — Zamorna's 'little blue-bell' — to resist his fascination; we trace again the anguish of Zenobia's infatuated mind which 'wellnigh overthrew its equilibrium'; we watch the proud Maria Sneachi being subdued by the oriental despot; and with

Warner, we see the faithful Mina Laury living in seclusion at Grassmere Manor, the guardian of Zamorna's two sons, and entangled in the father's spells 'past hope of rescue'. Zamorna is likened to the Grand Sultan of Turkey surrounded by his Seraglio: 'he humours them, understands every avenue to their hearts, possesses universal influence amongst them but he pays them no deference.'

By 1835 Zamorna has indeed become an Eastern potentate. In *A Late Occurrence* Lord Charles Wellesley lists twenty-two noble girls who are Zamorna's 'stock in trade'. They all have the 'peculiar Wellesley cast of face and form': the daughters of the Marquis of Wellesley, Lord Maryborough, Lord Cowley, Dr Wellesley, Lord Burghersh and Earl Seymour, all relatives or associates of the real Duke of Wellington. The first four fathers, brothers of Wellington, appeared in Charlotte's early manuscript describing a Wellesley family gathering.[9] Lord Burgersh (later 11th Earl of Westmorland) was a diplomat who married Wellington's favourite niece Priscilla Wellesley-Pole; and Seymour was probably modelled on Admiral Sir George Seymour, friend of William IV, although there were many Seymours connected with Wellington during his life.

Wellington's personal qualities, however, have now been superseded as a source by those of Byron and his hero. Zamorna still maintains the Wellingtonian glamour in war, but it is the fatal magnetism of the Byronic hero that now fascinates Charlotte. Her heroines are equally mesmerized. They display their allegiance to Zamorna by dressing in uniform black satin with scarlet flowers — 'a splendid bouquet for Beelzebub, a magnificent regiment of Lucifer's own raising'.[10] Lord Charles laments that Mary Henrietta's destiny should be linked with her husband's 'insatiable ambition and fiery impetuosity'. He sees in Zamorna's portrait the ambivalent beauty of Milton's fallen angel:

> O Zamorna! what eyes those are glancing under the deep shadow of that raven crest! They bode no good. Man nor woman could ever gather more than a troubled, fitful happiness from their kindest light. Satan gave them their glory to deepen the midnight gloom that always follows where their lustre has fallen most lovingly. This, indeed, is something different from Percy. All here is passion and fire unquenchable. Impetuous sin, stormy pride, diving and soaring enthusiasm, war and poetry, are kindling their fires in all his veins, and his wild blood boils from his heart and back again like a torrent of new-sprung lava. Young duke? Young demon!

This Zamorna of *A Peep Into A Picture Book* is very different from the young Marquis of Douro who pledged his faith to Marian Hume.

The increasingly complicated personality of Charlotte's hero is explored still further in *The Spell; An Extravaganza* (21 June — 21 July 1834). As the subtitle suggests, it is an extravagant dramatization of Zamorna's dual personality. Lord Charles invents a twin brother for Zamorna to account for the multiplicity of interests and relationships now connected with him: 'there cannot be two Zamorna's on this earth; it would not hold them.'[11] A spell is placed on the twins at birth in the form of a poetic incantation which recurs at crises: for a time they are to be as one and death will result if they are seen together. We watch their ingenious efforts to keep their lives separate until they are defeated by Mary's jealous curiosity to discover the parents of Ernest Edward Fitzarthur, the four-year-old companion of baby Julius (Marian's son) whom we met under the care of Mina Laury in *High Life In Verdopolis.* Zamorna's background is becoming ever more mysterious as Charlotte delves into his past and creates early marriages and romantic affairs. We learn in *The Spell* that Ernest is the son of the 'other' Zamorna who has married a Scottish woman, a Roman Catholic resembling Mary Stuart. It is not until *A Brace of Characters* (30 October 1834), however, that we learn that Zamorna was allied as a youth to 'the dark — malignant, scowling Gordons',[12] as was Byron himself. 'Fitzarthur' is, in fact, 'Ernest Edward Gordon Wellesley; Baron Gordon', the son of Zamorna and Lady Helen Victorine, 'the young and beautiful lily of Loch Sunart' who died in childbirth.

Zamorna now has three marriages to his credit and many more illicit love affairs. It is possible to gather from casual references in different stories that Marian Hume and Mary Henrietta Percy were preceded by Lady Helen Victorine, Baroness Gordon. Some manuscripts hint at yet another early marriage to Sofala, a Moor whom the eighteen-year-old Marquis of Douro forsook after she bore him the cursed offspring Finic, Zamorna's devoted dwarf servant. The issue is confused, however, when in *A Brace of Characters* Zamorna refers to Ernest Edward Fitzarthur (Lady Helen's son) as 'Sofala's son'. Are Lady Helen and Sofala one person? Lord Charles Wellesley's comment at the end of *High Life In Verdopolis* would suggest not: he says, 'I have heard that his mother was Sofala, the Moorish-lady with whom Arthur fell in love some years ago, but if so his complexion betrays no traces of his origin and I rather lean to the other opinion.' Lord Charles, a now self-conscious narrator, is deliberately mystifying his imaginary reading public. And Charlotte occasionally confused herself with her multitude of characters: the reference to 'Sofala's son' in *A Brace of Characters* may simply have been a mistake. It is unlikely that Sofala was ever married to Zamorna: she appears to have been one of his many past mistresses who proliferate as Charlotte falls further under Byron's charm.

The Spell is a fabrication of Lord Charles Wellesley's, woven in revenge against his elder brother, who has now excluded Charles's 'prying curiosity' from his house. Many of the characters do not appear again in the juvenilia and the events must be seen as separate from the main conception of the Glass Town Saga. *The Spell* is an imaginary excursion from the central plot. Lord Charles sets out to show 'that there is one person at least in Verdopolis thoroughly acquainted with all the depths, false or true, of [Zamorna's] double-dealing, hypocritical, close, dark, secret, half-insane, character'.[13] In the postscript he explains further:

> Reader, if there is no Valdacella there ought to be one. If the young King of Angria has no *alter-ego* he ought to have such a convenient representative, for no single man, having one corporeal and one spiritual nature if these were rightly compounded without any mixture of pestilential ingredients, should, in right reason and in the ordinance of common sense and decency, speak and act in that capricious, double-dealing unfathomable, incomprehensible, torturing, sphinx-like manner which he constantly assumes for reasons known only to himself.

Lord Charles warns that should the talisman of Zamorna's influence which holds together so many contradictory interests fail, then a veil of doom will be drawn over the whole scene: 'There is a sound, a stun, a crash, a smothered but deep dull desperate peal of thunder heard amidst the volumed fold of clouds which hide and pervade futurity. But farther I dare not look, more I dare not hear.'[14]

Charlotte and Branwell planned well in advance the movements of their empire. While Angria is still in its infancy and Zamorna at the height of his power, destruction and desolation are foretold. At the beginning of the year, on 17 January 1834, Charlotte had already glanced twenty-four years into the future lives of her Verdopolitan characters in *A Leaf from an Unopened Volume*. Zamorna is to be even more splendid: the Emperor Adrian, 'surnamed the magnificent'. The hero of *The Spell* and *High Life In Verdopolis* is only halfway towards Charlotte's ultimate conception of him. Zamorna is to become almost a god:

> the superb mould of his form, the withering keenness of his glance, the high soaring of his insatiable ambition, and the dark, yet deep and exhaustless genius which looked out through all his thoughts, words and actions, gave those who saw him the idea of something more than mortal. It looked . . . as if Heaven, being wrath with mankind, had sent Lucifer to reign on earth in the flesh.[15]

This future Emperor has finally exterminated Quashia and his people. He has built marble mansions for his old favourites in the arts: Sir William Etty, Sir Edward de Lisle, Sir Henry Chantry, Sir Edwin Hamilton and Alexander Soult, Duke of Dalmatia. The court beauties are still the 'renowned' Zenobia, the 'brilliant' Julia, the 'graceful' Harriet (Castlereagh) and the 'stately' Ellen. All, however, including the Emperor and Empress

(Mary Henrietta), are middle-aged. The drama now centres on Zamorna's sons and especially on the twins whose birth Charlotte records later in the year.[16] They embody the old rivalries of Zamorna and Northangerland. When Prince Adrian Percy falls in love with Zorayda,[17] his twin brother, Alexander Ravenswood, plans to thwart him and marry Zorayda himself. Earl Montmorency, who discovers that Zorayda is his grand-daughter, prevents Alexander from gaining access to her. She learns that her mother was Julia Montmorency but still believes her father was Quashia and that she must avenge his death. Her attempt to stab Zamorna, however, fails and her true father turns out to be Sir William Etty, RA, the unrecognized son of Northangerland by his first wife, Maria di Segovia.

There is now a profusion of characters and relationships for a student of Charlotte's juvenilia to sort out. The royal family alone has increased dramatically in number. Zamorna and Mary have five sons and one daughter, Princess Irene, who is later to marry John Augustus, Prince of Fidena, whom we met as a child in *Lily Hart*. With an eye to the future, Charlotte notes at the foot of the page that John's father, John the 1st (Duke of Fidena), 'was almost the only African potentate whose dominions remained uninjured by Zamorna's grasping and rapicious hand' and, 'Shortly after John the second came to the throne, the universal revolution took place which brought so many crowned heads to the block, and both he and his lovely queen suffered the doom which ought to have fallen on their rebellious subjects.'[18]

The note of future destruction is sounded throughout this manuscript. Society is voluptuous and despotic. Evil spreads like the Upas tree, contaminating the minds of the characters. We glimpse the lovers, Hermione and Arthur Julius, enjoying the 'sunshine of present prosperity', ignorant 'by what path of blood and mourning they were to descend to their untimely grave'. Charlotte had not yet intended Arthur Julius (Marian's son) to die. Here he is seen as 'the haughty and exclusive Arch-Duke' of twenty-three whom Charlotte planned to marry to Hermione Marcella, the nineteen-year-old daughter of Northangerland and Zenobia. Even Zamorna's appearance is described in retrospect from the 'numerous coins, busts, and whole-length statues which . . . escaped the rapid ruin of civil commotions'.[19] Melodramatic as this story is, it is an important indication of how far ahead Charlotte and Branwell planned their saga. The future African scene has been clearly established. As we shall see in successive manuscripts, each story, sketch or poem is another step towards the completion of this unified imaginary world.

17

Angria Arise!

Since *A Leaf from an Unopened Volume* is set in 1858 and Zamorna has ruled Angria for twenty-five years, one is led to believe that the kingdom was founded in December 1833. Charlotte's manuscripts show that by the following January Angria was an established part of her imaginary world; yet Branwell's first Angrian manuscript, in which he described the conferring of the kingdom on Zamorna by the Verdopolitan Parliament, was not written until 18 February 1834.[1] We could assume then, that Charlotte may have played a much larger role in planning its original creation than has previously been thought. Branwell described the wars which won the new territory,[2] but *A Leaf from an Unopened Volume* is the first manuscript to describe this new world. It is interesting, however, to note that in the preface Lord Charles Wellesley disowns all responsibility for his story. He tells how, on returning home to Thornton Hotel where he is now living, he found a stranger in his chair and was 'compelled' to copy down the manuscript read by this 'Unfortunate Author'. Was this 'author' Branwell, relating his plans for the new Kingdom of Angria? We may speculate that *A Leaf from an Unopened Volume* is the result of Charlotte's attempt to embellish Branwell's new ideas. But all we really know is that Lord Charles Wellesley, and probably Charlotte, felt that he had 'sworn allegiance to some foreign power'.

Yet it is not until October 1834 that the full influence of Angria is felt on Charlotte's writing. Until then we are aware of its presence only in titles and passing references. Branwell had described the efforts of Zamorna and his Generals, such as Northangerland, Fidena, Thornton, Warner, Castlereagh and Frederick Lofty in 'the late hard-fought war' of December 1833. On 18 February 1834, Zamorna demanded recompense

from the Verdopolitan Parliament for the labours of the last quarter of a
year:

> Hear me, Kings and Noblemen of Verdopolis. I have rejoined a shattered
> Government, I have conciliated a divided army, I have reconquered this
> City from the Enemies, I have totally defeated 200,000 foes. Oh, your
> Majesties, I have brought booty into the Exchequer, £5,000,000 of
> money — Hah! — Now, for these services rendered by me to my
> country, I demand from it the possession of my fields of Battle. I
> demand, My Lords the Provinces of Angria, Calabar and Northangerland
> and Gordon, to be yielded up to me unconditionally and immediately in
> just right to myself and my heirs and successors in due and rightful
> sovereignity now and hereafter, and to this effect I move that tomorrow
> night, February the 9th, A.D. 1834, a bill be brought forward in the
> Commons House of Parliament for the direct conferring of the Kingdom
> of Angria upon His Grace the Most Noble Arthur Augustus Adrian
> Wellesley, Duke of Zamorna, Marquis of Douro, and Lieut. General of
> the Verdopolitan Army.[3]

Soon after, Zamorna and his Queen are crowned in St Michael's Cathedral
amid much pomp and the scarlet and gold splendour of the Arising
Angrian Sun, symbol of the new nation.[4] Thus, in *High Life In Verdopolis,*
Charlotte refers to Mary as the 'Queen of Angria', Zenobia is seen
studying an Angrian map and Zamorna questions Warner (an Angrian by
birth) on his 'newly-obtained kingdom'; but the setting and the society are
still very much part of Verdopolis. In *A Day Abroad* we find Charlotte's
first note of enthusiasm for Angria:

> Adrianopolis is rising, soaring . . . the buildings spring like magic and I
> and Warner see that they are solidly put together. Men gather in my
> kingdom as if they came at beat of drum. There have been new inroads
> on the frontier, fresh raids on the borders, some of Ham's blood has
> been shed . . . don't tremble Mary, War we must have and it's drawing
> nigh. Angria lies naked to its gales and she loves them better than a
> land-locked sailor does the scent of the sea-breeze.[5]

Again in *The Spell* we glimpse for a moment Zamorna superintending
the building of his new capital, 'standing amidst the din and tumult of
uncreated squares and terraces, whilst the deep foundations of future
mansions were dug in the stubborn soil'.[6]

By October 1834 the building of Adrianopolis is complete. Charlotte is
at last ready to move her favourite Verdopolitan society to the new capital.
But it is not without reluctance that she describes the exodus from the old
city in *My Angria and the Angrians,* a medley of scenes of the new
society. The Angrians are scornful of the old world; they are the African
nouveaux-riches:

to hear them prefer the marble toy-shop of Adrianopolis, the mushroom of the Calabar, to a Babylon so steadfastly founded, an oak whose roots have struck so deep as the city of the Guinea-Coast, is most hateful, most maddening to any man cursed with a tithe less folly than themselves.[7]

As Lord Charles admits, this attitude is a pretence. They have a right to leave Verdopolis and 'if they chuse to shog simultaneously why let them.' But we suspect this is not Charlotte's attitude; for she remains sceptical about the new nation and its flamboyant despotic rule. Echoes of 'Angrian ostentation and loftiness' recur throughout her manuscripts. The very buildings exhibit a decline in taste: 'Here the hand of that great Architect Palladio could not be seen. The Venetian's classic elegance had given place to a profounder, a sterner, a more imperial style.' Captain Flower, now Branwell's Viscount Richton, had commented on the arrogance and uncouth behaviour of the Angrians at the coronation of their monarch. Yet when he is sent from Verdopolis as Ambassador Plenipotentiary to Adrianopolis, he is full of admiration for the new capital:

> We rolled swiftly through the unfinished portion of the City and soon entered under a vast Gateway of three Noble Arches into the great inhabited street of the Calabar, whose finished buildings, all resembling rather palaces than houses, and the noble shops blazing on each hand of us, with the thickly-peopled state of the promenade and the air of life and bustle which seemed to reign through this thoroughfare of an almost unborn City, all conspired to fill me with sensations of unmixed astonishment and admiration. As we neared the top of this very long and fully finished street which swept and curved most grandly before us, the majestic colonnades and royal entrances of the Palace of Adrian the First rose up and unfolded its splendour before and beyond the Ministerial Square. This square of vast size, and surrounded by just roofed houses of Regal Magnificence, is to be devoted entirely to the residences of the Ministry of the Angrian Parliament. Above it stretches the entrance of the Palace. On one side, the street sweeps on to the vast roofs of Northangerland House, and on the other side it makes an opening down toward the wide, bright, oceanlike Calabar.[8]

Angria lies to the east of the Glass Town Federation. Its geography is planned, mainly by Branwell, in exact detail. Such phrases as the 'Warner moors', the 'Sydenham Hills', the 'forests of Hawkscliffe' and the 'savannah of Arundel' now echo throughout the manuscripts. Angria has four rivers: Olympia, Guadima, Calabar and Douro. It is basically a flat land and, as Zamorna explains in his *Ad[d]ress To The Angrians* (15 September 1834), its borders are vulnerable.[9] The country is divided into seven provinces, each with a capital city and a Lord Lieutenant. As in *The History Of The Young Men* and *Letters From An Englishman*, Branwell provides us with a checklist of meticulous detail:

ZAMORNA. 170 miles long, 112 miles broad.
Capital. The City of Zamorna.
Lord Lieutenant. Lord Viscount Castlereagh.
Population.   1,986,000

ANGRIA. 80 miles long, 180 broad.
Capital. The City of Angria.
Lord Lieutenant. W. H. Warner, Esq.
Population.   1,492,000

ARUNDEL. 165 miles long, 90 broad.
Capital. The City of Seaton.
Lord Lieutenant. The Earl of Arundel.
Population.   971,000

NORTHANGERLAND. 200 miles long,
270 broad.
Capital. The City of Pequene.
Lord Lieutenant. The Earl of Northangerland.
Population.   376,000

DOURO. 130 miles long, 100 broad.
Capital. The City of Douro.
Lord Lieutenant. Earl of Jordon.
Population.   71,000

CALABAR. length 190 miles,
breadth 130 miles.
Capital. The City of Gazemba.
Lord Lieutenant. Wilkin Thornton, Esqr.
Population.   59,000

ETREI. length 120 miles, breadth 95 miles.
Capital. The City of Dongola
Lord Lieutenant. Henri Fernando Di Enara.
Population.   4,000
                                                  _____
        Total population of Angria   4,959,000[10]

Charlotte's description of this new land takes for granted her brother's
detailed census:

> The sun is on the Calabar, the dawn is quenched in day,
> The stars of night are vanishing, her shadows flee away;
> The sandy plains of Etrei flash back arising light,
> And the wild wastes of Northangerland gleam bright as heaven
>   is bright.
> Zamorna lifts her fruitful hills like Eden's to the sky,
> And fair as Enna's fields of flowers her golden prairies lie;
> And Angria calls from mount and vale, from wood and heather-dell,
> A song of joy and thankfulness on rushing winds to swell.

For Romalla has put his robe of regal purple on,
And from the crags of Pendlebrow the russet garb is gone;
And Boulsworth off his giant sides rolls down the vapours dim;
And Hawkscliffe's bright and bowery glades uplift their matin hymn.
The ancient hills of Sydenham have never felt the glow
Of such a dawn as that which burns their blushing summits now.
The fields, the woods of Edwardston are full of song and dew;
Olympia's waves glance clear along their wandering line of blue.
Green Arundel has caught the ray upspringing from the East;
Guadima rolls exultingly with sunshine on his breast.
All Angria through her provinces to arms and glory cries:
Her sun is up and she has heard her battle-shout,'Arise!'[11]

Angria is a nation founded by war and by war it must be maintained. At his coronation Zamorna is symbolically dressed in armour. He exchanges the crown which Gravi (Arch-Primate of Verdopolis) gives him for a steel helmet and replaces the sceptre by a sword 'which alone can be swayed over Angria'.[12] The new kingdom's emblem is the rising sun, its banner is scarlet and its battle cry 'Arise!'. Angria has its own patriotic anthems composed by its own new 'Poet of Angria' — Henry Hastings. He is the author of 'Sound the loud Trumpet o'er Afric's bright sea', 'Welcome heroes, to the War!' and 'Shine on us, God of Afric, shine'.[13] When twin sons are born to Mary and Zamorna on 5 October 1834, they are greeted in typical Angrian style: 'There must be flash and bustle and rising sunism about all her affairs, especially where the King is concerned.'[14] A twenty-

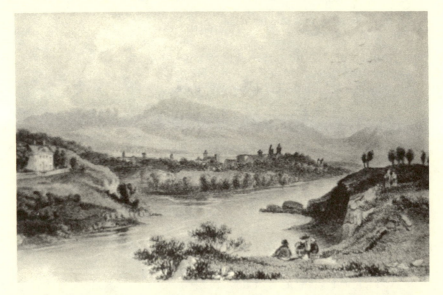

20   *Charlotte Brontë's copy of W. Finden's engraving 'Geneva', 23 August 1834,*
evocative of the Angrian landscape in the province of Zamorna

gun salute rings through Adrianopolis, the hotels, inns and ale houses are open at Zamorna's expense and Henry Hastings composes a new song: 'Hurrah for the Gemini!' With great ceremony the twins are christened in Trinity Cathedral and then formally presented to the Angrian people in Saldanah Park — 'that immense Green Plain stretching behind Zamorna Palace'.

At the christening of the royal twins in *My Angria and the Angrians* we meet the chief members of this new society. They are essentially Zamorna's coterie of *High Life In Verdopolis*. Frederick Lofty is now the Earl of Arundel, Grand Chamberlain of Angria, and married to his loyal Edith Sneachi, who remained faithful to his memory when he was presumed dead in the Battle of Velino during the late 'War of Encroachment'.[15] Maria Sneachi has married Edward Percy, the eldest disowned son of Northangerland.[16] Dr Henry Warner, Warner's wayward clerical brother of *A Day Abroad,* is now Primate of Angria Province. With Dr Porteous (Primate of Northangerland Province) he assists Dr Stanhope (Primate of the Kingdom) at the christening. General Thornton also plays a prominent role in Angria. When Julia leaves Sydney (now Lord Strafford) to his politics in Verdopolis she flees to Zamorna Palace in Adrianopolis.[17] Soon, however, we see her in the company of 'honest Thornton' whose frank, 'hearty countenance' wins her heart. His 'doric accents' are reminiscent of the Yorkshire dialect and his name echoes Charlotte's birthplace, only six miles from Haworth. Such features endear him to his creators and he becomes one of Zamorna's most trusted Generals and an Angrian minister.

There is a certain mystery surrounding Thornton that is not explained in any of the extant juvenile manuscripts. He appears first in Charlotte's writings in *A Fresh Arrival* where he is referred to as Lord Thornton Wilkin Sneaky. There are hints that he has been 'shamefully wronged'.[18] In *High Life In Verdopolis* we learn that Thornton is both a nobleman and a gentleman: 'Injustice has deprived him nominally of the first mentioned rank but it was not of its power to render the deprivation more than nominal.'[19] In *A Peep Into A Picture Book* his resemblance to John, Duke of Fidena, is noted, and in *Letters From An Englishman* there is reference to John and Wilkin Sneaky — 'John Sneaky the coolest, Wilkin Sneaky the gayest'.[20] It would seem that Thornton is the brother of John, Edith and Maria Sneachi and the son of Alexander Sneachi, King of Sneachiesland. In *The Politics of Verdopolis,* in fact, Thornton addressed Maria as 'sister' but the relationship between him and his relations is cold and distant. There is a passing reference in another of Branwell's unpublished manuscripts (*The Wool Is Rising,* chapter 7) to Maria's uneasiness at the persecution and 'expulsion from the royal family' of her brother, 'whatever his faults'.[21] The last scene of *The Secret* implies that the King of Sneachiesland has only one son: John, Duke of Fidena. It would seem that about mid-1833, Thornton was disowned by his family, probably for transgressing the strict moral code of the dour King of Sneachiesland.[22] By 15 November 1833, having been left a fortune by 'Old Girnington' and having recovered from rheumatism, he intends to make a dashing appearance in society again. He has also in some way acquired the guardianship of Lord Charles Wellesley, who now lives with him in Thornton Hotel and Girnington Hall. When Thornton leaves Verdopolis for Angria in *My Angria and the Angrians,* Lord Charles refuses to go with him, but boredom and curiosity soon make him change his mind. There is an amusing description of Thornton's righteous indignation, his 'puckered eyebrows and ruddied forehead', when he finds the nine-year-old Lord Charles loitering on the suspension bridge in the city of Zamorna.[23]

Comic characters are now an important element in Charlotte's writing. She has changed Arthur O'Connor, the bully of Branwell's *Letters From An Englishman,* into the swaggering drunk supporter of Warner's clerical brother. With great gusto he intrudes on the Warner family breakfast in *A Day Abroad* — a conference of Howards, Warners and Agars — but is soon sobered when Warner dismisses him from his post in the Angrian Excise. This episode might well be acted on the stage and could be said to be Charlotte's first successful comic scene.[24] The Warner family provides further comedy in *My Angria and the Angrians* when Julia goads Charles Warner and his 'loving cousin John' into speaking at the Zamorna County Meeting.[25] But Charlotte's most interesting comic figures in these manuscripts are based on her observation of Branwell and his changing interests. Maurice Flanigan, or 'Pratee' as he is known to patrons of 'the ring', embodies Branwell's new enthusiasm for boxing. Despite Flanigan's unreliability as an under-secretary Zamorna finds it difficult to resist re-employing his old boxing master when he favours him with a punch in the stomach, a 'scientific settler', 'a regular potato in the bread-basket' as it is described.[26] Pugilistic slang comes as readily to Lord Charles's tongue as it must have done to Branwell's. Charlotte records with sensitivity her younger brother's awareness of himself and his failure to measure up to the boxing physique he admires so much:

> His form was that of a lad of sixteen, his face that of a man of twenty-five, his hair red, his features not bad for he had a Roman nose, small mouth and well-turned chin. His figure too though diminutive was perfectly symmetrical and of this he seemed not unconscious from the frequent and complacent looks he cast down on his nether man. A pair of spectacles garnished his nose and through these he was continually

gazing at Flanigan whose breadth of shoulder appeared to attract his sincere admiration, as every now and then he touched his own with the tip of his forefinger and pushed out his small contracted chest to make it appear broader.[27]

This is Patrick Benjamin Wiggins, whose enthusiasm for boxing and music keeps pace in Charlotte's manuscripts with Branwell's varying tastes.[28]

Angria is a society where hard work and individualism thrive. The old agricultural society is reflected in such characters as Charles Warner and John Howard[29] but there is a pride in the developing industrialism personified in the figure of Edward Percy. Wiggins prostrates himself before Percy as he rides by and James Harborough an 'intelligent Angrian lad' admiringly describes him:

> Edward Percy is in sooth a first rate Angrian as to appearance, firmly and symmetrically made, with a springing step, a proud domineering deportment, a handsome set of features, crisply curled auburn hair and an eye whose penetrating blue light pierces through the heart like that of an eagle of the Gordon Mountains.[30]

Edward Percy has risen by hard labour in a combing house[31] to become 'a benefactor to the Commerce of Angria'. His factories dominate the main towns: 'Edward Percy's New Mill with its colossal chimney towered nobly from the sloping banks of the Olympia, and the cottages and combing-shops of his work-men clustered about it like Pigmies guarding a Giant.'[32] Edward has recently married Maria Sneachi, one of the belles of the Angrian court and an old favourite of Zamorna. In the *Duke of Z[amorna] & E[dward] Percy* (24 January 1835), Charlotte glances at the relationship between Zamorna and Percy, now 'one of his ablest and highest ministers'.[33] Their early friendship of *The Spell* has declined into 'extreme coldness'. Zamorna knows that Edward Percy is rising in the world and will 'reach the top of the tree', but it will be with 'heavy reluctance' that he rewards Percy with the honours he has earned.

Nor is any love lost between Edward Percy and his younger brother William. Although they were both disowned by their father (Northangerland) at birth, they were determined to work their way back into society. Together with Timothy Steaton, son of the steward of Ellrington Hall, they began a wool-combing business. As Edward explains to Sir John Flower, who stumbles across their workshop:

> we, deprived of house and home, block and penny, have just, as you observe, set up in a small way and in a smaller corner for ourselves, beginning here as combers on our own account with capital of £9 among us. We intend through a course of labour and honesty (hem) to

rise as it were from our present position to large trade, wealth and consequence. If such sequels do not follow the course of Edward (by right) Lord Viscount Percy, the Honourable William Percy, and Timothy Steaton Esqr. Attorney at Law, why may HE catch us, that's the humour of it.[34]

In *The Spell,* Edward has become a 'celebrated eastern Merchant' but he is a hard taskmaster to his younger brother. When William marries Cecilia, one of Zamorna's seven Seymour cousins, he decides to quit the commercial life for the military. The Duke of Wellington encourages his move with a large cheque but Edward merely gives his brother his clerk's salary. Necessity had previously held the brothers together; now they become estranged. In *My Angria and the Angrians,* William forbids his wife to enter his brother's house. Zamorna, at variance with the elder brother, frequents the home of the younger at Elm Grove Villa, 'formerly Lily Hart's place of romantic seclusion' when the city of Zamorna was still a village and the countryside as solitary as it is now populous.[35]

18

Political Rivalry

But the central rivalry of the Angrian manuscripts is not that of two brothers. It is the continuation, perhaps the culmination, of a struggle which began in the early manuscripts of this second period of Charlotte's juvenilia. From the time Rogue enters the Glass Town Saga his interests conflict with those of the Marquis of Douro. In September 1834, the antagonism between these two, now Northangerland and Zamorna, reaches a climax in a series of inflammatory speeches. The political situation in England itself had deteriorated; there was new material for this rivalry between the Angrian King and his Prime Minister. The manuscripts are fragmentary: Charlotte's all belong to *The Scrap Book. A Mingling of Many things,* consisting of eleven items in verse and prose 'Compiled by Lord C A F Wellesley'. They have been dismissed as 'pages of wearisome and absurd newspaper and platform oratory'.[1] Yet they are important for several reasons: they embody the central theme of the early Angrian Saga; they express the continued enthusiasm of the young Brontës for politics; and they show more dramatically than any other manuscripts the close relationship between Charlotte and her brother at this time.

In November 1833, Zamorna and Northangerland formed an alliance for mutual aggrandizement. With Northangerland's help Zamorna won the Kingdom of Angria. He was now married to Northangerland's daughter, Mary Percy. He made his new father-in-law Prime Minister of Angria and an uneasy coalition existed between these old enemies. Charlotte's manuscripts of 1834 repeatedly attempt to analyse the relationship between them. Northangerland, the former demagogue, parricide and pirate, is now a 'proud Aristocrat and stern upholder of thrones'. Zamorna is constantly unsure of his own attitude towards him: 'that illustriously infamous relative of mine, whom I abhor and yet admire, detest and yet love; that bundle of contradictions and yet that horribly consistent whole. He forsooth will share in the power and I cannot hinder him.'[2] As Adrianopolis is built, Northangerland remains a remote sullen figure: 'his ice will *not* thaw.' His tireless energy for evil is not extinct: in *A Day Abroad* we see him planning to destroy the friendship of Zamorna and Fidena. Like Zamorna, he has the grandeur and fascination of Milton's Lucifer: 'bright with beauty, dark with crime'.[3] The Lord of Pandemonium cannot rest long in peace.

After the coronation Sir John Flower had had grave misgivings about the future of a nation whose King was Arthur Wellesley and whose chief ruler was Alexander Percy.[4] And his fears are soon justified. By September 1834 we find that the Prime Minister of Angria has retired to Stumps Isle, the original Stump's Island of the Glass Town Saga which together with Monkey's Land is now considered 'antediluvian' by Zamorna and his friends. The inhabitants speak in a 'long, prosy old-fashioned drawl' (possibly the earlier 'young men tongue') and live on rice and melons.[5] The islands are a popular resort with the older inhabitants of Verdopolis and so Northangerland retreats there ostensibly for reasons of health: Stumps Isle provides the seclusion and anonymity he requires for plotting a coup. His old role as leader of the Democratic Party had asserted itself over his temporary alliance with kings. He had become unpopular with the other Angrian ministers. Yet he still asserts his insidious influence over Angria. On 15 September Zamorna denounces him in an *Ad[d]ress To The Angrians.* He accuses Northangerland of inciting rumours against him, and especially against his foreign favourites Soult, Murat and Rosier, Zamorna's favourite French page. Like Alexander Soult, Joachim Murat, 'the flower of French Chivalry', is a survivor of the Young Men's Play. He fought with the Ashantees against Zamorna in the 'War of Encroachment'; now he has changed sides and become an Angrian Minister. He is of course based on the brilliant French cavalry officer whom Napoleon made King of Naples in 1808 and who also changed his allegiance several times during Napoleon's decline in power.

In his speech Zamorna identifies Angria's enemies as 'the ferocious Ethiop [Quashia], the scoundrelly Scot [Ardrah] and shall I add the inscrutable Percy'.[6] Still Zamorna is hesitant in his attitude to Northangerland, who soon replies from his voluntary exile in a manuscript by Branwell.[7] Northangerland's 'Letter to the Men of Angria' appears in the Verdopolitan newspaper 'The Glory of Africa' on 16 September. With skill and duplicity of language, he justifies his actions of the last year. Zamorna's reception of the letter, delivered to him by S'Death, is described by Charlotte in *My Angria and the Angrians*.[8] Mary, who is suffering from the conflict between her father and husband, hopes the letter will bring reconciliation.

Brother and sister are now working hand in hand; each is the spokesman for his particular hero. The effect of Zamorna's *Ad[d]ress To The Angrians* is reported by Flower (Branwell).[9] It gives rise to provincial meetings throughout the country. Handbills from Castlereagh, Lord Lieutenant of Zamorna, announce the Great Provincial Meeting at the County Field in the city of Zamorna. Charlotte describes the event in *My Angria and the Angrians*. Northangerland now returns from Stumps Isle for the Opening of the First Angrian Parliament. The *Speech Of His Grace The Duke Of Zamorna* (20 September) is reported by Charlotte. Zamorna's main concern is whether to regard Northangerland as friend or foe. His attitude is still ambivalent: Northangerland is 'a Strong Friend, a mighty stay to Angria as a nation, but a most deadly and implacable Foe to the Angrians as Individuals'.[10] Zamorna leaves parliament to decide whether or not to re-elect Northangerland as Prime Minister. Branwell now quotes from Zamorna's speech in his own description of the Opening of Parliament.[11] When Flower returns from Verdopolis on 14 October, he finds three of Zamorna's Angrian ministers have resigned and Northangerland is premier again.

But the conflict does not end here. Branwell had reported a new alliance between Northangerland and the Marquis of Ardrah at the Opening of the Verdopolitan Parliament.[12] Northangerland supports Ardrah's moves to reform the Verdopolitan Constitution. In return Ardrah uses his position as editor of 'The Northern Review' to attack the despotism of Zamorna.[13] In this manuscript (5 December 1834) Charlotte mentions the aimless war against Quashia which Zamorna is about to embark on.[14] Next day she replies on behalf of Zamorna in a *Letter to the right honourable Arthur Marquis of Ardrah* (6 December).[15] In the *Duke of Z[amorna] & E[dward] Percy* (24 January 1835) we see Zamorna set off in great style for Verdopolis to defend himself. His speech in the Verdopolitan House of Lords is reported in *From the Verdopolitan Intelligencer* (16 March 1835);[16] it is addressed almost solely to Northangerland and, again, Zamorna demands that the Premier of Angria relinquish his seals of office.

Branwell gives his account of Zamorna's latest speech and Northangerland's defeat in his new story of *Verdopolis and the Verdopolitans* (19 January—10 May 1835).[17] In the introduction to this manuscript, Flower (now Sir John Richton) hands over the documentation of Angrian events to the rising young author Captain Henry Hastings. Through the enthusiastic eyes of this inexperienced young soldier we view the changing political situation in Verdopolis during the months from March through to May 1835. In chapter 2 he recounts the long speech of John, Duke of Fidena, the leader of the Constitutionalists and Prime Minister of the Verdopolitan Union, at the opening of the Verdopolitan Parliament in March. Fidena explains how 'the newly risen feature in our social organization', the Kingdom of Angria, has radically changed the current of politics: it has polarized men into parties either for or against Angria. Only the Constitutionalists have tried to maintain a moderate view, placing the law of fair government before polemics. On the formation of Angria in February 1834 the government, though basically Constitutional, was divided and the following August the premier, the Earl St Clair, resigned. 'Their magesties' (the original Kings of the Glass Town Federation) then called upon John, Duke of Morena, to form a cabinet, but this too was divided and lasted only a few months. On 20 November 1834, the Kings dismissed this new ministry and asked Fidena to form a government for the Union, which he did after a successful election.

This feverish speech-writing by Charlotte and Branwell was inspired by contemporary political activity. News of a government crisis in 1834 soon reached the Haworth parsonage by newspaper and by word of mouth. In November Emily notes that 'This morning Branwell went down to Mr Driver's and brought news that Sir Robert Peel was going to be invited to stand for Leeds.'[18] The Whig ministry under Lord Melbourne was divided, chiefly over their Irish Policy. The previous Whig ministry under Lord Grey had had to resign only four months before. Now on 14 November the King dismissed Melbourne's ministry. Tory hopes were rising. The King called on Wellington to form a government: Wellington suggested Peel. In December 1834, Peel formed his first ministry, only to be defeated six times in six weeks. Charlotte wrote to Ellen Nussey:

> What do you think of the course Politics are taking? . . . Brougham you see is triumphant. Wretch! I am a hearty hater, and if there is any one I thoroughly abhor, it is that man. But the Opposition is divided, red hots, and luke warms; and the Duke (par excellence *the* Duke) and Sir Robert Peel show no sign of insecurity, though they have already been twice beat; so 'courage, mon amie.' Heaven defend the right! as the old chevaliers used to say, before they joined battle.[19]

Only an election, as we saw in the Angrian situation, could resolve the crisis. On 8 May 1835, Charlotte writes with excitement and feeling:

> The Election! The Election! that cry has rung even amongst our lonely hills like the blast of a trumpet, how has it roused the populous neighbourhood of Birstall? Ellen, under what banner have your brothers ranged themselves? The Blue or the Yellow? Use your influence with

them, entreat them if it be necessary on your knees to stand by their Country and Religion in this day of danger.[20]

Branwell and his father were playing an active part in the campaign in Haworth. Mr Brontë spoke on the 'Blue' hustings outside the Black Bull.[21] It was only natural that this new experience should be transposed into the Angrian scene.

But May also brought a feeling of disruption within the parsonage itself. Charlotte wrote again to Ellen:

> We are all about to divide, break up, separate, Emily is going to school, Branwell is going to London, and I am going to be a Governess. This last determination I formed myself, knowing that I should have to take the step sometime, and 'better sune as syne' to use the Scotch proverb and knowing also that Papa would have enough to do with his limited income should Branwell be placed at the Royal Academy, and Emily at Roe-Head. Where am I going to reside? you will ask — within four miles of yourself dearest at a place neither of us are wholly unacquainted with, being no other than the identical Roe-Head mentioned above. Yes I am going to teach in the very school where I was myself taught.[22]

Charlotte arrived at Roe Head on 29 July 1835, to begin her life as a teacher. With great reluctance she had left behind her a 'Grand Drama now preparing West of the Niger for enactment on the Stage of the Universe'.[23] Angria was at war again with the Ashantees. Branwell was immersed in reporting 'The Campaign of the Calabar' in the voice of his new persona Captain Henry Hastings.[24] But far more sinister to Charlotte was the growing dissension within Angria itself. A new round of political upheavals was also being initiated by Branwell.[25] Zamorna had said of Northangerland: "'His sun should have set before mine rose, if their blended shining was not destined to set Earth on fire. By the Great Genii! it spreads! what! farther, farther, a deeper, longer gorier vista."'[26] In Charlotte's last manuscript before leaving home, Zamorna had threatened vengeance on Northangerland.[27] So desperate had he become that he determined to strike at the only thing Northangerland really loved: his daughter Mary. But Mary Henrietta was also Zamorna's beloved wife. The Angrian saga had reached a crisis when Charlotte was forced to abandon it.

PART III

The Angrian Legend
(1836—1839)

19

The 'Roe Head Journal'

For nearly three years, from 29 July 1835, to 23 May 1838, Charlotte remained a teacher at Miss Wooler's school. It was a period of intense emotional and spiritual strain. She had had to leave the freedom of home and the excitement of the developing Angrian situation for a life of drudgery. As she confessed to Ellen Nussey in June 1837:

> My life since I saw you last has passed on as monotonously and unvaryingly as ever, nothing but teach, teach, teach, from morning till night. The greatest variety I ever have is afforded by a letter from you, or a call from the Taylors, or by meeting with a pleasant new book.[1]

The enforced routine left her little time for writing; but in moments of quiet, while supervising her pupils' preparation or while alone in the bedroom in the evening, her thoughts would wander back to Haworth and Angria. When she had been a pupil at Roe Head, her dream-world had provided solace and escape; now even more it took possession of her hungry imagination. She was being mentally and emotionally starved, and her mind fed on itself. But her conscience was too fastidious to allow such self-indulgence without a growing feeling of guilt. After her first five months of teaching, she began to realize the extent to which she was becoming obsessed:

> When I sat 'neath a strange roof-tree
> With nought I knew or loved round me,
> Oh how my heart shrank back to thee,
> Then I felt how fast thy ties had bound me. . . .

Where was I ere an hour had passed:
Still listening to that dreary blast,
Still in that mirthless lifeless room,
Cramped, chilled, and deadened by its gloom?

No! thanks to that bright darling dream,
Its power had shot one kindling gleam,
Its voice had sent one wakening cry,
And bade me lay my sorrows by,
And called me earnestly to come,
And borne me to my moorland home.
I heard no more the senseless sound
Of task and chat that hummed around,
I saw no more that grisly night
Closing the day's sepulchral light.

The vision's spell had deepened o'er me:
Its lands, its scenes were spread before me,
In one short hour a hundred homes
Had roofed me with their lordly domes.[2]

The above extract is from the long untitled poem whose first few verses, beginning 'We wove a web in childhood', are often anthologized. It was written during Charlotte's first Christmas holidays, on 19 December 1835. In it she traces a series of Angrian visions which she experienced during her first term as a teacher. The prose conclusion to the manuscript vividly illustrates the conflict in her situation for the next two and a half years:

> Never shall I, Charlotte Brontë, forget what a voice of wild and wailing music now came thrillingly to my mind's — almost to my body's — ear; nor how distinctly I, sitting in the school-room at Roe-Head, saw the Duke of Zamorna leaning against that obelisk, with the mute marble Victory above him, the fern waving at his feet, his black horse turned loose grazing among the heather, the moonlight so mild and so exquisitely tranquil, sleeping upon that vast and vacant road, and the African sky quivering and shaking with stars expanded above all. I was quite gone. I had really utterly forgot where I was and all the gloom and cheerlessness of my situation. I felt myself breathing quick and short as I beheld the Duke lifting up his sable crest which undulated as the plume of a hearse waves to the wind, and knew that that music . . . was exciting him and quickening his ever rapid pulse.
>   'Miss Brontë, what are you thinking about?' said a voice that dissipated all the charm, and Miss Lister thrust her little rough black head into my face! 'Sic transit' &c.

Early the next month Charlotte again expressed the conflict of her divided life in two rambling poems. With no attempt to name or polish these verses she wrote rapidly some 760 lines of doggerel, wandering from one Angrian vision to another. The significance of these unpublished poems lies in their change of tone and in the evidence they show of Charlotte's poetic method. In the first fragment,[3] Charlotte recalls the martyrdom of St Stephen which she had read of in childhood. Now a young teacher surrounded by those she dislikes, she wishes for 'that lofty faith/which made him bless his foes'. With a kind of despair that seeps through all her writing at this time, she wrote in the margin opposite: 'This hope's divine'. She agonizes over whether her supplication to Christ is motivated by a contrite heart or merely by her inward agony. She yearns for her childhood dreams of heaven when she was blindly pious, unconscious of evil; now sinful terrors plague her mind, spectral visions foretell her death and the church tower bears down on her spirit like an awful giant. She is afraid to pray. She speaks of the 'ghastly power' and 'grinding tyranny' of her thoughts, fed in infancy by books 'of ghostly and spectral dread'.

The inspiration of books gives way to images of one's own creating. In the wakeful hours of the early morning, Charlotte's mind returns to the solace of its own world and her anguish subsides. Her mood changes to one of excitement, even enthusiasm, as she forgets the real world. She is not only creator but actor — sharing vicariously the life of her characters:

> Succeeding fast and faster still
>   Scenes that no words can give,
> And gathering strength from every thrill
>   They stir, the[y] breathe, they live.
>
> They live! they gather round in bands,
>   They speak, I hear the tone;
> The earnest look, the beckoning hands,
>   And am I *now* alone?
>
> Alone! there passed a noble line!
>   Alone! there thronged a race!
> I saw a kindred likeness shine
>   In every haughty face.
>
> I know their deeds, I know their fame,
>   The legends wild that grace
> Each ancient house, and round each name
>   Their mystic [?signals] trace.
>
> I know their parks, their halls, their towers,
>   The sweet lands where they shine,
> The track that leads through [blank] bowers,
>   To each proud gate, is mine.

Charlotte then recalls scenes from 'Fancy's pictured play'; but her visions are fitful, they come and go. Eventually she is interrupted by a summons to get up. The busy parsonage day intervenes before the prospect of another night of soothing dreams.

In the second poem,[4] Charlotte bids farewell to Haworth. She is writing on the day of her departure for another term at school but she is not going willingly. Her heart is bound to home: to her family and to her imaginary friends. She cannot love those she will live amongst:

> Just us and those we've formed in dreams,
>   Our own divine creations;
> These are my soul's unmingled themes,
>   I scorn the alien nations.

Such strangers would not understand her dream world: to them her visions would be simply names — 'thought in language dressed'. Her heroes, the great houses of the West, of Wellington's Land, and the clans of the North, would appear to them like the substance of an old song or magic story. But to Charlotte they vie with reality. They have a life of their own — more inspiring than the deadening routine of a teacher. They are the comrades who will offer solace in the coming months from the loneliness of night, twenty miles from Haworth.

For the first time, Charlotte acknowledges unequivocally what Zamorna means to her. She tells us that she speaks, on this 'farewell day', without the mask of an egotistical narrator. She admits her debt to her 'mental King':

> I owe him something, he has held
>   A lofty, burning lamp to me,
> Whose rays surrounding darkness quelled
>   And showed me wonders, shadow free.
>
> And he has been a mental King
>   That ruled my thoughts right regally,
> And he has given a [?steady] spring
>   To what I had of poetry. . . .
>
> He's not the temple but the god,
>   The idol in his marble shrine:
> Our grand dream in his wide abode
>   And there for me he dwells divine.

Zamorna and his consort are not random sparks that fly when the mind is feverish: they are the principals in the 'great Pantheon' of childhood gods, whose dwellings are as substantial as Haworth and the moors. No sooner does Charlotte recall the names of Alnwick, Mornington, Grassmere Grange and Percy Hall, than she is lost in reveries of their inmates.

The poem ends with a detailed description of Zamorna's first wife — Lady Helen Victorine the 'Highland Baroness' — posed as in a medieval painting beside an ivy-covered Norman door dreaming of her young Lord Douro who has left her for 'academic groves'. Lady Helen recalls her courtship and imagines her Lord now on Philosopher's Island, the University for Glass Town Nobles. Like Charlotte's own visions, Lady Helen's image of Douro is so vivid that she imagines him standing nearby. She starts when he calls her name, but on rising she is greeted only by the rustle of her own gown and the soft moan of the nearby Wansbeck. Douro is 600 miles away, thinking of her he will never see again: Lady Helen dies before her young husband returns. We know from other juvenile manuscripts that she left behind her a son whose own tragic death has already been planned.

This sequence of composition — the movement from the autobiographical to the imaginary, and the documentation of the conflict between the two — is the typical pattern of Charlotte's fragmentary manuscripts over the next few years. It is the pattern of her so-called 'Roe Head Journal': a series of six fragmentary autobiographical manuscripts written between 1836 and 1837 in her characteristic minuscule script, on single sheets of paper folded in half to form four pages of approximately 11.3 × 18.6 cm. Although it has been assumed that all six manuscripts were written during 1836, the dating is uncertain and it is likely that several fragments were written a year later. The individual manuscripts vary in length from one to seven pages and are referred to by their first lines:

'Well here I am at Roe Head', 4 February 1836.
'Now as I have a little bit of time', [5 February], 1836.[5]
'All this day I have been in a dream', 11 August—14 October 1836.
'I'm just going to write because I cannot help it', [c. October 1836].[6]
'My Compliments to the weather', [c. March 1837].[7]
'About a week since I got a letter from Branwell', [c. October 1837].[8]

The 'diary' content of these fragments constitutes the most important evidence we have of Charlotte's situation during these years. It provides a valuable record of her efforts to cling to her Angrian dream-world in the face of 'this wretched bondage',[9] her life as a teacher.

It is clear that during 1836 this imaginary world became an obsession. At certain times she would be whirled away to a reality beyond that of her Roe Head situation. She began to live in two conflicting worlds, so that the intrusion of the one upon the other had the force of physical pain. As she explains in her journal: 'All this day I have been in a dream half-miserable and half ecstatic, miserable because I could not follow it out uninterruptedly, ecstatic because it shewed almost in the vivid light of reality the ongoings of the infernal world'.[10] The sound of distant church bells from Huddersfield, south of Roe Head, was enough to kindle associations of home and flood her mind with images of 'The spirit of all Verdopolis, of all the mountainous North, of all the woodland West, of all the river-watered East'. When this Angrian vision was interrupted by some unsuspecting pupil she wrote angrily: 'But just then a Dolt came up with a lesson. I thought I should have vomited.'

As the year wore on Charlotte became increasingly frightened of her 'morbidly vivid realizations'. A good example is provided by the 'Roe Head Journal' fragment completed on 14 October:

> I grew frightened at the vivid glow of the candle, at the reality of the lady's erect and symmetrical figure, of her spirited and handsome face, of her anxious eye watching Brandon's and seeking out its meaning, diving for its real expression through the semblance of severity that habit and suffering had given to his stern aspect. I felt confounded and annoyed, I scarcely knew by what. At last I became aware of a feeling like weight laid across me. I knew I was wide awake and that it was dark, and that moreover the ladies were now come into the room to get their curl-papers. They perceived me lying on the bed and I heard them talking about me. I wanted to speak, to rise — it was impossible — I felt that this was a frightful predicament — that it would not do. The weight pressed me as if some huge animal had flung itself across me. A horrid apprehension quickened every pulse I had. I must get up I thought and I did so with a start.[11]

These visions made Charlotte feel sinful, but it may well be that she was never conscious of the precise significance of her sensual dreams. One can only speculate as to their nature, but they were vivid enough to cause her to pant (as she records) and their interruption would make her feel physically sick. Mary Taylor, observant but unaware of the Angrian world, later told Mrs Gaskell that Charlotte's 'imaginations became gloomy or frightful; she could not help it, nor help thinking'.[12] Visions would seize her — 'rushing impetuously all the mighty phantasm . . . conjured from nothing to a system strange as some religious creed'.[13] More and more Angria came to seem sinful, an 'infernal world' or a 'world below', to be expiated only in confession; but Charlotte could not betray her secret. The nearest she came to revealing the truth to the unsuspecting Ellen Nussey was on 10 May 1836, when she wrote: 'If you knew my thoughts; the dreams that absorb me; and the fiery imagination that at times eats me up and makes me feel Society as it is, wretchedly insipid, you would pity and I dare say despise me'.[14] Her confessional letters to Ellen tell only half the story of her religious melancholia at this time. As we have seen, Charlotte had a deep need for escapism, but felt profoundly guilty about it.

The resulting conflict, although it lessened in intensity after 1836, was only to be resolved by her departure from school in May 1838.

The 'Roe Head Journal', then, provides a valuable commentary on her state of mind at this time and an illuminating corollary to her sometimes hysterical correspondence with Ellen Nussey, to whom she wrote in the tone of a lover. Charlotte's biographers have acknowledged her 'journal' as a unique account of her visual imagination and her method of composition, which will be discussed in the following section; but our concern here is with its importance to the Angrian Saga — an issue seldom examined since few of the 'Roe Head Journal' manuscripts have been published in their entirety. Because of the scarcity of manuscripts for the years 1835—36, we must turn to these autobiographical fragments for an account of Charlotte's efforts to keep pace with Branwell's rapidly changing initiatives on the Angrian front.

20

War-torn Angria

A Leaf from an Unopened Volume (17 January 1834), has shown us that Charlotte planned a magnificent and prosperous reign for Zamorna in Angria; but she also warned of imminent destruction. Her departure for Roe Head had left Branwell in sole charge of their imaginative world, and he was only too willing to precipitate disaster in a series of bloody battles. On 3 October 1835, he triumphantly announced:

> Reader, if you have any knowledge or observation, I have no need to assure you that we stand on the brink of wonderful times; that another year is not destined to pass over us without scenes and changes which might fill a century. Neither you or I can guess what these events will be, but we can guess that they will be.[1]

The following December, while Charlotte was still at school, Branwell launched the Second Angrian War which threatened the very existence of the kingdom and threw the whole of Africa into civil war. He traced this protracted struggle in a series of manuscripts from December 1835 until June 1837, and then continued to trace the adventures of the fugitive Revolutionaries until April 1839. These manuscripts have now been broken up and fragments are scattered among various libraries.[2] Most of them describe in tedious detail the various battles and changing allegiances throughout the war. It is, however, necessary to reconstruct as far as possible the main events in Branwell's manuscripts if we are to see his continuing influence on Charlotte's writing. It seems that he kept her aware of his plans for Angria, either by letter[3] or by discussion in the holidays, when she made every effort to make her own summaries of the situation: *Passing Events,* written in Easter 1836, is an excellent example.

Not only do the 'Roe Head Journal' manuscripts reveal her frustration in not being able to restrain Branwell's wild schemes for Angria, but most of her poems and her four major stories of 1836—37 are written against the background of events described by Branwell: Charlotte assumed that her fictitious reader was as familiar as she was with her brother's latest productions.

Branwell had brought the political situation in Africa to a crisis. The ministry in Verdopolis, now under Ardrah and his Reform Party, was bent on destroying the Kingdom of Angria; on 19 December 1835, it expelled her from the Verdopolitan Union. Zamorna immediately issued a proclamation urging all Angrians to rise in revolt. The Reform Ministry called to its assistance the French and the Ashantees, Angria's natural enemies. The members of the Angrian Government were declared outlaws, their property in the Verdopolitan Union was confiscated, and Zamorna, together with other Angrian leaders, spent a short time in prison.[4] In the *History of Angria II* (1—7 January 1836),[5] Henry Hastings (Branwell's new pseudonym) relates his experiences in the ensuing war. Zamorna's generals (Thornton, Hartford, Arundel, Castlereagh and di Enara) fight bravely, but after a series of battles at Grantley (Battle of Danceton Bridge), Westbeach, Ludlow and Anvale they are gradually forced to withdraw from the borders of Angria. Charlotte sadly lamented her now-deserted countryside. After the Battle of Anvale she wrote:

> Turn not now for comfort here;
>   The lamps are quenched, the guests are gone;
> Cold and lonely, dim and drear,
>   Void are now those halls of stone.
>
> Sadly sighing, Anvale woods
>   Whisper peace to my decay;
> Fir-tree over pine-tree broods
>   Dark and high and piled away.[6]

The Verdopolitan Reform Army under Sir Jehu MacTerrorglen (alias Jeremiah Simpson) is particularly strong: supported by Ardrah and the Verdopolitan Navy, their allies include the French under General Massena,[7] the Ashantees under Quashia, other friendly negro tribes under King Boy and King Jack, and the Arabs under Abdulla Medina (otherwise known as the Earl of Jordon). Ardrah sails the navy up the Calabar and threatens Adrianopolis. Besieged on all sides, Zamorna is forced to retreat to 'the Ancient Ecclesiastical City of Angria' among the Warner Hills, leaving his capital to the ravages of the Ashantees. Under MacTerrorglen, the Province of Zamorna becomes a scene of 'never ending cruelty and horror'.

Charlotte carried this image of destruction with her when she returned to school in February 1836:

> My dreams, the Gods of my religion, linger
>   In foreign lands, each sundered from his own,
> And there has passed a cold destroying finger
>   O'er every image, and each sacred tone
> Sounds low and at a distance, sometimes dying
> Like an uncertain sob, or smothered sighing.[8]

She records that as she sat alone in the dining-room one evening when her pupils were at tea, 'the trance seemed to descend on a sudden and verily this foot trod the war-shaken shores of the Calabar, and these eyes saw the defiled and violated Adrianopolis shedding its lights on the river from lattices whence the invader looked out and was not darkened'.[9] In her vision, Charlotte ascends the great marble terrace and peeps through the windows of Zamorna Palace. She sees a familiar room, one she had often seen in the stillness of evening when the lamp-light revealed Mary Henrietta, the young Queen of Angria, reading in solitude beneath the imposing portrait of Zamorna. Charlotte describes in great detail Mary's attitude on such occasions, her dress and her features, her proud white brow 'spacious and wreathed with ringlets', her chaste image contrasting sharply with the drunken Ashantee chief who now occupies the room:

> the cushions of a voluptuous ottoman which had often supported her slight fine form, were crushed by a dark bulk flung upon them in drunken prostration. Aye where she had lain imperially robed and decked with pearls every waft of her garments as she moved diffusing perfume, her beauty slumbering and still glowing as dreams of him for whom she kept herself in such hallowed and shrine-like separation, wandered over her soul on her own silken couch, a swarth and sinewy moor intoxicated to ferocious insensibility had stretched his athletic limbs weary with wassail and stupified with drunken sleep. I knew it to be Quashia himself and well could I guess why he had chosen the Queen of Angria's sanctuary for the scene of his solitary revelling.

Throughout the juvenilia, Quashia has envied and fought against Zamorna; and since Mary's appearance in Branwell's *The Politics of Verdopolis,* Quashia has lusted after her. Now in a scene of morbid sensuality he is seen 'savagely exulting' — 'triumphant Lord in the halls of Zamorna! in the bower of Zamorna's lady!'

By 23 March 1836, after six weeks in a military hospital, Hastings reports: 'Our Capital has been taken, our Monarch forced to retreat into Angria [province], half our Nation in possession of our foes, Verdopolis made one mighty warlike depot.'[10] Charlotte complained the following month in *Passing Events:* 'All the body politic of Africa seems delirious with raging fever: the members war against each other. Parties are confounded, mutual wrath increases.' She was tired of war and had no intention of competing with Branwell in its glorification. At the opening of *Passing Events* (21—9 April 1836), written during the Easter holidays at Haworth, she stated clearly the limitations of her subject and interest. She was quite content to let Branwell play the epic role through his two narrators, Viscount Richton and Henry Hastings:

> Let Richton take his seat at the council board of war or peace, let him paint to the life, the members gathering round that table . . . let Hastings familiarise us with the terms and tactics of war, let him stir us up with the sweet and warlike national airs of Angria . . . let them rush upon that noble quarry, they are eagles, let them travel that broad road, they are mounted on chargers of the Ukraine. For me I am but a crow, so I must dwell content in the rookeries that shade Africa's ancestral Halls, I have but my own shanks to go on, therefore I can travel no farther than the groaning park-gates of the magnates.[11]

The truth was that Charlotte had no interest in war: she returned to her favourite subject, the domestic life of her characters.

Passing Events is a series of vaguely related scenes described by Charles Townshend, the new successor to Lord Charles Albert Florian Wellesley. He is still Zamorna's brother and therefore granted access to the royal palaces; but he is less obtrusive in his narration, being 'secure from remark in the thorough alteration that had taken place' in his person. His vindictiveness has disappeared, but his ironic voice remains. Unable to find a suitable subject for an extended narrative, Charles (or rather Charlotte) is content to highlight certain incidents in the lives of favourite characters in order to convey the effects of Branwell's recent wars on them. We witness a crisis in the relationship between Zenobia and Northangerland; a brief pastoral scene at Hawkscliffe during a lull between battles; and Mary's desperate efforts to maintain a separate existence, to escape being a pawn in the power struggle between her father and her husband. With Warner's help she travels secretly to Angria to gain an interview with Zamorna, who now refuses to see her. *Passing Events* records the last meeting before their separation: Zamorna's anguish is obvious, but he shows no lack of resolution.

The manuscript also shows Charles Townshend's satirical attitude to Methodism and to Northangerland's sinister activities in Verdopolis. Zamorna's behaviour is censured by the Calvinist Warner and various newspaper reports describe the former's increasingly fickle character, his vanity and dwindling popularity. In the final scene we stand with Charles Townshend among the crowd at an auction, the sale of the contents of Douro Villa, once the retreat of Marian Hume but now the confiscated property of the Verdopolitan Government. Townshend's attention is arrested by an old portrait of the young Marquis of Douro painted by De Lisle. He reflects on the contrast between its subject and the present Zamorna of the news reports:

> The contrast of past and present times stood bright as the sun and black as midnight before me. Could the Duchess of Wellington have foreseen this hour how miserably she would have died, but she thought her son a God whom all Africa and the world must worship. This picture could not be disposed of that night but I afterwards learnt it was bought by a publican, who had a fool's cap painted on the head, a pot of porter in one hand and a pipe in the other, and as a good joke hung it over his door by way of sign.[12]

Although Charlotte's poetry of this period preserves Zamorna's heroic role, he becomes an increasingly anti-romantic figure in the prose manuscripts.

After Charlotte's return to school, Branwell continued to document Zamorna's declining fortunes. By May 1836, the Reform Army has also occupied the province of Angria; Zamorna and his army can sustain little more than guerilla warfare in the Olympian Hills. Their only hope is help from the Verdopolitan Constitutionalists — Wellington, Sneachie, and his son Fidena — who enter the war in late May. Parry and Ross, the other two kings of the original Glass Town Federation, support Parry's son, Ardrah, and the Reform Army against Zamorna. There is now civil war in the Verdopolitan Union. Fidena takes Freetown on the Niger River in an effort to reach Angria and march south to Verdopolis. The old Generals Hill and Murray of the early juvenilia are sent from Wellington's Land (now called Senegambia) to Parry's and Ross's capitals. Branwell has managed to create confusion throughout Africa, from the River Gambia in the west to the Guadiana in the Angrian east.[13]

Meanwhile, his hero Northangerland has not been idle. He is still Prime Minister of Angria after his new alliance with Zamorna on 10 May 1835;[14] but by April 1836, as Zamorna's army is gradually defeated, he has taken refuge in Verdopolis with his old mistress Louisa Vernon, and is again in league with Zamorna's enemies Ardrah and Montmorency. Charlotte had said in *Passing Events*, 'It is not for nothing he has dismissed Northangerland and recurred to Rogue', his former name; for Northangerland's real aim is to create revolution in Verdopolis, an obsession since his early Glass Town days as 'Rogue'. Again, under the disguise of 'Brother Ashworth', an evangelical preacher, he pretends to identify with 'the people' and their leader Richard Naughty, a 'rare lad' of the early manuscripts, often called Richard Magne. In *Passing Events* Charlotte gives us an amusing and lively picture of the now-pious

Northangerland hard at work, winning souls in the Wesleyan Chapel in Slugg Street, Verdopolis. His text is appropriate: 'I came not to save but to destroy', and to the narrator, his congregation is not unlike 'the crowd of a suburb schism-shop!'[15]

On 26 June 1836, the eve of the reopening of the Verdopolitan Parliament, Northangerland is successful: the city rises and overthrows the Reform Ministry. Northangerland declares a Republic and establishes a Provisional Government on the French model; again Branwell is merely repeating the pattern of Rogue's earlier rebellion of 1833 and attempting to re-create the career of his early hero Napoleon. Meanwhile Zamorna, in a desperate attempt to reach Verdopolis and join Northangerland against the Reform Ministry, is defeated at the Battle of Edwardston, ironically, on the very day of Northangerland's success. Zamorna escapes to the Warner Hills, but is eventually captured in early July and tried in Zamorna City by his victor, MacTerrorglen (who has joined Northangerland since Ardrah's defeat). Zamorna is found guilty and brought to Verdopolis for execution, but to the fury of his new allies, Northangerland has Zamorna conveyed on board his old pirate ship the *Rover,* under S'death, and banished 2,000 miles to Ascension Isle. Angria becomes an occupied nation subject to a Reign of Terror.[16]

When Charlotte arrived home for the summer holidays, she again took stock of the latest events and their effect on her characters in a long untitled narrative poem referred to as *Zamorna's Exile,* Canto I (19 July 1836). The stanza form and the mood are Byronic. Zamorna bursts forth in an impassioned analysis of his feelings for Northangerland and the bitter consequences they have had for his marriage and his country. Charlotte was still fascinated by the love-hate relationship between them and its implications of evil:

> You are a fiend! I've told you that before;
> I've told it half in earnest, half in jest.
> I've sworn it when the very furnace-roar
> Of Hell was rising fiercely in my breast,
> And calmly I confirm the oath once more,
> Adding, however, as becomes me best,
> That I'm no better, and we two united,
> Each other's happiness have fiend-like blighted.[17]

Zamorna traces the events which led to his exile. He watches the water as the *Rover* speeds towards Ascension Isle, and thinks of his wife Mary who lies dying 'far off at Alnwick'. He had told Warner in *Passing Events:*

> But two living creatures in the world know the nature of the relations that have existed between Alexander Percy and myself. From the very beginning in my inmost soul, while I resisted his devious and eccentric

course, I swore that if he broke those bonds and so turned to vanity and scattered in the air sacrifices that I had made and words that I had spoken; if he made as dust and nothingness causes for which I have endured jealousies and burning strife and emulations amongst those I loved; if he froze feelings that in me are like living fire, I would have revenge. In all but one quarter he is fortified and garrisoned.[18]

Thus Mary must be sacrificed for Zamorna's vengeance:

> I've pledged my faith
> I'll break the father's heart by Mary's death.[19]

21   *The Duke of Zamorna. Pen and ink drawing by Branwell Brontë, 1835*

As the *Rover* passes along the coast of France (the 'Frenchy Land' of the early Glass Town Saga), the faithful Mina Laury steals on board the ship disguised as a flower-girl. Zamorna spurns her at first 'for my Mary's sake', but relents when she brings news of Angria, so enabling Charlotte to weave into her story the events of Branwell's latest manuscripts. Mina tells how she struggled to protect her charge, Ernest Edward Gordon (the 'Fitzarthur' of *High Life In Verdopolis* and eldest son of Zamorna by his first wife, Lady Helen Victorine). When Angria was invaded Mina had fled with the child under Lord Hartford's protection to Zamorna City, but her escort was overpowered by Quashia's troops and the boy dragged from her.[20] He had been found later by Warner, a sightless 'gory corpse', and had died in his arms:

> Doomed on a cold and stormy heath
> In the arms of a noble mourner
> To breathe his last and struggling breath
> On the heart of the gallant Warner.[21]

Quashia had fulfilled his earlier drunken boast to put out Ernest's eyes with a red-hot iron.[22] The loyal Warner, roused by horror, had addressed his men and vowed 'deep vengeance for the dead'.[23] This news increases Zamorna's hatred of Northangerland and all connected with him; he turns to Mina, a companion in adversity:

> Faithful, devoted martyr! Through the eye
> Her soul its ray of fevered joy is flinging
> Because I said she might the victim be
> Of a chained vulture, caged amid the sea.[24]

Like a 'faithful dog' she follows her master into exile.

From August to December 1836, Angria is an occupied country. The Provisional Government in Verdopolis under Northangerland declares Angria part of the Grand Republican Union and appoints Richard Naughty as Lord Lieutenant. But Branwell had no intention of allowing the situation to remain static: his soldiers could expect no respite. Fidena was still preparing to invade Arundel Province; Warner and his insurgents were still struggling for liberty in the Warner Hills; and Fort Gazemba under General di Enara in the East remained undefeated. Northangerland's brief period of power is fraught with troubles. As he prepares to fight Fidena and Warner, he knows that he is plotted against in Verdopolis by Montmorency, Macara and Strafford (members of his government since Ardrah's fall), and on 19 September Mary, his beloved daughter, finally dies at Alnwick.

Charlotte, unaware of this event, assesses the effect it would have on Northangerland, now broken in constitution himself. In the 'Roe Head

Journal' fragment beginning 'I'm just going to write because I cannot help it' (*c.*October 1836), she wonders if Branwell has really killed Mary: 'Is she dead, is she buried, is she alone in the cold earth on this dreary night'? Charlotte is full of sympathy for her characters left at the mercy of Branwell: 'I hope she's alive still, partly because I can't abide to think how hopelessly and cheerlessly she must have died, and partly because her removal if it has taken place must have been to North[angerland] like the quenching of the last spark that averted utter darkness'.[25] But Branwell had indeed killed the Queen of Angria and Northangerland is wallowing in detailed death-bed scenes in poetry and prose.[26] An oil painting attributed to Charlotte reproduces exactly Branwell's scene:

> This chamber of death was opened now in all its dreary magnificence, lofty and airy, but hung and fashioned with velvet so dark as to seem shadowy in despite of the softly shining silver lamps that glistened from their white marble pedestals and centred their radiance on the bed where lay the shadow rather than the substance of the forsaken wife and crownless Queen. Over her the vast festoons of drapery hung from the coronetted tester as if even they were mourning . . . right opposite Mary's eyes, a wide and lofty arch opened sublimely to the sky; its curtains were drawn aside to display the full extent of waste midnight heaven and sad struggling moon. Trees waved too beneath this window which looked toward the south-west, where every thought, every feeling

22   *Alexander Percy at the death-bed of his daughter Mary.*
Watercolour attributed to Charlotte Brontë

of her soul were hovering round the Ascension Isle. What was she like? For such things as I have hitherto mentioned were only auxiliaries in the picture. Here was the principal figure, cold, white, and wasted, supported by a pile of pillows, with attenuated hands clasped, and glassy eyes fixed in unutterable anguish. All the once rich auburn curls were fallen back, and parted in long locks from her brow which, with her cheeks and lips, was stricken with the glistening light of death . . . Into this room, then, came Lord Northangerland . . .[27]

If the painting shown in plate 22 is by Charlotte, then the co-operation between brother and sister during this period can be said to be very close indeed.

Northangerland is shattered by his daughter's death; and his haggard face, 'thin, sallow, and gloomy, with saturnine eyes and brow, and hollow-whiskered cheeks', attests to his sufferings. Nor can he expect sympathy from his self-centred mistresses in Verdopolis: only Lady Georgiana Greville can offer him understanding, but this is smothered by the hysterics of Louisa Vernon and Madame LaLande,[29] whose rivalry recalls that of the Duke of Wellington's admirers.[30] Northangerland's wife Zenobia has been living alone in the north, 'among the stately solitudes of Ennerdale', since the start of the war.[31] Northangerland is alone with his ambition, yet he has little time for self-pity. By November, the Grand Provisional Army has been assembled and awaits his command. The following month Fidena's Constitutional troops join Warner's Army of Vengeance in the Olympian Hills. In the so-called *History of Angria IX* by Viscount Richton, Branwell records Warner's heroic speech demanding vengeance for the death of Queen Mary and Zamorna's son.[32] A silent figure listens to this speech before revealing himself; it is Zamorna who has suddenly returned to lead Angria to victory at the Battle of Ardsley. His return, via France, is recorded by Charlotte in *Zamorna's Exile Canto II* (9 January 1837), another poem expressing his Byronic feelings about his wife's death.[33] Zamorna then marches with Fidena and Warner on Republican Verdopolis, while MacTerrorglen retreats and Northangerland flees. A popular rising inside the city secures victory for the Constitutionalists.[34] The rejoicing, however, is subdued; Mary is dead and Angria has been ravaged.

21

Charlotte Restores Peace

During the Christmas holidays of 1836, Charlotte rebelled against Branwell's control of Angrian events. She was not only tired of war, but she was determined to preserve Mary Henrietta, Queen of Angria, as her heroine. On Christmas Eve Charles Townshend, now lodging with Surena Ellrington, sits down to write a story in lieu of rent: *The Return of Zamorna* (*c.*24 December 1836).[1] His aim is to refute a recent book by Lord Richton (Branwell) and to relate instead his own version of events. According to him, Queen Mary is not dead. Richton, 'the wise and wary politician', saw an opportunity to serve Angria. When Northangerland was called away suddenly to Alnwick, Richton 'poured out a glowing and impetuous . . . effusion' (Charlotte's opinion of Branwell's writing?) on the death of Mary. The alert, 'far-seeing Warner' immediately took up Richton's story, sent it echoing through his hills and roused his men to battle.

Meanwhile Mary is not dead but has been wasting away at Alnwick throughout the autumn. As winter approaches she receives news of the wreck of the *Rover* and Zamorna's death. Weakness forces her to abandon her solitary walks in the corridor, consumption threatens, her memory fails and she grows delirious. When she is alone on stormy nights, 'a superstitious horror' creeps over her mind and her shattered nerves are unable to resist the 'wild awakening of woes', not unlike Charlotte's own experiences of the past year: 'She seemed to comprehend at once that she had been living in a world of hideous phantasms which till now she had mistaken for realities'.[2] At the end of chapter 1, Mary is suddenly transformed by a letter from Zamorna, assuring her that he is alive. Its healing effect is as powerful as Haworth and Angria were to Charlotte herself: 'its perusal seemed to change almost her very being. It came like a gush of reviving air breathing a healthy tone over her shattered nerves and spirit'. Mary sees Zamorna pass by Alnwick Park on his way to Angria, and she resolves to go to Ellrington Hall to watch her father in Verdopolis.

The narrator then asks us to imagine 'a chain of black moors': it is 17 December, the very day on which Branwell had recorded Warner's heroic speech among the Olympian Hills. As night falls Warner is met by the huge stag-hound Roswal, Zamorna's favourite dog, and is led to its master, now at Ardsley, by the faithful Mina Laury. Ardsley is the headquarters of the combined Constitutional and Angrian army. In chapter 3, we see Arundel, Thornton and Castlereagh camping in the derelict Ardsley House, once the home of the patriotic George Turner Grey and his brave daughter Catherine — both victims of the war. News is brought of Zamorna's return and all rush to offer their allegiance to him.

We do not see the victorious Battle of Ardsley; this is Branwell's subject matter. Instead, with Mary, we learn of the battle and its consequences from the newspapers of the following day. We see Northangerland's household in panic, his mistresses in hysterics, and Mary's concern for her father. As Charles Townshend says: 'I leave to other and abler pens the description of the approach of the Constitutiona-lists — of the onslaught of the Angrians . . . and again I sink back to the details of private life.' The climax of chapter 4 is not the victorious entry of the army into Verdopolis, but the reunion of Mary and Zamorna.

Branwell's fund of invention, never really rising above the early battles of the toy soldiers, was now becoming exhausted; Charlotte was beginning to assert her authority over Angria again. She was anxious for the peace she had often imagined at school. Her 'Roe Head Journal' records just such a peace on 'a day whose rise, progress and decline seemed made of sunshine': 'It seemed to me that the war was over, that the trumpet had ceased but a short time since and that its last tones had been pitched on a triumphant key'.[3] The scene is Hawkscliffe forest in the Sydenham Hills: Zamorna and his general, Henry di Enara, converse in 'the soft vowels' of Italian. As the sun sets, a calm diffuses over the scene, 'a power to stir and thrill the mind such as words can never express'.

Peace is soon restored to Africa and all that remains for Branwell is to trace the fortunes of his miscreants who had created such havoc. The remnants of the Provisional Army are massing on the plains of Fala and Cirhala; they hope for help from Parry's and Ross's Lands. When Charlotte returned to Roe Head for another year in January 1837, Branwell launched yet another 'Campaign of the West'. His narrator is now Henry Hastings and the accent is on his personal experiences. He begins his tale on 23

January 1837,[4] by defending himself against the recent charges of drunkenness, gambling and recklessness made by his 'late patron' Richton in his recent narrative of the invasion and resurrection of Angria, which the reading public seem to have 'stamped with such decisive approbation'. He then concentrates on 'a new and perhaps equally important scene of civil and warlike strife', describing the triumphal entry of the Angrian army into Verdopolis and the efforts of Fidena and Warner to rearrange the affairs of state, while Zamorna pursues the retreating foes.

The next surviving manuscript by Hastings (*c.*June 1837)[5] plunges us into the midst of the Battle of Leyden, near Alnwick. Hastings has changed sides and is fighting with the Provisional Army (now called the Revolutionary troops) against his 'own old [Angrian] comrades'. As Charlotte later tells us in her untitled manuscript known as *Henry Hastings* (24 February — 25 March 1839), he had become a wanted man and a deserter after shooting his superior officer in a drunken fit of pride.[6] The Revolutionary troops are routed at Leyden, Lord Jordon (Sheik Abdulla Medina) is killed and, after another defeat at Westwood, they retreat towards Evesham. They reach Evesham on the Cirhala River on 13 March, fortify the town and wait for reserves from the south (Parry's and Ross's Lands) which never appear. Charlotte, anxious for news from Haworth, 'calls up' characters from her imagination for the purpose of 'holding half an hour's converse with them'.[7] Mr Saunderson appears and tells her that 'March has left the Angrians madder than ever.' Charlotte is surprised that they are still fighting, but Saunderson (Sneachie)[8] assures her that Mr Wellesley senior (Wellington) thinks peace will soon be restored.

Sure enough, on 30 June 1837, the last major battle of the Angrian legend is fought at Evesham. As if to express her relief from the restrictive chronology imposed by Branwell, Charlotte wrote two long narratives in one month during her summer holidays. Neither of these manuscripts has a title, but they are known as *Julia* (29 June 1837) and *Four Years Ago* (21 July 1837). Each is about 15,000 words long, written in Charlotte's minuscule script on loose sheets of note-paper, folded in half to form four pages approximately 11.2 × 18.3 cm in size. All Charlotte's later juvenile manuscripts (1836—39) are written on these loose leaves: the miniature handsewn booklets with detailed title-pages and covers were now a thing of the past. Both the physical appearance and the content of her manuscripts had changed. There is little accent on plot; this was provided by Branwell. Instead, Charlotte concentrates on the development of character and scene. *Julia* is an excellent example of this: it is a constantly changing medley of scenes which comment at random on aspects of Branwell's developing saga. Charles Townshend, the narrator, allows himself to 'be rattled away' by his imagination; he has no subject but merely records the thoughts and visions that occur on his travels:

> There is, reader, a sort of pleasure, in sitting down to write, wholly unprovided with a subject. There now lie before me a quire of blank sheets which it is my intention to cover with manuscript, and not a word have I prepared for the occasion, not a scene, not an incident.[9]

Yet *Julia* does have a skeletal plot, drawn from the writings of Branwell, which we are still expected to be aware of. Charlotte makes only fleeting references to the larger Angrian drama. We are told that Zamorna's troops now surround the town of Evesham, but we are never shown their movements or informed why they are there. We are at the mercy of Charles Townshend and see only as much of the war as he elects to show us. By an unexplained coincidence, he is now lodging with his disreputable old associate Macara Lofty in the very town which is being besieged.[10] Charles and Macara, formerly a member of the Verdopolitan Government under Ardrah, go for a walk along the banks of the Cirhala. They hear in the distance the guns of the two armies, Zamorna's and MacTerrorglen's. Charles, the omniscient spy, has connections in both camps. Eugene Rosier, still Zamorna's valet, invites him to the Angrian headquarters at Clarence Wood, where he reports on 'the Great-Gun', his elder brother Zamorna. Thornton and Enara look solemn; a council of war is to be held. Apparently 'Evesham is doomed' and MacTerrorglen 'grows savage'. Charlotte knows a battle is brewing but she has no intention of describing it. At the close of *Julia,* Charles and Macara are off to Verdopolis; they have no interest in war: '"What may take place after our departure I know not — but rumours such as men scarce dare whisper above their breath, are thickening daily — Good bye Reader, 'tis a sweet evening. Can such lovely summer days forbode the advent of a Storm? — — — Such a Storm!"'

Julia, then, is set in the days preceding the Battle of Evesham, but the accent is on the 'private life' of the characters. Louisa Vernon, rather than Julia (who appears in only one scene), is the female protagonist. She has boasted in *The Return of Zamorna:* 'I am the woman who has had power to fascinate Northangerland, to make him desert his wife and banish his friend, to make him revolutionize Africa.'[11] In *Passing Events* she had escaped from Zamorna's clutches and lived incognito in Verdopolis with Northangerland, until he came to power and made her 'Lady Protectress' of Republican Verdopolis.[12] But when Northangerland refused her request for Zamorna's death, she had left him and had had an *affaire* with Macara Lofty. Now, in *Julia,* she is again the prisoner of Zamorna and has come from Fort Adrian, where she is kept by Enara, to Evesham to plead her cause. We see Zamorna alone at dusk with his thoughts. He thinks of Mary and curses war and ambition. Charlotte says that Warner, and one suspects Branwell too, would have been distraught to see him now: 'His troops were arranged, his plans were laid for an awful crisis. it was at hand and he was sick of it.'[13]

A childish figure interrupts him: it is Caroline Vernon, the natural daughter of Louisa and Northangerland. She is thrilled to meet Zamorna, to sit on his lap and prattle about her father who is in self-exile in Monkey's Isle, 'beneath equatorial suns wasting out that life which decay and sorrow and disappointed ambition are fast undermining'.[14] We learn from Charlotte's 'Roe Head Journal' a few months later that another daughter, now returned to Zamorna Palace in Adrianopolis, is also concerned for Northangerland: as Mary looks across at Northangerland House she ponders the plight of its owner, 'a homeless Man' in a distant sea-port watching the Atlantic 'to whose green waves he will to-morrow commit himself in that steamer' — a hint of his imminent return urged strongly by Branwell in a recent letter.[15]

The quiet interlude between Zamorna and young Caroline Vernon in *Julia* is cut short by the entry of her mother Louisa. This former opera singer, 'Miss Allen', and one-time wife of Lord George Vernon (or Dance) and of the Marquis of Wellesley, is well-known for her 'whimsical infatuations' and histrionics. She enters the room, magnificently dressed, her eyes wet with tears for the occasion: Caroline cries delightedly, 'There's going to be a scene!' and we witness Louisa's unsuccessful efforts to obtain a release from her royal jailer.

In another scene, Charles Townshend lays down the last volume published by Henry Hastings and muses over the recent machinations of Richton, Warner and Hartford against the young soldier-author. Here Charlotte is referring to Branwell's latest manuscript which she has just read and in which Hastings complains of the repulses and jealousies of his 'lofty associates and patrons'.[16] This reminds her of a confrontation two years ago between Hartford and Hastings and she sets out to describe the scene in detail to the reader. Hastings is 'in the blaze of his fame'. He is seen taking tea at Girnington Hall, the home of Julia and General Thornton. Julia and her sister-in-law, Maria Percy, are highly amused at Hastings' enthusiastic narration of his exploits in the Campaign of the Calabar: 'he spoke fast and eloquently — not very discreetly or correctly — but at every little slip the ladies laughed again and encouraged him to proceed!'[17] Like Branwell, Hastings is naively confident of his ability to charm and is mortified when Thornton explains that the ladies are mocking him. His vanity dashed, he affects a moody silence, but is soon consoled by Julia's flattery. He is piqued again, however, when Lord

Hartford enters, treats him contemptuously and steals the attention of the ladies. His pride is wounded and he leaves angrily.

It is interesting to compare Charlotte's sensitive presentation of Hastings's character in this scene with Branwell's crude 'effusions' in the voice of Hastings himself. Branwell seemed to be unconcerned, and was perhaps unaware, that Hastings' boastful justifications of drinking and debauchery were a reflection on his own character. He was contemptuous of Charlotte's more delicate domestic scenes; Charles Townshend had even found it necessary to apologize for his narration of the above episode, for he pleads that 'amid the daily deeds of strife passing round me, the recollection of domestic scenes is singularly soothing'.[18]

From mid-1837, as Charlotte relied less on Branwell's manuscripts as a framework for her own stories, she gradually saw him more objectively as a character, until in *Henry Hastings* she was able to present him without illusions and to analyse her own relationship to him. The old partnership seems to have become one of conscious indulgence on Charlotte's part. Like his alter ego Hastings, Branwell was now drinking heavily. He was becoming an embarrassment to his family. Charlotte, always eager to help her brother, would have seen in the Angrian Saga the same secure haven from reality for Branwell which she had found comforting in fits of depression at Roe Head. She disapproved of his subject matter — the drunken debauchery of Hastings and his cronies — but she continued to acknowledge his latest writing. Her indulgence paid off. She was able to turn Branwell's increasingly egotistical rambling to good effect, using his hero as a butt for the playful satire she was to employ so effectively against the conceited clergy in *Shirley*.

Until now, Branwell had always provided the basic plot for her stories, but she would no longer allow him to alter the scene with constant battles. From mid-1837 Angria had been re-established; Charlotte had asserted her independence. Brother and sister still wrote within the framework of their imaginary world but, despite Charlotte's efforts to please Branwell, their choice of material continued to diverge.

In *Four Years Ago* (21 July 1837), Charlotte completely ignores recent Angrian events. She returns instead to the past, embellishing old scenes and inventing further motivation for the present relationships of her characters. Her narrator is again Charles Townshend and his pretext for writing this manuscript is the discovery of an old society newspaper cutting: 'Four years is but a short time, yet what a change it has wrought in kingdoms, in parties, in families!'[19]

Released from the pressure of Branwell's rapidly changing events, Charlotte now takes stock of her characters. Lord Jordon has been slain at the Battle of Leyden, and Arthur O'Connor — the 'dissipated roué' of *A*

Day Abroad — is now 'a dead maniac', buried in the yard of the lunatic asylum in Adrianopolis. General Thornton is a very different man from the drunk Wilson (or 'Wilkin') Thornton who attacked Marian in *The Tea Party*. He was then 'a young man living on his means, the door of his father's house bolted on him in excommunication; the portals of the tavern and Hell open in seduction'. We see him serenading Lady Julia Sydney (now his wife) in the gardens of York Villa, until he is suddenly attacked by Douro (Zamorna) disguised as the devil.

The image of the innocent young Lord Douro of the early juvenilia has vanished. The evening on which Douro thrashed Thornton was the same evening on which he seduced Lady Honor O'More. Zamorna recalls the event and recognizes the 'Prince of Air' as the exact shadow of himself — his own 'grim evil shade' or *doppelgänger*: 'How he winked and nodded at me, who stood so quietly, gentlemen, so innocently listening to the great deceiver making love.' His satanic qualities are explained by an early association with Northangerland, then known as Lord Ellrington: 'to that man he [Douro] has shown more of his real heart than to any other living thing: the mutual communications of those two have been singular . . . each placed in the other unlimited confidence.' After his marriage with Zenobia, Ellrington became a leader of the 'Ton'. His home was frequented by French society, Revolutionists and infidels, like Montmorency, O'Connor and Gordon. Douro gathered round him a rival set of young African nobles. Thus:

> the great world was at that time divided into two parties, with the former Star of the West, and the future Sun of the East, at their head.

Between the two leaders there exists an intense personal rivalry in public and an equally intense intimacy in private. Charlotte illustrates this contradictory relationship, which had always fascinated her, in a series of vignettes. Douro and Ellrington, for example, meet accidentally at Monsieur Chenille's perfume shop and compete for the favours of a 'mere Parisian shop-girl' by showering her with expensive gifts.

The chief scene of their rivalry 'four years ago' was the Elysium, probably a successor to the Rotunda of Bravey's Inn in the manuscripts of 1829—30. This 'splendid temple of Hell' is a mysterious men's club in Verdopolis, which Branwell had recently referred to in a manuscript dated 31 August 1836: *The Life of feild Marshal the Right Honourable Alexander Percy*, by John Bud.[20] This manuscript traces Percy's (Northangerland's) ancestry to the Northumberland 'Percies of Rayestracke'; it explains yet again the early history of the Verdopolitan Union, its geography and constitution and it describes the emigration of Northangerland's father to Senegambia (Wellington's Land). Northangerland's own life is then retold in detail: his murders, his mistresses and his wives are enumerated, and many of the hiatuses of the early Glass Town Saga are filled in.

Charlotte and Branwell had probably discussed the early lives of their characters recently and thought it necessary to record them more exactly. *The Duke of Zamorna* (21 July 1838) which Charlotte wrote in her next summer holidays, again returns to the early life of Northangerland and his relationship with Zamorna; and in the same year Branwell described the early life of Warner Howard Warner.[21] It is interesting to note here that Emily and Anne were also writing the 'lives' of characters in their Gondal Saga at this time. Emily noted in her diary paper of 26 June 1837, a few days before Charlotte wrote *Julia,* that she was writing 'Augustus-Almedas life 1st V'. Moreover, she was aware of the Angrian situation, for she wrote: 'Northangerland in Monceys Isle — Zamorna at Evesham'.[22] This is the only evidence we have that Charlotte and Branwell still shared their imaginary world with Emily and Anne; it may imply a closer relationship between Gondal and Angria than has previously been supposed.[23]

Four Years Ago is a history of the relationship between Ellrington and Douro. Charlotte dwells on their mutual fascination, their wild midnight rides together down the Freetown Road,[24] and their regular visits at night to each other's houses, when in 'breathless interest they have for hours listened to each other, and forgot even to sneer and to upbraid.'[25] Such meetings, however, usually ended in abuse. We witness just such a scene in which Marian, Douro's wife at this time, is mentioned. Ellrington accuses Douro of causing her death: 'She is now a little shadow, but you have a strange power of withering every flower you touch.' Presumably Charlotte was also thinking here of Mary and her recent ordeal at Alnwick. She shows us several 'pictures' of the late Marchioness of Douro, on her marriage day and, later, alone with Ellrington, her 'evil genius'. In the latter scene, Charlotte introduces a new cause of Marian's death: to a broken heart and consumption is added Ellrington's baleful effect on her spirits. His stare has always haunted her; he knows her past, her connections with his second wife (her mother's friend) and her early marriage to his son Henry, whom he murdered. She tells Ellrington that this crime must be 'amongst the darkest feelings of your heart, and there I am inextricably mingled up'.[26] He haunts her life at times of sorrow and death, and we see him here, six weeks before her death in December 1833, announcing that Douro no longer loves her as he did, that he is 'about to launch on a voyage where he will require a different consort'.

Thus Charlotte shows in *Four Years Ago* that Northangerland played an important role in Zamorna's early life; there is good reason for their inability to ignore each other. She is at pains to provide her audience with a greater understanding of their often confusing and motiveless political alliances, initiated by Branwell in the years 1835 to 1836. Even their political coalition in the earlier war of 1833, in which Zamorna won the Kingdom of Angria, is now attributed to their common interest in dissolving the Elysium, a 'pandemonium' of their joint creation. The story, if this loosely constructed series of recollections can be called that, is Charlotte's attempt to rationalize her characters' recent actions and to re-establish their background. After her religious and emotional crisis of 1836, *Four Years Ago* is a reaffirmation of her commitment to the old Angrian world.

22

Mina Laury

Six months later, she wrote the most perfectly constructed of her later manuscripts: *Mina Laury* (17 January 1838). If *Four Years Ago* endorsed her commitment to her subject, then *Mina Laury* marked a new confidence in her role as a writer. The cynical voice of Charles Townshend has gone; and Charlotte herself is the narrator, presenting her characters objectively to us but still intruding at times to comment on their situation. She says of Zamorna's behaviour: 'People say I am not in earnest when I abuse him — or else I would here insert half a page of deserved vituperation — deserved & heart-felt — as it is I will merely relate his conduct without note or comment.'[1] This may be a confession of her partiality for Zamorna, but it is also an acknowledgement of the author's duty to present character in action.

Mina Laury is essentially a reworking of an old theme, the devotion of Mina for the unworthy Zamorna; yet it shows a remarkable advance in narrative technique. The episodes are no longer recollections of the past or commentaries on the changing events in Branwell's manuscripts; they are all closely related by the description of character and action and by chronology to the central theme. As with Charlotte's manuscripts of 1837, there are no chapters, but the story divides naturally into two parts: Lord Hartford's proposal to Mina, her refusal and Hartford's duel with Zamorna; and Zamorna's subsequent treatment of Mina. A secondary plot, Zamorna's duplicity and neglect of Mary, underlines his selfish exploitation of Mina. The relationship between Northangerland and Zamorna, which Charlotte usually drags to the centre of her stories, is confined to the background in *Mina Laury*. We see them together only once, at the opening: Zamorna and Mary have been spending Christmas at Alnwick with Northangerland and Zenobia, who are now reunited. The furious reaction of Angria to Zamorna's renewed relations with that 'baleful North Star' is shown indirectly through newspaper reports, through Warner's complaints and in Hartford's depressing thoughts. Charlotte has made a conscious effort here to confine her story to a central action and theme.

She had probably planned *Mina Laury* well in advance, for there is a prelude to it in *Passing Events,* written almost two years earlier. Here, in the presence of Hartford, we see Mina affirm her loyalty to Zamorna.[2] As in *Mina Laury,* she is the hostess of the Cross of Rivaulx,[3] the lodge of Hawkscliffe, and is entertaining her few friends, Hartford, Enara, Arundel and Warner. Hartford, who now becomes increasingly important in the Angrian saga, is presented as 'a sort of Angrian Great-heart in the field & in the council',[4] but he is also an arrogant, ambitious aristocrat who is not unsusceptible to the charms of Miss Laury. His offer of friendship 'on terms such as it was never given to a beautiful woman before' is prophetically interrupted by the arrival of Zamorna. Here we are shown what we are told in *Mina Laury,* that Mina is devoted to Hartford and Zamorna's other loyal followers only 'because she believed them to be devoted as unreservedly to the common Master of all'.[5]

In *Mina Laury* Hartford's friendship has developed into passion. He is a man of 'strong & ill-regulated feelings'; his awareness of Mina's attitude to Zamorna throws him into a dilemma:

> he stood beset & nonplussed — Miss Laury belonged to the Duke of Zamorna — She was indisputably his property as much as the Lodge of Rivaux or the stately woods of Hawkscliffe, & in that light she considered herself . . . She had but one idea — Zamorna, Zamorna —! it had grown up with her — become part of her nature — Absence — Coldness — total neglect — for long periods together — went for nothing — she could no more feel alienation from him than she could from herself.[6]

We therefore see Hartford alone in his stately Angrian mansion, 'retired with all his blushing honours thick upon him — from the Council, the Court, the Salon', drowning his hopeless love for Mina in a drunken stupor. Once he has proposed to Mina and been rejected, he becomes a desperate man. So long as his love remained undeclared and therefore, unrejected, he could cherish 'a dreamy kind of hope'; but, 'No web of self-delusion could now be woven, the truth was too stern.'[7] Like a madman, he stops Zamorna's carriage as it passes Hartford Hall on its way from Verdopolis to Zamorna City; he insults Zamorna and precipitates a duel in which he is seriously wounded. He hovers between life and death for some time, his passion for Mina undimmed by pain, as we see in a untitled poem written by Charlotte about this time:

> Again if raised from this death-bed
>   I'll peril life to try
> If she for whom I fought and bled
>   Will let me hopeless die;
> And if an angel's voice divine
>   From God should bid me tell
> In what bright heaven of glorious shine
>   My spirit longed to dwell,
>
> I'd say let it be shadowy night,
>   On earth let stars look down,
> And let her lips in their dim light
>   Confess her heart my own.
> Be it in black and frozen wild,
>   Be it in lonely wood,
> So she but loved and cheered and smiled
>   I'll buy such bliss with blood.[8]

The relationship between Mina and Zamorna has remained unchanged since we first saw her as Zamorna's mistress, 'entangled in his spells past hope of rescue' in *High Life In Verdopolis*.[9] We are reminded in *Mina Laury* that she was Zamorna's 'first love'; a poem inserted in the text ('Holy St Cyprian! thy waters stray') recalls 'the fire of that first passion' which we encountered in *Something about Arthur*. The poem was written by the young Lord Douro and dated 'Mornington-1829': Mina had then worked for Zamorna's mother, the Duchess of Wellington, at the country estate of Mornington (surname of the real Duke of Wellington's parents). They are both 'Westerns' — that is, 'Irish' — from Senegambia (Wellington's Land), and thus endowed with a warmth of feeling foreign to eastern Angria. In her interview with Lord Hartford, Mina's reaction is that 'born of a warm & Western heart'; her eyes burn with 'a wild bright inspiration — truly, divinely Irish'. But the 'sweet West' is also associated with decadence and profligacy not found in youthful, vigorous Angria, and Zamorna and Mina are not exempt from this stigma. Zamorna is branded a 'double-dyed infernal Western profligate', and there is something perverse in Mina's delight in being totally subservient to her 'master'. She is a masochist, Zamorna a sadist. In the second part of *Mina Laury*, we see Mina checking her accounts with 'a most business-like sharpness & strictness'. She is 'strong-minded beyond her sex', yet in the presence of Zamorna she is 'as weak as a child — she lost her identity'. She accepts unquestioningly his cruel threats which cause her to faint, and her reaction to the news of his duel expresses a perverse satisfaction: 'Miss

23   *Watercolour by Charlotte Brontë after W. Finden's engraving of*
      'The Maid of Saragoza', representing Mina Laury

Laury shuddered, but so dark & profound are the mysteries of human
nature, ever allying vice with virtue, that I fear this bloody proof of her
master's love brought to her heart more rapture than horror'.[10]

Charlotte did not return to this relationship in her early manuscripts.
Mina falls into the background, her role of selfless lover having been fully
exploited. *Caroline Vernon* (*c.*July—December 1839) traces the beginnings of a similar infatuation, but it was in the conflict between adoration
and moral conscience in the mind of Elizabeth Hastings that Charlotte
was to find a more rewarding model for her later novels.

23

High Life in Angria

On 30 January 1838, thirteen days after completing *Mina Laury,* Charlotte returned to Miss Wooler's school in a mood of stoical resignation:

> So there's no use in weeping,
>   Bear a cheerful spirit still;
> Never doubt that Fate is keeping
>   Future good for present ill![1]

The intensity of her guilt about the 'world below' had subsided but her situation remained unchanged. She was still separated from home and those she loved, and had long felt that her life was slipping by:

> The thought came over me: am I to spend all the best part of my life in this wretched bondage, forcibly suppressing my rage at the idleness, the apathy and the hyperbolical and most asinine stupidity of those fat-headed oafs and on compulsion assuming an air of kindness, patience and assiduity?[2]

Teaching had become abhorrent to her. Moreover, she was now carrying a much greater work load. Since Easter 1837, the school had been moved from Roe Head to a more depressing situation on Dewsbury Moor,[3] so that Miss Wooler might be near her ailing parents at Rouse Mill. Charlotte's letters from mid-1837 show that she was often left alone in charge of the school and that she also had to act as babysitter for the children of one of Miss Wooler's married sisters — 'so that between nursing and teaching' she had her time 'pretty well occupied'.[4]

Angria remained a consolation to her at school. On 17 November 1837, she wrote a sequel to her poem 'We wove a web in childhood': the

spring which she had created in infancy 'Of water pure and fair' is still a
mighty torrent:

> A single word — a magic spring
>   That touched, revealed a world,
> A tone from one sweet trembling string
>   That deepest feelings stirred.
>
> I cannot tell and none can tell
>   How flashed the mighty stream
> At once, as on the vision fell
>   Its silent, written name.
>
> The Calabar! The Calabar!
>   The sacred land it laves,
> I little thought, so lone, so far
>   To hear its rolling waves.
>
> To see and hear them in their course
>   As clear, as they who stand
> And watch the unbridled torrent force
>   Its way through Angria's land.[5]

Charlotte wrote many poems during the years 1837 and 1838 which
relate to the Angrian Saga. Most are undated, untitled fragments, jotted
down in precious moments alone unplagued by the demands of her young
pupils. She tells us that on sleepless nights her bright dream descends to
soothe the 'dark day's despondency':[6]

> If thy love were like mine, how best
>   That twilight hour would seem,
> When, back from the regretted Past,
>   Returned our early dream![7]

She records in detail those momentary glimpses of her Angrian characters
— the lonely heroine pining for her western home, Zamorna's sleeplessness
after the carnage of the Battle of Evesham, Lord Hartford's close encounter
with death, Mary's increasing scepticism and her disillusion with her
husband.[8]

Other Angrian poems appear as part of the text of Charlotte's stories.
Seven of her nine 'novelettes' written between 1836 and 1839 include
poems and the remaining two, *The Return of Zamorna* and *Julia,* are each
followed by a poem which bears some relationship to their texts.
Occasionally Charlotte would insert a poem that she had written some
time earlier, into her story; but usually the poems included in the text of a
story are the earliest drafts existing of later versions found in 'copy books'
made by Charlotte herself. For example, 'Deep the Cirhala flows' is a
twenty-four-line poem included in the prose manuscript known as

Stancliffe's Hotel (28 June 1838): when Charlotte transcribed this poem about five years later into a copy book of poems she made various alterations and entitled it 'The Town besieged'.[9] It describes the sleeping town of Evesham before the decisive battle the following day.

In 1838, however, there was no time at school for writing even the shortest poem. That year Charlotte wrote approximately ten separate poems and another six included in prose manuscripts, but it seems that all of them (a few dates are uncertain) were written either in January before she returned to school or in the summer holidays of June and July. Her brief Easter holidays were cut short by an unexpected summons back to Dewsbury Moor as a result of the death of Mr Wooler. Charlotte wrote on 5 May: 'Since that time I have been a fortnight and two days quite alone.' For her, depression and a resulting physical illness always accompanied solitude; her concern for Ellen Nussey at this time reflects her own morbid state of mind: 'How have your spirits been? I trust not much overclouded — for that is the most melancholy result of illness'.[10] She later spoke of 'weeks of mental and bodily anguish'.[11] By the end of the month her health and spirits had failed, and the doctor advised her that if she valued her life she must return home. Her parting gift from Miss Wooler was an edition of Scott's poem *The Vision of Don Roderick* illustrated by Westall.[12]

The atmosphere of home at once 'roused and soothed' her; it gave her the freedom to write again. She began a long story which was finished before the end of the month. This is an untitled narrative of thirty-four pages (11.5 × 19 cm), closely written in her minuscule script and dated 'June 28, 1838'; it has never been published and for want of a better title I refer to it as *Stancliffe's Hotel*.[13]

The structural unity of *Mina Laury* has gone; like *Julia, Stancliffe's Hotel* is a loosely connected story crowded with characters and scenes, giving us a panoramic view of Angrian life. It is especially important in the canon of Charlotte's early manuscripts for its description of Macara Lofty's opium addiction, for the introduction of the heroine Jane Moore, and for Charlotte's changing attitude to Zamorna in both his public and private roles. Since *Stancliffe's Hotel* is Charlotte's only 'novelette' of 1836—39 not yet published, a detailed description of its plot is necessary for an appreciation of its place in the Angrian saga.

The manuscript opens in Ebenezer Chapel, Verdopolis; the satire against Methodism, begun in *Passing Events* and continued in *The Return of Zamorna* and *Julia,* is again an important source of comedy. Charles Townshend has resumed his role of narrator; he accompanies Louisa Vernon home from the evening service, entertaining her with the titillating information that Northangerland no longer wears pantaloons,

24 The first page of Charlotte Brontë's unpublished manuscript known as
Stancliffe's Hotel, *28 June 1838, typical of her later juvenile manuscripts.*
The manuscript measures 11.5 cm × 19 cm

but 'sports white tights and silks'. When they arrive at Louisa's house, they find Macara Lofty slumped in an armchair, with 'a rapt expression — as if every faculty were spell-bound in some absorbing train of thought'. Charles watches him while the ecstatic smiles give way to 'an air of fatigue'. Macara is no longer able to appreciate the beauty of a summer evening; his thoughts echo Charlotte's 'Roe Head Journal':

> Memory whispered to me that in former years I could have sat at such an hour in such a scene and from the rising moon, the darkening landscape on which I looked, the quiet little chamber where I sat, have gathered images all replete with bliss for the present, with softened happiness for the future . . . but the gloom, the despair became unendurable: dread forebodings rushed upon me — whose power I could not withstand. I felt myself on the brink of some hideous disaster and a vague influence ever and anon pushed me over, till clinging wildly to life and reason, I almost lost consciousness in the faintness of mortal terror. Now Townshend, so suffering, how far did I err when I had recourse to the sovereign specific which a simple narcotic drug offered me?

Macara's justification for taking opium is an interesting amalgam of Charlotte's recent experiences at school and her awareness of Branwell's new tendencies. For a year from May 1838 Branwell worked as a portrait painter at Bradford. He had little success and little money. Since opium was cheaper than drink, it seems likely that he was introduced to the drug by one of his artist friends. He had hoped to imitate De Quincey[14] but without De Quincey's talent opium became 'the sovereign specific' for failure.

This opening episode bears no relation to the remainder of the manuscript[15] which is centred round Stancliffe's Hotel in the city and province of Zamorna. The month is June (the actual time of composition), the season is over in Verdopolis, town residences are closing and country houses coming to life again: Summerfield House (Arundel), Stuartville Park (Castlereagh), Girnington Hall (Thornton), Edwardston Hall (Edward Percy) and Warner Hall (Warner) — the homes of Angria's elite — are occupied once more. Charles longs for 'pastoral hills and bright pebbled becks'; he sits in Grant's Coffee House musing over newspaper announcements and wondering where he will spend the summer. Charlotte pauses to take stock of his character, for he plays an active part in this manuscript. He is a self-opinionated young dandy of twenty:

> I'm a neat figure — a competent scholar, a popular author, a gentleman and a man of the world — who then shall restrain me?

We, the readers, are asked to make an inventory while he packs his carpet-bag, and while Charlotte decides on her next move. All we can expect from *Stancliffe's Hotel* is an episodic journey through Angria: 'Now reader if you're ready so am I.'

Charles arrives by coach in Zamorna on market day. He takes refuge in the crowded travellers' room of Stancliffe's Hotel, where he eventually decides to stay. We are presented with a vivid picture of the noise and bustle, and the conversation of the Angrian commercial travellers. He meets his old friend Sir William Percy, who is also staying at Stancliffe's. After a long introduction of 'brilliant sallies' and narrative description, William relates his recent life to Charles and, hence, to us. He is now Colonel Sir William Percy, having distinguished himself as Captain of the 10th Hussars in the recent Angrian war. For the last six months the papers have praised his efforts in the east to exterminate 'the savages'; despite Angria's huge war debt and Warner's protests, Zamorna was determined to wreak vengeance on the Ashantees for their part in the war.[16] He has now been recalled by Zamorna and tells of his recent meetings with General di Enara and Lord Hartford at Gazemba, Warner at the Treasury in Adrianopolis, and his brother Edward Percy, now President of the Board of Trade. Through Sir William's eyes we are shown Enara, 'the Tiger', surrounded by a cut-throat staff; we also see his friend Hartford, breathing asthmatically since 'that wound he received last winter' (in *Mina Laury*), Warner's annoyance in the face of Sir William's insolent boredom, and the continuing hostility between the two Percy brothers.

Sir William Percy has now become a major character in Charlotte's manuscripts. Apparently she had forgotten that in *The Spell* and in *My Angria and the Angrians,* William Percy was married to one of Zamorna's Seymour cousins. In *Passing Events* he is reintroduced as a bachelor: a promising young officer with a 'light and rather reckless eye'. He works hard and his promotion is rapid, in obvious contrast to the sad career of Captain Henry Hastings whom he is later sent to pursue and bring to justice. He has little communication with his 'illustrious sister' Mary, Queen of Angria; while his brother Edward ignores both his siblings. In *Stancliffe's Hotel,* the similarity between William Percy and Charles Townshend is emphasized:

> We were both young, both thin, both sallow and light-haired and blue-eyed, both carefully and somewhat foppishly dressed, with small feet set off by a slender chaussure and white hands garnished with massive rings. My friend however was considerably taller than I and had besides more of the air military.[17]

The resemblance of the narrator to his friend is significant. William Percy is destined first to share and then to take over (as William Crimsworth in *The Professor*) Lord Charles's role of narrator. In *Julia* we had been warned of William's disconcerting omnipresence: he resembles Lord Charles Wellesley, in that 'no one could fix his place — he was at your elbow when you least dreamed of his presence.'[18] In *The Duke of Zamorna,* Charlotte's next manuscript, written a month later than *Stancliffe's Hotel,* William Percy and Charles Townshend become joint narrators.

The introduction of the Angrian beauty Jane Moore is another innovation of Charlotte; Branwell makes no mention of her in his manuscripts. It appears that Charlotte had had a picture of Jane in her mind for some time. Charles says in *Stancliffe's Hotel:* 'Perhaps my readers may recollect a description of this young lady which appeared some time since — in a sort of comparison between Eastern and Western women.' This comparison, which extends to the nature of the land itself (and implies a contrast between England and Ireland), is a favourite theme in Charlotte's later juvenilia. The description Charles refers to here can be found in the 'Roe Head Journal' fragment beginning 'My Compliments to the weather' (*c.*March 1837). Writing at school, in the company of Anne who was doing her lessons on the opposite side of the table, Charlotte was unable to imagine her usual Western heroines: 'far from home I cannot write of them except in total solitude. I scarce dare think of them.'[19] Instead, she wrote for the first time about Jane Moore, the youngest daughter of George Moore, a merchant who is later presented as an eminent Angrian barrister 'but lightly burdened with principle',[20] the 'oily-tongued, smooth-faced toady' of Lord Hartford on whose estate the Moores' new house, Kirkham Lodge, lies. We see Jane at home, thinking of her dead sister Harriet,[21] who was to marry Mr Charles Kirkwall. She is emotionally limited, 'as matter of fact as any manufacturer of Edwardston' and, like all Angrian women, she lacks 'the deep refined romance of the West'.

Jane is the heroine of *Stancliffe's Hotel.* She is admired from a distance by Charles Townshend who is pleased to find that Sir William Percy has heard of her. Together they decide to visit her, under the assumed names Clarke and Gardiner; they pretend to be calling on her father whom they know is away attending assizes at Angria City. Their vanity is wounded, however, when Jane treats their visit with complacency and mistakes them for 'two chits . . . counting-house clerks or young surgeons or something of that kind'. Sir William concludes that 'there's no mind there and very little heart', and General Thornton's untimely call curtails the visit. The following episode is no more flattering to Jane. She is staying at Girnington Hall with Thornton and Julia, entertaining them with patriotic songs of the recent Angrian war. She sings of the siege of Evesham and of the heroic charge of George Turner Grey and the men of Ardsley,[22] events Charlotte had already described in *The Return of Zamorna* and

Julia. Julia thinks that Jane will never marry — she is too proud and saucy — but as we learnt in the 'Roe Head Journal' fragment, Jane has ambitions: she will settle for nothing less than an Angrian coronet, wealth and estates. Her eye is on Lord Hartford. When Castlereagh, now Earl of Stuartville, hastily enters with important news he fails to notice her, but she thrusts herself forward and interrupts the conversation. Charlotte's beauties are no longer the 'transcendently fair and inaccessibly sacred beings'[23] of the earlier manuscripts.

Castlereagh brings the news that because Zamorna is expected in Zamorna City next day, there is the possibility of a riot. Mary and Zamorna have been staying with Northangerland in his new home, Selden House, in Ross's Land; the Angrians are furious that their King should stay so long with the 'old harlot-ridden buck' who caused such havoc in their country. Edward Percy refuses to help protect Zamorna and even loyal followers of the Angrian King now have misgivings. Thornton grumbles in his 'strong twang' that Zamorna is 'allus brewing bitter drink for hisseln and now he mun sup it for aught I know'. Zamorna is no longer the heroic leader worshipped by all. His arrival next day is marred by angry crowds who surge forward in protest. Stuartville is ordered to disperse them with the cavalry. Zamorna is now 'the Czar', 'the Great Mogul', who accuses his friends of inaction and threatens to deprive the city of its corporate privileges. Sir William Percy tells Charles Townshend of Zamorna's tyranny at a meeting of the city leaders. The King apparently sees all protests against his behaviour as an infringement of his freedom. Northangerland is now dying and, as Zamorna told Warner in *Mina Laury,* he will not forsake his former comrade simply because 'Angria mutinies & Verdopolis sneers'.[24]

Zamorna and Mary also stay at Stancliffe's Hotel. After the meeting with the city leaders, Zamorna seeks his wife and finds her sleeping. His tyranny now extends to the bedroom: Mary is woken and expected to soothe his ruffled feelings. However, she too has changed; she is no longer the perfect heroine of *High Life In Verdopolis,* but a more realistic character: 'Her temper is changeful. She is not continual sunshine. She weeps sometimes and frets and teazes him not infrequently with womanish jealousies.'[25] She still bears some vestige of saintliness but Zamorna's recent neglect of her has changed her into a 'haughty jealous little Duchess'. Her illness at Alnwick has 'weakened her nerves — & made them a prey to a hundred vague apprehensions, fears that never wholly left her except when she was actually in his arms'.[26] We seldom see her with her children now. On two occasions only is she seen as a mother in the manuscripts of 1836—39: in *Passing Events* she bids farewell to her children — the twins of *My Angria and the Angrians* and a new baby, 'little Arthur', born just before Zamorna left her[27] — and in *Henry Hastings* there is a family scene at Wellesley House in which another child, Maria, appears to have been born recently.[28] Charlotte is more interested in Mary's relationship with Zamorna, which gradually degenerates into domestic comedy in *Henry Hastings* (24 February — 26 March 1839). Charles reminds us that Zamorna has now loved Mary longer than any other woman. She still has the power to awaken him at intervals to her worth[29] but she is constantly haunted by his unfaithfulness. In *Henry Hastings* her jealousy of Jane Moore is unfounded, but in *Caroline Vernon* the rapacious Zamorna steals furtively home 'like a large Tom-cat' to write a letter to his latest conquest.

Not only are Charlotte's characters and their relationships more realistic now, but the landscape is very definitely that of England rather than Africa. Since the founding of Angria, the various kingdoms of the Verdopolitan Union and the different regions of Angria itself had been modelled on landscapes which Charlotte and Branwell had read about or drawn from art, rather than from life (see plate 20); the deserts, the palm trees and the sultry climate of the earlier manuscripts had gone, yet the scenes were still idealized. Now the Claude-like landscape of Grassmere in *High Life In Verdopolis* and the awesome splendour of Verdopolis which so impressed Edward Sydney in *The Foundling,* have also vanished. In fact, Verdopolis is seldom described in the later manuscripts: it is no more than a name, a 'mighty Megatherian — the Old Capital of the country'.[30] Adrianopolis, the former 'mushroom of the Calabar', and centre of Angrian society, is even less popular with Charlotte or her characters since it was evacuated during the Angrian war. The new focus of society is the thriving commercial city of Zamorna, situated in the west of Angria on the main highway between the two capitals.

Zamorna City had been occupied in the recent war, but there was now 'no mark of recent tyranny, no trace of grinding exaction, no symptom of a lately repulsed invasion, of a now existing heavy national debt'.[31] It is as thriving as any industrial Yorkshire town of the 1830s. The 'Piece-Hall' is the centre of activity. Edward Percy's 'tobacco pipe' has been joined by other mills which line the banks of the Olympian River and pollute the air.[32] The inns are full of commercial travellers drinking North Country ale and, outside, gigs speed through the streets driven by 'market-fresh' manufacturers who have just dined at their local pubs — 'The Wool-pack' and 'The Stuart Arms'. The mob which confronts Zamorna is composed of 'mad mechanics and desperate operatives'. Special constables are sworn in to handle the crisis and the cavalry are ordered to charge on the people as they did in Wellington's day at 'Peterloo'. The gleaming sabres, the stampeding crowd, the fierce sun and blood-stained victims are all

reminiscent of that fatal day in August 1819, when the Manchester
Yeomanry Cavalry and the 15th Hussars charged a reform meeting of
Lancashire weavers in nearby St Peter's Field, Manchester:

> With horse-hair waving and broad sabres glancing, with loud huzza and
> dint of thunder, the cavalry charged on the mob. Lord Stuartville led the
> van, waving his hat and mounted on a horse like a devil. Nothing could
> stand this — not even the mad mechanics and desperate operatives of
> Zamorna. They flew like chaff; it was the whirlwind chasing the sand of
> the desert. Causeway and carriage were cleared, the wide street lay bare
> in the fierce sun behind them. A few wounded men alone were left with
> shattered limbs lying on the pavement. These were soon taken off to the
> infirmary, their blood was washed from the stones, and no sign remained
> of what had happened.[33]

Charlotte was only two years old when the 'Peterloo' massacre occurred,
but she would have heard of it from her father and possibly been aware of
Byron's verdict that 'It was a yeoman's holiday' for a lot of 'bloody
Neros'.[34]

Beyond the factories and Great Bridge of Zamorna, the landscape is
that of rural England. The Olympian Valley broadens and the road runs
through rich pastures and extensive woods. Here lie many of the country
estates of the Angrian nobility — the 'bloody Neros' of Zamorna — and in
particular Hartford Hall, Girnington Hall and Edwardston Hall. Across
the nearby Olympian Hills in the northern province of Angria lie Warner
Hall and the Howard Moors; and far in the distance are the Sydenham
Hills and Hawkscliffe forest, where Mina Laury keeps the Lodge of the
Cross of Rivaulx, halfway between Verdopolis and Adrianopolis.
Charlotte's descriptions of these areas are recollections of real scenes. The
town of Howard in the Warner Hills was identified as Haworth in *My
Angria and the Angrians;* the Haworth landscape is seen again in *Henry
Hastings* when Elizabeth, alone in the countryside surrounding Zamorna,
longs for Pendleton and the Warner Hills:

> So wild was her longing that when she looked out on the dusky sky —
> between the curtains of her bay-window — fancy seemed to trace on the
> horizon the blue outline of the moors — just as seen from the parlour at
> Colne-moss — the evening star hung over the brow of Boulshill — the
> farm-fields stretched away between.[35]

We know from Charlotte's 'Roe Head Journal' that a scene from the classroom window would also remind her of home. It is interesting to compare
the above passage with Charlotte's description of an actual scene:

> I started up and mechanically walked to the window. A sweet August
> morning was smiling without. The dew was not yet dried off the field,
> the early shadows were stretching cool and dim from the hay-stack and

the roots of the grand old oaks and thorns scattered along the sunk fence. All was still except the murmur of the scrubs about me over their tasks. I flung up the sash. An uncertain sound of inexpressible sweetness came on a dying gale from the south. I looked in that direction. Huddersfield and the hills beyond it were all veiled in blue mist, the woods of Hopton and Heaton Lodge were clouding the water's edge and the Calder, silent but bright, was shooting among them like a silver arrow.[36]

But for the names, this could be a description of the countryside around Zamorna with its 'rich pastures and waving woods of the dale . . . the gentle hills . . . the glorious river! bright flowing!'[37] Experience and visual memory were now playing an important role in Charlotte's creative writing.

24

William Percy and Elizabeth Hastings

Immediately after completing *Stancliffe's Hotel,* Charlotte wrote another long untitled manuscript known as *The Duke of Zamorna* (21 July 1838). She intended this to be a more romantic work. As Charles Townshend explains in chapter 8:

> I began this work with the intention of writing something high and pathetic. To the more perfect attainment of such an aim, I had withdrawn myself from the mercantile suburbs of Zamorna to a soft seclusion on the farthest verge of green Arundel. There amid summer gales and July suns, I strove to lull myself into a sort of dream which should recall all the fair, the wild, the wondrous of the past.[1]

But he finds it impossible to keep his feelings 'wound up to the pitch of romance and reverie'; he returns to the world of 'common clay'. The thirteen short chapters of this manuscript can therefore be divided into two sections: the recollections of 'the far departed past' and present Angrian events. Charles Townshend is the narrator throughout, although he relies for the latter half of his story on the letters of his friend Sir William Percy.

The Duke of Zamorna was Charlotte's only major excursion into the epistolary style. She had often included the odd letter in her earlier stories, such as *Tales of the Islanders;* and her most extensive use of letters before *The Duke of Zamorna* can be found in *The Spell,* where two chapters are written in the form of letters. But in *The Duke of Zamorna,* Charles is like the provident legatee of *Tales of My Landlord:* he has a pocketbook of relics from the past which he now presents to the 'general reader':

> They were letters — yellow many of them with time — stained and faded with the damp of old drawers and cabinets where they had lain.

Ask not how these came into my possession — my eye is quick, my fingers are light — I had sought these autographs in houses long deserted, in receptacles long unopened — and aided by chance I had found them.

Scott had a marked influence on Charlotte's early writing, especially in the years 1831—35, and it is very likely that this introduction to her story owes something to his narrative method, in particular to his *Tales of My Landlord* which had made a deep impression on Branwell six months earlier.[2]

With the assistance of the letters, Charlotte's narrator is able to describe 'the wicked Aristocracy of the West', many members of which he is too young to remember, while at the same time attempting to disassociate himself from his scandalous subject. Most of the letters are related to Northangerland's early life, the main subject of *Four Years Ago*. Charles has always been fascinated by society scandal and Northangerland's first wife, Lady Augusta Romana di Segovia, 'an Italian of the highest birth and most easy morality'[3] was a veritable Clytemnestra. The young Percy, as Northangerland was then, is bewitched by this 'beautiful and imperial' woman; she, in turn, is violently jealous of Percy and lavishes her fortune (and that of her young brother Lord Jordon, the Sheik Medina) on her protégé. Augusta is in league with old Lord Caversham, Mr Jeremiah Simpson (later MacTerrorglen) and Mr Daniel Montmorency, to whom Percy owes money. In *The Duke of Zamorna,* her letter to Simpson, dated 'Jordan Villa, August 1811', hints that should Percy's father be removed they would receive payment from the estate of Percy Hall. Using Robert King (alias S'Death), Branwell's hatchet-man of the early juvenilia, Augusta contrives the murder of Edward Percy senior, but is herself poisoned by her accomplices for withholding their payment.

Charles's letters concern a confusing number of early characters which belong more to Branwell's than to Charlotte's manuscripts. The most important of these is Harriet O'Connor, the tragic heroine of several long poems by Branwell.[4] Harriet was an early victim of Percy's dissolute youth. Her childhood had been made miserable by her termagant stepmother and in her youth 'one fatal fault destroyed her peace of mind forever.'[5] Without describing her fate, Charles includes in his story a hasty note in a school-boy hand from Percy to Harriet, suggesting a secret moonlight meeting.[6] Branwell tells us that Montmorency, the banker friend of Percy and of Harriet's brother Arthur O'Connor, later married her but her affections were thrown away on her husband's 'hollow and revengeful heart'. She therefore repeated the former costly error and eloped with Percy to Fidena City in Sneachiesland, soon after his conspiracy against St Clair. There he neglected her and she died a sad, lonely death,

1,000 miles from her home in Wellington's Land, 'the atonement which an outraged conscience and broken heart exacted for the double sin':[7]

> An exile from her country
> She died on mountain ground,
> The Flower of Senegambia
> A northern tomb has found.[8]

Two of Charles's letters refer to Mrs Alexander Percy who was 'much admired in the metropolis'. This is Percy's second wife, Mary Henrietta Wharton, the mother of Mary, Queen of Angria. Dr Sinclair writes to the surgeon about Mrs Percy's illness after the birth of her third son Henry, who (as we learnt in *The Secret*) was removed from her by her husband's 'unnatural barbarity'. When the Duchess of Wellington visits Mrs Percy, the three-year-old Douro is an unhappy reminder of her own lost sons. This child, 'all laughing selfishness even then', is now the Duke of Zamorna, riding a fiery horse in the midst of his generals to review 10,000 troops at Gazemba.[9] Charles reflects on the saintly character of Mrs Percy, her consumptive decline which is aggravated by the removal of her sons, and her effect on Percy. She is recalled throughout the juvenilia as 'that soft spirit which had once charmed him to alienation from his evil genius'. Her untimely death 'changed the destiny of Africa': for Percy became a desolate and altered man, his 'life and motives utterly perverted'.[10] Charlotte felt she must continually justify Percy's demonic personality.

When Charles Townshend's letters are exhausted, Charlotte is at a loss for a subject. In desperation she returns to the old relationship of Douro and Ellrington (alias Percy and Northangerland), but admits: 'All this I have written before.' There is no sense of planning in *The Duke of Zamorna;* Charlotte's total reliance on the framework of her saga appears to hinder any advance in the structure of her individual stories. She remembers that in her last manuscript she alluded to Zamorna's recent visit to Selden House, and merely re-creates the scene. She says, 'Here it was that the latest renewal of the Ellrington and Douro's conferences took place. Let me sketch one if I can.'[11] Northangerland is an old man now, ill and lethargic; Zamorna is flippant and delights in teasing his father-in-law. Their relationship, once so dramatic and explosive, has degenerated into comedy.

In *The Duke of Zamorna,* all Charlotte's thoughts are committed to paper; we have followed her wandering through old melodramatic scenes in search of a subject. Tiring of the Douro/Ellrington plot and the deathbed of Augusta di Segovia, she finally consigns such material to Branwell, who is capable of 'far higher language than I can use!': 'I grew weary of heroics and longed for some chat with men of common clay.'[12]

This, of course, is Charles Townshend speaking, and his friend Sir William Percy steps forward to oblige.

Sir William sends four letters to Charles describing his recent activities. His tone is robust and debonair, and his writing betrays the 'clear mercantile strokes' of his former occupation. He reports from Zamorna City on the sensation which Jane Moore caused at Hartford's County Ball, but his most important news is of his appointment as an ambassador, despite Hartford's opposition. Sir William is to perform a mysterious diplomatic mission for Zamorna in Paris and his last letter is written at Doverham where he is about to board a ship for Calais in Branwell's original 'Frenchyland' to the south of the Verdopolitan Union. For the first time we see behind the suave exterior of Sir William's personality. The poverty of his childhood and early youth is no longer a hindrance to his ambition; he is 'discovering' his own strength, but he is also aware of a new feeling of loneliness. He turns to his sister Mary for affection and a new dimension is added to our understanding of the rivalry of the two Percy brothers. Until now they have both been presented as cold and unfeeling; but one, at least, has suffered from this relationship:

> When Edward and I were in penury, kept chained together by want, and abhorring each other for the very compulsion of our union, I used to endure worse torments than those of Hell. Edward overwhelmed me by his strength and bulk. He used his power coarsely for he had a coarse mind, and scenes have taken place between us which remembrance to this day, when it rushed upon my mind, pierces every nerve with a thrill of bitter pain no words can express.
>
> I always affected indifference to his savage, hard, calculating barbarity, and I always will affect indifference to it to my dying day. But if there be a power superior to humanity, that power has witnessed feelings wringing my heart in silence which will never find voice in words.[13]

Sir William Percy remains in Paris for about four months. His return is recorded in Charlotte's next untitled manuscript, known as *Henry Hastings* (24 February—26 March 1839). Meanwhile Charlotte herself had stayed twice with Ellen Nussey, now home after an extended stay in London, and had reluctantly paid a visit to the Walkers at Lacelles Hall, Mirfield. Ellen and the Taylors also stayed at Haworth in January 1839: thus there had been little time for writing.[14] Late in February, however, Charlotte settled down to write about two themes which demanded both self-analysis and insight: the choice in love between romantic desire and moral conscience, and the relationship of a sister to her increasingly degenerate brother.

Henry Hastings is comprised of two parts, dated 24 February and 26 March 1839, respectively. In the former, Charles Townshend (with the help of Sir William's diary) traces the capture of Henry Hastings by Sir

William Percy and Lord Hartford despite Henry's sister's efforts to help him; and in the latter, Charles describes in six chapters, Hastings' trial and Sir William's attempted seduction of Elizabeth Hastings. The opening of the second part of this manuscript summarizes Charlotte's 'last volume', an intervening manuscript (possibly dated sometime in early March) which has since been lost and which described Hastings' escape and unsuccessful attempt on Zamorna's life.[15]

In *The Duke of Zamorna,* Sir William had said:

> I will never marry till I can find a woman who has endured sufferings as poignant as I have done — who has felt them as intensely — who has denied her feelings as absolutely and in the end, has triumphed over her woes as successfully.
>
> A woman so gifted with youth and refined education, would attract my love far more irresistibly than the beauty of Helen or the majesty of Cleopatra. Beauty is given to dolls — majesty to haughty vixens — but mind, feeling, passion, and the crowning grace of fortitude are the attributes of an angel.[16]

The introduction of the insensitive beauty Jane Moore was Charlotte's first attempt to illustrate the superiority of intellect and feeling over beauty and wealth. The character of Elizabeth Hastings is an even more positive step on the road towards the creation of Jane Eyre. Like the later Rochester, Sir William has had an *affaire* in 'the pastil-perfumed bowers of the South', but he decides that the Marquise de Franceville did not measure up to his ideal of womanhood. In *Henry Hastings,* he gradually becomes aware that Elizabeth is the person he is looking for. His initial scorn of her outward appearance is recorded in his diary. At the opera in Zamorna, she is the ideal foil for the magnificent Jane Moore, as her prototype was for the superb Mary Lonsdale.[17] Sir William is horrified when he arrives late at Thornton's dinner and finds there are no ladies left for him to patronize 'but the same little dusk apparition' he had seen at the opera. He pretends to ignore her, but during the evening he watches her closely and realizes that:

> the creature, on a close examination, was by no means ugly — her eyes were very fine & seemed as if they could express anything . . . but her features were masked with an expression foreign to them — her movements were restrained & guarded — she wanted openness — originality — frankness . . . A careful gleaner finds corn of good grain where a fool passes by & sees only stubble.[18]

Some months previous to *Henry Hastings,* Charlotte had drafted an early sketch of Elizabeth Hastings. This unpublished two-page manuscript of only 800 words[19] describes the character of Miss West, a companion/governess to the three vivacious daughters of Mr Lonsdale.

Like the later Elizabeth, she is seen in society as an unimpressive, shadowy figure, gliding stealthily through the crowded rooms of Adrianopolis in the same dark, simple dress which enabled her to avoid unwanted observation. But as the first line of this fragment suggests, 'it is not in Society that the real character is revealed.' Alone in her own humble bedroom, the 'shade of habitual and studied reserve' which Sir William remarked in Elizabeth lightens: her features 'overflow with meaning and strange meaning too'. Miss West is aware that one individual at least is as capable of estimating character as herself. He had seen her during one of 'those moments of awakened feeling, those sudden flashing fits of excitement which she could not always control'. Thus, she always shunned this unnamed person, who is surely Sir William Percy.

When Elizabeth tries to prevent her brother's capture in *Henry Hastings,* Sir William witnesses one of those intense moments of feeling:

> here was a being made up of intense emotions — in her ordinary course of life always smothered under the diffidence of prudence & a skilful address, but now when her affections were about to suffer almost a death-stab — when incidents of strange excitement were transpiring around her — on the point of bursting forth like lava — still she struggled to keep wrapt about her the veil of reserve & propriety.[20]

Again, in her interview with the Duchess of Zamorna (Mary, Queen of Angria) Elizabeth, who would normally have put to good use her intuitive knowledge of human nature, fails in her petition for her brother because a heated argument with Warner had 'raised her Dander'.[21] Sir William considers his fancy for Miss Hastings as a 'freek of taste' yet she still lingers in his recollection. When next in Zamorna, some time after Henry Hastings' trial, he contrives to meet her as if by accident. Elizabeth now runs a school and is proud of her independence; yet she was 'always burning for warmer, closer attachment' than that which she derived from her acquaintances in Zamorna. She would think of her brother, but he 'was changed, she was changed, those times were departed for ever'; then she would remember Sir William Percy 'with an intensity of romantic feeling that very few people in this world can form the remotest conception of'.[22]

Sir William's solitary walk with Elizabeth in the country forms the climax of their relationship. As in Charlotte's first love story, *Albion and Marina,* the romance is undercut by the rather coy, garrulous narrator: 'Of course my readers know him, Sir William Percy & no mistake, though what he could possibly be doing here ruralizing in a remote nook of the Girnington Summerings I candidly confess myself not sufficiently sagacious to divine.'[23] Yet there is in the narration a maturity of feeling and purpose absent from the earlier manuscript. Sir William proceeds to woo Elizabeth with skill and caution; Charlotte is now more familiar with the way of the world. With an appropriate touch of irony, Charlotte allows Sir William to seat Elizabeth on a gravestone beside Scar Chapel at Ingleside. It bears no inscription except the word 'Resurgam', an obvious link with *Jane Eyre.* It is the grave of Lady Rosamund Wellesley, whom Zamorna lured away from her family and then forsook. Rosamund and her sister Lucy were first introduced in *A Late Occurrence:* their cousin Zamorna had lured them to Adrianopolis from the Episcopal Palace at Lismore in the West of the Verdopolitan Union. Their father is Dr Gerald Wellesley, Primate of Wellington's Land, modelled on the Reverend Gerald Valerian Wellesley, a younger brother of the real Duke of Wellington who made unsuccessful attempts to obtain a bishopric for him. In the *Duke of Z[amorna] & E[dward] Percy,* Rosamund, 'a daring girl and at times rather eccentric', has become Zamorna's mistress: she is 'the Rose of Woodstock', the 'Flower of Fort Adrian'. A year later, however, her infatuation for Zamorna is rewarded by his neglect. Shame and heartbreak follow and her brief life of seclusion is thought to have ended in suicide.

Unlike Zamorna's easy loves, Elizabeth has a moral conscience, but, as with her successor Jane Eyre, it hinges more on self-respect than social repute. She acknowledges that the world's scorn would be dreadful but the miseries of self-hatred would be a worse torment should she become Sir William's mistress. She is afraid of nothing but herself. She is tempted to yield to Sir William's proposal and suffers 'the hard conflict of passionate love — with feelings that shrank horror-struck from the remotest shadow of infamy'. Self-respect wins, for she prides herself on the consciousness that 'though I have been left entirely to my own guidance, I have never committed an action or narrated a word that would bring my character for a moment under the breath of suspicion!'[24]

Here, more than ever before, Charlotte was searching the depths of her own character for a model for her heroine. It is of course a mistake to treat all Charlotte's manuscripts as biographical evidence: Brontë scholarship has suffered greatly from this approach and the juvenilia have been plundered for ideas in the absence of biographical fact. But at the same time we cannot ignore the large role that autobiographical material plays in Charlotte's early creative writing, as it does in her later novels. Where we already have biographical evidence, in the form of letters or autobiographical fragments, for example, it is possible to gauge the extent to which Charlotte's experience affected her writing; but simply to read her stories as accounts of her life would elicit fantasy not fact.

Miss West feels for her pupils the same scorn Charlotte felt: she has Charlotte's quiet confidence in her own intellectual superiority which, together with her natural reserve, make her appear aloof to all but her closest friends and family: 'She never by inadvertent breath or glance betrayed the scorn that often swelled at her heart. She listened to all, sympathized with all and never for a moment required sympathy or attention in return.'[25] The tensions which she experiences in her situation were those peculiar to Charlotte's own life:

> I know my place is a favourable one for a Governess — what dismays and haunts me sometimes is a conviction that I have no natural knack for my vocation — if teaching only were requisite it would be smooth and easy — but it is the living in other people's houses — the estrangement from one's real character — the adoption of a cold frigid apathetic exterior that is painful.[26]

Lucy Snowe in *Villette* practises the same studied suppression of her natural feelings, veiling her emotions in what she refers to as 'catalepsy and a dead trance'.[27]

Like Charlotte, Elizabeth Hastings paints landscapes, is proud of her knowledge of French and takes a great deal of interest in politics — 'people who live in retired places often do.' She comes from Pendleton in the province of Angria, a rough moorland country where there is 'no good society' and 'such stony roads'; yet as Jane Moore remarks: 'I really believe she likes those dreary moors & that old-manor-house far better than Zamorna or even Verdopolis — isn't it odd —?'[28] Alone in Massinger Hall, four miles from Zamorna, Elizabeth paces to and fro down the length of the old parlour, her expression 'fixed & dreamy' and her mind excited by 'feverish Dreams'. The Brontë sisters too paced up and down the sitting room at home 'like restless wild animals', lost in thought or in excited discussion of their latest stories.[29] There is surely an element of wish-fulfillment in the satisfaction which Elizabeth derives from her school, so different from Roe Head:

> She was now settled to her mind, she was dependent on nobody — responsible to nobody — She spent her mornings in the drawing-room surrounded by her class, not wearily toiling to impart the dry rudiments of knowledge to yawning, obstinate children — a thing she hated & for which her sharp-irritable temper rendered her wholly unfit — but instructing those who had already mastered the elements of education — reading, commenting, explaining, leaving it to them to listen — if they failed, comfortably conscious that the blame would rest on her pupils, not herself . . . she was as prosperous as any little woman of five feet high & not twenty years old need wish to be.[30]

The Rev. Henry Nussey's proposal of marriage to Charlotte in March 1839, about three weeks before she wrote *Henry Hastings,* included the suggestion that she might run a nearby school.[31] Before refusing, Charlotte must have thought hard about this offer and the extent to which Henry

Nussey fell short of her 'ideal' husband: it is possible that *Henry Hastings* embodies many of these thoughts. Certainly the parallels between Charlotte and Elizabeth are numerous; they culminate in the relationship between Elizabeth and her brother.

Henry Hastings is now a wanted man, not only for the murder of his senior officer and his desertion from the army, but for his attempt on Zamorna's life. Charlotte emphasizes the contrast between his former hopes and present degradation: 'He had gone away a young soldier full of hope, & what career of life must that have been which had brought him back a Cain-like Wanderer with a price upon his blood.'[32] In *Henry Hastings* he is introduced first as the mysterious, drunk Mr Wilson, whom Charles Townshend meets at Macara Lofty's one evening. Next day Charles is arrested and asked to disclose the identity of Mr Wilson. Sir William Percy and Lord Hartford trace Hastings, alias Wilson, to Massinger Hall where he has taken refuge with his sister. Elizabeth has not seen Henry for two years; we witness an intimate scene in which brother and sister talk together before the fire. He tries to explain the reasons for his crimes, but his sister understands already: she knows that his passions are 'naturally strong, & his Imagination . . . warm to fever'. She distinguishes between him and his faults. Encouraged by her sympathy, Henry becomes excited and builds 'Castles in the air'; Elizabeth, 'Instead of softening the renegade's excited ferocity, & reasoning against his malignant vindictiveness . . . caught his spirit & answered in a quick excited voice'.[33] Their joint hopes and old enthusiasm are not yet dead. It was for her brother's sake that Elizabeth had forsaken her father and her beloved home. Jane Moore had remarked how strange it was that Elizabeth never mentioned Henry and she dared not speak to her on the subject; Elizabeth had certain 'peculiarities'. Even after Henry's trial, in which he gains 'life without Honour' by turning King's evidence, he is still not degraded in the eyes of his sister:

> It was very odd but his sister did not think a pin the worse of him for all his Dishonour — it is private mean-ness — not public infamy that degrade a man in the opinion of his relatives — Miss Hastings heard him cursed by every mouth — saw him denounced in every newspaper. still he was the same brother to her he had always been — still she beheld his actions through a medium peculiar to herself.[34]

Charlotte was obviously very concerned about Branwell. Since she left school in May 1838, he had been at Bradford trying to make a living as a portrait painter. This new chance to establish himself in a profession had been made possible by his aunt's generosity: she had paid for further lessons in Leeds with his old master William Robinson for several months before he went to Bradford. The family must have had fresh hope at this time, after the London fiasco of autumn 1835 when Branwell failed to gain admittance to the Academy Schools. As Branwell's biographers tell us, not only did he not present his letters of introduction but he squandered his father's money on 'little squibs of rum', and apparently told his family that he had been robbed. His spirit, like that of Charles Wentworth, a character introduced into Branwell's manuscripts soon after this experience,[35] was crushed by the magnitude of London: he was overawed by the realization of an event so long anticipated.[36] London was not Verdopolis, and he was certainly not Alexander Percy.

The Bradford enterprise, however, was also unsuccessful and by May 1839 Branwell had returned home to Haworth.[37] *Henry Hastings* was completed on 26 March, before his sister and family had suffered this disappointment. Yet Branwell came home almost every weekend from Bradford and although he tried to hide things from his family, Charlotte was probably aware that commissions were not coming his way. We have already seen his introduction to opium reflected in Charlotte's recent writing. Still willing at this stage to offer moral encouragement as well as financial help, she expresses in *Henry Hastings* her faith in her brother despite social misfortune. Her opinion of Henry is very different from Branwell's own idea of his alter ego at this time.

If we can judge from the surviving poems and prose fragments, Branwell wrote very little during his time in Bradford. His interests were now well removed from the parsonage and he had very soon become bored with a peaceful Angria. Richton, once more his narrative voice, complains:

> The unopposed domination of Fidena and Zamorna, the wearied slumber of the forgotten Northangerland, the fruitless repining of the defeated Ardrah, the utter annihilation of the ferocious Montmorency, though a blissful prospect seems but tame to one who has mingled with all these when universal Africa was in a flame of exciting and tremendous change.[38]

While Charlotte was still at school, he had turned from 'the unvarying round of uneventful happiness' to contemplate 'the greatest *Creation* of the Storm': *The Life of Warner Howard Warner* (February—8 March 1838). But before Warner reached the age of seven, the manuscript was abandoned in favour of Branwell's old subject of Henry Hastings. A two-page fragment dated 25 April 1838, describes the 'penniless and proscribed' debauchee in 'an overwhelming confusion of shame' rising from the floor of a sordid inn after a night of revelry. He is now completely under the power of his new mentor, George Frederic Ellen of Hallows Hall — an unredeemed character whose object in life was 'to root out morality from the natures of all his acquaintances'.[39]

Branwell had recorded Hastings' meeting with this man seven months earlier in a group of fragmentary manuscripts known as *Percy* (20 October — 30 December 1837).[40] In March 1837, the besieged town of Evesham (under MacTerrorglen and the Revolutionary troops) had sent a deputation led by Montmorency and Macara Lofty to the court of Rossestown to rouse assistance from the south.[41] Hastings' regiment had been sent to escort them and while in Rossesland he fell deeper into drunkenness and debt. One morning in July, oblivious of his duty, he leapt on to a coach bound for Sneachiesland.[42] There he had met Squire Ellen, the veritable 'son of Nicholas'. Branwell delights in describing the violent Bacchanalian scenes caused by Ellen and Hastings in the 'beer-shops' of the secluded Coomassie Mountains. On one such occasion, Montmorency, Simpson and Quashia burst into the room where Hastings and his cronies are drinking; they are on the run after the defeat of Evesham and are closely pursued by Sir William Percy and his Angrian troops. Ellen, Hastings and the revolutionary renegades are forced to defend themselves. All escape except Joynes, a degenerate preacher who is taken to Verdopolis as a prisoner.[43] Hastings then becomes the tool of the revolutionaries and after hiding for some time in France (the reason for Sir William Percy's secret mission to Paris in *The Duke of Zamorna*), he returns with a commission to murder Zamorna; his return is documented in a group of manuscripts known as *Love and Warfare*.

Love and Warfare (15 December 1838 — April 1839)[44] is almost the last of Branwell's prose manuscripts. He was later to write a story entitled *And the Weary are at Rest*,[45] a reworking of these earlier manuscripts, but apart from his poetry, these fragments were the last to have any obvious influence on Charlotte's writing. The influence is slender: it consists solely in Charlotte's awareness of Hastings' latest escapades. On January 1839, Hastings lands at Wilson's Creek in the east of Angria in a French smuggler craft containing armed Frenchmen and negroes. They massacre the inhabitants of a nearby farm and then Hastings makes his way alone to Verdopolis; there he attempts to shoot Zamorna at the state opening of parliament. The bullet ricochets off a gold star on Zamorna's breast and he is unhurt. Hastings flees with the police in hot pursuit. We know from *Henry Hastings* that he made his way to Massinger Hall, where his sister Elizabeth was living. Zamorna knew his attempted murder had been planned in Paris, and so it is against Montmorency and Simpson, now lurking 'among the lowest saloons of Paris', that Hastings is asked to inform at his trial in *Henry Hastings*. In return for his life, he gives evidence against his associates (Montmorency, Simpson, Macqueen, Caversham and Quashia) on the 'late massacre in the east & the disembarkation of French arms at Wilson's creek'. Major King, who assists Sir William in Hastings' capture, is the 'John King' who first warned Zamorna of Hastings' return to Angria in Branwell's *Love and Warfare* manuscript of January 1839. Quashia has now retreated far into the deserts of Etrei. Branwell depicts Warner busily working on maps for an 'invasion against the Negroes'; in *Henry Hastings,* Zamorna bores Zenobia with details of these same Angrian maps.[46] It seems that Branwell will not be satisfied until the prophecies of *A Leaf from an Unopened Volume* are fulfilled.

25

Farewell to Angria

Caroline Vernon, Charlotte's last 'Angrian' manuscript, totally ignores Branwell and his writing. Any boredom with the peaceful African scene is dismissed in Charles Townshend's jaunty introductory poem:

> There's not always
>   An Angrian campaign going on in the rain,
>   Nor a Gentleman Squire lighting his fire
>   Up on the moors with his blackguards & boors,
>   Nor a Duke & a lord drawing the sword,
>   Hectoring & lying, the whole world defying,
>   Then sitting down crying.[1]

As Charles says, 'one can't expect earthquakes & insurrections every-day . . . a constant renewal of such stimulus would soon wear out the public stomach & bring on indigestion.' A view of morality might be just as interesting as lurid guilt; and a 'book-wright' need never be at a loss so long as he may observe 'the face of society'. Although her promise is broken by this manuscript, Charlotte had resolved after *Henry Hastings* to 'write no more till [she] had somewhat to write about'.[2] This more critical attitude of Charlotte towards her material in *Caroline Vernon,* despite its return to old themes, marks another step towards greater realism in her writing.

The advance in technique can partly be explained by Charlotte's new experience of society. Branwell's failure at Bradford had meant she again had to find work. Anne had already gone as a governess to the Inghams at Blakewell Hall, Mirfield, when Charlotte left Haworth to join the Sidgwick family for three months at Stonegappe, an estate four miles from Skipton. The position of a private governess was the only employment open to her.

On 30 June 1839, she wrote a vivid description of her situation at Swarcliffe, where the family had moved for the summer holidays:

> imagine the miseries of a reserved wretch like me, thrown at once into the midst of a large family — proud as peacocks and wealthy as Jews — at a time when they were particularly gay, when the house was full of company — all strangers, people whose faces I had never seen before — in this state of things having the charge given me of a set of pampered, spoilt, and turbulent children, whom I was expected constantly to amuse as well as instruct.[3]

Yet she had time to 'look on and listen',[4] and alone in the schoolroom with 'oceans of needlework', she had time to think.

On her return to Haworth the following month Charlotte made use of her recent experience of North Yorkshire. *Caroline Vernon* is peppered with 'oat-cake & grouse', red wheat and manure. Hawkscliffe is now given over to farming in preference to forestry. Zamorna is seen in his shirt sleeves —

> with a straw hat on his head — swearing at the hay-tinkers, now & then giving a hand to help to load the waggons — & at noon or drinking-time sitting down on a cock — to eat his bread & cheese & drink his pot of ale like a King & like a clod-hopper.[5]

Mr Sidgwick's 'large Newfoundland dog' guards Zamorna's lodge, and the conversation recalls the difference between Stonegappe soil and that of Haworth moor:

> 'Humph — wha ye see, ye cannot err mich, for where trees grow as they do here, there's hardly any mak o' grain but what'll prosper — I find t'truth o' that at Girnington — now up i't North, about Mr Warner's place, it's clear different —' 'Yes, Warner has a great deal of bother with tillage & manure — that bog-soil is so cold & moist — it rots the seed instead of cherishing it.'[6]

The roomy but rather plain house, the 'pleasant woods, winding white paths, green lawns, and blue sunshiny sky' which Charlotte saw but could not enjoy at Stonegappe, are all transposed into Angrian scenery:

> the remoter hills of the same range [the Sydenhams] rolled away clad in dusky woodland — till distance softened them & the summer sky embued them with intense violet. near the centre of the Park stood Hawkscliffe-House, a handsome pile — but by no means so large nor so grand as the extent of the grounds seemed to warrant — it could not aspire to the title neither of Palace nor Castle — it was merely a solitary Hall — stately from its loneliness — & pleasant from the sunny & serene effect of the green region which expanded round it.[7]

Palaces have been reduced to country houses and heroes to North Yorkshire farmers. The conversation is more realistic and characters

SONNET.

Why hold young eyes the fullest fount of tears,
  And why do happiest hearts most sadly sigh
When fancied friends forsake, or lovers ~~fly~~ die,
Or others heart strings crack, oerstrained by cares?
Ah! Thou who askest me art young in years
  Or Time's rough voice had long since told thee why!
  Increase of days increases misery,
And misery brings selfishness, which sears
The souls best feelings — Mid the battle's roar,
  In Death's grim grasp the soldiers eyes are blind
To others dying — he whose hopes are oer
  Smiles sternest at the sufferings of mankind.
A wounded spirit will delight in gore —
  A tortured heart will make a tyrant mind.

                                Northangerland.

The results of Sorrow.

25 'Sonnet' and pen and ink profile of Northangerland by Branwell Brontë,
written in a commonplace book belonging to Mary Pearson, 'at Ovenden Cross
in the Autumn of 1846'

exhibit the commonplace vagaries of human nature. Zamorna invents a headache to elicit sympathy and elude cross-examination; the haughty Mary Percy, Queen of Angria, has become a fussy, doting wife who indulges in gossip and chitchat, though she has not lost her ability to judge her husband's mood and act accordingly. Zenobia has emerged from retirement, middle-aged and 'magnificently round', with the 'weight of as much pride & cholor to support as would overwhelm any two ordinary mortals'.[8] Northangerland has returned from another brief escapade with his mistresses. He and Zamorna no longer clash like blazing meteors, they merely oppose each other 'like two bulls'. Northangerland is now the furious father, not the dissipated rake of the earlier manuscripts; Charlotte's description of his 'pallid features & marble brow' accords with Branwell's final conception of him in an unpublished sketch and poem of autumn 1846 (see plate 25). Quashia, still in league with Northangerland and still determined to marry one of his daughters, writes in his usual style — a mixture of biblical phrases and drunken slang — to Northangerland demanding Caroline and financial support. If he cannot have Mary after all this time (he began his pursuit in Branwell's *The Politics of Verdopolis* of 1833), then he will settle for the younger half-sister — a possible prefiguring of Zamorna's rapacity in claiming both daughters for himself. Northangerland has no trouble rejecting Quashia's belligerent demand, but he is powerless to avert 'the basilisks's fascination'.

In *Caroline Vernon* we see Northangerland lose his 'last & only comfort', for the central theme of the story is the seduction of Caroline. She was first introduced in *Passing Events,* at the beginning of this third period in Charlotte's early writing. She was Northangerland's 'animated intelligent daughter', and in her first meeting with Zamorna in *Julia,* this eleven-year-old had 'a foreign wildness, a resemblance which stirred sensations'[9] in Zamorna. Already Caroline is determined to do exactly what she wants: she has uncurbed, ardent feelings like her mother Louisa, but 'her heart has no vice yet, whatever it may acquire.'[10] Such early hints suggest that Caroline was being groomed for a major role in the Angrian saga.

Caroline Vernon is divided into two parts, of five and six chapters respectively. In the first part we encounter Caroline as a child living with her mother near Hawkscliffe under the guardianship of Zamorna; part II shows the effect of a Parisian education and the abandonment of the adolescent Caroline to the charms of her former protector. The plot does not allow Zamorna to remain a staid Yorkshire farmer for long: in part II, he reassumes 'the genuine character of Arthur Augustus Adrian Wellesley' of the early juvenilia. The climax of *Caroline Vernon* is but another conquest in Zamorna's long career:

in this crisis, Lord Douro stood true to his old name & nature —

Zamorna did not deny by one noble & moral act the character he had earned by a hundred infamous ones. Hitherto we have seen him rather as restraining his passions than yielding to them — he has stood before us rather as a Mentor than a Misleader — but he is going to lay down the last garment of light & be himself entirely.[11]

The spectre of Rosamund Wellesley is again raised, but, unlike Elizabeth Hastings, Caroline has not the will to resist temptation. Zamorna deposits her in his old 'treasure-house': Scar House, sheltered by Ingleside and hidden in a wood in the heart of Angria. We are left to infer that Caroline's fate will be the same as that of Rosamund:

> The Duke undertook to be her Guardian & Tutor — He executed his office in a manner peculiar to himself — Guarded her with a vengeance & tutored her till she could construe the Art of Love at any rate — She enjoyed the benefit of his protection & instructions for about a year — & then somehow she began to pine away.[12]

Caroline Vernon has been called Charlotte's 'last Byronic fling'.[13] The creation of yet another heroine dominated by passion was a bold move by the twenty-three-year-old Charlotte, who must by now have been aware of society's disgust at the openly expressed passion of Claire Clairmont and Caroline Lamb, whose name may have suggested that of Caroline Vernon. Obviously her story was not meant for public consumption, but it clearly shows that lack of interest in conventional morality which brought her such condemnation on the publication of *Jane Eyre*.[14] More than any other of her manuscripts, *Caroline Vernon* reverberates with Byronic echoes. The young Caroline is imbued with Republican ideals. Her heroes include Bonaparte and Lord Edward Fitzgerald (the latter, because his biographer was Byron's friend Moore). Zamorna thinks that 'reading Lord Byron has half-turned her head, yet his own motto is 'Crede Zamorna!'[15] He is 'Satan's eldest Son', he simulates the 'bearded Turk', and his eyes sparkle 'from the depths of Gehenna'. The attraction of evil plays a large part in Caroline's seduction, as the play on the name of 'Eden' Cottage, her mother's old home indicates: 'infatuation was stealing over her — The thought of separation or a return to Eden was dreadful'. Caroline experiences 'a thrill of nameless dread' — 'Here he was — the man that Montmorency had described to her — all at once she knew him — Her Guardian was gone — Something terrible sat in his place'.[16] But for the author, Zamorna is almost ridiculous as he hovers about his prey 'like a large Tom-Cat'. Charlotte no longer identifies whole-heartedly with her hero. The feeling of compelling fascination for this heir of 'the dark — malignant, scowling Gordons',[17] which is so strong in *The Spell,* has finally subsided. The 'farmer' image and rustic domestic comedy have destroyed any such illusions and we are now confronted with an objective narrator who, like Thackeray, leads us by the hand and cries:

> Oh, human nature! human nature! & Oh, Inexperience! in what an obscure, dim unconscious dream Miss Vernon was envelloped — How little she knew of herself — However, time is advancing & the hours, those 'wild-eyed Charioteers' as Shelley calls them — are driving on — She will gather knowledge by degrees — She is one of the Gleaners of Grapes in that Vineyard — where all man & woman-kind — have been plucking fruit since the world began, the Vineyard of Experience.[18]

Caroline Vernon is well-constructed. Whereas *Henry Hastings* was weighed down by two main plots, Caroline is at the centre of almost every chapter here. The story is a study of human nature: the heroine progresses 'on stage' from childhood to adolescence, from innocence to experience. Quashia's letter asking for Caroline's hand sends Northangerland in search of his daughter whom he left under the surveillance of Zamorna. He had ignored her until now, although we have already been told of her 'strange likeness'[19] to him. She is now fifteen years old. Northangerland wishes to give her an establishment of her own; her 'guardian' objects. He has studied her character:

> it is one that ought not to be exposed to dazzling temptation — She is at once careless & imaginative — her feelings are mixed with her passions — both are warm & she never reflects — Guidance like yours is not what such a girl ought to have — she could ask you for nothing which you would not grant — Indulgence would foster all her defects, when she found that winning smiles & gentle words passed current for reason & judgement — She would speedily purchase her whole will with that cheap coin.[20]

Irony is now implicit in the story, not merely in the voice of the narrator. In chapter 4 we see Caroline for ourselves: the wilful school-girl who infuriates her neurotic mother by 'jigging' over 'Jim Crow' on the piano. Northangerland is struck by the incongruity of her childish dress and her mature figure. Her behaviour contrasts favourably with the hysterics of her mother, but Northangerland's questions elicit 'the pent-up enthusiasm of her heart': her penchant for Republicanism, Miss Martineau, Bonaparte and Byron. During this interview we are shown character in action, and the self-conscious narrator is determined we should appreciate this: 'By this time the reader will have acquired a slight idea of the state of Miss Caroline Vernon's mental development, & will have perceived that it was as yet only in the chrysalis form'.[21]

At the close of part I, Caroline bids farewell to Zamorna; she is leaving Hawkscliffe for Republican Paris. Zamorna warns her against the vicious 'immodesty' of French society and pretends to be unmoved by her parting tears. Charlotte is careful to preserve credulity in the relationship here: had Zamorna shown his true feelings for Caroline, as in Charlotte's first draft of this scene, their friendship would no longer have been innocent. The climax of part II would have been anticipated and Caroline would have lost the illusions about Zamorna which were necessary to make her pursuit of him anything but ungoverned lust.[22]

In part II, a period of 'about four months' has elapsed: we are told that 'It was in July when affairs reached their climax. It is now November, nearly December.' Since Charlotte made a habit of setting her stories at the time of composition, we can guess — with the help of biographical information — that the two parts of *Caroline Vernon* were written about late July/early August and late November/early December. While Caroline had been in Paris, Charlotte herself had been on a seaside holiday with Ellen Nussey. She had experienced her first feeling of real independence; now she described how Caroline had fared alone in the 'Atmosphere of Paris': 'She learnt life & unlearnt much fiction — the illusions of retirement were laid aside with a smile, & she wondered at her own rawness when she discovered the difference between the world's reality & her childhood romance'.[23] Caroline had been patronized by the Northangerland faction — the Dupins, the Barras, the Bernadottes — all the Republican and Revolutionary coteries of the early juvenilia. Branwell's old passion for things French was still alive in Charlotte's writing; and her grasp of the French language had been recently improved by reading French novels. These she had borrowed from her friend Mary Taylor's father, who spoke fluent French, held Republican views and often visited France on business. Such novels — 'clever, wicked sophistical and immoral' — confirmed her early views of French society. Caroline could hardly remain in Paris long without hearing of the seamy side of Zamorna's character and of his *affaires* with such women as Mina Laury. She began to see Zamorna in a new light and longed to meet him again. It becomes only a matter of time before the interview takes place; but it is appropriate that the final scene of Charlotte's last truly 'Angrian' story should end in conflict between Northangerland and Zamorna.

It would seem that late in 1839, Charlotte was becoming critical of her previous writing. In March 1837, Southey had warned her against indulgence in day-dreams which were likely to induce 'a distempered state of mind'.[24] Her reaction to his well-meaning strictures on the propriety of women writers shows her inability to relinquish what had already become a necessary mode of self-expression:

> I felt a painful heat rise to my face when I thought of the quires of paper
> I had covered with what once gave me so much delight, but which now
> was only a source of confusion; but after I had thought a little, and read

it again and again, the prospect seemed to clear. You do not forbid me to write; you do not say that what I write is utterly destitute of merit. You only warn me against the folly of neglecting real duties for the sake of imaginative pleasures.[25]

On her twenty-first birthday she had labelled this letter 'Southey's advice to be kept for ever'.[26] Now, three years later, she was reconsidering her attitude to those 'quires of paper'. Charles Townshend's weariness 'of heroics' in *The Duke of Zamorna* echoes throughout the later novelettes; it is symptomatic of Charlotte's growing awareness that the mature author should mix with 'men of common clay'. The self-analysis necessary for the creation of Elizabeth Hastings and the more convincing portrait of female fascination for Zamorna in *Caroline Vernon* are indicative of Charlotte's growing sense of realism.

In an untitled fragment written about this time, Charlotte views her Angrian world as an artist. She has exhausted her model and is ready to paint 'from the life':

> I have now written a great many books and for a long time have dwelt on the same characters and scenes and subjects. I have shown my landscapes in every variety of shade and light which morning, noon, and evening — the rising, the meridian and the setting sun can bestow upon them. . . . So it is with persons. My readers have been habituated to one set of features, which they have seen now in profile, now in full face, now in outline, and again in finished painting — varied but by the change of feeling or temper or age; lit with love, flushed with passion, shaded with grief, kindled with ecstasy; in meditation and mirth, in sorrow and scorn and rapture; with the round outline of childhood, the beauty and fulness of youth, the strength of manhood, and the furrows of thoughtful decline; but we must change, for the eye is tired of the picture so oft recurring and now so familiar.[27]

Charlotte warns, however, that it will not be easy for her to dismiss from her imagination 'images which have filled it so long'; a few succeeding unpublished manuscripts confirm this.[28] Yet if her 'Farewell to Angria' does not mark the end of an era in her writing, it is a clear statement of future intention, which is reaffirmed in the preface to her first novel, *The Professor*. William Crimsworth's sober destiny is determined here:

> Still, I long to quit for awhile that burning clime where we have sojourned too long — its skies flame — the glow of sunset is always upon it — the mind would cease from excitement and turn now to a cooler region where the dawn breaks grey and sober, and the coming day for a time at least is subdued by clouds.[29]

The sagas of Glass Town and Angria have finally been dismissed by a more discriminating author. *Caroline Vernon* can be said to mark the end of Charlotte Brontë's juvenile writings; but it is an arbitrary milestone. There would be 'many a crude effort' yet before *The Professor,* many a sketch 'destroyed almost as soon as composed' before she relinquished her taste for 'ornamented and redundant composition'.[30]

PART IV

The Juvenilia
and the Later Writings

26

Ashworth and Angria

It is very edifying and profitable to create a world out of one's own brain and people it with inhabitants who are like so many Melchisedics . . . If you have ever been accustomed to such society Sir you will be aware how distinctly and vividly their forms and features fix themselves on the retina of that 'inward eye' which is said to be 'the bliss of solitude'.

So Charlotte wrote to Hartley Coleridge on 10 December 1841[1] nearly a year after she had completed *Caroline Vernon* and her 'Farewell to Angria'. She was obviously referring to her old imaginary world and was probably aware that her correspondent, the creator of Ejuxria, would be sympathetic to her thoughts. She had sent him the draft of a 'demi-semi novelette' in the hope that he might judge it worthy of publication. Coleridge's reply has since been lost but it seems that he intimated that 'Messrs Percy and West', the leading characters in her story were 'not gentlemen likely to make an impression upon the heart of any Editor in Christendom'. He apparently gave her no encouragement and censured her proliferation of fanciful characters. She decided to commit them to oblivion 'with several tears and much affliction' and hoped she could get over it. Yet she soon regained her confidence, as she had done after Southey's criticism two years previously, for she could not bring herself to lay aside for long her first attempt at a realistic novel. She recast it some months later in an incomplete, untitled manuscript known as *Ashworth*, after the principal character in the story. Although when this failed to satisfy her more discriminating taste she abandoned it, she returned again and again throughout her career to certain episodes in an effort to rework this first realistic adaptation of Angria.

Although *Ashworth* is later than Charlotte's juvenile writing, it must be looked at in detail if we are to follow the trend of her early work towards greater realism. It seems that she first began writing this story in the winter of 1839—40, soon after completing *Caroline Vernon* and possibly within days of her 'Farewell to Angria'. Several fragments survive in the Pierpont Morgan Library relating to an early version of *Ashworth*, the Percy/West story which Charlotte sent to Hartley Coleridge in the late summer of 1840.[2] These fragments refer to the background of Alexander Percy of the West Riding of Yorkshire, the character of his daughter Miss Percy who was a pupil in Mrs Turner's Seminary in London, the relations between Miss Percy and Miss Thornton in Yorkshire once they have left their London school, and the grief of an unnamed man over the death of a woman referred to as 'his own snow-drop'. While a glance at the names of the characters is enough to identify their Angrian counterparts, the close relationship of these early drafts to Charlotte's juvenilia is traced in the following discussion of the final version of *Ashworth*.

From her letter to Hartley Coleridge, it is clear that Charlotte sent only the early chapters of a proposed novel to him. She must have revised these original Percy/West fragments (and possibly others which are now lost) and sent a fair copy to Coleridge. He returned the manuscript,[3] and she replied on 10 December 1840, promising to lock up her 'precious manuscript' until she had a specific object in writing. In March 1841, she went as a governess to Upperwood House, Rawdon, where she remained until December. After this she returned briefly to Haworth leaving for Brussels in February 1842. It would seem that she had little opportunity to break her promise to Coleridge; but some time between December 1840 and March 1841 she again revised her story and wrote the manuscript we now know as *Ashworth*.[4] The idea of 'seeing all my characters at full length in three vols',[5] was too tempting to resist.

Only three chapters and an early draft of chapter 4[6] of *Ashworth* exist, but it is possible to see the direction Charlotte's first attempt at a full-scale novel was taking. The central figure of this manuscript is Mr Alexander Ashworth, a landowner in West Yorkshire and master of Gillwood Hall. His early life, which is identical in almost every detail to that of Alexander Percy (or Northangerland, as we know him in the later juvenilia), is traced throughout the first three chapters: chapter 1 relates 'his birth, his bridal, and his bankruptcy'; chapter 2 describes the fate of his two disowned sons, and his daughter's experience at a private boarding school in London; and chapter 3 shows the attitude of his neighbours, General West and Mr De Capell, to his entrance into Yorkshire society. In chapter 4 the interest moves to his daughter Mary, and her relationships with the younger Yorkshire generation of Wests and De Capells.

On the evidence of these surviving chapters one would assume that

Charlotte had intended to rewrite the history of Alexander Percy; yet she protests at the opening of Chapter 2 that her intention is not biographical. After a brief introduction of Arthur Ripley West in the final scene, she announces that he is going to be the hero, 'for if we did not reveal this secret, the reader would soon find it out'. She obviously intended to change the emphasis of her writing and the long opening devoted to Alexander Ashworth may be one of the reasons why she abandoned her story. The close relationship of the existing chapters to the world of Angria, however, gives us some indication of her intention. It seems we are to witness yet another episode in the Percy/Douro—Northangerland/ Zamorna relationship, thinly disguised by an English setting.

The plot and the characters of *Ashworth* are reminiscent of the juvenilia. Charlotte herself was well aware of this and it is implicit in her narrative pretence to verisimilitude:

> There is also a certain narrative whose particulars I have often heard from different individuals and which I wish to condense into something like the form of a story, that the names and events therein detailed may not wholly slip from my memory. I have not heard these incidents lately; nor did they come to my ear all at once. Every scene and character to which I shall refer has formed the theme of many anecdotes communicated in the evening talk of sundry homely firesides.[7]

One might read Senegambia (or Wellington's Land) for Hampshire, where Ashworth spent his childhood at an ancestral home differing only in name from Percy Hall. After constant quarrels with his father, he is sent away to Eton and Oxford. His scandalous early life is associated with the 'softer names' of Harriet and Augusta: 'To the former, there appertains a sad, to the latter a wild, story.'[8] These we heard of in the tales of Percy's *affaire* with Harriet O'Connor and his early marriage to Augusta di Segovia. In the early manuscripts we also heard of Ashworth's dissolute life in London, the English equivalent of Verdopolis, and of his musical talents and his relations with the opera singer Miss Allen (later Louisa Vernon). His infamous associates are drawn directly from the juvenilia: George Charles Gordon, Frederick Caversham, Robert King (or S'Death), and Jeremiah Simpson. As the narrator of *Ashworth* says, their 'names I need only record to express their characters.'[9] Even Thaddeus Daniels and Arthur Macshane, both of Irish extraction, are obviously Hector Montmorency and Arthur O'Connor of the juvenilia. As in the case of the young Percy, Daniels and King were the youthful Ashworth's mentors in vice;[10] and after his bankruptcy, the old gang of 'Percy & Co' (now 'Ashworth & Co') followed his career as a drover in north Yorkshire.

Ashworth's marriage to the gentle Miss Mary Wharton is identical to Percy's relationship with his second wife, Maria Henrietta. Even her maiden name belongs to the juvenilia. Charlotte had referred to her only as Lady Maria Henrietta Percy and as Mrs Alexander Percy but Branwell described in detail the young daughter of Lord George Wharton of Alnwick who was to become the future Lady Percy.[11] Another of Branwell's manuscripts is recalled minutely in Charlotte's picture of Mrs Ashworth walking along the country lanes attended only by her large Newfoundland dog Roland and her face shaded by a straw hat: in *The Politics of Verdopolis,* Branwell had described Lady Percy's daughter Mary walking alone through the sequestered 'English-like' lanes of Wellington's Land with a large hat shading her face and accompanied by 'her usual guard dog Roland'.[12] We learnt in *High Life In Verdopolis* that Roland was a Newfoundland dog, though it has been suggested that the appearance of a similar dog in *Caroline Vernon* may be attributed to Charlotte's recent position as governess at the Sidgwicks who owned just such an animal.[13] As in Charlotte's early manuscripts, Ashworth's wild habits were subdued for a time after his second marriage to Mary Wharton whom he dearly loved. Her death left him desolate: he received a shock 'whose severity was attested by the great change it wrought in the whole course of his subsequent life',[14] words which echo the same description of his predecessor in *The Duke of Zamorna.* He espoused the cause of Republicanism and, like Percy, set about subverting the masses with a religious doctrine varying 'from the lowest Arminism to the highest Calvinism'. The 'smutty' mechanics of Manchester and the West Riding whom he attempts to convert recall the 'mad mechanics' of Zamorna City who were dispersed by the cavalry in *Stancliffe's Hotel,* and the mills and combing shops of *Ashworth* were already a vital part of the industrial areas of Angria in the later juvenilia.

Alexander Ashworth's disowned sons, Edward and William, disparate as their characters are, are forced together as they 'shake hands with poverty'. There are hints of individual enterprise, of a 'counting house' future, of ledgers and profits, which lead one to suspect that they are to rise in life through the wool trade as their prototypes did in Branwell's *The Wool is Rising.* Edward was a 'strong and hardy boy', untroubled by sentiment and constantly thrashing his quieter younger brother. The latter, however, treasured up his brother's offences: he had no readiness to forgive and his character, like that of Captain William Percy, was marked by a certain cynicism and a lack of candour. William's fondness for books, rather than for a military life, however, and Edward's contempt for learning, look forward to the more subtle antagonism between the Crimsworth brothers in *The Professor.*

Ashworth's preference for his intelligent and beautiful daughter Mary is also paralleled in the juvenilia. Charlotte adopts the same detached admiration for her that we see in her attitude to the remote but regal Queen of Angria. Her person demanded consideration: 'I select the word "consideration" in preference to warmer terms, such as "affection" or "attachment," for the young lady had the character of being thought somewhat proud and exclusive.'[15] In the juvenilia, however, her haughty aloofness is accepted as requisite in a Queen. Here, in *Ashworth,* Mary has only her position as a Yorkshire heiress to justify Amelia De Capell's view of her as 'Proud as Lucifer!' Mary, with all her Angrian overtones, must become a more realistic character if she is to fit into her upper-middle-class Yorkshire setting. In *Mina Laury* and *Stancliffe's Hotel,* Charlotte had begun to make this 'inaccessibly sacred' heroine a little less perfect by the introduction of 'womanish jealousies'. In *Ashworth,* Mary's intelligence is emphasized. Her aloofness is presented in an equivocal manner, promising future strength of character: 'She seemed careless to the regard of most of those about her. Whether this carelessness was the result of cold-heartedness and want of feeling or whether it had another source, it shall be our business to inquire hereafter.'[16] We are reminded here of the mask assumed by Miss West, the governess, and the efforts of Elizabeth Hastings to hide her true character as self-protection. In *Ashworth* we are shown the 'new' Mary's compassion for poor Ellen Hall (an advance on Mary Percy's harsh treatment of Elizabeth Hastings) and her sensitivity towards the retiring Marian Fairbourne, both of which are emphasized by contrast with Amelia De Capell's behaviour.

After a whole chapter devoted to narrating the main incidents in Alexander Ashworth's past life, Charlotte tires of this Angrian marsh-spirit. He is leading her back into the old imaginary realms of Glass Town and Angria. At the beginning of chapter 2 she interrupts her narrative and announces her intention to return to the world of 'Hampshire gentlemen', 'Newmarket coats' and Doncaster races:

> What but an ignis fatuus, that carries its lantern over moor and moss through impossible places, can be expected to trace the steps of such a rover. I should be lost if I attempted to venture into the dusk wilds where I see his wandering light gleaming for a moment on the reedy pools among which it flits. No, reader, if you go with me you must keep the highroad, the railway across Chat Moss. We will talk with all whom we meet, and sometimes, at intervals, Ashworth with his light will flit across our path, perhaps pause and turn twice or thrice in his strange gyrations, then glide away, where we must never follow.[17]

Ashworth's light refuses to fade until the later part of Chapter 2; the following episodes, however, which exclude the narrative of his life, show Charlotte's growing sense of realism and ability to portray character in action.

The last part of chapter 2, for example, includes a sharply realized scene at Mary's London school on the eve of the Christmas vacation. Charlotte herself saw the necessity for a change in style: 'We have had enough of narrative and *didactic;* I must now come more closely to the point and endeavour to illustrate character by the occasional introduction of scenes and dialogue.'[18] She reproduces something she must have heard often as a pupil and then as a teacher at Roe Head: the excited prattle of girls in the dormitory after prize-giving. She first compares the 'brilliantly lighted drawing-room' and the gaiety of the girls there with the dim light of a solitary candle in the dormitory above where the 'drudge-like' half-boarder, Ellen Hall, silently packs the trunks of those who, more fortunate than herself, have homes to return to for the holidays. Soon the selfish talk of 'pampered girls' invades the dormitory and Ellen is bullied into repacking the trunk of Amelia De Capell. Like so many of the girls Charlotte mentions in her letters to Ellen Nussey and Mary Taylor, Amelia is not ill-natured, she is merely spoilt and unthinking: 'Her mother was a proud and senseless woman, and she had been taught from early childhood that inferiors were persons to be kept at a distance and treated haughtily.'[19] It is tempting to suggest that the name 'Amelia' is not coincidental here; for in a letter to Ellen Nussey Charlotte had mocked her godparents' niece, Amelia Walker, and complained that she was 'spoilt utterly spoilt by the most hideous affectation'.[20] When the girls retire for supper Ellen is left alone in the dormitory with Mary Ashworth. Mary's concern and questions reveal Ellen's lonely background in a more interesting manner than the long narrative of Ashworth's past life. Mary's scorn of Ellen's proposed future as a nursery governess reflects Charlotte's loathing of her similar role at the Sidgwicks, and her considerate gift to Ellen of some volumes of Scott and Byron recalls Charlotte's own farewell present from Miss Wooler when she left her employment in 1838.

In this scene Charlotte had returned to the autobiographical approach she had found so successful in her portrait of Elizabeth Hastings and which she was to employ in her later novels. Her recent experience with the Sidgwick family and her memories of Roe Head have been skilfully combined and transposed into a new scene, more realistic than any relating to Angria. The parts of *Ashworth* which provide glimpses of Charlotte's later mastery of scene and character are those which are free from the restraining influence of the Angrian plot: namely, the dormitory scene above, the conversation in chapter 3 between General West and Mr De Capell about their wayward sons and the corrupting influence of Ashworth, and the final scene in which Mary Ashworth visits Amelia De Capell.

General West, a 'trucculent Tory' and veteran of 'the field "of red

Assaye"',[21] has the same overtones of Wellington as has the Duke in *Tales of the Islanders;* and Mr De Capell with his 'broad Yorkshire', forthright manner and readiness 'to dig for lucre' among the manufacturers of Leeds and the clothiers of Bradford, recalls General Thornton and more particularly his father, Alexander Sneachie. They are not weighed down, however, as Ashworth is, with an unnecessarily detailed past. Their characters speak for themselves in what Charlotte calls 'a slight sketch of one of their dolorous dialogues'.[22] Their conversation is reminiscent of both the early conversations among military men in Bravey's Inn, reported in the *Young Men's Magazine,* and the later frankness of the dialogues between Mr Helstone and Hiram Yorke in *Shirley.*

Although there are aspects of the unthinking Jane Moore and the superficial Julia in Amelia De Capell, her character is not greatly illuminated by comparing her with these prototypes. It is more clearly revealed in her relations with her cousin Marian, with Ellen Hall and Mary Ashworth. One nicely timed sentence speaks volumes about her character: '"Oh! I had forgotten to introduce to you my cousin, Marian," exclaimed Miss De Capell. "I beg pardon, but she is so tiny, it is easy to overlook her."'[23] Marian Fairbourne's name, auburn hair and symbolic association with the purity of a snow-drop, recall Marian Hume; but her attitude to Arthur Ripley West, the 'new' Zamorna, has the qualified admiration of Elizabeth Hastings or the later Jane Eyre. With a fluency and discernment unknown to her earlier namesake, Marian tells Arthur, 'You are rather satirical, and, when you see me so foolish and bashful, you often feel tempted to amuse yourself at my expense.'[24] The dependent governess is again distinguished, as was Charlotte herself, by her ability to draw; and, as in *Jane Eyre,* Marian's portfolio of drawings leads to a more intimate dialogue between her and her admirer. The scene is very different from the open declarations of the former Marian and her Marquis of Douro.

The contrast between the early narrative chapters and the later scenes of *Ashworth* are evidence that Charlotte found that once her African setting had been totally rejected in favour of a solid Yorkshire one, the plot of the juvenilia and especially the lurid details of Percy's early life became incongruous. Her early imaginary world was now hindering her progress as a writer.

27

Branwell's Influence

Charlotte's repetition in *Ashworth* of the old Angrian events, almost a year after she had rejected the Angrian Saga, can be explained mainly by her long partnership in writing with Branwell. We have seen how Branwell had always taken the lead in plot-making in the juvenilia. With less practice, Charlotte had either less confidence or less interest in plot. Thus, in her first attempt to write independently of her Angrian material, she had felt (as she had feared she would in her 'Farewell to Angria') like a stranger in a distant country. The first four chapters of *Ashworth* show confusion in their planning. Their interest centres in the younger generation of characters; but in an effort to give these characters a realistic background, Charlotte has seized on the nearest available framework: the early life of Branwell's hero, Alexander Percy, and the Glass Town Saga.

Branwell was no longer an obvious influence on Charlotte's writing at this time, but the effect he had had on her development must not be forgotten. Charlotte's return to the early life of Percy as late as July 1838 in *The Duke of Zamorna* shows the fascination this subject still had for her as well as for Branwell, despite his attachment to Henry Hastings. Charlotte would have known that six months earlier, towards the end of 1837, Branwell had reviewed the early life of Alexander Percy in a story about the Thurstons of Darkwell Manor.[1] Details from this 'Percy' fragment, such as the scandal associated with Thurston's wife and Percy's partners in cattle-dealing, all recur in *Ashworth*. Charlotte may have been relying on her memory here, but it is possible that she was still consulting her brother's manuscripts, for the name Thurston occurs only in this fragment by Branwell and in *Ashworth*.

The Thurston episode is also significant for its reliance on the Yorkshire landscape, an unusual feature in Branwell's writing: the 'lonely farmhouses', the 'stone-fenced fields that skirt the heather', the linnet-peopled hills', and the legend of the 'Darkwell Gytrash' later found in *Jane Eyre*.[2] We saw in the early Glass Town Saga and especially in *A Day at Parry's Palace* that Emily was the first to protest against the lack of realism in Charlotte's stories; but Branwell, while seldom following his own precepts, may have had some influence on Charlotte's later adaptation of her Angrian story to a Yorkshire setting in such manuscripts as *Stancliffe's Hotel* and *Henry Hastings,* for he writes in the Thurston fragment of 30 December 1837:

> I will never believe that our minds can be so well awakened by the poetry of distant and unknown images as by that of the things we have long been used to know. I would doubt the genius of that writer who loved more to dwell upon Indian palm-groves or genii palaces than on the wooded manors and cloudy skies of England.

This is a very different Branwell from the boy who tried to preserve his role as leader of the four Chief Genii.

Branwell's early initiatives in magazine writing, his introduction of things Greek and French, his insistence on a solid geographical setting and his enthusiasm for poetry, were constructive forces in Charlotte's development as a writer; but his impact on her later writing was largely negative. Because of his constant reliance on war and political intrigue to perpetuate the Angrian Saga, Charlotte had lost that early interest in story-telling which is so evident in *Tales of the Islanders. Passing Events, Julia, Four Years Ago, Stancliffe's Hotel* and *The Duke of Zamorna* have little sense of structure. They are basically a series of scenes relying for coherence on the outside framework of the events in Branwell's manuscripts. In *The Return of Zamorna* Charlotte asserts her independence and insists on reversing Branwell's plot in order to save her heroine from destruction; but the manuscript is again simply a series of loosely connected episodes. *Mina Laury* has a unity that is rare in Charlotte's manuscripts. Here, her concentration on a single character and on the theme of love has focused her interest on one aspect of the Angrian Saga. Charlotte was always more accomplished in the handling of a single plot: one is tempted to compare not only the more successful *Caroline Vernon* with the dual plot of its predecessor *Henry Hastings,* but the simple linear structure of the three plots in *Jane Eyre* with the less successful, more diffuse double plot of *Shirley.*

The subject of romantic love provided Charlotte's sole concern in plot-making. It was this which had preserved her interest in the Glass Town Saga after the four Brontë children had dissolved their early partnership, and which had sustained her writing through the years 1834 to 1835 when the creation of the new kingdom of Angria threatened to alter her imaginary world. Branwell had embraced Angria and its perpetual wars with enthusiasm, but *High Life In Verdopolis* shows how reluctant Charlotte was to move her stories of romance and scandal to the new kingdom. Not until *Passing Events,* two years later, did she accept Angria as the setting for her review of aristocratic life. For a time she was swept along by the fervour of the political activity around her and by Branwell's insistence on its transposition into the new Angrian scene; but when she left for Roe Head to become a teacher in July 1835, her concern lay not with the new round of political upheavals initiated by her brother, but with the deteriorating relationship between Mary and Zamorna.

Romantic love continues to form the basic subject of Charlotte's later juvenile manuscripts (1836—39). This is particularly true where she can be seen as initiating her own plot rather than relying on Branwell's: in *The Return of Zamorna, Mina Laury,* and especially in *Henry Hastings* and *Caroline Vernon.* Harriet Martineau was later to accuse Charlotte of being obsessed in her novels by the idea of love, and by the need to be loved.[3] She spoke of the heroines in Charlotte's novels as loving 'too readily, too vehemently and sometimes after a fashion which their female readers may resent'[4] — a judgement which might more aptly be applied to the self-effacing heroines of the early manuscripts. In the juvenilia, certainly, Charlotte's invention in plot-making seldom wanders from this subject.

28

The Search after Love

The theme of the abandoned child, of the destitute person deprived of parental love, who struggles to come to terms with a hostile environment, fills the pages of Charlotte's novels with the persistence of obsession. Aside from any psychological interpretation, this theme can be traced to the early fairy-tale beginnings of the juvenilia.

The unloved orphan is first seen in *The Enfant* (13 July 1829),[1] a short fairy story set in Paris and originally written as a contribution to *Branwell's Blackwood's Magazine.* Here, a thin, pale little child is pressed into labour as a chimney-sweep by the 'farfamed madman PIGTAIL', whose habit it is throughout the early Glass Town Saga to steal, exploit and murder children. The child is kicked and trampled by his master until he becomes insensible; but he is eventually rescued — through the intervention of 'a party of Gendearmes' and the Emperor Napoleon — by Monsieur Hanghimself, who turns out to be the child's father. The gruesome details of Pigtail's activities are described in a very matter-of-fact way with little sense of horror and with the same perverse fascination that one finds in children's reactions to fairy tales and folklore.

The abandoned, wandering child is the ideal vehicle for an adventure story. In *The Search after Happiness*, an old man tells how he was lured away from home as a child by a magician and forced to encounter many terrible adventures in strange lands. Charlotte elaborates and expands this tale in many of her early stories. In *The Adventure's of Mon Edouard de Crack,* for example, Edouard leaves his simple country life in the south of France when his parents die of a fever and travels to Paris, a city of magnificence and squalor. He is struck by its haggard inhabitants, their bleached bones 'peeping ghastly' through their withered skins. Robbed of his money, Edouard is forced to join their ranks and to serve a Tavern Master who trades in corpses. But, as in many fairy tales, his situation is reversed by a good genie and he is transported to the magical world of the Glass Town.[2]

Foster-parents and disowned children abound in the juvenilia, from the orphaned Quashia, who is adopted by the Duke of Wellington, to General Thornton, disowned as a young man by his royal family in Sneachiesland. Northangerland, who sought to murder his male offspring, is the rejecting father figure *par excellence.* The Duke of Wellington's initial role as a protector of children fades as he is replaced in the saga by his eldest son Zamorna, the sinister guardian—seducer of Caroline Vernon. Two of Zamorna's own sons are deprived of a mother at birth: Arthur Julius dies early from consumption and Ernest Edward 'Fitzarthur' suffers a violent death when he is dragged from his foster-mother, Mina Laury. Even in Zamorna's own background there are hints of a foster-mother, seen in an enigmatic unpublished poem addressed to 'Justine'. We learn that Justine was Mina's mother, the wife of Ned Laury and the young Zamorna's beloved nurse. Northangerland later taunts Zamorna with his singular gratitude to his 'young French foster-mother', who nursed him with her own child and whom Zamorna repaid by making that child his concubine.[3] In the poem to Justine, the unrepentant Zamorna pays homage to the grave of his mistress's mother and recalls her death:

> Then her daughter and her foster-son she'd to her bosom press
> And say with such a bitter moan God my children bless,
> And then I called her mother and weepingly I said
> I would be Mina's brother when she was cold and dead.

> That vow has since been broken, as when lightning shivers trees,
> These words in anguish spoken have been scattered to the breeze.
> Justine if God has given a glance of earth to thee
> Thou hast even wept in heaven my withering crimes to see.

> But let me not remember those hours of darkness past
> Nor blow the dying ember, to light with such a blast,
> I do not know repentance, I cannot bend my pride
> Nor deprecate my sentence even at thy cold grave's side.[4]

Zamorna appears to love children: he is often seen playing with young 'Fitzarthur' or Caroline Vernon on his knee. But his is an ambiguous love entangled in his Byronic pride. All young females who come within his orbit are subject to what he refers to as his 'comet-fires'.[5] All are affected by his magnetic charm and all must suffer because of it. This accounts for 'the touch of saddness'[6] which haunts the beautiful faces of Charlotte's early heroines. As Mr Warner studies the hostess of Grassmere Manor, he sees in the features of Mina Laury a face that 'all too plainly whispered of a heart that had known its hours of anxiety, of neglect, desertion, coldness, and was eager to enjoy to its full warmth the moment of sunshine now vouchsafed to it'.[7] Mina has no thoughts of relinquishing her devotion to Zamorna, no matter how he treats her. His infidelity is accepted as part of his male prowess. It is gratifying simply to be one of the chosen.

Yet that wistfulness which haunts a succession of heroines is the result of Zamorna's unfaithfulness. Some, like Lady Helen Victorine and Marion Hume, die from neglect; others, like Rosamund Wellesley, commit suicide — ashamed of having loved Zamorna 'not wisely but too well'.[8] Even Mary Percy is reduced by 'hideous phantoms of jealousy'[9] to a shadow of her former self, subject to nervous fits of weeping. Yet at no time do Zamorna's loves lay the blame for that unhappiness at his feet. They believe, as he does, that such adulation is his destiny and his due:

> He has too little of the moral Great-Heart in his nature, it is his creed that all things bright & fair live for him — by him they are to be gathered & worn as the flowers of his Laurel Crown — The green leaves are victory in battle — they never fade, the roses are conquests in Love — they decay & drop off — Fresh ones blow round him, are plucked & woven with the withered stem of their predecessors — such a wreath he deems a glory about his temples.[10]

Nor is there any hint of moral dilemma in Charlotte's attitude to him. He is condemned and mocked by his priggish younger brother, through whose eyes we see Zamorna's 'crimes', but he is never punished by events in the saga. Like Lucifer, he is magnificently sinful and irresistible.

For Charlotte Zamorna's guilt is largely absolved by the willingness of the child-heroine to be possessed by an all-absorbing love. From the earliest manuscripts, the orphan is in search of happiness which he finds in the protection of a benefactor and father figure. Women do not have the same attraction. Zenobia's patronage of the young Ellen Grenville is the only case of a female benefactor in the juvenilia and this relationship is based not on emotional need but on Zenobia's superior learning. Zenobia herself is dictatorial and mentally unstable. In the juvenilia the loving mothers all die young. Mary Percy is an exception, but her preoccupation with her husband usually obscures her devotion to her children. Other mothers, like Louisa Vernon, are hysterical, devious and shallow, scorned by their more intelligent daughters. Whether Charlotte is reflecting here her family situation, her lack of a loving mother and the security of a stern father—protector, or whether she is simply reflecting Byron's attitude to women, the image of an unloving, even deceitful, older woman extends into her later writing in such figures as Mdlle Reuter, Mrs Reed and Madame Beck, and elements of the father—protector—lover can be seen in William Crimsworth, Mr Rochester and especially Paul Emanuel. Even in Charlotte's final fragmentary sketch, *Emma,* the urbane Mr Ellin protects bewildered little Matilda Fitzgibbon against bullying Miss Wilcox.

It is simplistic, of course, to suggest that such later characters owe their origins solely to the juvenilia. Charlotte's experience in Brussels and the development of her critical faculty would belie any such crude equation; but there is no doubt that her lonely experience in Brussels and her later yearning for the understanding love of an older man reinforced earlier images in her imagination.

The motherless heroines of Charlotte's later writing — Jane Eyre, Shirley Keelder, Lucy Snowe, Paulina Holme — all have their precursors in the juvenilia. All betray a hunger for affection. But the heroines of the novels possess a discrimination, a pride in their own worth which allows them to reject temptation. As Charlotte grew older she became more interested in the moral aspects of love and passion. The early Mina Laury is careless of her reputation and honour; her world is the man she loves as 'master'. Her self-effacement is accepted as admirable. In the later Caroline Vernon Charlotte explores carefully the development of a mind destined for such wilful self-destruction. Fed by those romantic dreams Southey warned Charlotte against, Caroline confuses her love for her guardian with adolescent fantasy. Her conscience is feeble compared to the powerful fascination of dawning passion. She is 'as clay in the hands of the Potter'.[11] It is Zamorna who provides the opportunity for temptation, but it is Caroline's own nature, predisposed to wilfulness and imaginative excess by a neglected childhood, that causes her to identify her indulgent guardian with fictional idols. When Zamorna takes the young Caroline to Scar House, Ingleside, where Rosamond Wellesley died, her fate is sealed.

Of all Charlotte's juvenile heroines, only Elizabeth Hastings and her prototype Miss West have the strength of will to suppress the dictates of passion. Unlike the typical early heroines who are chiefly the products of fairy tale and fiction, Elizabeth is almost wholly a creature of experience. As the fairy-tale element of the juvenilia diminishes, the abandoned child and the neglected heroine are no longer simply the products of legend. The theme of estrangement assumes autobiographical significance.

In the 'Roe Head Journal' and *Henry Hastings,* the figure of the lonely governess emerges: the dependent female who despite her plain appearance and vulnerable position in society insists on her right to win self-respect and affection. Charlotte's position at Roe Head had made her more aware of her own plight in society. Like many educated single women of the 1830s and 1840s, she was forced to earn her living as a governess because there was no alternative occupation. Her letters and prose manuscripts of the years 1836 to 1839 bear witness to overwork and to the humiliation of having to earn her living with people who were her social equals or inferiors.[12] At Roe Head, her position was one of bondage: she felt 'chained' to her chair while 'the year is revolving in its richest glow and declaring at the close of every summer day the time I am losing will never come again.'[13] She was not temperamentally suited to teaching but felt forced as a dependent female into a life of drudgery:

> I cannot get used to the ongoings that surround me. I fulfil my duties strictly and well, but so to speak, if the illustration be not profane, as God was not in the wind nor the fire nor the earthquake so neither is my heart in the task, the theme or the exercise.[14]

We have seen how Charlotte's resentment found release in writing, but her experience also heralded a new type of heroine. In the portraits of Miss West and Elizabeth Hastings, she gives a poignant account of the duplicity needed to sustain the roles of teacher, governess and lady companion. Her heroines must disguise their true feelings if they are to listen to and advise those they secretly despise:

> With indulgence [Miss West] listened to the tale of conquests won, of vanity flattered, of admiration attracted, with profound wisdom she gave warning against the sorrows and heart-breakings of imprudent love, though in all these confessions there was to her high-wrought feelings something weak and low and vapid, an absence [of] intellect, of the colouring of imagination, of the force of passion and intense energy of enthusiasm. She never by inadvertent breath or glance betrayed the scorn that often swelled at her heart. She listened to all, sympathized with all and never for a moment required sympathy or attention in return.[15]

Charlotte had recorded how her pupils bored her with their 'vulgar familiar trash': 'If these Girls knew how I loathe their company they would not seek mine so much as they do.'[16] Elizabeth Hastings' outward demeanour hides a being of intense passions which only the most astute observer can discover: 'here was a being made up of intense emotions — in her ordinary course of life always smothered under the diffidence of prudence & a skilful address.'[17] Beneath the reserved exterior of this lonely, Quaker-like little governess there was a heart that, like her creator, yearned for a 'warmer, closer attachment'. Elizabeth Hastings gains the satisfaction of economic independence but conventional attitudes to her profession deny her the security of love. William Percy recognizes her worth but is too proud to marry a school-teacher.

After a week or so with the Sidgwick family at Stonegappe, Charlotte wrote: 'I see now more clearly than I have ever done before that a private governess has no existence, is not considered as a living and rational being

except as connected with the wearisome duties she has to fulfil.'[18]
Ashworth contains her protests against the Amelia De Capells she met at
the Sidgwicks and the 'oceans of needlework, yards of cambric to hem,
muslin nightcaps to make, and, above all things, dolls to dress', which
came the way of a young woman in the ill-defined occupation of 'nursery-
governess':

> In the name of common sense, how can she expect it [correct school-
> work] when the moment she has given you [Ellen Hall] the pages of
> history to study or three pages of French prose to learn by heart, she
> sends you into the laundry to clearstarch a basketful of lace and
> muslin?[19]

This theme of sympathy for the underdog — for the orphaned and the
oppressed — which runs through so much of Charlotte's juvenile and
mature writing, clearly has its roots in autobiography. Ellen Hall, Miss
West and Elizabeth Hastings are the obvious antecedents of Jane Eyre and
her later counterparts. The abandoned child is preserved in the moving
portraits of Helen Burns, Paulina Holme, Willie Ellin and Matilda
Fitzgibbon; and the child's countless oppressors of the early manuscripts
reappear in such figures as Mr Brocklehurst and Mrs Reed.[20]

Two Rival Brothers

Related to the orphan/governess theme is Charlotte's preoccupation with two mutually antagonistic brothers, disowned from birth and forced to live by their wits. Their most recognizable prototypes are to be found in the figures of Edward and William Percy in Branwell's manuscript *The Wool is Rising*. Edward is first introduced by Charlotte as the scoundrelly accomplice of Miss Foxley in *The Secret*. From the beginning he is unencumbered by principle and his sole aim is to rise in society by the accumulation of money. In Charlotte's manuscripts he is initially more important than his younger brother, and was possibly introduced to replace his ageing father in the central rivalry with Zamorna. Edward is referred to as 'young rogue'; he has his father's 'auburn ringlets', imposing stature, and violent energy. In *The Spell* Edward has become a celebrated Angrian merchant and friend of Zamorna; but their relationship soon deteriorates into one of expediency between the new Angrian monarch and his able Minister for Trade. Their open conflict, however, never replaces the central rivalry between 'Old Rogue' (Northangerland) and Zamorna. In Charlotte's later juvenile manuscripts interest in Edward is gradually replaced by the fascination of his more subtle brother William, but not before his relationship to this brother has been clearly defined. The story of Cain and Abel was to haunt Charlotte's writing to the last.

The antagonism between two brothers existed in Charlotte's stories from the beginning. The Duke of Wellington's two sons, the Marquis of Douro and Lord Charles Wellesley, are of very different dispositions and become estranged after an initial attachment in the *Tales of the Islanders*. Lord Charles is excluded from his elder brother's house because of his prying curiosity and malicious pen. As he degenerates into a mere reporter of his brother's liaisons, he ceases to be a plausible character. In order to overhear Northangerland's private reminiscences of his scandalous past, for example, Lord Charles becomes a thumb-sucking 'Diminutive Idiot' who wanders ghoul-like through the Verdopolitan palaces with his pet cat tucked under his arm.[1] Meanwhile, his brother, who was only two years older than he in the Glass Town stories, is now twenty and has been married twice. But it is unfair to expect consistency in the early juvenilia: the tales abound in such minor anomalies, whatever germs of the later novelist we may discern in them. With the emergence of Charles Townshend in the manuscripts of 1836 to 1839, the relationship between these royal brothers is thrust into the background and their previous antagonism survives only in the cynical attitude of Charles towards the absurdities of 'the great Gun', his elder brother.

Other contrasting pairs of brothers are to be found in Charlotte's early stories, in particular, John Augustus (Duke of Fidena) and Thornton Wilkin (General Thornton) Sneachie. Prince John has a legal mind, is reserved and unforgiving, but noble and honest; whereas 'honest' Thornton (disowned in his wayward youth by his father) is frank, hearty and generous. Even their speech is contrasted: John's language is 'classic and refined'; Thornton's is distinguished by his blustering 'doric accents'. Both of these characters reappear in *Ashworth* as John and Thornton De Capell: the eldest is studying law in London — 'a proud, correct young man, gifted with a power of perfect self-command' — and the younger is 'a thorn in his father's side', a mere scamp whose father is 'on the point of disowning and disinheriting him every day'. Even the early friendship between Prince John and Zamorna, and the latter's influence on Thornton in the juvenilia is reflected in *Ashworth*.[2]

But it is in Branwell's manuscripts that we find the earliest delineation of the story Charlotte was to rework so constantly in her later writing. This Branwell first described in an early draft of chapter 1 of *The Wool is Rising* on 18 February 1834,[3] and he recast it the following June, while Charlotte was writing *The Spell*. Charlotte was quick to echo (in *The Spell*) Branwell's story of Edward and William Percy's early deprivation of home and family, their exclusion from rank by the 'black, unnatural justice' of their father, and the tyranny Edward exercises over his younger brother. William soon leaves his position as a clerk in Edward's woollen mill and makes a successful career in the army. Apart from an occasional clash in the streets of Zamorna when William offers supercilious insults and Edward wields his gig-whip,[4] the antagonism between the brothers is revealed through the mind of the cynical but idealistic William Percy. As we saw in *The Duke of Zamorna*, William was not insensitive to Edward's brutality, though in his pride he affected indifference.

In *Ashworth,* Charlotte transposed this story into a Yorkshire setting. The early Northangerland had hated his sons, believing that they represented the demonic in his nature, and he therefore paid S'Death to murder them. Less melodramatically, Mr Ashworth has his sons 'put out to nurse' in a farmhouse on his estate and left there to become parentless urchins. Charlotte leaves the motive for this callous act unexplained: 'Have I not hinted that he hid eccentric fantasies in his nature that seemed bordering sometimes on the frenzies of a madman?' A 'faithful chronicler' can tell only what has been told to him;[5] but she presumes that Ashworth's feelings must be motivated by the same principle which caused the Empress Catherine's hatred of her son, a possible source of the idea of child rejection in the juvenilia.[6] The boys are rescued for a time from obscurity by their grandmother and sent to Harrow, where Edward 'pushed his way through the rough life of a school boy', while William merely endured by cynicism, day-dreaming, and 'Indian doggedness'. When their grandmother dies they are again plunged into poverty, 'into the darkness and vacuum of cold waves'; and we are left with the thought that 'The divers may rise into daylight again, ere long, bearing in their hands pearls, such pearls as are found in the dreary seas of adversity.'[7]

When the brothers are next seen in *The Professor,* as Edward and William Crimsworth, one suspects that the pearls they find are not quite those intended for the Ashworth brothers; but the Crimsworths' way through life is also one of adversity, as Charlotte promised in the Preface, and their relationship is essentially that of their Percy and Ashworth predecessors. Charlotte wisely omits the lurid parent-figure, however, and concentrates on the brothers' early efforts to rise from obscurity. The relationship is seen from the point of view of the younger brother as it had been in *The Duke of Zamorna.* Timothy Steaton, the obsequious evangelical clerk of the juvenilia, reappears as Tim Steighton, so reviving in name and relationship the early role of his father, who was the subservient steward of Northangerland's estates and his minion in various crimes.[8]

Allied to the recasting of his early material in *The Professor* is the irrelevant introduction, in the opening chapter, of William Crimsworth's old friend Charles, characterized as he was in the juvenilia — 'a sarcastic, observant, shrewd, cold-blooded creation'. The explanation for this lies in the former William Percy's friendship with Charles Townshend, which gradually developed in the manuscripts of 1836 to 1839. William's old habit of confiding the details of his life to Charles by letter presented Charlotte with a familiar conventional opening for her first novel. She never saw its incongruity to the remainder of the narrative. Although she offered *The Professor* to Smith, Elder & Co. for publication several times after its initial rejection and even wrote a preface for it, this opening chapter was never altered. Charlotte recognized that the beginning of her novel was 'very feeble' but never seemed to identify the extraneous letter to Charles as a possible cause. For her first novel, Charlotte was also probably eager to imitate the writings of those she admired, in this case Scott, who almost invariably used the discovery of an old letter or journal to reveal past events. Her letter however is rendered unnecessary by the fact that its writer and the narrator of the story are the same person; but its survival is perhaps the most obvious example of the persistence of an Angrian convention in her mature writing.[9]

The Professor was not published in Charlotte's lifetime, yet she clung to her 'martyrised MS' with the fondness of 'a doting parent towards an idiot child'.[10] She admitted that the narrative was 'deficient in incident and in general attractiveness',[11] but she was reluctant to put aside a work which she still believed had merit. Although she acknowledged that the Brussels section of the book contained 'more pith . . . more reality', one suspects that much of her fondness was for the old Angrian theme of two rival brothers, for at the commencement of each new novel she returned to the material in the early sections of *The Professor.*

After the success of *Jane Eyre,* in which there is no more than a hint of the theme of the two brothers in Rochester's unhappy background, Charlotte tried to salvage her first novel. She wrote to her publishers: 'My wish is to recast "The Professor," add as well as I can what is deficient, retrench some parts, develop others, and make of it a three-volume work — no easy task, I know, yet I trust not an impracticable one'.[12] Charlotte had begun three drafts of this new story already and the survival of one of these, an untitled manuscript known variously as *John Henry* and *The Moores,*[13] shows an effort to expand the early section of *The Professor* relating to Edward and William Crimsworth. The contents of the first eight pages of *The Professor* fill approximately sixteen pages of *John Henry.* Although their names have been altered to John Henry and William Calvert Moore, the situation and personalities of the brothers remain the same. So close was their identification in Charlotte's mind that at one place in the manuscript she mistakenly wrote 'Edward' for 'John Henry'.[14] Even Edward's Methodist book-keeper (the original Tim Steaton from the juvenilia) reappears as Tim Flute.[15] The letter convention has also been preserved in chapter 1, but is now more relevant: William writes to John Henry rather than to Charles, asking for work in his counting house and describing his rift with their maternal relatives, Mr Calvert and Dr Greatorix,[16] who have offered him a career in the Church and a cousin for a wife. His attitude to marriage recalls the scrupulous William Percy: 'I look too high, and as I won't descend one inch, I may after all be doomed to celibacy';[17] and he has Percy's ability to divine immediately the true character of his acquaintances.

John Henry was rejected by Charlotte after the commencement of chapter 3, when she began to rethink the opening of the novel that was to become *Shirley;* but it is obvious from this fragmentary draft that she was intending to subdue the antagonism of the two brothers which was so obvious in her first novel. When she wrote the final version of *Shirley,* she preserved in the relationship of Robert and Louis Moore only a mild contempt for each other's occupation. It is also interesting to note that *Shirley* bears other marks of the earlier *John Henry.* Charlotte had introduced Miss Alicia Wynne, 'the Rose of De Walden Hall' (a recasting of Amelia De Capell and possibly Jane Moore who was the 'Rose of Zamorna') into the *John Henry* manuscript to enliven the beginning of *The Professor* and to define by contrast William's views of his ideal woman. Alicia Wynne's family, the Wynnes of De Walden Hall, reappear in the background of *Shirley* with all the class pretensions she expressed in *John Henry.*

In *Villette,* Charlotte returned to the orphan/governess theme; but not before she had again proposed the publication of *The Professor* and written a preface for it. This famous preface — in which Charlotte states that her hero 'As Adam's son . . . should share Adam's doom, and drain throughout life a mixed and moderate cup of enjoyment' — was probably written at the end of 1849, soon after the publication of *Shirley* in August of that year. It was printed in the posthumous first edition with a note by Charlotte's husband and has appeared in all subsequent editions.

There is, however, an earlier preface to *The Professor,* about which little is known. This unpublished manuscript of one and a half pages seems to have been written much earlier, possibly after the publication of *Jane Eyre.* At this time, 14 December 1847, Charlotte had written to her publishers stating that she had attempted 'three commencements'.[18] We have seen that *John Henry* was one of these; and it is quite possible that this so-called early 'preface' to *The Professor* is another, for this preface is quite unlike the later one.

It begins with an interesting critique of the narrator (William Crimsworth) by the author Charlotte, pointing out personal defects he himself is unaware of and explaining that she, who had known him well and could vouch for his respectability, had undertaken to edit his manuscript. Here, for the first time, is a reworking of the inappropriate letter to Charles at the beginning of *The Professor.* Charlotte excuses the shortness of *The Professor* (one of the causes of its rejection by publishers) by explaining how she adapted this manuscript for her friend:

In its original form it extended to nearly twice its present length, but upon his entrusting it to me for correction and retrenchment (which he did on finding that the various publishers to whom he offered it regarded the MS as a — — and — — at it accordingly) I took the liberty of cutting out the whole of the first seven chapters with one stroke of the scissors. A brief summary of the import of these chapters will content the reader.[19]

Then follows the same summary of the early lives of the two brothers, Edward and William, that we find in *The Professor,* in *John Henry,* and in the juvenilia; after which the manuscript ends abruptly. Besides being an obvious recasting of the early plot of *The Professor,* this unpublished 'preface' is possibly another of the three early 'commencements' to *Shirley, John Henry* being the only one scholars have known of until now.

The writing of a second preface for *The Professor* after the appearance of *Shirley* again failed to tempt Smith, Elder & Co. into publication. Once more Charlotte was forced to relinquish the idea 'under protest', although she was able to incorporate much of the central Brussels section into her new novel. Three fragments relating to Edward and Willie Ellin[20] survive to show that immediately after the publication of *Villette,* Charlotte tried once more to revive the neglected early chapters of *The Professor.* In these fragments, William is a small orphan deprived of his position as a gentleman and forced by his brutal elder brother to become a shop apprentice. Edward, like his various precursors, is 'athletic and red-whiskered'; but his character is now presented in its most extreme form. Willie runs away to his ancestral home, Ellin Hall, but is pursued by the tyrannical Edward with his gig-whip (wielded before in both *The Duke of Zamorna* and *The Professor*).[21] A kindly Jewish merchant, Mr Boas, in a role similar to that of the earlier Yorke Hunsden, prevents Willie's punishment; but the check only strengthens Edward's vindictiveness and, in the final scene we witness Willie's brutal punishment. Again, the two brothers are antipathetic: the sensitive mind of the child is incomprehensible to the gross nature of the mercantile man. Again in her writing, only two years before her death, Charlotte was recasting old material and 'new moulding'[22] her old characters.

30

The Authorial Voice

All Charlotte's novels except *Shirley* are narrated in the first person. Here again, she has preserved a stylistic convention of the juvenilia. The majority of the early manuscripts are signed with a male pseudonym; and where a signature is missing, the voice of Lord Charles Wellesley, Captain Tree or Charles Townshend can almost always be recognized in the tone of the writing and the attitude of the narrator to his characters.[1] It is worth noting how early Charlotte shows the ability to convey the voice of a particular character.

It is not difficult to see the link between the roles the Brontë children acted in their early impromptu plays and their later habit of writing as characters in their Glass Town Saga. Personal involvement may account for the saga's having continued for so long. Certainly in Charlotte's case her imaginative world became an important source of security: it gave her a sense of 'belonging', and took on proportions which threatened to blur different levels of reality in her mind. Well before her emotional crisis at Roe Head, she had considered reality from the point of view of her creations. So real had the world of Glass Town become by August 1830, that she could view with amusement Lord Charles Wellesley's uncertainty 'as to whether I am or am not'. In a surrealistic dream he senses his symbiotic relationship with his creator:

> It seemed as if I was a non-existent shadow — that I neither spoke, eat, imagined, or lived of myself, but I was the mere idea of some other creature's brain. The Glass Town seemed so likewise. My father, Arthur, and everyone with whom I am acquainted, passed into a state of annihilation; but suddenly I thought again that I and my relatives did exist and yet not us but our minds, and our bodies without ourselves.

Then this supposition — the oddest of any — followed the former quickly, namely, that WE without US were shadows; also, but at the end of a long vista, as it were, appeared dimly and indistinctly, beings that really lived in a tangible shape, that were called by our names and were US from whom WE had been copied by something — I could not tell what.[2]

Like Lemuel Gulliver, he feels himself raised to the ceiling by a hand 'wide enough almost to grasp the Tower of all Nations' and stationed opposite two immense sparkling blue globes. Having been returned to the floor again, he sees a huge personification of himself 'hundreds of feet high' and is now convinced of his non-existence 'except in another corporeal frame which dwelt in the real world, for ours I thought was nothing but idea'. An imaginary character's view of reality is a sophisticated concept for a girl of fourteen.

One of the most unusual features of the early manuscripts is their strange amalgam of precocity and naivety. The initial assumption of different voices allowed Charlotte to practise a variety of styles but, as in *Something about Arthur,* the increasing use of the witty satirical narrator (Lord Charles) who must play the role of a child in his own story is often awkward and inappropriate. Because Charlotte fails to observe the limitations of the first person narrator, Lord Charles becomes an implausible character, crouching under tables and behind locked doors in order to be able to overhear and later repeat conversations. He is omniscient and omnipresent, his single viewpoint being used to comment on characters and events. Later, when he becomes Charles Townshend, Charlotte makes an effort to preserve verisimilitude. In the *Duke of Zamorna,* for example, she uses William Percy's letters to Charles to supplement Charles's lack of experience. In *Stancliffe's Hotel,* Charles Townshend again uses William Percy's experience to report on royal events he is now excluded from. But he is always removed from the emotional centre of the stories he tells and he remains an insipid observer.

It was natural that Charlotte should continue the same narrative technique in her first novel: the bloodless hero/narrator of *The Professor* owes much of his pallor and cynicism to Charles Townshend. His narration lacks the emotional intensity of the later Jane Eyre who, unlike Charles Townshend, is the focus of her story. Charlotte is able to identify imaginatively with her because she is female, whereas the preservation of a male narrator in *The Professor* limits her use of experience. In the juvenilia, Charles constantly sympathizes with Zamorna's wives, but nowhere does Charlotte adopt the voice of a female character. When she explores the thoughts of Miss West, Elizabeth Hastings and Caroline

Vernon, she remains an outside observer, despite the autobiographical nature of her material.

Why, then, did Charlotte not use a female narrator in the juvenilia, since this would be the most obvious outlet for autobiographical material? Part of the answer must lie in the fact that to the Brontës writing was very much a male domain. It was Branwell who was taught the classics and so gained entry to the male world of knowledge. It was Branwell who was to have a career, to be first a professional writer and then an artist. It was Branwell who was the first of the Brontë children to appear in print[3] and who had the confidence to send work to the editor of *Blackwood's Magazine*. Above all, it was Branwell who initiated the *Young Men's Magazine* and persuaded Charlotte to contribute. It was accepted that if the girls wrote under assumed names and at the dictation of Branwell, they should impersonate men. Besides, there were no females in the early Branwell-dominated games of war and colonization.

Secondly, when women were introduced into the saga, their roles were restricted by their sex. Marian Hume, with her fairy-tale beauty and timid personality, was hardly the ideal persona for a young girl eager to play her part in controlling events. Charlotte automatically identified in her saga with the power and privilege of the male world which allowed her independence of expression. Such freedom and authority enabled her to think out her own unrealized ambitions. Unequal to Branwell in the nineteenth-century world, she could be a strong rival to his control over their dream world.

As she grew older, Charlotte saw that to write as a man allowed her to exercise the same freedom she had wielded as a child. If violence and passion were male prerogatives then she would be identified as 'male' since these emotions were the grist of her imaginative mill. The later adoption of a male pseudonym for publication was a natural development of this early bid for independence in writing. 'Currer Bell' sought to conceal her identity in an effort to avoid the limitations of the stereotyped 'female novelist'.

It is not obvious in the juvenilia that the assumption of a male voice was a conscious decision; but about the time that she wrote to Southey, in March 1837, she had clearly been considering her position as a female writer. Southey's simultaneous recognition of the talent she possessed 'in no inconsidereable degree'[4] and his strictures that she limit herself to her proper sphere left Charlotte in a dilemma. She replied:

> You do not forbid me to write; you do not say that what I write is utterly
> destitute of merit. You only warn me against the folly of neglecting real

duties for the sake of imaginative pleasure; of writing for the love of fame; for the selfish excitement of emulation.[5]

Her duties as a Victorian woman were in conflict with her emotional need to express herself. If she persisted in writing, she might be neglecting her duty. She knew her perfervid dreams were unhealthy and now the very act of committing them to paper was to be associated with guilt.

The elements of conflict which complicated Charlotte's attitude towards her writing are worth spelling out clearly, since they affected not only her subject matter but also the style of her narration. The ambiguity of her feelings about her writing had its roots in the fact that she delighted in stories of love and sexual passion, yet she felt moral discomfort over the rakish nature of her material. As a woman and as a Christian she seems to have felt considerable unease about her favourite subject matter. In addition there was the fear, brought into sharp focus by Southey, that in writing at all she was tending to neglect the duties proper to a woman for a frivolous and unrewarding occupation. And finally there was her intellectual conviction that the head and not the heart should rule, a conviction which many of her juvenile stories seemed designed to overturn.

Charlotte's moral equivocation about her writing helps to explain her reluctance to replace her narrator, Charles Townshend, with a more central character in the Angrian drama. For a time she had written poetry as the romantic pompous young Marquis of Douro, but as his character altered and he developed into the fascinatingly wicked Zamorna, Charlotte preferred to describe his exploits from a respectable distance. The 'Roe Head Journal' shows the guilt she felt about her increasing attachment to Zamorna and her 'world below'; and Southey's letter had reinforced this. As narrator of Zamorna's deeds, she chose to shelter behind the cynicism of his younger brother. As Lord Charles Wellesley and the later Charles Townshend, she could pretend to disapprove of Zamorna's sinful career.

It is not always easy, however, to judge the moral tone of Charlotte's juvenile writing. Lord Charles's attitude to the central characters is inconsistent and reflects Charlotte's own ambiguous moral attitude to her creations. Lord Charles is not always disapproving: beneath his witty cynicism lurks a vicarious delight in his brother's wicked deeds. His disapproval of Zamorna is rooted in envy. At times in the early stories his cynicism vanishes altogether and Charlotte takes over the narration herself. *Something about Arthur,* for example, begins with a moral maxim. Lord Charles preaches the value of punishment for truancy, but when he begins his exemplum — a tale of one of Zamorna's early peccadilloes — he forgets his intention was critical. None of his usual ridicule is evident in the narration of the romantic part of the story and Zamorna is not criticized for disobeying his father or for his callous treatment of Mina Laury. It is difficult to decide too whether Charlotte is mocking her hero or whether she endorses his exaggerated code of honour. Her tone suggests that she admires his wild posturing and directly contradicts that of her opening chapter.

This ambiguous moral tone is related to her ambivalent attitude to passion. Throughout the juvenilia, so noted for Charlotte's expression of her romantic imagination, there is a distinct theme of anti-romanticism. William Crimsworth's aversion to displays of passion and sentimentality in *The Professor* is clearly anticipated by Charles Townshend. At the beginning of *Stancliffe's Hotel,* for example, Charles deflates Louisa Vernon's romantic reveries of her former elderly husband, the Marquis of Wellesley:

'Charles,' said my fair companion in her usual voice, half a whisper, half a murmur. 'Charles, what a sweet night, a premature summer night. It only wants the moon to make it perfect, then I could see my villa. These stars are not clear enough to bring out the white front fully from its laurels. And yet I do see a white glittering there. Is it not from my drawing-room window?'

'Probably,' was my answer and I said no more. Her ladyship's softness is at times too surfeiting, more especially when she approaches the brink of the sentimental.

'Charles,' she pursued, in no wise abashed by my abrupt coolness. 'How many fond recollections come on us at such a time as this. Where do you think my thoughts always stray on a summer night? What image do you think "a cloudless clime and stormy skies" always suggest?'

'Perhaps,' said I, 'that of the most noble Richard, Marquis of Wellesley as you last saw him reposing in gouty chair and stool, with eyelids gently closed by the influence of the pious libations in claret with which he has concluded the dinner of rice-currie, devilled turkey and guava.'[6]

In *Henry Hastings,* Charles Townshend mocks the heroine, Mary Percy, as she displays her displeasure at her husband's philandering and in *Caroline Vernon,* he pillories Zamorna's Byronic pretensions. But it is the mockery of romanticism in the early juvenilia, so pervaded by fairy-tale motif, that is surprising. In the *Young Men's Magazine* for November 1830, Charlotte includes a song by Lord Charles Wellesley in which he jibes at his brother's penchant for lugubrious subjects. The song was suggested by Edward Young's *Night Thoughts on Life, Death and Immortality* which Mr Brontë owned and which Charlotte had read earlier that year;[7] and it parodies the work of the 'graveyard poets':

Some love Sorrow's dismal howls,
Write verses on her sighs and scowls
And rant about her mourning dress,
Her long black funeral array,
Her veil which shuts out light and day
    And love her not the less;

Although She sits with woeful face
On some old monumental tomb,
Where yellow skulls and bones have place,
Where corpses rot in churchyard gloom.

I wish some eve as thus she's weeping,
While sober men are soundly sleeping,
Hid [by] the obscurity of night,
From out its grave a ghost would start
And make her throat receive her heart
    And give her sore affright.[8]

Charlotte was taught early that reason was superior to passion. Her early reading reinforced this. In *The Poetaster,* Lord Charles satirizes his brother's adolescent illusions of romantic love. He describes a dream in which he sees the Marquis of Douro's bleeding heart delivered to Marian Hume by Cupid. The smiling Marian then lacerates the heart with very fine scissors, while the Marquis frowns, weeps and sighs pitifully, as Lord Charles suggests he does in his nauseously sentimental rhymes. Charlotte had been reading Jonson's *Poetaster* in which Ovid is criticized for wasting his talents on erotic poems. Charlotte was not slow to learn that the device of a cynical narrator allowed her simultaneously to criticize and to indulge in her romantic fantasies.

Until the end of 1830, her romantic and anti-romantic themes were more or less distinguished by the separate voices of the Marquis of Douro and Lord Charles Wellesley; but when Lord Charles, the anti-romantic, begins to dominate the narration Charlotte's natural preference for romance caused confusion. This is especially marked in the second period of her juvenile writing when she is often carried away by the narration of a love story and, as in *Something about Arthur,* forgets the cynicism of Lord Charles. The two conflicting attitudes run side by side through a single narration. In the later juvenilia, Charlotte became more adept at masking her feelings; but the basic conflict between her attachment to her subject and her critical conscience, expressed by her narrator, extended throughout her writing. Even the outwardly sober Lucy Snowe who protests, 'Of an artistic temperament I deny that I am,' betrays her nature in every character sketch and literary allusion.

Charlotte gradually learned to confine her view to the limitations of a single character and to use that narrator's personality in her writing. Lord Charles's perversity, for example, allows her to change styles rapidly and to play with the reader. In *Henry Hastings*, he writes with approval of the Verdopolitan Parliament, then immediately undercuts his previous assertion by saying that he wrote it 'merely as a specimen of a certain style':

> my dear reader, when you are inclined to grow enthusiastic about such things — just recall my image — leaning over the gallery with my hat on & alternately squeezing & sucking a remarkably fine madeira orange — & meantime cocking my eye at the honourable gent on his legs with an expression sufficiently indicative of the absorbing interest I take in his speechifications.[9]

Except in the 'Roe Head Journal', 'the reader' plays an important part in Charlotte's early writings. Lord Charles's aim is always to please: his literary efforts are likened to a 'frail bark' launched on the 'boistrous tide of public opinion.'[10] The concept of an audience (however imaginary) and the need to communicate, which appear in the earliest of Charlotte's stories, are underlined by her constant reference to the image of a stage, especially at the beginning and end of chapters.[11] The 'first scene' of *High Life In Verdopolis,* for example, 'is placed in the breakfast-room of Warner Hotel'. Chapter 1 concludes when the grand party at Wellesley House moves off-stage to the supper room 'through wide-flung folding doors and uplifted draperies, and so for the present (Exeunt Omnes)'. The image is even more explicit at the end of chapter 2 when the 'voile du théâtre' is dropped by the author and then 'raised again' in the following chapter.[12]

Charlotte's role as stage-manager, implicit in her early position as landlord and controlling genie in her stories, is not unlike that of Thackeray or Fielding. Particularly in her later stories, we are conducted through a series of scenes, sometimes with moral judgements but always with the prejudiced comments of Lord Charles Wellesley or Charles Townshend. At the beginning of *The Return of Zamorna,* Charles explains the pictorial nature of his method:

> Oh reader what a strange aspect of uncertainty hangs over everything. Do you not now feel in doubt as to what picture the sketchy and airy Townshend will first present to your fancy. I have you by the hand and am your guide, and we are in a long gallery, the paintings of which are all veiled. . . Sit down on that antique chair in the centre and I will pass silently round and draw the curtains one by one.[13]

The self-conscious author is present in Charlotte's earliest productions: in the frequent apostrophes to the reader; in the detailed documentation of the formation of the 'plays' and the noting of the exact time that a story took to write; in the title-pages and careful production of her magazines; and in her detailed *Catalogue of my Books,* 'with the periods of their completion up to August 3, 1830'. The fourteen-year-old Charlotte notes for example in the Preface to *The Adventure's of Mon Edouard de Crack:*

> I began this Book on the 22 of February 1830 and finished it on the 23 of February 1830, doing 8 pages on the first day and 11 on the second. On the first day I wrote an hour and a half in the morning and an hour and a half in the evening. On the third day I wrote a quarter of an hour in the morning, 2 hours in the afternoon and a quarter of an hour in the evening, making in the whole 5 hours and a half. CB[14]

Her care in dating and signing almost all her manuscripts also reflects her early awareness of her role as an author. What has been seen as the 'suspicious multiplicity'[15] of signatures in some of Charlotte's writings is common in all her volumes of more than one work. In *Corner Dishes,* for example, Charlotte has signed each of the three items and the Preface to the whole volume.

Albion and Marina explicitly 'sets up no pretensions' to being a novel; but by the end of the second period of her writing, Charlotte is at pains to include in her stories what she sees as the necessary conventions of a novel: 'A novel can scarcely be called a novel unless it ends in a marriage, therefore I herewith tack to, add, and communicate the following *postscriptum.*'[16] In *The Spell,* she includes not only this conventional ending but she also experiments with the use of letters and extracts from a journal as part of her text, a possible borrowing from Richardson. It is interesting to compare the opening scenes of *Shirley* with Charlotte's early notion that it is 'good policy in an author to make the first pages of his book of a light and miscellaneous character'.[17] In the later juvenilia, all her comical and satirical episodes, such as those relating to Methodism, occur in the first chapters of her stories. The author of *High Life In Verdopolis* explains that he opens his narrative with an extract from Captain Tree's 'Verdopolitan Magazine' not because he agrees with it, but because 'it serves well as an introduction to a book which treats principally of lords, ladies, knights and squires of high degree'. In this same manuscript Charlotte prefaces each chapter with an appropriate quotation from Byron's *Childe Harold's Pilgrimage,*[18] a method probably derived from Scott.

Authors hold a high position in Glass Town society. Their ambitions are dramatized in the early rivalries between Captain Tree and Lord Charles Wellesley. The variety of narrative techniques used by Charlotte — the portrait, the allegory, the dream sequence, the tale-within-a-tale,[19] the dialogue, the newspaper review — show an early critical attitude to the art of writing. As this awareness increases, Charlotte's view of the 'book-wright's' material changes. We see a gradual progression towards realism. Charlotte becomes more aware of her redundant style: 'I keep heaping epithets together and I cannot describe what I mean.'[20] Occasionally she reins herself in:

> I could have grown poetical. I could have recalled more distant and softer scenes touched with the light of other years, hallowed by higher, because older, associations than the campaign of — 33, the rebellion of — 36. I might have asked how Sunshine yet became the elms and the turret of Wood-Church, but I restrained myself.[21]

Probably with the juvenilia in mind, William Crimsworth refers in *The Professor* to 'pictures chequered with vivid contrasts of light and shade'.[22] These could be avoided, he states, if novelists never allowed themselves to weary of 'the study of real life.' We have seen that Charlotte was already attempting to observe this principle in *Henry Hastings* and *Caroline Vernon.*

31

A Visual Imagination

Observation of the real world was not new to Charlotte. Ellen Nussey tells how her friend 'began to analyze character when she was five years old'[1] and even the earliest juvenile writings show a marked attention to detail. The habit of close observation was fostered by her early lessons in drawing and lies at the basis of her later mastery of character and scene.

Mrs Gaskell speaks of the strong yearning which the whole Brontë family had towards the art of drawing: 'the girls themselves loved everything connected with it — all descriptions or engravings of great pictures; and, in default of good ones, they would take and analyse any print or drawing which came in their way'.[2] Branwell too showed much enthusiasm and some talent for painting, talent which was encouraged by Mr Brontë who employed several art teachers for his children. Charlotte's first letter tells how she and her sisters have been copying 'some views of the lakes' which her Uncle Fennell had brought from Westmoreland.[3] She often describes in her stories a scene she has just copied, usually from a current periodical. Her imitation of Gilpin's 'Cross of Rivaulx' (see plate 26), for example, inspired her verbal picture of the surroundings of the hunting lodge of the same name in *Passing Events.*

> there are no decided grounds laid out about the Cross of Rivaulx, but a lawn-like greenness surrounds it & the last remnants of Hawkscliffe shade it in the form of many wild rose trees & a few lofty elms. You look in vain for anything like a wall or gate to shut it in — the only landmark consists in an old Obelisk with moss & wild flowers at its base and an half obliterated crucifix sculptured on its side.[4]

Charlotte's copies of several of Finden's Byronic landscapes and heroines survive[5] and it is well known that the historical painter Martin, four of whose engravings hung on the parsonage walls, inspired some of her

26   *'The Cross of Rivaulx' by Charlotte Brontë after Gilpin,*
23 December 1834

earliest scenic descriptions.[6] It was Martin's vast architectural scenes of massive rectangular palaces and towers, punctuated by rows of cylindrical columns, that suggested Charlotte's original conception of Glass Town. Her 'Tower of All Nations', rising in the midst of the Glass Town landscape (see plate 15), is a copy of The Tower of Babel in Martin's painting 'The Fall of Babylon'.[7] Her descriptions of Adrianopolis, the imperial capital of Angria, are even more obviously influenced by 'Martin' — Martin, whose name now appeared among the artists of the new city as Sir John Martin Dundee.

> At first the scene that burst so unexpectedly on my vision only inspired vague ideas of boundless grandeur, but soon I was able to take a calmer and more careful view. What seemed solemn, vast, undefined, as the hoary cone of CAUCASUS ere long settled down into an edifice of mason's work. It stretched indeed far away and ascended to a sublime height but still its limits were well and clearly outlined. A mighty row of marble pillars, pale and gleaming as ice receded in their grand perspective before me. Their eternal basements, their Giant shafts, their gorgeous capitals, the long, long, high-uplifted cornice that ran above them, were all of the purest, the noblest Grecian moulding. All breathed of Ionia in her loftiest times.[8]

Among the earliest surviving manuscripts, written when she was about thirteen, is a *list of painters whose works I wish to see,* which includes such well-known names as Titian, Raphael, Michaelangelo, Guido Reni, Fra Bartolomeo and Correggio.[9] The names of local Yorkshire painters, such as William Etty, have their counterparts in the juvenilia. There they are associated with the Verdopolitan aristocracy. When William Etty, RA follows Zamorna to Angria he is knighted for his services to art in the new kingdom. He is shown at work in his artist's studio, a sensitive man unwilling to be disturbed by the garrulous Lord Charles who surveys and comments on his latest paintings.[10]

The Young Men's Magazine includes advertisements and reviews of paintings,[11] stories about artists and discussions on the 'sublime art of painting' — not the 'mechanical skill' of the portrait painter but 'the higher art' of painting the 'bold and rugged mountains'.[12] Charlotte had

27   *Manuscript page of an early draft of Charlotte Brontë's poem*
'The moon dawned slow in the dusky gloaming', January 1834

heard of the wild romantic scenes of Salvator Rosa.[13] Her manuscripts are often embellished with hasty sketches of heroes and heroines (see plate 27).

At fourteen she was writing her own critiques of engravings: she would study a picture for hours although she knew that 'gazing at small and exquisitely finished pictures is apt to ruin one's eyesight'.[14] In *Cam[p]bell Castle* (30 September 1830), based on an engraving in *Friendship's Offering* (1829), Charlotte discusses the perspective, the variation of light and shade which throws the castle into focus, the mountains which are 'not very picturesque', the action in the foreground which enlivens the scene, and the sky, 'variegated by light fleecy clouds that have assumed the form of a grand aërial arch spanning the space above the castle like an irregular rainbow'.[15]

The same analytic approach is used by Charlotte in the description of her imaginary scenes. In *Liffey Castle,* 'A Tale by C Wellesley', Lord Charles goes on a 'pedestrian escursion' in southern Ireland. The result is a detailed natural description of an early morning scene:

> snails and worms luxuriate in dampness under the heath and hawthorn hedges glittering with dew or white with blossoms, and star-eyed robin-flowers and stately fairy-caps are seen gleaming from trailing underwood by the roadside, or crowning with crimson bells the sloping green banks.[16]

In *The Spell,* Charlotte paints a 'lovely prospect of Douro Villa' in terms reminiscent of the pictures in Humphrey Repton's little red books: the 'vast slopes of verdure, varied by large stately trees', the deer, the 'low knoll of shaven lawn' leading to the Grecian villa and the contrasted planting of light and dark greenery. For Charlotte, no landscape was complete without figures, and her 'pencil, or rather pen' proceeds to draw 'one or two of these animating adjuncts on the canvas.'[17] Throughout her writing she retained this method of ordering her material: a character is seldom introduced until a scene has been drawn in detail. The character is then provided with a context which both defines and acts upon him.

All Charlotte's experience appears to have arranged itself in pictorial form, in much the same way as it does for William Crimsworth in *The Professor.*[18] For Jane Eyre, too, a new face was 'like a new picture introduced to the gallery of memory'.[19] People are described in the juvenilia as if they are portraits. Indeed, many of Charlotte's verbal pictures correspond to drawings of Angrian characters and scenes. The description of Mina Laury with her 'profusion of dark hair', her 'complexion of the richest brunette' and dress of black satin with gold chain, cross and earrings,[20] is closely related to Charlotte's copy of 'The Maid of Saragoza' (see plate 23), an engraving by Finden for Byron's *Childe Harold's*

Pilgrimage. Caroline Vernon's forehead is 'pencilled with soft dusk curls — dark & touching eyes & a round youthful cheek, smooth in texture & fine in tint — as that of some portrait hung in an Italian Palace'.[21] Colour is an important adjunct to character: Marian is always dressed in white, Zenobia 'in her usual attire of a crimson-velvet robe and black plumes'.[22] Crimson is worn by all Zamorna's admirers: it has associations of luxury and decadence whch extend even to Mr Rochester's den in *Jane Eyre.*[23]

Yet it is the facial features that distinguish a portrait, for here Charlotte can minutely observe and 'read' the true character.[24] William Moore, though his eyesight is defective (as Charlotte's was), is able to perceive Alicia Wynne's true nature: 'The fact was, he had dived into Alicia's eyes and seen covetousness at the bottom of them. He had run his glance along her features and felt where the illiberal heart gave harshness to their outline, narrowness to their significance.'[25] When Ellen Grenville discusses her suitors, her initial reaction to Lord Macara Lofty is based on her interpretation of his eyes: 'I feel afraid of him. He has such strange eyes, so sly and dangerous and with an obliquity of vision that is absolutely startling.'[26] By contrast, Warner — despite his 'little silly hands' and smooth, beardless chin — has 'eyes like living diamonds' which reflect a depth of character and he is therefore preferred. It is in Mr Rochester's eyes in particular, that Jane Eyre can read his worth, and he, in turn, warns her of his ability to interpret the 'language' of her eyes.[27]

In the juvenilia, as in the later novels, the ability to judge character from facial features is indicative of intelligence. Warner's powers of judging character and predicting the future are treated with great respect by his associates. William Percy, Miss West and Elizabeth Hastings pride themselves on their ability to understand human nature: their moral judgements are based firmly on observation. William Percy, like his later counterpart William Crimsworth, practises his physiognomy on everyone he meets. Charles Townshend tells us how William 'searched' the countenance of the beautiful Jane Moore and was not particularly pleased with the result of his 'scrutiny'. He decides that 'there's no mind there and very little heart.'[28]

Charlotte's intelligent characters also have the ability to observe natural phenomena patiently, in particular the sky. Elizabeth Hastings finds solace and excitement in the sky: her curtains are left undrawn and her feverish dreams feed on the rising moon.[29] Charlotte herself believed that the sky was a valuable companion for anyone living in solitude, more important even than her beloved moors. She impressed Mrs Gaskell by her 'careful examination of the shape of the clouds and the signs of the heavens, in which she read, as from a book, what the coming weather would be'.[30] In *Cam[p]bell Castle* it is the engraver's handling of the sky which for Charlotte gives the picture its 'consummate genius'.[31] Her early manuscripts show that she was as sensitive to the sky in landscapes as she was to the language of the eye in portraits.

Constant references to the weather and the time of the year give the Angrian stories solidity. Climate (which becomes increasingly English rather than African) is an accompaniment to personal feelings: as the last days of autumn decline and the 'leaf-strewn walks and embrowned groves' prophesy winter, Mary Henrietta, 'wasted and blanched' herself by the desertion of Zamorna, paces the corridors and terraces of Alnwick (see plate 28). When damp December draws on she becomes corpse-like.[32] Before his visit to fairyland, Ernenst Alembert is 'often chilled by frost and icy winds, and saddened by the absence of the cheering warmth of the sun.'[33] By contrast, in 'the land of Faery' the sun never sets.

The warm, fecund atmosphere of Africa obviously appealed to Charlotte, and the sun rises and sets with the varying fortunes of Zamorna's Angrian faction throughout the pages of the early manuscripts. Angrian characters are affected by sunrise and sunset: Zamorna reflects, 'ever since I can remember the rays of the setting sun have acted on my heart, as they did on Memnon's wondrous statue.'[34] In *The Professor* too, William Crimsworth's first real sense of freedom is associated with the rising sun: 'Liberty I clasped in my arms for the first time, and the influence of her smile and embrace revived my life like the sun and the west wind. . . my imagination was with the refulgent firmament beyond.' Later in the novel,

28   *The Duchess of Zamorna at Alnwick. Pencil drawing by Charlotte Brontë, c. 1836*

a vivid sunset takes on supernatural significance.[35] Both the sunset and later vision are described in pictorial terms.

Charlotte's love for the sun and her later use of it as a symbol of hope and warmth of character, probably reflected a basic reaction to the inhospitable Yorkshire climate. In the early manuscripts, however, the image carries mythic and biblical associations. In the manuscripts of 1834, with the formation of Angria, the image of the sun becomes associated with Zoroastrianism. Charlotte's knowledge of this ancient Persian religion may have come from recent history lessons at school or from books in the Brontë parsonage. Certainly the *Bibliotheca Classica* on her father's shelves[36] contained references to Alexander the Great's campaigns against the Persians, to Mithras, god of light (whom Charlotte mistakenly identifies as the sun) and to such Persian leaders as Darius and Zenobia.[37]

In her poem *Death of Darius Codomannus* (1 May 1834), Charlotte describes the doom of the Persian Empire in words that recall her prophecy of the violent destruction of Angria in *A Leaf from an Unopened Volume,* written four months earlier. Both manuscripts refer to the evil deeds of the 'Persian Satrap'. In death, Darius is deserted by 'the glorious host/That bowed to Mithras' beam', his empire's streams are dyed with blood and 'Mithras' gorgeous standard' is furled.[38]

Angria reflects the glory and despotism of the ancient Persian Empire. Zamorna and his new kingdom, founded to the east of the Glass Town Federation, are constantly associated with the rising sun. Lord Charles Wellesley scorns the 'flash and bustle and rising sunism' in Angria's affairs. The Angrians are 'fire-worshippers', their banner is 'fire-dyed' and their motto is 'Arise'. Their monarch is likened to Apollo in his beauty and his actions:

> At that instant a splendid chariot was thundering in from Grenville Street. The first flash of its rich emblazonry told who was the occupant. The vehicle of polished, glorious green, the rising sun blazing in gold on its panels, the outriders in the emerald livery of the house of Wellesley, the magnificent horses foaming and tossing their heads like charges of the Sun, all as they dashed glancing and flashing forwards proclaimed the young monarch of awakening Angria.[39]

A Leaf from an Unopened Volume tells us that Zamorna is to become the Emperor Adrian, an 'African Potentate', an 'imperial despot'.[40] In other manuscripts of 1834 he is already 'the young satrap of Angria'.[41] When Lord Charles describes a recent painting of him by De Lisle, he describes a sun-god: 'Fire! Light! What have we here? Zamorna's self, blazing in the frontispiece like the sun on his own standard.'[42]

Another possible source for Charlotte's identification of the rising sun with Angria may be the Book of Isaiah lix, 19, which is paraphrased by Zamorna in his *Letter to the right honourable Arthur Marquis of Ardrah:* 'So shall they hear my name from the West and my glory from the rising Sun, when the enemy shall come like a flood I will lift up my Standard against him.'[43] Zamorna tells his audience to 'Read, mark, learn and inwardly digest' this text: it is his guiding principle. Ellen Nussey remembered that at Roe Head Charlotte was particularly familiar with Isaiah 'in which she took great delight'.[44]

The Bible was a fertile source of imagery and inspiration for the young author. The drama and colour of the Old Testament and the prophetic visions of the New Testament appealed especially to Charlotte's pictorial imagination. The world of the genii owes as much to the Book of The Revelation as it does to the *Arabian Nights* and the *Tales of the Genii.* A fairy palace in *The Search after Happiness* is as fabulous in conception as the new Jerusalem with its brilliant light and its buildings of precious stones and streets of pure gold:

> The tall stately pillars reaching from heaven to earth were formed of the finest and purest diamonds the pavement sparkling with gold and precious stones and the mighty dome made solem and awful by its stupendous magnitude was of one single emerald. In the midst of this grand and magnificent palace was a lamp like the sun the radiance of which made all the palace to flash and glitter with an almost fearful grandeur. The ruby sent forth a stream of crimson light the topaz gold the saphire intensest purple and the dome poured a flood of deep clear splendour which overcame all the other gaudy lights by its mild triumphant glory.[45]

Many of Charlotte's tales have a moral drawn explicitly from the Bible: in *Leisure Hours,* for example, 'charity and mercy shall have their reward'.[46] Several stories in *Tales of the Islanders* are based on religious themes;[47] there are constant references to Catholic emancipation and Calvinist doctrines; much of Lord Charles Wellesley's cynicism is couched in Biblical terms (as in the opening of *My Angria and the Angrians*); and Charlotte's chief source of comedy is the extravagances of Methodism and the wayward clergy of the Established Church.[48] Northangerland's blighted life and frustrated ambitions are always associated with his denial of the after-life and his confessed atheism: he has 'hid [his] face from the light and then denied its existence'.[49]

The juvenilia show that Charlotte herself drew comfort from the stories of early Christians. On 30 August 1832, she wrote a poem on St John the Divine describing how through his heavenly visions he overcame exile on the Isle of Patmos, 'The doom of thraldom and captivity'. His revelation is described in terms like those used to describe the fairy world of Charlotte's earliest manuscripts:

> The armèd hosts of God, in panoply
>   Of splendour most insufferably bright,
> Rush forth triumphant from the parting sky,
>   Whose wide arch yawns before those floods of light.
>
> He hears the voices of Archangels tell
>   The doom, the fiery, fearful doom of Earth;
> And as the trumpet's tones still louder swell,
>   On the dark world red plagues are poured forth.[50]

Again, the brilliance of the angel host, the trumpets, the thunder, the 'rainbow radiance' of the new Jerusalem, the harmonious music, and the plagues sent to punish sinful men are echoed in the world of the all-powerful Chief Genii.

In her frustrated 'exile' as a teacher Charlotte felt nothing but resentment towards her pupils. She longed for 'that lofty faith' which made St Stephen, the first martyr, bless his foes. At the beginning of a long unpublished poem, written about January 1836, she recalls how as a child she wept when she read of Stephen's calmness in the face of violent death:

> Oh! could I feel the holy glow
>   That brightened death for him;
> I'd cease to weep that all below
>   Is grown so drear and dim.
>
> Could I but gain that lofty faith
>   Which made him bless his foes,
> I'd fix my anchor, firm till death,
>   My hope's divine repose.[51]

Troubled too at this time by Branwell's new series of wars against Angria which threatened her 'world below', Charlotte wrote in the margin beside these lines 'This hope's divine'.

Zamorna also acknowledges the example of the Patriarchs and Christian martyrs, and recognizes the 'exalted soul of the Christian philosopher'[52] in his righteous friend John Sneachie, Duke of Fidena:

> the greatest man is he who has the strongest control over his rebellious passions, who can best separate his mortal from his immortal part, his corruptible body from his incorruptible spirit, who can give the last government over the first, and thereby obtain and keep a more exalted order of feeling than belonged to him by nature: such a man is higher than humanity.[53]

Similarly, Elizabeth Hastings struggles to control and hide her passionate nature but cannot deny its existence. Zamorna, like Jane Eyre, can bow before such stern embodiments of intellect and religion as John Sneachie and St John Rivers, but 'cannot and will not follow [their] precepts'. His destiny lies down another pathway and, like a pilgrim, he must 'travel forward through the wilderness of this world'.[54]

Even Charlotte's view of her creative process is described in biblical phrases:

> It is the still small voice alone that comes to me at eventide; that which like a breeze with a voice in it over the deeply blue hills and out of the now leafless forests and from the cities on distant river banks of a far and bright continent. It is that which takes my spirit and engrosses all my living feelings, all my energies which are not merely mechanical and, like Haworth and home, wakes sensations which lie dormant elsewhere. Last night I did indeed lean upon the thunder-wakening wings of such a stormy blast as I have seldom heard blow and it whirled me away like heath in the wilderness for five seconds of ecstasy.[55]

Her imagination was essentially visual. Her method of writing was trance-like. She had merely to shut her eyes to see those forms and features which, as she told Hartley Coleridge, were so realistic that, like Pygmalion's statue, they appeared to have a life beyond that of their creator.[56] In her 'Roe Head Journal', Charlotte stresses the reality of her visions: the accent is always on sight:

> I see distinctly their figures and, though alone, I experience all the feelings of one admitted for the first time into a grand circle of classic beings — recognizing by tone, gesture and aspect hundreds whom I never saw before, but whom I have heard of and read of many a time, and is not this enjoyment?[57]

Romantic stories — from the Bible, from antiquity, from Persian tales, from the lives of historical personages or local legend — are glimpsed by the precocious child 'as through a glass darkly'.[58] They are recalled later by the adolescent and woven into that 'web of waking visions' which relate to 'a far and bright continent.'

Charlotte built up a whole pictorial world from which to select her material for writing. An etching or a name would activate her imagination:

> Linked with the name of every land
>   Some thought will rise, some scene unfold,
> The bending wood, the barren sand,
>   The lake, the Nile, the dreary wold.[59]

Her writing was a retreat into this 'other' world: her visions became 'the ark', a haven from 'this world's desolate and boundless deluge'.[60]

Conclusion

In renouncing her commitment to the world of Glass Town and Angria, Charlotte renounced also the framework in which her imagination could work. Slowly she built up a view of her own experience which was to replace her imaginary world. She had already begun to do this in the later juvenilia, as her attitude towards her writing grew more critical. Yet, as we have seen in *Ashworth,* it was a struggle to explore those 'cooler' regions which were to be the material of *The Professor.* With its Yorkshire setting but heavy reliance on the Angrian saga, *Ashworth* merely confirmed the fears expressed in her 'Farewell to Angria' and indicated the need for new material.

As Charlotte grew older and saw more of life, especially during her years in Brussels, her new fund of experience would replace the Angrian plot. She would have new characters from life to analyse, as was her habit, and to introduce into her writing. Occasionally their looks, habits or background would smack of the old imaginary world; for as Charlotte later said, very little of her work was founded solely on experience of reality: 'We only suffer reality to *suggest,* never to *dictate.*'[1] Echoes of Angrian characters and plot can be found in all Charlotte's novels and later fragmentary writing and there has been an effort to note many of these in the previous pages; but it would be wrong to exaggerate the importance of the juvenilia to the later work. There are similarities, for example, between Shirley and the patriotic Angrian beauty Jane Moore, who has been said to represent Emily Brontë;[2] but unlike Shirley or Emily, Jane Moore is insensitive, 'flashy' and 'overbearing'. Nor is Rochester a Europeanized Angrian: he is as much a product of Charlotte's more mature imagination as he is a representative of either Angria's hero or

Monsieur Heger, the Brussels school-master whom she grew to love and respect.

The world of Glass Town and Angria provided the stimulus to create but it also had its drawbacks for the young author. We have seen how Charlotte eventually became tired of the repetitive Angrian scene with its emphasis on high life and romantic intrigue. Yet she had realized that to quit her familiar 'world below' would leave her like a stranger in a distant country, where 'every face was unknown and the character of all the population an enigma which it would take much study to comprehend and much talent to expound'.[3] Self-discipline was needed if she was to reject the most readily available source of material. It was relatively easy to change the setting of her stories from Africa to England; but it took time to wean herself from the multiplicity of characters related to Angria. This excessive proliferation was obviously one of Hartley Coleridge's criticisms of the *Ashworth* draft which Charlotte had sent him. She admitted that she had materials in her head for at least half a dozen volumes:

> I should have made quite a Richardsonian concern of it. Mr. West should have been my Sir Charles Grandison, Percy my Mr. B——, and the ladies should have represented Pamela, Clarissa, Harriet Byron, etc. Of course, it is with considerable regret that I relinquish any scheme so charming as the one I have sketched.[4]

Working within a smaller framework became one of Charlotte's aims in her later writing. The tight interrelationship of characters and plot in *Jane Eyre,* for example, marks a major departure from the juvenilia. Only *Mina Laury* and perhaps *Caroline Vernon* could be said to show this concision. With no Angrian framework, Charlotte was forced to plan her stories in detail, as we see from the surviving *Scheme of a Mag[azine] Tale* written inside the front cover of an old French exercise book.[5] This was probably written at home in the months preceding the creation of *The Professor,* although it contains elements relevant to each of Charlotte's later novels. One of her main concerns in this plan appears under the heading 'Characters', where she noted 'Moderation to be observed here. Friends — avoid Richardsonian multiplication'. A postscript follows: 'As much compression — as little explanation as may be.' The advice of Hartley Coleridge and the failure of *Ashworth,* her first attempt at a non-Angrian story, had taught her the necessity of restraint. This had been reinforced by Monsieur Heger's correction of her *devoirs.*[6] He had censured her tendency to redundancy and digression, and her 'bad habit' of 'seeing everything through "the coloured glass" of simile'.[7]

With this experience in mind, she had written *The Professor* according to a set of realistic 'principles'.[8] Her style and subject were to be 'plain and homely'; her hero, like every son of Adam, was to share Adam's doom and to 'drain throughout life a mixed and moderate cup of enjoyment'. A negative response from the publishers soon proved her system wrong. She found that principles 'generally approved in theory' were not always true in practice. *The Professor* was too mundane, too realistic and devoid of interest. Chastened by the restraint she had imposed on her imagination, however, Charlotte was able to return with a more critical attitude to the world of romance. If *The Professor* can be seen as an over-reaction to the extravagances of her juvenilia, then in *Jane Eyre* she found a successful compromise.

In *Jane Eyre* Charlotte dispensed with the male narrator she had used throughout her juvenilia and preserved in *The Professor*. Until then she had lacked the confidence to relinquish the cynical voice that protected her from admitting, sometimes even to herself, her attachment to the passionate world of Angria. She had felt guilty about the nature of her visions and her idolatry of Zamorna. Lord Charles had allowed her to feel less guilty, to distance herself from her 'sinful' creations; but he had also drained her stories of the emotional commitment found in *Jane Eyre* and glimpsed in the juvenilia only in the 'Roe Head Journal' and in the passages related to Miss West and Elizabeth Hastings. As Charlotte became more aware of her position in society, her writing became more consciously autobiographical and more realistic; but she was slow to learn that her narrator and heroine might share the same imaginative experience.

A study of the world of Glass Town and Angria provides evidence of Charlotte's apprenticeship in writing, of her early awareness of her role as an author and of the formation of her visual imagination; but it is not a formula by which to interpret the novels. As Mrs Gaskell recorded, Charlotte took pleasure in 'new moulding characters, giving unthought of turns to incidents, rejecting carefully-elaborated old ideas, and suddenly creating and adopting new ones'.[9] What is remarkable about the juvenilia is not that Charlotte had a creative childhood, but that the imaginary world of that childhood should have continued to preoccupy her for so long. Not until the age of twenty-three did she have the courage to reject it. The hypnotic attraction of Angria had stunted her development as a writer of realistic fiction; it was only grudgingly, and over a period of years, that childhood romance gave way to the balanced perception of reality that marks her mature work.

Appendix A: A List of Other Principal Characters in the Juvenilia

Ardrah, Arthur Parry, Marquis of: contemporary and rival of Zamorna. Heir to Parrisland (or Parry's Land).

Bud, Captain John: an eminent Glass Town political writer and contemporary of the Duke of Wellington. Friend of the young Lord Charles Wellesley and father of Sergeant Bud, a rascally lawyer. (A pseudonym of Branwell.)

Castlereagh, Frederick Stuart, Viscount Lord: Earl of Stuartville after the creation of Angria. Married to Harriet. Contemporary and friend of Zamorna.

De Lisle, Frederick (or Sir Edward): an eminent Verdopolitan portrait painter. Patronized first by St Clair and then by Zamorna.

Enara, Henry Fernando di: an Italian known as 'The Tiger'. Commander-in-Chief of the Angrian forces and friend of Lord Hartford and Zamorna.

Flower, Sir John, Viscount Richton: an eminent scholar and Verdopolitan Ambassador to Angria. Contemporary of the Duke of Wellington. (A pseudonym of Branwell in the later juvenilia.)

Grenville, General: an eminent mill-owner and father of Ellen Grenville who marries Warner Howard Warner.

Hartford, General Edward, Lord: an Angrian nobleman, who, after an unsuccessful attempt to win the affections of Mina Laury, recovers to court Jane Moore.

Hastings, Elizabeth: a loyal Angrian and sister of Captain Henry Hastings. Companion to Jane Moore.

Hastings, Captain Henry: a popular young Angrian soldier and author, who degenerates into a drunken murderer. (A pseudonym of Branwell in the later juvenilia.)

Jordon, Lord: brother of Augusta (or Maria) di Segovia, who squanders his fortune on her lover and later husband, Alexander Percy. As the Sheik Medina, he and his troops are a constant threat to Angria.

Laury, Mina: daughter of Sergeant Ned Laury, a 'rare lad' and retainer of the Duke of Wellington. Loyal mistress of Zamorna and hostess of the Cross of Rivaulx, the lodge of Hawkscliffe Estate.

Lofty, Lord Macara: the scoundrelly younger brother of the Earl of Arundel and friend of Lord Charles Wellesley.

Montmorency, Hector Matthias Mirabeau: a Verdopolitan nobleman, contemporary of the Duke of Wellington and 'familiar' of the young Alexander Percy. Married Harriet O'Connor, sister of Arthur O'Connor. Montmorency's daughter Julia married Sir William Etty, a disowned son of Alexander Percy by his first wife Maria di Segovia.

Moore, Jane: an Angrian beauty known as 'The Rose of Zamorna'; youngest daughter of George Moore, lawyer and toadie of Lord Hartford whom Jane intends to marry.

Naughty, Richard (Young Man Naughty): a Glass Town villain and associate of Ned Laury. Later, as Richard Naughten (or, Mange) he rouses the lower classes of Verdopolis in support for Northangerland (Alexander Percy).

O'Connor, Arthur: a profligate associate of Alexander Percy, who seduces O'Connor's sister, Harriet, and then deserts her.

Parry, Sir William Edward: king of Parrisland (Parry's Land) and father of Arthur, Marquis of Ardrah.

Quashia Quamina: son of Sai-Too-Too, King of the Ashantees. When his father dies, he is adopted by the Duke of Wellington; but he becomes the enemy of the Duke's son, Zamorna, and his new kingdom of Angria.

Rosier, Eugene: Zamorna's French page.

Ross, Captain John: king of Rossesland (Ross's Land) and father of Edward Tut Ross, Marquis of Harlaw and friend of Arthur, Marquis of Ardrah.

S'Death, or Robert King: the hideous red-haired minion of Alexander Percy.

Simpson, Jeremiah: a banker and associate of Montmorency. As 'Macterrorglen', he joins Lord Jordon, Julian Gordon and Quashia in support of Northangerland (Alexander Percy) in the war against the Verdopolitan Union and an independent Angria.

Soult, Alexander, Marquis of Marseilles, Duke of Dalmatia: known as 'The Rhymer' in the early juvenilia. A Glass Town poet patronized by Zamorna and later made Angrian Ambassador to Verdopolis. (A pseudonym of Branwell in the early juvenilia.)

St Clair, Lord Roslyn: a highland chieftain, who marries Lady Emily Charlesworth. Friend of the Duke of Wellington.

Tree, Captain: a Glass Town novelist and rival of Captain Bud and Lord Charles Wellesley. Father of Sergeant Tree, the Glass Town book-seller and publisher. (A pseudonym of Charlotte in the early juvenilia.)

Warner, Warner Howard: prime minister of Angria and head of one of the oldest Angrian families of Warners, Howards and Agars. Known to have a hereditary gift of 'second sight'. Contemporary and important ally of Zamorna.

Appendix B: A Chronological List of Charlotte Brontë's Early Prose Manuscripts

Manuscript volumes are listed first and the separate items which comprise them are included in the main list of manuscripts, since many items were originally written well before they were included in the volumes. Manuscripts are referred to either by their titles or, if they are untitled, by their first lines. Those with well-known titles not given by Charlotte are indicated by square brackets, followed by the first line or phrase of the manuscript.

Information on Charlotte Brontë's poetry manuscripts, school exercises and miscellaneous notes can be found in my *A Bibliography of the Manuscripts of Charlotte Brontë,* published by The Brontë Society in association with Meckler Publishing, 1982.

MANUSCRIPT VOLUMES

1829

12 March — 30 July 1830	*Tales of the Islanders* (NYPL: Berg)
15 — 28 April	*Two Romantic Tales* (formerly in Law Collection, untraced)
August	*Blackwoods Young Mens Magazine* (HCL: MS. Lowell I(6))
September	[*Blackwood's Young Men's Magazine*] (BPM: SG.95)
October	[*Blackwood's Young Men's Magazine*] (HCL: MS. Lowell I(5))
November	[*Blackwood's Young Men's Magazine*] (HCL: MS. Lowell I(4))

December	[*Blackwood's Young Men's Magazine*] First Issue (BPM: 10)
December	[*Blackwood's Young Men's Magazine*] Second Issue (BL: Ashley MS.157)

1830

August	*Young Men's Magazine. Second Series. No. 1* (BPM: B84)
September	*Young Men's Magazine. Second Series. No. 2* (untraced)
October	*Young Men's Magazine. Second Series. No. 3* (BPM: B85)
November	*Young Men's Magazine. Second Series. No. 4* (BPM: 12)
December	*Young Men's Magazine. Second Series. No. 5* (formerly in Law Collection; untraced)
December	*Young Men's Magazine. Second Series. No. 6* (BPM: B86)

1833

7 November	*The Secret and Lily Hart. Two Tales by Lord Charles Wellesley Verdopolis* (Ellis Library, University of Missouri—Columbia)
20 November	*Arthuriana or Odds & Ends Being A Miscellaneous Collection of Pieces In Prose & Verse By Lord Charles A F Wellesley* (PML: MA29)

1834

28 May— 16 June	*Corner Dishes Being A small Collection of Mixed and Unsubstantial Triffles In Prose and Verse By Lord Charles Albert Florian Wellesley* (HL: HM2577)
15 September— 17 March 1835	*The Scrap Book. A Mingling of Many things Compiled by Lord C A F Wellesley* (BL: Add.MS.34255)

PROSE MANUSCRIPTS

*c.*1826—28	'There was once a little girl and her name was Ane' (BPM: B78)

1829

12 March	*The History of the Year* (BPM: B80(11))
12 March	'The origin of the O'Deans' (BPM: B80(11))
12 March	'The origin of the Islanders' (NYPL: Berg)
15 April	*A Romantic Tale* (formerly in the Law Collection; untraced)

28 April	*An Adventure in Ireland* (formerly in the Law Collection; untraced)
30 June	*Tales of the Islanders Volume I* (NYPL: Berg)
8 July— 2 October	*Anectdotes of the duke of Wellington* (BPM: B81)
13 July	*The Enfant* (BPM: B80(9))
13 July	*The Keep of the Bridge* (NYPL: Berg)
14 July	'Sir it is well known that the Geni' (BPM: B79)
28 July— 17 August	*The Search after Happiness A Tale by C Brontë* (BL: Ashley MS.156)
8 August	*A Fragment August the 7 1829,* 'One Cold dreary night in the month of December' (BPM: B80(12))
8 August	*Fragment August the 8 1829,* 'On the third day I came to a wide plain' (BPM: B80(10))
20 August	*A True Story by CB* (HCL: MS. Lowell I(6))
20 August	*A True Story By CB* (BPM: SG.95)
21 August	*Revi[e]w of the painting of the Spirit of Cawdor ravine By Dundee a private in the 20.* (BPM: SG.95)
August	*Review of the causes of the late War by the Duke of Wellington* (HCL: MS. Lowell I(6))
August	*Military Conversations* (HCL: MS. Lowell I(6))
September	*Military Conversations* (HCL: MS. Lowell I(5))
1 September	*The Silver Cup A Tale* (HCL: MS. Lowell I(5))
September	*Scene On The Great Bridge By The Genius CB* (HCL: MS. Lowell I(4))
8 September	*A scene in my Inn* (HCL: MS. Lowell I(4))
9 September	*An American Tale* (HCL: MS. Lowell I(4))
20 November	*The Swiss Artist* (BPM: 10)
2 December	*Tales of the Islanders Volume II* (NYPL: Berg)
9 December	*Review of The Cheif Geni in Council by Edward De Lisle* (BL: Ashley MS. 157)
10 December	*The Swiss Artist Continued* (BL: Ashley MS. 157)
17 December	*Characters of the Celebrated Men of the Present Time. By Captain Tree* (formerly in the Law Collection; untraced)
December	*Conversations* (BL: Ashley MS. 157)

1830

| 16 January | *Description of the Duke of Ws small palace situated on the Banks of the Indirce* (PML: Bonnell) |
| 16 January | *A Visit to the Duke of Wellington's small palace situated on the Banks of the Indirce* (untraced) |

22 February	*The Adventure's of Mon Edouard de Crack By Lord C Wellesley* (HCL: MS. Lowell I(3))
8 May	*Tales of the Islanders Volume III* (NYPL: Berg)
25 May	*The Adventures of Ernenst Alembert a Tale by C. Bronte* (Pforzheimer Library: CHPL Misc.MS. 187)
18 June	*An Interesting Passage in the Lives of Some eminent men of the Present time By Lord Charles Wellesley* (HCL: MS. Lowell I(1))
22 June	'The following strange occurrence' (HCL: MS. Eng.35.3)
29 June	*Leisure Hours* (BPM: B83)
6 July	*The Poetaster. A Drama In Two Volumes Vol I By Lord Charles Wellesley* (HCL: MS. Lowell I(2))
12 July	*The Poetaster A Drama In Two Volumes Vol II By Lord Charles Wellesley* (PML: Bonnell)
30 July	*Tales of the Islanders Volume IV* (NYPL: Berg)
3 August	*Catalogue of my Books with the periods of their completion up to August 3 1830* (PML: Bonnell)
12 August	*Liffey Castle. A Tale by C Wellesley* (BPM: B84)
13 August	*Journal of a Frenchman* (BPM: B84)
13 August	*Conversations* (BPM: B84)
c.14–21 August	*A Letter from lord Charles-Wellesley* (untraced)
c.14–21 August	*A Frenchmans Journal continued by Captain Tree* (untraced)
22 August	*A Day at Parry's Palace By Lord Charles Wellesley* (BPM: B85)
23 August	*Conversations* (BPM: B85)
26 August	*Silence* (BPM: 12)
28 August	*A Frenchmans Journal Continued by Tree* (BPM: 12)
29 August	*Strange Events by L Wellesley* (formerly in the Law Collection; untraced)
30 August	*A Frenchmans Journal Continued. By Tree* (formerly in the Law Collection; untraced)
1 September	*Conversations* (formerly in the Law Collection; untraced)
2 September	*An Extraordinary Dream By lord Charles Wellesley* (BPM: B86)
4 September	*A Frenchmans Journal Concluded by Tree* (BPM: B86)
30 September	*Cam[p]bell Castle* (HCL: Lowell)
12 October	*Albion and Marina: A Tale by Lord Charles Wellesley* (Wellesley College Library: English Poetry)

7—11 December *Visits in Verreopolis. By Lord Charles Wellesley. In*
               Two Volumes. Volume First (formerly in the Law
               Collection; untraced)

18 December   *Visits in Verreopolis. By the Honourable Charles*
               Albert Florian, Lord Wellesley, aged 10 years. In Two
               Volumes. Volume the Second (formerly in the Law
               Collection; untraced)

1831

11 July   *A Fragment,* 'Overcome with that delightful sensation
               of lassitude' (BPM: B82 and B87)

*c.*December   'About 9 months after my arrival at the GT' (The
               King's School Library, Canterbury); continued by the
               fragment 'in green shady hills, looking quietly down'
               (BPM: B112)

1832

14 July—   [*The Bridal*] 'In the Autumn of the year 1832 being
20 August   weary of study' (PML: Bonnell); includes the fragment
               'With a smiling blush she took a little ivory lyre' (BPM:
               B88)

1833

12 February   *The African Queen's Lament* (BPM: B91 (3))
1 May   *Something about Arthur Written by Charles Albert*
               Florian Wellesley (HRC: Stark)
31 May—   *The Foundling A Tale Of Our Own Times By Captain*
27 June   *Tree* (BL: Ashley 159)
2 September   *The Green Dwarf A Tale Of The Perfect Tense By*
               Lord Charles Albert Florian Wellesley (HRC: Stark)
27 September   *The Post Office* (PML: MA29)
1 October   *Brushwood Hall* (PML: MA29)
6 October   *The Tragedy and The Essay* (PML: MA29)
7 October   *The Fresh Arrival* (PML: MA29)
7 October   *The Tea Party* (PML: MA29)
*c.*9 October 'Every-body knows how fond Arthur is of patronizing
               rising talent' (PML: MA29)
*c.*October   *The Vision* (untraced)
*c.*7 November *The Secret* (Ellis Library, University of Missouri—
               Columbia)
7 November   *Lily Hart* (Ellis Library, University of Missouri—
               Columbia)

1834

5 January
Last Will And Testament Of Florence Marian Wellesley Marchioness Of Douro Duchess Of Zamorna And Princess Of The Blood Of The Twelves (PML: Bonnell)

17 January
A Leaf from an Unopened Volume Or The Manuscript of An Unfortunate Author. Edited By Lord Charles Albert Florian Wellesley. (BPM: 13.2)

20 February—
20 March
High Life In Verdopolis or The difficulties of annexing a suitable title to a work practically illustrated in Six Chapters. By Lord C A F Wellesley. (BL: Add.MS.34255)

30 May
A Peep Into A Picture Book (HL: HM2577)

15 June
A Day Abroad (HL: HM2577)

21 June—
21 July
The Spell, An Extravaganza By Lord Charles Albert Florian Wellesley (BL: Add.MS.34255)

15 September
Adress To The Angrians By his Grace The Duke of Zamorna (BL: Add.MS.34255)

20 September
Speech of His Grace The Duke of Zamorna At the Opening of the First Angrian Parliament (BL: Add.MS.34255)

14 October
My Angria and the Angrians By Lord Charles Albert Florian Wellesley (formerly in the Law Collection: untraced)

30 October
A Brace of Characters. John Augustus Sneachie E E G Wellesley (BL: Add.MS.34255)

*c.*5 December
'"Well Etty" said I' (BL: Add.MS.34255)

5 December
Extracted from the last number of the Northern Review (BL: Add.MS.34255)

6 December
Letter to the right honourable Arthur Marquis of Ardrah (BL: Add.MS.34255)

1835

*c.*January
A Late Occurrence (BL: Add.MS.34255)

24 January
Duke of Z & E Percy (BL: Add.MS.34255)

16 March
From the Verdopolitan Intelligencer (BL: Add.MS.34255)

19 December
[*We wove a web in childhood*] 'I now heard the far clatter of hoofs on the hard milk-white road' (HL: HM2578)

1836

4 February
'Well here I am at Roe-Head' (PML: Bonnell)

*c.*5 February	'Now as I have a little bit of time' (PML: Bonnell)
21 — 29 April	*Passing Events* (PML: MA30)
11 August —	'All this day I have been in a dream'
14 October	(BPM: B98(8))
*c.*October	'I'm just going to write because I cannot help it'
	(BPM: B98(6))
*c.*24 December —	[*The Return of Zamorna*] 'Reader I'll tell you what —
January 1837	my heart is like to break' (formerly in the Law
	Collection; untraced)

1837

*c.*March	'My Compliments to the weather. I wonder what it
	would be at' (BPM: B98(6))
29 June	[*Julia By Charles Townshend*] 'There is reader a sort
	of pleasure, in sitting down to write, wholly unprovided
	with a subject' (HRC: Wren)
21 July	[*Four Years Ago*] 'A day or two ago, in cleaning
	out an old rubbish drawer, I chanced to light upon a
	pile of newspapers bearing dates of some four or five
	years back' (formerly in the collection of Adrian H.
	Jolin and subsequently in that of John L. Clawson;
	untraced)
*c.*October	'About a week since I got a letter from Branwell'
	(BPM: B92(1))

1838

17 January	[*Mina Laury*] 'The last scene in my last book'
	(PUL: Robert H. Taylor)
28 June	[*Stancliffe's Hotel*] 'Amen! Such was the sound given
	in a short shout which closed the evening Service at
	Ebenezer-Chapel' (BPM: B114)
21 July	[*The Duke of Zamorna. By Charles Townshend and
	Sir William Percy*] 'In a distant retreat very far indeed
	from the turmoil of cities' (formerly in the Law
	Collection; untraced)
*c.*late 1838	'But it is not in Society that the real character is
	revealed' (BPM: B113(7))

1839

24 February —	[*Henry Hastings. By Charles Townshend*] 'A young
26 March	man of captivating exterior, elegant dress'
	(HCL: Widener)
*c.*July —	[*Caroline Vernon*] 'When I concluded my last book

December   I made a solemn resolve' (HCL: Widener)

c.late 1839   'I have now written a great many books'
                    (BPM:B125(1))

c.late 1839   [*Ashworth*] 'Alexander Percy esq^re was a man much
                    known about the country' (PML: Bonnell)

c.late 1839   [*Ashworth*] 'Miss Percy was a pupil in Mrs Turner's
                    Seminary at Kensington' (PML: Bonnell)

c.late 1839   [*Ashworth*] 'Miss Percy and Miss Thornton being
                    both now settled in Yorkshire' (PML: Bonnell)

c.late 1839   [*Ashworth*] 'hand over the heart & seemed to look into
                    the marble face for life' (PML: Bonnell)

1840

c.December —   [*Ashworth*] 'Long disuse of a pen that was once
March 1841   frequently handled' (HCL: Widener)

Notes

INTRODUCTION

1 Mrs Gaskell to George Smith, 25 July 1856; J. A. V. Chapple and Arthur Pollard, eds., *The Letters of Mrs Gaskell* (Manchester: Manchester University Press, 1966), p. 398.

2 Clement Shorter, *Charlotte Brontë and Her Circle* (London: Hodder and Stoughton, 1896), p. 25.

3 Manuscript fragment beginning 'With a smiling blush she took a little ivory lyre', 20 August 1832; originally part of *The Bridal*, Bonnell Collection, PML.

4 F. B. Pinion, *A Brontë Companion: Literary Assessment, Background, and Reference* (London: Macmillan, 1975), p. 71.

5 See Winifred Gérin, *Charlotte Brontë: The Evolution of Genius* (Oxford: Clarendon Press, 1967), p. 31.

6 Winifred Gérin, for example, refers to 'the absence of all reference, either direct or indirect, to religious or clerical influences' in the juvenilia: *Charlotte Brontë*, p. 33). Tom Winnifrith (in *The Brontës and Their Background,* pp. 43 and 232, n.72) speaks of 'a remarkable reluctance to handle religious themes' and, while acknowledging that the absence of religious references is not quite as complete as Winifred Gérin, suggests, he asserts that it is 'nevertheless impressive'. This view is accepted in such recent articles as 'Literary and Biblical Allusions in *The Professor*', by Michael Wheeler, *BST*, vol. 17, part 86 (1976), p. 46.

7 B. C. Southam, *Jane Austen's Literary Manuscripts: A study of the novelist's development through the surviving papers* (Oxford: 1964), p. vii.

CHAPTER 1: CHILDHOOD INFLUENCES

1 Unpublished manuscript, *c.* 1826—28 (BPM: B78). My dating of this manuscript is later than that of previous writers. It is based on the

similarity of writing and spelling to Charlotte's next surviving manuscript dated 1829 and the fact that the final pages of this first manuscript are unlikely to have been written before December 1827 (see pp. 32 and 262 n.15).

2   Mrs Gaskell, *The Life of Charlotte Brontë*, vol. 1, pp. 55 and 59—60.

3   Mr Brontë to Mrs Gaskell, 24 July 1855; *BST* (1932) 8:43:92.

4   A printer who worked for Mr Thomas Inkersley apparently remembered seeing Charlotte correcting the proofs of Mr Brontë's sermon on the Eruption of Bog on the moor at Crow Hill, published in 1824 (William Scruton, *Thornton and the Brontës*, pp. 66—67). Judging from the poor spelling and punctuation in Charlotte's early manuscripts, it seems more likely that Mr Brontë allowed his eldest daughter Maria to help him and not the eight-year-old Charlotte.

5   Compare, for example, the title-page of Charlotte's unpublished manuscript, *The Adventure's of Mon Edouard de Crack*, 22 February 1830 (HCL: MS. Lowell I(3)) and that of Mr Brontë's *The Cottage in the Wood* (see plate 5).

6   Mrs Gaskell, *The Life of Charlotte Brontë*, vol. 1, p. 49.

7   Thomas à Kempis, *An Extract on the Christian's Pattern: or, a Treatise on the Imitation of Christ*, Abridged and Published in England by John Wellesley (London, 1803), inscribed 'C Brontes 1st Book . . . July 1826' and 'M. Branwell July 1807' (PML); and Thomas Browne, *The Union Dictionary* (London: 1806), inscribed 'C Bronte' and 'M. Branwell Sept. 9 1808' (BPM: 237).

8   Unpublished manuscript, *A Fresh Arrival*, 7 October 1833 (PML: MA29).

9   *SHCBM*, vol. 2, p. 13.

10 *Ibid.*, pp. 11—12.

11 See the discussion of *Tales of the Islanders*, vol. 2, ch. 4 (21 November 1829), pp. 49—50.

12 Hannah More, *Moral Sketches of Opinions and Manners* (London: 1819), inscribed by Mr Brontë (BPM: 214).

13 Ellen Nussey, 'Reminiscences of Charlotte Brontë', *BST* (1899) 2:10:70.

14 For example Winifred Gérin writes: 'However religiously they were brought up (and Charlotte's early knowledge of the Bible was phenomenal) and however deep and genuine were their later religious convictions, no word of religion enters into their voluminous juvenilia,' British Council pamphlet: *The Brontës*, vol. 1, 1973, p. 9.

15 See, for example, the unpublished manuscript, *Tales of the Islanders*, vol. 2, chs. 4 and 5 (NPL: Berg Collection).

16 *SHCBM*, vol. 2, p. 65 (facsimile only).

17 *Ibid.*, p. 53 (facsimile only).

18 Mr Brontë to Mrs Gaskell, 30 July 1855, *BST* (1932) 8:43:95.

19 See Jane W. Stedman, 'The Genesis of The Genii', *BST* (1965), 14:75:16—19.

20 See, for example, 'Saul', *SHCBP*, pp. 176—8; 'St. John in the Island of Patmos', unpublished poem (B); 'O Hyle thy waves are like Babylon's streams', *SHCBP*, p. 137; and 'The Wounded Stag', *SHCBP*, pp. 187—8.

21   For example, the religious fanatic Warner has the gift of 'second sight' which is presented as 'a kind of inspiration', *SHCBM,* vol. 2, p. 249. Rochester's cry is prefigured by Marina's cry to Albion across the sea in another land, *SHCBM,* vol. 1, pp. 32—5.

22   *Ibid.,* vol. 2, p. 53 (facsimile only).

23   T. Weymss Reid, *Charlotte Brontë: A Monograph,* pp. 24—6.

24   *A Description of London; containing a Sketch of its History and Present State, and of all the most celebrated Public Buildings* (London: 1824), inscribed 'PB Bronte aged 10 years and 9 months. March 21 — 1828 —' (BPM: 141).

25   Rev. J. Goldsmith, *A Grammar of General Geography* (London: 1823) (BPM: B45).

26   Ellen Nussey, 'Reminiscences of Charlotte Brontë', *BST* (1899) 2:10:79.

27   Abbé Lenglet Du Fresnoy, *Geography For Youth* (Dublin, 1795), signed by two of Mr Brontë's brothers: Hugh Bronte in 1803 and Walsh Bronte in 1884 (BPM: 238). The name Brontë originated from the Irish Prunty or Brunty. It was Charlotte who adopted the now accepted form of Brontë: her father preferred to sign his name either Bronte or Bronté.

28   Unpublished manuscript, *Branwell's Blackwood's Magazine,* July 1829 (HCL: MS. Lowell I (9)).

29   Transcription from manuscript, *The History of the Year,* 12 March 1829 (BPM: B80(11)); see also *SHCBM,* vol. 1, pp. 1—2. All other quotations from Charlotte's work are taken where possible from a printed source and unpublished texts have been regularized to facilitate reading. This exact transcription, however, gives some idea of Charlotte's poor early spelling and punctuation which survived her juvenilia. She later relied on her publishers to repunctuate her novels as she 'found the task very puzzling', *SHLL,* vol. 2, p. 142.

30   *SHCBM,* vol. 1, p. 1.

31   Mrs Gaskell, *The Life of Charlotte Brontë,* vol. 1, pp. 54 and 63.

32   Emily Brontë's diary paper, 30 July 1841, *SHLL,* vol. 1, p. 238.

33   Mrs Oliphant, *Annals of a Publishing House,* vol. 2, p. 178.

34   For example, the unpublished manuscript *Branwell's Blackwood's Magazine,* June 1829 (HCL: MS. Lowell I (8)).

35   Printed in *BST* (1950) 11:60:344—58.

36   For example, *The Poetaster* is based on Jonson's *Poetaster or His Arraignement* (1601) and the rivalry between the Glass Town authors was probably inspired by the War in the Theatres.

37   Unpublished manuscript by Branwell, *A Collection of Poems by Young Soult the Rhymer,* 30 September 1829 (BPM: 114).

38   Fran Carlock Stephens, 'Hartley Coleridge and the Brontës', *TLS,* 14 May 1970, p. 544; compare *Shirley,* p. 440.

39   Charlotte quotes especially from Cowper, Young, Wordsworth, Coleridge, Scott, Southey and Shelley in her juvenilia.

40   Unpublished manuscripts, *Laussane: A Dramatic Poem* (BPM: B138) and *The Revenge A Tragedy* (BPM: 116).

41   Draft of letter from Charlotte Brontë to Hartley Coleridge, 10 December 1840, *BST* (1940) 10:50:17. The Marquis of Douro's maid in the

unpublished manuscript *Visits in Verreopolis,* vol. 1, 7—11 December 1830 (untraceable: transcript lent to author by Professor Ian Jack) is called Clarissa, which may indicate an even earlier knowledge of the book.

42 *Jane Eyre,* p. 5.
43 *SHLL,* vol. 1, p. 122.
44 *The Violet, SHCBP,* p. 112.
45 John Dryden, *The Works of Virgil* (London: 1824) (BPM: 240).
46 *SHCBM,* vol. 1, p. 81.
47 See especially the discussion of *A Leaf from an Unopened Volume,* pp. 120—1.
48 *SHCBM,* vol. 2, p. 37.
49 The twelve volumes of Gibbon's *Decline and Fall of the Roman Empire* were in the Keighley Mechanics' Library in 1841, *BST* (1950) 11:60:348.
50 J. B. Bury, ed., *The History of the Decline and Fall of the Roman Empire,* by Edward Gibbon (London: 1900), pp. 302—3.
51 See *SHCBM,* vol. 1, pp. 258, 358 and 336; and the unpublished manuscripts, *Visits in Verreopolis,* vol. 1 (untraceable: transcript lent to author by Professor Ian Jack) and 'Every-body knows how fond Arthur is of patronising rising talent', in *Arthuriana* (PML: MA 29).
52 Unpublished manuscript, *Tales of the Islanders,* vol. 3, ch. 1 (NYPL: Berg Collection).
53 Ellen Nussey, 'Reminiscences of Charlotte Brontë, *BST* (1899) 2:10:79.
54 See p. 46.
55 Mr Brontë to Mrs Gaskell, 24 July 1855, *BST* (1932) 8:43:91—2.
56 Unpublished manuscript (BPM: B81).
57 Unpublished manuscript, *Fragment August the 8 1829* (BPM: B80(10)).
58 Mrs Arbuthnot, quoted by Elizabeth Longford, *Wellington: Pillar of State,* p. 129.
59 Mrs Chadwick, *In the Footsteps of The Brontës,* p. 87.
60 It has always been assumed that the Brontë children's 'play' originated with Charlotte and Branwell. But Mr Brontë states in a letter to Mrs Gaskell (30 July 1855) that 'when my children composed and acted their little plays, Maria was in the eleventh year of her age, Elizabeth in her tenth', *BST* (1933) 8:43:94. This would have been early in 1824 before Maria and Elizabeth went to Cowan Bridge on 21 June.
61 Mrs Gaskell, *The Life of Charlotte Brontë,* vol. 1, p. 55.
62 *SHCBM,* vol. 1, p. 1.
63 *Ibid.,* pp. 1—2.

CHAPTER 2: THE YOUNG MEN'S PLAY

1 Transcription of original manuscript (BPM: B80(11)): published inaccurately in *SHCBM,* vol. 1, p. 2. Above and below the word 'mine' in line 4 are the words 'Auther' and 'Athur' respectively; 'Arthur' was the Duke of Wellington's Christian name.
2 See Fannie Ratchford, *Gondal's Queen,* Appendix II, p. 185.

3   *The History Of The Young Men, SHCBM,* vol. 1, p. 76. Winifred
    Gérin suggests that Branwell was mocking Anne's lisp in his spelling
    here (*Charlotte Brontë,* p. 26).
4   *SHCBM,* vol. 1, p. 63.
5   *Ibid.,* p. 63.
6   *Ibid.,* pp. 3—4. This is one of the few specific references in Charlotte's
    juvenilia to *The Arabian Nights' Entertainments.* Winifred Gérin says
    that 'The edition . . . accessible to the Brontë children was the translation
    of the French text by Galland, pub. 1706 (the definitive was that of
    1787)' (*Charlotte Brontë,* p. 26, n. 2). The source of this statement is
    not indicated and it is yet to be verified.
7   *The History Of The Young Men, SHCBM,* vol. 1, pp. 78—9.
8   Namely, *Battell Book,* 1827 (BPM: 110), *History of the Rebellion In
    My Fellows,* 1828 (BPM: 112), and *Branwell's Blackwood's Magazine,*
    January 1829 (HCL: MS. Lowell I (8)). These are all unpublished
    manuscripts.
9   Unpublished manuscripts: *Branwell's Blackwood's Magazine,* June 1829
    (HCL: MS. Lowell I(7)) and July 1829 (HCL: MS. Lowell I(9)). The
    main contents of Branwell's three surviving magazines include a detailed
    description of a 'Journey To The Mons and Wamons Islands', a pedantic
    discussion of Ossian's poems, and songs, letters and references to
    Branwell's favourite theme of the Young Men's rebellion against the
    Genii.
10 *SHCBM,* vol. 1, p. 6.
11 *Ibid.,* p. 9: cf. Revelation 4: 1—6.
12 *Ibid.,* p. 12.
13 All publications of Branwell's map have been unsatisfactory as the
    writing is very faint and difficult to read. The original map can be seen in
    the British Library as a frontispiece to Branwell's manuscript *The
    History Of The Young Men* (BL: Ashley 187). Winifred Gérin notes in
    Five Novelettes, p. 10, that the map of the Gulf of Guinea published in
    Blackwood's Magazine for June 1826 is much closer to Branwell's map
    than the usually recognized source of the map of Africa in Goldsmith's
    Grammar of General Geography, London: 1825.
14 One of the Duke of Wellington's many titles was 'Duke of Vitoria', but
    the name of this map is more likely to refer to the later 'Princess Vittoria'
    of the Islanders' Play, where it is an allusion to the early Queen Victoria.
    Winifred Gérin sees this character as a main source of inspiration of the
    Gondal Saga: see *Emily Brontë,* pp. 21—3, 25.
15 C. W. Hatfield dates this manuscript *c.* 1824 ('The Early Manuscripts of
    Charlotte Brontë: A Bibliography', *BST* (1922) 6:32:97). But there is
    further evidence for my later dating. Charlotte was at Cowan Bridge
    from 10 August 1824, until 1 June 1825. The school register of 1824
    states that she 'Knows nothing of Grammar, Geography, History or
    accomplishments' yet the lists of countries in this manuscript show that
    Charlotte knew something of geography. If the Young Men's Play began
    in June 1826, then the map could not have been drawn before this date

and the names 'Parry' and 'Vittoria' suggest a later date still. Charlotte's next surviving manuscript (*The History of the Year*, March 1829) reveals a similar though more mature cursive hand. In the hand-printed script of these two manuscripts only Charlotte reverses the letter 's' ('s'), again suggesting that these two early manuscripts are closer in time than was previously thought.

16 *The History Of The Young Men: SHCBM*, vol. 1, pp. 65—6.

17 *Ibid.*, p. 71.

18 Unpublished manuscript (HCL: MS. Lowell I(8)).

19 Daphne Du Maurier, *The Infernal World of Branwell Brontë*, p. 13. She also states that the reason for this language was 'to make the game more secret still' and describes it as 'a blend of Yorkshire, Greek and Latin', but there is no evidence to support either of these claims.

20 *SHCBM*, vol. 1, p. 101.

21 *Ibid.*, p. 69.

CHAPTER 3: THE YOUNG MEN'S MAGAZINE

1 Unpublished manuscript: (HCL: MS. Lowell I(9)).

2 *The Enfant* is an interesting example of Charlotte's earliest method of composition, and leads one to suspect that many of the surviving juvenile manuscripts may in fact be fair copies rather than original drafts, as previously assumed. As noted, the first draft of *The Enfant* was copied (with minor variations) by Branwell into his *Branwell's Blackwood's Magazine* for May and June 1829. The following month Charlotte made a fair copy from her original draft which she probably then destroyed. This may account for the neat appearance (and relatively few corrections) of many of the smaller early manuscripts. Other longer early manuscripts, however, such as *Tales of the Islanders*, are obviously first drafts though presented as a final version in booklet form.

3 Unpublished manuscript: (HCL: MS. Lowell I(9)).

4 Unpublished manuscript: (HCL: MS. Lowell I(7)).

5 Winifred Gérin, *Branwell Brontë*, p. 40.

6 'Lines spoken by a lawyer on the occasion of the transfer of this magazine', *BST* (1919) 5:29:270.

7 'Lines by one who was tired of dullness upon the same occasion', *BST* (1919) 5:29:271.

8 *Ibid.*, 272.

9 Mrs Gaskell, *The Life of Charlotte Brontë*, vol. 1, p. 98.

10 It is possible that Charlotte helped to compose some of the articles in Branwell's magazines; certainly, he copied one of her manuscripts for his *Branwell's Blackwood's Magazine*, June 1829 (see n. 2 above). The tone and content of his three surviving magazines, however, are typical of Branwell rather than of Charlotte.

11 *SHCBM*, vol. 1, pp. 37—43.

CHAPTER 4: OUR FELLOWS' PLAY

1   Winifred Gérin reads 'O'Deays' for 'O'Deans' (*Charlotte Brontë*, p. 25). Her reading may have been influenced by the word 'O'Deay' occurring rather mysteriously under the heading 'Natural History' at the beginning of *Branwell's Blackwood's Magazine,* January 1829.

2   Transcription of original manuscript (BPM: B80(1)).

3   Only the characters of Boaster and Clown can be found in the titles of Aesop's *Fables*; Hay Man and Hunter are not even mentioned in the 1825 edition, translated by Samuel Croxall, which Winifred Gérin suggests the young Brontës used (Winifred Gérin, *Charlotte Brontë*, p. 25).

4   This title has always been incorrectly transcribed as the 'History of the Rebellion in My Army' and so its relationship to Our Fellows' Play has been obscured.

5   Unpublished manuscript (BPM: 112).

6   This could support Winifred Gérin's suggestion that the 'babyishness' of the manuscript 'makes one suspect it was considerably post-dated', *Branwell Brontë*, p. 35.

7   Unpublished manuscript (NYPL: Berg Collection).

8   Unpublished manuscript by Branwell, 'The Ammon Tree Cutter', *A Collection of Poems by Young Soult the Ryhmer,* 30 September 1829 (BPM: 114).

CHAPTER 5: THE ISLANDERS' PLAY

1   The relationship of 'The origin of the Islanders' to these two early manuscripts has not been recognized before as it is bound as part of vol. 1 of *Tales of the Islanders,* 30 June 1829 (NYPL: Berg Collection). The fragment forms p. 1 of this bound volume but is really a separate manuscript. Ch. 1 of *Tales of the Islanders,* vol. 1, actually begins on p. 3 of the bound volume.

    Mrs Gaskell rearranged these two accounts (see *The Life of Charlotte Brontë*, vol. 1, p. 92). She combined the more dramatic elements of 'The origin of the Islanders' (MS. p. 1) with those of the first part of *Tales of the Islanders,* vol. 1 (MS. p. 3), and quoted them as one manuscript. All subsequent writers have perpetuated this mistake; no one has checked the original manuscript to find that there are two accounts of the origin of the Islanders' Play separated by an interval of four months yet bound possibly by Charlotte in the same little volume.

2   This title for ch. 1 of *Tales of the Islanders,* vol. I, is not given in the original manuscript but in Charlotte's *Catalogue of my Books:* Mrs Gaskell, *The Life of Charlotte Brontë*, vol. 1, p. 89.

3   Unpublished manuscript (NYPL: Berg Collection); the layout of the original manuscript has been altered here for clarity.

4   Unpublished manuscript, *Tales of the Islanders,* vol. 2, ch. 2 (NYPL: Berg Collection).

5   Unpublished manuscript, *Tales of the Islanders,* vol. 1, ch. 2 (NYPL: Berg Collection).

6 The Palace of Instruction, in Emily and Anne's later Gondal Saga, was also for 'young sovereigns' and their relations, and may have originated in this Palace School, as Fannie Ratchford notes in *Gondal's Queen,* p. 21. The Palace School is a forerunner of the school for nobles on Philosophers' Island, which appears in the manuscripts of the second period of Charlotte's juvenilia (1832–35).

7 Unpublished manuscript, *Tales of the Islanders,* vol. 1, ch. 2 (NYPL: Berg Collection).

8 *Ibid.* The layout of the original manuscript has been altered here for clarity.

9 Not to be confused with Lord Arthur Hill, another minor character in *Tales of the Islanders,* vol. 3, who is probably based on Arthur Hill, Lord Dungannon, the Duke of Wellington's maternal grandfather.

10 See Winifred Gérin, *Emily Brontë,* p. 21.

11 Unpublished manuscript, *Tales of the Islanders,* vol. 2, ch. 1 (NYPL: Berg Collection).

12 Charlotte Brontë to Mr Brontë, 23 September 1829; *SHLL,* vol. 1, p. 82: 'Charlotte's First Letter'.

13 The estate of Stratfield Saye in Hampshire was presented to the Duke of Wellington by the nation in 1817.

14 Unpublished manuscript, *Tales of the Islanders,* vol. 2, ch. 2 (NYPL: Berg Collection).

15 William Vesey Fitzgerald was chosen by Wellington in 1828 as President of the Board of Trade, but although a 'Catholic' Tory, he lost his re-election in June of the same year. Eldon (an 'Ultra Tory'), Hardinge (who lost his arm at Ligny fighting under Wellington in 1815), Rosslyn (a Whig) and Peel were all members of the Duke's cabinet at this time. Castlereagh had died in 1822.

16 Named after Seringapatam, the stronghold of Tipoo Sultan in India; Wellington, then Colonel Wellesley, took part in its capture in 1799.

17 Sir Robert Peel inherited his baronetcy on the death of his father on 3 May 1830.

CHAPTER 6: THE FUSION OF THE PLAYS

1 Cf. Fannie Ratchford, *The Brontës' Web of Childhood,* p. 11, for a contrary view.

2 Unpublished manuscript, *Tales of the Islanders,* vol. 2, ch. 3 (NYPL: Berg Collection).

3 Unpublished manuscript, *A Fragment August the 7:* 'One Cold dreary night in the month of December', 8 August 1829 (BPM: B80(12)).

4 *SHCBP,* p. 90. Lord Charles Wellesley speaks again of his love for the African climate compared to that of England in an unpublished poem, 'Verses by Lord Charles Wellesley', 11 February 1830 (PUL: Robert Taylor Collection).

5 T. A. J. Burnett, ed., *The Search After Hapiness: A Tale By Charlotte Brontë,* p. 18.

6 Based, like Hill, on an old Peninsular officer: General Sir George Murray who served in the Duke's cabinet (1828–30).

7 *SHCBM,* vol. 1, p. 28.
8 See 'Lines on seeing the portrait of — —, Painted by De Lisle' (10 November 1830) *SHCBP,* pp. 117—18; and 'Matin' (12 November 1830), *SHCBP,* pp. 121—3.

CHAPTER 7: THE GREAT GLASS TOWN

1 *Tales of the Islanders,* vols. 3 (8 May) and 4 (30 June) are the main exceptions to this. Other unrelated manuscripts include *The Adventures of Ernenst Alembert* (25 May), 'The following strange occurrence' (22 June), *Catalogue of my Books* (3 August) and *Cam[p]bell Castle* (30 September).
2 8 January 1830, *SHCBP,* p. 82.
3 Unpublished manuscript, *Description of the Duke of Ws small palace situated on the Banks of the Indirce* (PML: Bonnell Collection). An alternative version is published in *BST* (1933) 8:43:78, *A Visit to the Duke of Wellington's small palace situated on the Banks of the Indirce,* but the original manuscript is missing.
4 Unpublished manuscript, (HCL: MS. Lowell 1 (3)).
5 *Letters From An Englishman,* vol. 2; *SHCBM,* vol. 1, p. 106.
6 This is Charlotte's earliest description of industrial Yorkshire.
7 Unpublished manuscript, *Conversations* (in *Young Men's Magazine*), 13 August 1830 (BPM: B84).
8 Preface to *Visits in Verreopolis,* vol. 1 (7—11 December 1830), *SHCBM,* vol. 1, p. 44 (facsimile only).
9 *Characters of the Celebrated Men of the Present Time, SHCBM,* vol. 1, p. 38.
10 Marshal Soult was Wellington's opponent in the Peninsular Campaign and again at Waterloo, under Napoleon. De Lisle, Le Brun and Dundee were all well-known artists of this time.
11 *The Violet A Poem With Several Smaller Pieces By The Marquis Of Douro* (14 November 1830), *SHCBP,* p. 109.
12 See *Brushwood Hall,* 1 October 1833, included in the unpublished manuscript volume *Arthuriana* (PML: MA29).
13 Unpublished manuscript, 'About 9 months after my arrival at the GT', *c.* December 1831 (King's School Library, Canterbury): see Christine Alexander, 'Some New Findings in Brontë Bibliography', *Notes and Queries,* June 1983, pp. 235—6, for a more detailed discussion of this MS.
14 *SHCBM,* vol. 1, p. 39.
15 Judith Chernaik, ed., *TLS,* 23 November 1973, p. 1453. Lord Charles reveals another scandal involving Tree in the unpublished manuscript, *Conversations* (in *Young Men's Magazine*), 13 August 1830, (BPM: B84).
16 See especially Branwell's first volume of *Letters From An Englishman* (6 September 1830), *SHCBM,* vol. 1, pp. 97—102.

17   Melodie Monahan, ed., 'Charlotte Brontë's *The Poetaster:* Text and Notes', *Studies in Romanticism,* 20 (Winter 1981), pp. 491—492; 'nearly' altered to 'neatly' from the manuscript.

18   Unpublished manuscript, *Visits in Verreopolis,* vol. 1 (location untraceable); extracts, including the verse-drama known as 'The Rivals', are published in *SHCBM,* vol. 1, 45—51.

CHAPTER 8: THE YOUNG AUTHOR

1   The original manuscripts of the *Young Men's Magazine* for August, October, November and December (second issue) 1830 are extant. The numbers for September and December (first issue) are untraceable. Their contents are listed in the General Index to the Second Series at the end of the *Young Men's Magazine,* December (second issue) 1830. Three contributions to the first December issue have been published: two in *SHCBM,* vol. 1, pp. 18—23, and one in *The Bookman,* December 1925, pp. 155—6.

2   Unpublished manuscripts: *Young Men's Magazine,* October 1830, and *Young Men's Magazine,* November 1830.

3   See in particular the following unpublished manuscripts which appear in the *Young Men's Magazine* for October, November and December 1830: *Conversations,* 23 August 1830; *Silence,* 26 August 1830; *A Frenchmans Journal Concluded,* 4 September 1830.

4   Unpublished manuscript (BPM: 114).

5   18—23 December 1829; unpublished manuscript (BPM: B138).

6   *Caractacus. A Dramatic Poem,* by Young Soult, 26 June 1830 (B), published in *SHCBM,* vol. 2, pp. 405—22; and unpublished manuscript, *The Revenge A Tragedy in 3 Acts,* by Young Soult, 18 December 1830 (BPM: 116).

7   *SHCBM,* vol. 2, pp. 405 and 408.

8   Unpublished manuscript by Branwell (BPM: B139).

9   *An Interesting Passage in the Lives of Some eminent men of the Present time, TLS,* 23 November 1973, pp. 1453—4.

10   'The Vision A Short Poem' (13 April 1830), *SHCBP,* pp. 91—3.

11   Unpublished manuscript, *Conversations,* 23 August 1830 (BPM: B85).

12   Melodie Monahan, ed., 'Charlotte Brontë's *The Poetaster:* Text and Notes', *Studies in Romanticism* 20 (Winter 1981, pp. 491—2; with minor alterations from the original manuscript.)

13   *SHCBM,* vol. 1, pp. 40—1.

14   The location of this book is unknown, but the 'Catalogue of the Property of Mrs Nicholls, July 1907' at the Brontë Parsonage Museum mentions the following item: 'Voltaire (M. de) las Henriade, Poëme, with inscription inside cover: "Charlotte Brontë's Book, price 3/- purchased May, 1830, anno Domini &c." uncut, 1825.' Dr Enid Duthie, to whom I am indebted for this information, also suggests that 'uncut' here most probably refers to the succeeding cantos of *La Henriade* which, as there are ten in all, form the bulk of the work.

15 See Ellen Nussey, 'Reminiscences of Charlotte Brontë', *BST* (1899) 2:10:62; and the introduction to Clement Shorter's privately printed edition, *Voltaire's 'Henriade' Book I Translated from the French* by Charlotte Brontë, London: 1917.

16 Enid L. Duthie, *The Foreign Vision of Charlotte Brontë*, London: 1975, p. 6.

17 Viz. *Young Men's Magazine* for August, September, November, December (first and second issues) 1830. The magazines for September and December (1) are untraceable.

18 *The Swiss Artist*, 20 November and 10 December 1829, contributions to *Blackwood's Young Men's Magazine* for December 1829, first and second issues respectively; the former only is published in *BST* (1919) 5:29:267—70.

19 *SHCBM*, vol. 1, pp. 96—102. Vols. 2 and 3 were not written until almost a year later on 8 and 11 June 1831. Another year intervenes before Branwell completes the letters with vols. 4, 5 and 6 on 2—3 August 1832.

20 Adam Scott. All the *Letters From An Englishman* are signed by James Bellingham except letter I. This is 'To Mr. Bellingham London, England' and signed 'Adam Scott', but Branwell seems to have confused the roles of his characters and addressed the subsequent letters 'To Adam Scott, London'.

21 Unpublished manuscript, *Visits in Verreopolis*, vol. 1, ch. 5; the original manuscript has not been traced but a transcript was kindly lent to the author by Professor Ian Jack.

22 'The following strange occurrence': Mrs Gaskell, *The Life of Charlotte Brontë*, vol. 1, p. 101.

23 The single exception to this is the unpublished manuscript *Cam[p]bell Castle* (30 September 1830), a critique on three engravings, discussed in ch. 31, pp. 237—9.

24 *SHLL*, vol. 1, p. 80.

25 Unpublished manuscript (NYPL: Berg Collection).

26 Clement Shorter and C. W. Hatfield, eds., *The Twelve Adventurers and Other Stories* by Charlotte Brontë, p. 50.

27 This is the first occurrence of the name 'Warner', later to appear as Warner Howard Warner, the Duke of Zamorna's trusted Prime Minister of Angria.

28 Cf. Revelation 21: 23—5, and 22: 2; there is a close relationship between Charlotte's idea of fairy land and the biblical paradise.

29 *Visits in Verreopolis*, vol. 2, ch. 2 (18 December 1830), *SHCBM*, vol. 1, p. 52.

30 On 15 December Branwell began *The History Of The Young Men* (completed 7 May 1831).

31 *SHCBM*, vol. 1, p. 52.

CHAPTER 9: GLASS TOWN ECLIPSED

1 *SHCBM*, vol. 1, p. 27.

2 Melodie Monahan, ed., 'Charlotte Brontë's *The Poetaster:* Text and Notes,' *Studies in Romanticism,* 20 (Winter 1981), p. 484.

3 Charlotte usually sets the scene of her story at the same time of year as she is writing (i.e. 30 July), a habit she continues in her later manuscripts.

4 *Young Men's Magazine,* (December (first issue) 1839), *The Bookman,* December 1925, p. 155.

5 'Lines on seeing the portrait of — — Painted by De Lisle' (10 November 1830) *SHCBP,* pp. 117—8; and 'Matin' (12 November 1830), *SHCBP,* pp. 121—3.

6 'The effect of her going upon the play was a subject of anxious discussion among the four children. They decided at last to take leave of the game in a grand spectacular finale . . . [the] wholesale wiping out of the machinery of the Young Men's Play [recorded in 'The trumpet hath sounded'], Fannie Ratchford, *The Brontës' Web of Childhood,* pp. 49—50. This poem was not written until 11 December 1831, almost a year after Charlotte went to school. If it did represent the desire to destroy the Glass Town Saga, then the desire was transitory.

7 Ellen Nussey, 'Reminiscences of Charlotte Brontë', *BST* (1899) 2:10:62—3.

8 Mrs Gaskell, *The Life of Charlotte Brontë,* vol. 1, pp. 113—6.

9 17 January 1831: inside cover of *A New and Easy Guide to the Pronunciation and Spelling of the French Language* By Mr. Tocquot, London: 1806 (BPM: 30).

10 Mrs Gaskell, *The Life of Charlotte Brontë,* vol. 1, p. 113; the manuscript of Mary Taylor's letter to Mrs Gaskell (18 January 1856) has not been traced.

11 *SHLL,* vol. 1, p. 88.

12 Branwell began this manuscript on 15 December 1830, while Charlotte was still at home. He wrote chs. 1, 2, 3, and the beginning of ch. 4 before he stopped on 25 January 1831. The 'history' was resumed on 23 April (soon after Charlotte's Easter holidays), ch. 6 being completed on 7 May.

13 Fannic Ratchford, *The Brontës' Web of Childhood,* p. 52.

14 *SHCBM,* vol. 1, p. 113.

15 He did not continue 'the saga of *Letters From An Englishman,* which he would send his sister every week throughout the term, thus keeping her abreast of African news' (Daphne Du Maurier, *The Infernal World of Branwell Brontë,* p. 38).

16 Their subject matter, however, is still very different: *Letters From An Englishman,* vols. 2 and 3 (8 and 11 June) introduce Glass Town's villains in detail (Pigtail, Tom Scroven, Young Man Naughty, Ned Laury and O'Connor). The most accomplished is 'Rogue' who leads a rebellion ending in a French-Revolutionary 'terror', which is finally overthrown by the four Kings and Crashie — 'their venerable Patriarch'.

17 See Christine Alexander, 'Some New Findings in Brontë Bibliography', *Notes and Queries,* June 1983, pp. 233—5, for a transcription and detailed discussion of this unpublished manuscript.

18 Mrs Gaskell, *The Life of Charlotte Brontë*, vol. 1, p. 116.
19 *SHCBP*, pp. 129—31.
20 Fannie Ratchford, *The Brontës' Web of Childhood*, p. 49.
21 'O There is a land which the sun loves to lighten' (25 December 1831), *SHCBP*, pp. 132—3.

CHAPTER 10: SUNLIGHT ON AFRICA AGAIN

1   *A Fragment* (11 July 1831), Christine Alexander, 'Some New Findings in Brontë Bibliography', *Notes and Queries,* June 1983, p. 234.
2   *TLS,* 23 November 1973, p. 1454. The earlier sketch of Rogue in *Characters of the Celebrated Men of the Present Time,* by Captain Tree (17 December 1829) appears to be of 'Old Rogue', forty-seven years old, whose attributes are later applied to his son: 'His manner is rather polished and gentlemanly but his mind is deceitful, bloody, and cruel', *SHCBM*, vol. 1, p. 42.
3   *Letters From An Englishman,* vol. 3 (9—11 June 1831), *SHCBM*, vol. 1, p. 123.
4   *Letters From An Englishman,* vol. 4 (19 April), vol. 5 (16 June) and vol. 6 (2 August 1832), *SHCBM*, vol. 1, pp. 125—58.
5   *SHCBM*, vol. 1, p. 204.
6   *Ibid.,* 45.
7   'Catalogue of Sale of Brontë effects at Haworth Parsonage', 1 October 1861 (BPM). Certainly by July 1834 Charlotte had read Moore's *Life of Byron* as she recommended it in a letter to Ellen Nussey: *SHLL*, vol. 1, p. 122. Charlotte's debt to Finden was first recorded by Winifred Gérin, *Charlotte Brontë,* p. 51.
8   *SHCBM*, vol. 1, p. 206.
9   Mrs Gaskell, *The Life of Charlotte Brontë*, vol. 1, pp. 120—3.
10 *SHCBM*, vol. 1, pp. 165—6. The Olympic Games, now a fixed occurrence in Verdopolis, are also celebrated at the end of *Letters From An Englishman,* vol. 3, *SHCBM*, vol. 1, p. 124.
11 *SHCBM*, vol. 1, p. 183: Branwell still spells 'chief' incorrectly as in his earliest manuscripts. The children's titles, Tallii, Brannii, Emmii and Annii, are spelt variously in the juvenilia with either a single or double 'i'.
12 *Ibid.,* p. 201.
13 *SHLL*, p. 124. The definitions of Gondal and Gaaldine were inserted by Anne into 'A Vocabulary of Names and Places' at the end of Goldsmith's *Grammar of General Geography* (BPM: B45).
14 *BST* (1899) 2:10:75.
15 It has previously been supposed that Ardrah is Parry himself (see Fannie Ratchford, *The Brontës' Web of Childhood*, p. 65), but a reference in Charlotte's manuscript *From the Verdopolitan Intelligencer* (16 March 1835) makes it clear that they are two distinct characters (*SHCBM*, vol. 2, p. 93: facsimile only). Moreover Arthur Parry appears in Branwell's *Letters From An Englishman,* vol. 3 (*SHCBM*, vol. 1, p. 116) amongst a

group of the sons of the four Kings of the Glass Town Federation including the Marquis of Douro, John and Wilkin Sneaky and Edward Tut Ross (later Marquis of Harlaw and ally of Ardrah). Branwell's manuscript *The Wool is Rising* (26 June 1834) confirms that Ardrah is Arthur Parry, 'the only son of His Majesty William Edward, King of Parrysland': Ardrah's character and appearance are described in ch. 7 of this manuscript, *SHCBM,* vol. 1, p. 429 (facsimile only).

16 'A Tale by Captain John Flower M.P. In I Vol', unpublished manuscript (B).

17 *SHCBM,* vol. 1, p. 174.

18 Unpublished manuscript (PML: MA29)

19 See especially *The Pirate, SHCBM,* vol. 1, p. 181, and *The Green Dwarf* (Fannie E. Ratchford and William Clyde DeVane, eds., *Legends of Angria* p. 52). As he becomes more respectable in the later juvenilia, S'Death's name changes to 'Robert King'.

CHAPTER 11: SOMETHING ABOUT ARTHUR

1 'The Bridal' (14 July), *SHCBM,* vol. 1, pp. 202—4; 'St. John in the Island of Patmos' (30 August), unpublished manuscript (B): and 'The cloud of recent death is past away' (27 November 1832), *SHCBP,* pp. 134—6.

2 Mrs Gaskell, *The Life of Charlotte Brontë,* vol. 1, p. 117.

3 *SHLL,* vol. 1, p. 103.

4 Mrs Gaskell, *The Life of Charlotte Brontë,* vol. 1, p. 135.

5 *SHLL,* vol. 1, p. 103.

6 *Ibid.,* p. 108.

7 See p. 22.

8 The only exception to this in the years 1832—35 is *The Foundling. A Tale Of Our Times,* By Captain Tree, *SHCBM,* vol. 1, pp. 220—95.

9 Christine Alexander, ed., *Something about Arthur,* p. 32.

10 Although a prominent character in this manuscript, Caversham plays only a minor role in the juvenilia. There is a passing reference to his callous attitude to his father's death in *A Day Abroad* (15 June 1834), unpublished manuscript (HL: HM2577); and although he features more frequently in Branwell's later manuscripts since he associates with Percy (Rogue) and his revolutionary gang, he appears briefly in only three of Charlotte's later manuscripts: *The Duke of Zamorna* (21 July 1838), *Henry Hastings* (24 February—26 March 1839), and *Ashworth* (*c.* December 1840—41).

11 The manuscript of *Something about Arthur* was in the private collection of Mrs H. J. Lutcher Stark, Orange, Texas, until January 1977 when she presented it to the Humanities Research Center, who kindly made it available for my inspection. See the introduction to Christine Alexander, ed., *Something about Arthur,* for a more detailed discussion of the manuscript.

12 Unpublished manuscript (BL: Add. MS. 34255).

13 George Edwin MacLean, ed., *The Spell: An Extravanganza,* p. 5.

CHAPTER 12: A NEW ALBION

1 *SHCBM,* vol. 1, p. 238.
2 *A Late Occurrence* (*c.* January 1835), *SHCBM,* vol. 2, p. 82 (facsimile only).
3 *The Post Office* (27 September 1833), *The Secret* (7 November 1833) and *High Life In Verdopolis* (20 February—20 March 1834).
4 *SHCBM,* vol. 2, pp. 5—7 and 15; and *ibid.,* p. 82 (facsimile only). Julia is eventually remarried to General Thornton.
5 *SHCBM,* vol. 1, pp. 180—1. Branwell's *The Pirate* was probably influenced by Scott's novel *The Pirate* (1812) and by Byron's poem *The Corsair* (1814).
6 Unlike Charlotte, Branwell continually spells 'Ellrington' with one 'l' in his manuscripts.
7 William Holtz, ed., *Two Tales By Charlotte Brontë: 'The Secret' & 'Lily Hart',* pp. 86 and 89.
8 *SHCBM,* vol. 1, p. 234.
9 Finic appears first in *An Interesting Passage in the Lives of Some eminent men of the Present time* (18 June 1830) and in *The Poetaster* vol. 1 (6 July 1830). In *A Leaf from an Unopened Volume* (17 January 1834) we are told that he haunts Douro for seven years until he is executed for trying to murder him. Finic is apparently the offspring of Douro and Sofala (or Soffala), a Mooress whom the young Marquis forsook. Charlotte, however, is never clear about this early *affaire* (which hints at marriage) and in other manuscripts such as *The Spell,* Finic appears as Douro's devoted dwarf servant.
10 Danash first appears in *The Bridal*; both he and Maimoune are Genii from the *Arabian Nights' Entertainments.*
11 *SHCBM,* vol. 1, p. 205.
12 *Ibid.,* p. 227.
13 *Ibid.,* p. 228.
14 Tom Winnifrith, *The Brontës and Their Background,* pp. 16 and 225—6 n.43, 44, 49. A facsimile of the title-page of *The Foundling* can be found in *SHCBM,* vol. 1, p. 221.
15 A possible exception is *The Bridal,* but there is no definite evidence for this.
16 *SHCBM,* vol. 1, p. 363.

CHAPTER 13: ALEXANDER PERCY

1 Clement Shorter and C. W. Hatfield, eds., *The Twelve Adventurers and Other Stories,* p. 137. The title of this tale was first devised by Shorter for a privately printed limited edition of the end of ch. 1 of *The Green Dwarf: Napoleon and The Spectre. A Ghost Story* by Charlotte Brontë (London: 1919). This episode, a digression from the main plot, is omitted from Fannie E. Ratchford and William Clyde DeVane, eds., *Legends of Angria. The Green Dwarf* has never been published in its complete form.

2 *Legends of Angria,* pp. 22—3.

3 *SHCBM,* vol. 1, p. 218: this verse was probably inspired by the prophecy of retribution in Psalm 137: 7—9. On the last page of *The African Queen's Lament* (BPM: B91(2)), Charlotte wrote the poem 'O Hyle thy waves are like Babylon's streams', in which she compares the defeated Ashantees to the Jews in captivity: cf. *SHCBP,* p. 137, and Psalm 137. Fannie Ratchford sees Byron's *Hebrew Melodies* as the source of this later poem rather than the Bible (*The Brontës' Web of Childhood,* p. 62); but the two sources are of course related.

4 September 1836: see Winifred Gérin, *Branwell Brontë,* p. 37. The Earl St Clair was probably based on James St Clair Erskine, Lord Rosslyn, a member of Wellington's Reform Cabinet who features in *Tales of the Islanders.*

5 *Legends of Angria,* p. 101.

6 *A Leaf from an Unopened Volume* (17 January 1834), A. Edward Newton, ed., *Derby Day And Other Adventures;* and *The Duke of Zamorna* (21 July 1838), *SHCBM,* vol. 2, pp. 90—3 (facsimile only). See also p. 181.

7 See Branwell's unpublished manuscript *The Politics of Verdopolis,* 23 October 1833 (BPM: B141).

8 15 November 1833 (BPM: B141).

9 Unnamed and undated fragment (possibly part of Branwell's missing manuscript *Real Life in Verdopolis*), *SHCBM,* vol. 1, p. 296 (facsimile only).

10 See unnamed and undated fragment, *ibid.,* p. 296; and 'An Hour's Musings' (10 November 1834), *ibid.,* vol. 2, p. 55.

CHAPTER 14: ARTHURIANA

1 The pages have since been mounted and bound in half red morocco binding.

2 Unpublished manuscript (PML: MA29); a facsimile of the first page of *The Post Office* is printed in *SHCBM,* vol. 1, p. 299.

3 C. K. Shorter, *The Brontës: Life and Letters,* vol. 2, Appendix V, p. 434, lists 'Real Life in Verdopolis: A Tale. By Captain John Flower, MP. In two volumes. P. B. Bronte, ... 1833.' The manuscript would have been written before 27 September and possibly begun in late August 1833.

4 Unpublished manuscript (PML: MA29).

5 Unpublished manuscript (BPM: B141).

6 *SHCBM,* vol. 1, p. 30.

7 See especially *A Frenchmans Journal Continued* by Tree (28 August 1830). *The Poetaster, A Drama* In Two Volumes (6—12 July 1830) and *Visits in Verreopolis,* vol. 1, ch. 3 (11 December 1830).

8 Stephen Price was manager of Drury Lane in 1833.

9 *SHCBM,* vol. 1, p. 302: the omitted sentence (marked *) has been replaced from the manuscript (PML: MA 29).

10 *SHCBP,* p. 142: the preamble explaining the circumstances in which the poem was written has not been published.

11 *Adress To The Angrians* (15 September 1834), *SHCBM,* vol. 1, p. 453.
   p. 453.
12 *Silence,* 26 August 1830 (BPM: 12).
13 He appears for the first time in *Lily Hart* (7 November 1833) although
   the title is not applied to him until *High Life In Verdopolis* (20
   February—20 March 1834). A detailed description of his appearance
   and character at six years old occurs in *A Brace of Characters* (30
   October 1834).
14 The date occurs at the end of the second tale *Lily Hart: The Secret* was
   probably written slightly earlier, in late October.
15 *SHCBP,* pp. 162—71.
16 Unpublished manuscript, 'Every-body knows how fond Arthur is of
   patronizing rising talent' (PML: MA29).
17 Unpublished introduction to the poem (*SHCBP,* pp. 145—6), written on
   7 October 1833, and included in *Arthuriana* (PML: MA29).
18 Unpublished manuscript, 'Every-body knows how fond Arthur is of
   patronizing rising talent' (PML: MA29) and *The Secret,* William Holtz,
   ed., *Two Tales by Charlotte Brontë: 'The Secret' & 'Lily Hart',* p. 44.
19 See unpublished manuscript by Branwell, *An Historical Narrative of the
   'War of Encroachment',* 18 November—17 December 1833 (HCL: MS.
   Eng.869).
20 *SHCBM,* vol. 2, pp. 82—7 (facsimile only).
21 The history of their relationship is traced in detail in *A Day Abroad* (15
   June 1834), *SHCBM,* vol. 1, pp. 365—76 (facsimile only).
22 *SHLL,* vol. 1, p. 122.
23 *SHCBM,* vol. 1, p. 307. Charlotte's poem has no title but bibliographers
   refer to it by the signature to the introduction: 'Captain Flower's Last
   [?Novel]'. The last word of this signature is usually ignored as it is
   difficult to transcribe: see C. W. Hatfield, 'The Early Manuscripts of
   Charlotte Brontë: A Bibliography,' *BST* (1923) 6:33:156, and Mildred
   G. Christian, 'A Census of Brontë Manuscripts in the United States',
   The Trollopian, vol. 2 (1947), p. 191. Mildred Christian lists the poem
   as 'Captain Flower's Last Moments' but it is difficult to support this
   reading from the original manuscript. Nor is there any indication of
   Captain Flower's death elsewhere; he continues as Branwell's pseudonym
   until mid-1834. The content of the poem (which refers to Branwell's last
   manuscript) and the actual script indicate that the word is likely to read
   either 'work' or 'novel'.
24 *SHCBM,* vol. 1, pp. 327—52 (facsimile only).
25 Unpublished manuscript by Branwell in two volumes 'By Sir John
   Flower' (HCL: MS.Eng.869). The first volume is mistakenly labelled
   'Vol II'. Vol. 2 is entitled *An Historical Narrative of the War of
   Agression* and dated at the end, 29 December 1833.

CHAPTER 15: MARY PERCY

1 *A Leaf from an Unopened Volume,* A. Edward Newton, ed., *Derby Day
   and Other Adventures,* pp. 347—80.

2   *A Peep Into A Picture Book* (30 May 1834), *SHCBM,* vol. 1, p. 359.
3   *SHCBP,* p. 169.
4   'Sneaky' is now changed to 'Sneachi' or 'Sneachie'. Other names are similarly changed at varying times in the juvenilia: for example, Gravi (Gravey) and Montmorenci (Montmorency). 'Alford' may be derived from the name of one of Anne's chief men in the Islanders' Play, namely, Henry Halford, a Palace School surgeon; or it is possible that Charlotte had heard of Henry Alford, Vicar of Wimeswould, Leicester, who wrote 'The School of the Heart and Other Poems', from *Blackwood's Edinburgh Magazine* (see especially the issue for May 1836).
5   *SHCBM,* vol. 1, p. 360.
6   G. E. MacLean, ed., *The Spell: An Extravanganza,* p. 16.
7   *Ibid.,* p. 6.
8   Mrs Gaskell, *The Life of Charlotte Brontë,* vol. 1, p. 142.
9   *SHLL,* vol. 1, p. 118.
10 Unpublished manuscript, *The Politics of Verdopolis* (BPM: B141).
11 *SHCBM,* vol. 1, p. 339 (facsimile only).
12 Unpublished manuscript in two volumes by Branwell, *An Historical Narrative of the 'War of Encroachment'* (HCL: MS.Eng.869).
13 Unpublished and untraced manuscript, 31 August 1836 (HCL: facsimile of p. 1 only).
14 See Lewis Parry Curtis, ed., *Letters of Lawrence Sterne* (Oxford: Clarendon, 1935) p. 302, n. 5.

CHAPTER 16: HIGH LIFE IN VERDOPOLIS

1   *SHCBM,* vol. 1, p. 331 (facsimile only).
2   Unpublished manuscript (PML: Bonnell Collection).
3   *SHCBM,* vol. 1, p. 331 (facsimile only).
4   20 February 1834; *SHLL,* vol. 1, pp. 119−120.
5   *From the Verdopolitan Intelligencer* (16 March 1835), *SHCBM,* vol. 2, p. 95 (facsimile only).
6   *SHCBM,* vol. 1, p. 366 (facsimile only).
7   Fannie Ratchford, *The Brontës' Web of Childhood,* p. 84.
8   *SHCBM,* vol. 1, p. 336 (facsimile only).
9   *A Fragment August the 7 1829:* 'One Cold dreary night in the month of December', 8 August 1829 (BPM: B80(12)).
10 *SHCBM,* vol. 2, p. 82 (facsimile only).
11 G. E. MacLean, ed., *The Spell: An Extravanganza,* p. 101.
12 *SHCBM,* vol. 2, p. 53 (facsimile only). Ernest's history, appearance and character at four years old are described here in *A Brace of Characters.*
13 G. E. MacLean, ed., *The Spell; An Extravanganza,* p. 2.
14 *Ibid.,* pp. 144−5.
15 A. Edward Newton, ed., *Derby Day and Other Adventures,* p. 370.
16 *My Angria and the Angrians* (14 October 1834), *SHCBM,* vol. 2, pp. 41−9.
17 Zorayda is also the name of Edward Sydney's mother in *The Foundling,* a name echoed in that of 'Zoraïde' in *The Professor.*

18 A. Edward Newton, ed., *Derby Day and Other Adventures*, p. 360.
19 *Ibid.*, p. 369.

CHAPTER 17: ANGRIA ARISE!

1 *SHCBM,* vol. 1, p. 326 (facsimile only).
2 Unpublished manuscript, *An Historical Narrative of the 'War of Encroachment',* 17—19 December 1833 (HCL: MS.Eng.869).
3 Manuscript fragment by Branwell, *SHCBM,* vol. 1, p. 328 (facsimile only).
4 *Ibid.,* p. 439 (facsimile only).
5 *SHCBM,* vol. 1, p. 371 (facsimile only).
6 G. E. MacLean, ed., *The Spell: An Extravanganza,* p. 9.
7 *SHCBM,* vol. 2, p. 5.
8 Manuscript fragment by Branwell, *ibid.,* vol. 1, pp. 437—8.
9 *SHCBM,* vol. 1, p. 453 (facsimile only).
10 *Ibid.,* p. 439 (facsimile only).
11 'A National Ode for the Angrians' (17 July 1834), *SHCBP,* pp. 172—5; lines 15 and 18 corrected from the original manuscript (BPM: B80(1)).
12 Manuscript fragment by Branwell, *SHCBM,* vol. 1, p. 440 (facsimile only).
13 Songs by Branwell, *ibid.,* pp. 435—7 and 464.
14 *SHCBM,* vol. 2, p. 41.
15 *High Life In Verdopolis, SHCBM,* vol. 1, p. 351 (facsimile only).
16 G. E. MacLean, ed., *The Spell: an Extravaganza,* p. 58, and the final pages of Branwell's manuscript *The Wool Is Rising Or The Angrian Adventurer,* by the Rt Hon. John Baron Flower and Viscount Richton (26 June 1834), *SHCBM,* vol. 1, p. 434 (facsimile only).
17 *A Late Occurrence, SHCBM,* vol. 2, p. 82 (facsimile only).
18 *Ibid.,* vol. 1, p. 360.
19 *Ibid.,* p. 337 (facsimile only).
20 *Ibid.,* p. 116; Branwell also refers to 'Alexander Wilkin Sneaky, a son of Alexander Sneaky', *ibid.,* p. 113.
21 *Ibid.,* p. 431 (facsimile only); echoed in Charlotte's manuscript *Four Years Ago,* see p. 162.
22 Possibly described in Branwell's lost manuscript *Real Life in Verdopolis,* written *c.* August 1833.
23 *SHCBM,* vol. 2, p. 15.
24 *Ibid.,* vol. 1, pp. 366—7 (facsimile only).
25 *Ibid.,* vol. 2, p. 17.
26 *A Day Abroad, ibid.,* vol. 1, p. 368 (facsimile only).
27 *Ibid.,* p. 369 (facsimile only).
28 Branwell's relationship to Patrick Benjamin Wiggins is explored in detail in Winifred Gérin's *Branwell Brontë,* p. 69.
29 *My Angria and the Angrians, SHCBM,* vol. 2, p. 22.
30 *Duke of Z and E Percy, ibid.,* p. 91 (facsimile only).
31 See Branwell's manuscript *The Wool Is Rising, ibid.,* vol. 1, p. 412 (facsimile only), which traces Edward's rise to power and his marriage to Maria Sneachi.

32 *My Angria and the Angrians, SHCBM,* vol. 2, p. 14.
33 *Ibid.,* p. 90 (facsimile only).
34 Manuscript fragment by Branwell, *ibid.,* vol. 1, p. 327 (facsimile only).
35 *Ibid.,* vol. 2, p. 23: Captain William Percy had purchased Elm Grove Villa from Fidena shortly after his marriage to Cecilia.

CHAPTER 18: POLITICAL RIVALRY

1 Fannie Ratchford, *The Brontës' Web of Childhood,* p. 99.
2 *High Life In Verdopolis, SHCBM,* vol. 1, p. 338 (facsimile only).
3 *A Peep Into A Picture Book, ibid.,* p. 357.
4 Manuscript fragment by Branwell, *ibid.,* p. 451.
5 Unpublished manuscript, 'Every-body knows how fond Arthur is of patronizing rising talent' (PML: MA29). See also *The Green Dwarf,* Fannie E. Ratchford and William Clyde DeVane, eds., *Legends of Angria,* p. 12.
6 *SHCBM,* vol. 1, p. 453 (facsimile only).
7 *Ibid.,* pp. 460—1 (facsimile only).
8 *Ibid.,* vol. 2, p. 28.
9 *Ibid.,* vol. 1, p. 458 (facsimile only).
10 *Ibid.,* p. 479 (facsimile only).
11 *Ibid.,* p. 467 (facsimile only).
12 *Ibid.,* p. 474 (facsimile only).
13 *Extracted from the last number of the Northern Review, ibid.,* vol. 2, p. 64 (facsimile only).
14 Related in detail by Branwell in an unpublished manuscript begun on 17 December 1834: '*A Narrative of the First War* with Quashia undertaken for the purpose of clearing his Ashantees from the rightful Territory of Angria By the Duke of Zamorna In the year AD 1834 The first of his glorious reign. Compiled from the personal experience of Henry Hastings's and written by himself' (HRC). This manuscript, like so many of Branwell's, is a conglomeration of fragments: half of it is unrelated to the 'First War' and refers to later Angrian events of June 1836. *A Narrative of the First War* is continued by the untitled fragmentary manuscripts known as 'The Massacre of Dongola' (B; facsimile in *SHCBM,* vol. 2, p. 70) and 'The Battle of Loango', last two pages only (PML). The story related in these manuscripts is referred to by Charlotte and Branwell as 'The Campaign of the Calabar', the subject of the first prose work of Captain Henry Hastings.
  The military situation at the end of the Battle of Loango, which was fought on 3 January 1835, and which marked the victorious end of the 'First War' for the Angrians, is summarized at the beginning of 'The Battle of Loango' manuscript (PML); this manuscript (as Hastings tells us in a fragment dated 3 October 1835, and mistakenly bound with 'The Battle of Loango') should really be known as *Verdopolis and the Verdopolitans* (19 January—10 May 1835).
15 *SHCBM,* vol. 2, pp. 67—9 (facsimile only).

16   *Ibid.,* pp. 93—7 (facsimile only).
17   Unpublished and untitled manuscript (PML); previously referred to as 'The Battle of Loango' because of the short recapitulation of this battle at the beginning of the manuscript (see note 14 above).
18   Diary note by Emily Brontë: *SHLL,* vol. 1, p. 124.
19   13 March 1835: *SHLL,* vol. 1, p. 126.
20   *Ibid.,* p. 127.
21   Eye-witness account in *The Bradford Observer,* 17 February 1894: see Winifred Gérin, *Branwell Brontë,* p. 90. Winifred Gérin shows the effect of the election on Branwell and especially on his manuscript *The History of Angria I* (15 June—25 July 1835).
22   6 May 1835; *SHLL,* vol. 1, p. 129.
23   *A Brace of Characters, SHCBM,* vol. 2, p. 51 (facsimile only).
24   After the conclusion of the 'First War' against the Ashantees on 3 January 1835, skirmishes continue along Angria's eastern borders and a 'Second War', which eventually threatens the very existence of Angria, is launched by Branwell in December 1835.
25   On 9 April 1835, the Reform Party under Ardrah (those opposed to Angria) force Fidena to resign. Ardrah, supported by his 'royal father' King of Parrisland, is then appointed Prime Minister and Lord High Admiral of the Verdopolitan Union. Elections follow and street fighting breaks out in Verdopolis between the supporters of the 'crimson' (Angrian) and the 'yellow' (Reformers, i.e. Whig) hustings. Richard Naughty, that 'antediluvian patriarch', rouses the rare lads in support of Northangerland, now retired to Alnwick but still politically active as his second letter to the people of Africa (10 May 1835) shows. Again he has changed sides: with Zamorna he now intends to oppose his old ally Ardrah who wants to reform Angria: see unpublished manuscript *Verdopolis and the Verdopolitans,* previously known as 'The Battle of Loango' (PML). The political upheaval is continued when Northangerland stands for election in Verdopolis against Montmorency (the 'yellow' government representative) in *The History of Angria I,* 15 June—25 July 1835: *SHCBM,* vol. 2, p. 100 (facsimile only: manuscript untraceable, formally in the Symmington Collection). This manuscript describes Captain Henry Hastings's entry into Angrian society, Zamorna's intention to form another alliance with Northangerland and Northangerland's speech (delivered on 17 June 1835) advocating Naval Reform.
26   *My Angria and the Angrians, SHCBM,* vol. 2, p. 30.
27   *From the Verdopolitan Intelligencer, ibid.,* p. 97 (facsimile only). Zamorna threatens Northangerland: 'I'll strike from under you the only prop left to support your exhausted and world-weary heart.'

CHAPTER 19: THE 'ROE HEAD JOURNAL'

1   *SHLL,* vol. 1, p. 159.
2   *SHCBP,* pp. 182—3.

3 Unpublished manuscript, beginning 'Long since as I remember well', *c.* 19 January 1836 (SUNY).

4 Unpublished manuscript, beginning 'But once again, but once again', 19 January 1836 (SUNY).

5 See Christine Alexander, 'Some New Findings in Brontë Bibliography', *Notes and Queries,* June 1983, p. 236, for an explanation of the dating of this manuscript.

6 The dating is based on the internal evidence of the weather, the Angrian situation, and on the physical appearance of the manuscript.

7 This fragment has previously been dated *c.*October 1836 but internal evidence indicates March 1837 as a more obvious date. The word 'March' occurs on p. 2 of the manuscript and the Angrian events described here are those of early 1837 rather than of October 1836.

8 Internal evidence points to October, but the year is uncertain. The previous dating of 1836 is incongruous with Angrian events. Mary is seen here in Zamorna Palace, receiving a letter from her exiled father. From February to December 1836 Adrianopolis was occupied by enemies and Northangerland was at the height of his power; by October 1837 Zamorna Palace was habitable again and Northangerland had fled into voluntary exile. Moreover, Charlotte was soon made aware of Mary's death in September 1836 and the decision to 'resuscitate' her was not made until the following December. It is possible that the fragment was written in 1835, but the internal evidence is less obvious and Branwell seems to have been less interested in Angria during the autumn of 1835 when he made his trip to London.

9 Unpublished manuscript, 'All this day I have been in a dream' (BPM: B98 (8)); see *SHCBM*, vol. 2, pp. 255—6 (ms. p. 1 only).

10 Unpublished manuscript, 'All this day I have been in a dream' (BPM: B98(8)).

11 *Ibid.,* the last three pages were probably written in October 1836, the date at the end of the manuscript, although internal evidence suggests the earlier date at the beginning of the manuscript, 11 August 1836.

12 *SHLL,* vol. 1, p. 136.

13 Unpublished manuscript, 'All this day I have been in a dream' (BPM: B98(8)).

14 *SHLL,* vol. 1, p. 139.

CHAPTER 20: WAR-TORN ANGRIA

1 Unpublished fragment included as ch. 6 at the end of *Verdopolis and the Verdopolitans,* formerly known as 'Battle of Loango' (PML).

2 Viz, BPM, Brotherton Library in Leeds, and PML in New York.

3 One fragment of the 'Roe Head Journal' begins 'About a week since I got a letter from Branwell': *SHCBM*, vol. 2, p. 256.

4 Unpublished manuscript by Branwell, *The Rising of the Angrians* (last half only), 24—8 December 1835 (PUL).

5 *SHCBM,* vol. 2, pp. 112—22 (part facsimile): pp. 121—2 come from another manuscript and have been wrongly included here. Scarcely any of the titles of Branwell's later manuscripts are original but have been added by the Shakespeare Head editors.

6 'Turn not now for comfort here', *c.* January 1836, *SHCBP,* p. 188; I have corrected 'moors' to 'guests' and 'hills' to 'halls' from stanza one of the original manuscript (BPM: B92(2)).

7 Marshal André Massena was one of Napoleon's most famous officers. He led the French 'Army of Portugal' against Wellington in the Peninsular Wars. Jordan, like so many of Branwell's characters, is derived from a similar source (Marshal Jourdan).

8 Untitled, undated poem, 'Again I find myself alone and ever', *c.* 1836; *SHCBP,* p. 201, entitled 'My Dreams'.

9 Unpublished manuscript, 'Well here I am at Roe Head', 4 February 1836 (PML).

10 Unpublished manuscript by Branwell, *The Rising of the Angrians* (first part only), 23 March 1836 (PUL).

11 *SHCBM,* vol 2, pp. 125—7 'grounds and' altered to 'groaning' from the manuscript (PML: MA 30).

12 *Ibid.,* p. 166.

13 *History of Angria IV* (4—23 May 1836) by Branwell; *SHCBM,* vol. 2, pp. 169—78 (part facsimile).

14 See p. 278, n.25.

15 *SHCBM,* vol. 2, pp. 142—3.

16 These events are related in a series of fragmentary manuscripts by Branwell known as: *History of Angria VI* (22 June 1836), *SHCBM,* vol. 2, p. 186; *History of Angria VII* (24 June 1836), *SHCBM,* vol. 2, p. 188; *A Narrative of the First War* (22—30 June 1836), unpublished manuscript — last section only (HRC); *History of Angria VIII* (22 July—8 August 1836), *SHCBM,* vol. 2, pp. 196—210 only. [*SHCBM,* vol. 2, pp. 210—21 (dated 3—19 September 1836) are irrelevant here and should be read after pp. 223—33 (dated 20—31 August 1836)].

17 Fannie E. Ratchford and William Clyde DeVane, eds., *Legends of Angria,* p. 111.

18 *SHCBM,* vol. 2, p. 156: 'watched' altered to 'resisted' from the manuscript (PML: MA 30).

19 Fannie E. Ratchford and William Clyde DeVane eds., *Legends of Angria,* p. 115.

20 Charlotte records this event later in *Mina Laury* (17 January 1838) when Hartford makes a bid for Mina's affections and reminds her of the assistance he gave her on 1 July 1836.

21 Unpublished poem, 'Long since as I remember well', *c.* 19 January 1836 (SUNY).

22 *History of Angria VIII* by Branwell, *SHCBM,* vol. 2, p. 203.

23 See Branwell's unpublished fragment (17 December 1836) included in his *History of Angria IX: SHCBM,* vol. 2, p. 267 (facsimile only).

24 Fannie E. Ratchford and William Clyde DeVane eds., *Legends of Angria,*

p. 126. Compare the frequent references to captured birds in *Jane Eyre:* for example, pp. 318, 414, 445, 552 and 562.

25 Unpublished manuscript (BPM: B98(6)).

26 See Branwell's *History of Angria VIII,* chs. 4—5, *SHCBM,* vol. 2, pp. 210—21, which is continued by an unpublished fragment (BPM: B145(1)), and two unpublished items in the private collection of Roger W. Barrett, Chicago: a fragment narrated by Richton (11 November 1836) and the poem 'Queen Mary's Grave' (10 December 1836).

27 *SHCBM,* vol. 2, pp. 218—19.

28 *Ibid.,* p. 217.

29 Unpublished fragment by Branwell (19 November 1836) included in the *History of Angria IX* (BPM: B143).

30 Such as Lady Jersey, Lady Shelley, Mrs Arbuthnot, Lady Charlotte Greville, and Lady Caroline Lamb. Elizabeth Longford explains that 'giving good advice to pretty women with problems' was one of the Duke's pleasures, and competition for his attention formed a bizarre feature of his social life for some years (*Wellington: Pillar of State,* p. 35).

31 Unpublished manuscript, 'I'm just going to write because I cannot help it' (BPM: B98(6)).

32 Two unpublished fragments by Branwell: 16 December 1836 (BPM: B145 (3)) and 17 December 1836 (B): the latter manuscript is reproduced in *SHCBM,* vol. 2, pp. 267—8, in facsimile.

33 *Ibid.,* pp. 322—3.

34 These events are recorded in a series of fragments by Branwell, grouped together by The Shakespeare Head editors under the title *History of Angria IX* (*SHCBM,* vol. 2, pp. 258—80).

CHAPTER 21: CHARLOTTE RESTORES PEACE

1 Untitled and undated manuscript (location untraceable: formerly in the Law Collection): published in *SHCBM,* vol. 2, pp. 281—314 as *The Return of Zamorna.* The dating has been based on internal evidence and on references in Branwell's manuscripts.

2 *SHCBM,* vol. 2, p. 292.

3 Unpublished manuscript, 'Now as I have a little bit of time', *c.* 5 February 1836 (PML).

4 Manuscript fragment by Branwell (BPM: 120), *SHCBM,* vol. 2, p. 334.

5 Prose fragment by Branwell (BPM: 111), *SHCBM,* vol. 2, p. 315: the manuscript has been placed too early in the sequence of Angrian events in the Shakespeare Head edition.

6 Winifred Gérin, ed., *Five Novelettes,* p. 210.

7 Unpublished manuscript, 'My Compliments to the weather', *c.* March 1837 (BPM: B98(6)).

8 In the original manuscript 'Sneachie' has been cancelled and 'Saunderson' inserted instead, perhaps to disguise his relationship to the Angrian Legend. Saunderson is, however, Sneachie, since he is referred to as 'John of the Highlands' and his closest friend is Wellington.

9 Winifred Gérin, ed., *Five Novelettes*, p. 87.

10 See Charlotte's original version of the poem 'The Town Besieged', beginning 'Deep the Cirhala flows' and included in her unpublished untitled story referred to as *Stancliffe's Hotel*, 28 June 1838 (BPM: B114).

11 *SHCBM*, vol. 2, p. 308.

12 *Ibid.*, p. 139.

13 Winifred Gérin, ed., *Five Novelettes*, p. 113.

14 Fragment by Branwell, *SHCBM*, vol. 2, p. 321.

15 'About a week since I got a letter from Branwell' (*c.* October 1837), *SHCBM*, vol. 2, p. 257.

16 Fragment by Branwell, 23 January 1837, *ibid.*, p. 334.

17 Winifred Gérin, ed., *Five Novelettes*, p. 94.

18 *Ibid.*

19 Unpublished, untitled manuscript known as *Four Years Ago,* a title used by C. W. Hatfield in his transcript (BPM) to which I am indebted. Formerly in a private American collection, the manuscript has not been traced.

20 See *SHCBM*, vol. 2, p. 223 (facsimile only). The facsimile of 11 pages from the manuscript (BL: Ashley 187) known as 'A New Year Story' and printed in *SHCBM*, vol. 2 as *The History of Angria VIII*, has not previously been related to Branwell's manuscript *The Life of feild Marshal the Right Honourable Alexander Percy,* now untraceable. A facsimile of the first page of this latter manuscript, however, which is to be found in the HCL and which includes the title and part of ch. 1, describes events which are continued in the former manuscript.

21 *The Life of Warner Howard Warner, Esq.,* By the Right Hon. John, Earl of Richton, February—8 March 1838 (BPM: B152(1)).

22 *BST*(1951) 12:61:15.

23 Emily also notes that Anne is writing a long narrative poem ('fair was the evening and brightly the sun', 1 July 1837) which concerns the separation and reunion of lovers, reminiscent of the situation between Zamorna and Mary in the Angrian legend.

24 Compare Charlotte's vision of two horsemen riding at midnight on the moor near Freetown, in the prose conclusion to 'We wove a web in childhood' (*SHCBP*, p. 186).

25 Transcript by C. W. Hatfield (BPM).

26 See earlier discussion of *The Secret* and 'Stanzas on the Fate of Henry Percy', p. 107.

CHAPTER 22: MINA LAURY

1 Untitled manuscript known as *Mina Laury:* Winifred Gérin, ed., *Five Novelettes*, p. 164.

2 *SHCBM*, vol. 2, pp. 132—8.

3 Spelt variously by Charlotte: 'Rivaulx' and 'Rivaux'. Winifred Gérin notes that this title is from Gilpin's sketch of the 'Cross of Rivaulx' (*Charlotte Brontë,* p. 118): in fact, Charlotte made her own copy of

Gilpin's picture but only a photograph of it exists (BPM: Symington Collection). She had also seen and possibly sketched Rievaulx Abbey in Rysedale, North Yorkshire.

4   Winifred Gérin, ed., *Five Novelettes*, p. 36: the pages of the juvenilia are full of obvious references to Bunyan.

5   *Ibid.*, p. 142.

6   *Ibid.*, p. 143: compare this passage with Catherine's attitude to Heathcliff in *Wuthering Heights* (pp. 110—12) and with that of Jane to Mr Rochester in *Jane Eyre* p. 219).

7   Cf. Branwell's manuscript fragment known as *History of Angria V* (28 May 1836): so long as Charles Wentworth could anticipate his visit to Verdopolis he was full of hope for the 'real life' he would begin there, but once there, his inability to cope with life in 'the mightiest City of the world', dispelled all the pleasure he had previously gained in self-deluding dreams — 'Happiness consists in Anticipation' (*SHCBM*, vol. 2, p. 180 (facsimile only)).

8   '"O! let me be alone" he said' (*c.* January 1838), *SHCBP*, 223—5, entitled 'The Death of Lord Hartford'.

9   *SHCBM*, vol. 1, p. 345 (facsimile only).

10 Winifred Gérin, ed., *Five Novelettes*, p. 165.

CHAPTER 23: HIGH LIFE IN ANGRIA

1   'Parting' (29 January 1838), *SHCBP*, p. 60. On 4 January 1838, Charlotte wrote to Ellen Nussey from Haworth: 'It will want three weeks next Monday to the termination of the holidays' (*SHLL*, vol. 1, p. 164).

2   Unpublished manuscript: 'All this day I have been in a dream', 11 August—14 October 1836 (BPM: B98(8)).

3   It has been thought that this move was made during the summer holidays of 1837, (Winifred Gérin, *Charlotte Brontë*, p. 112). However documentary evidence suggests an earlier date, possibly the Easter holidays. Charlotte was at home by 29 June for the summer holidays (the date of *Julia*) yet two letters addressed to Ellen Nussey in early June were sent by Charlotte from 'Dewsbury Moor' (*SHLL*, vol. 1, pp. 159—60).

4   *Ibid.*, p. 162.

5   *SHCBP*, p. 215.

6   'When Thou Sleepest' (*c.* May 1837), *SHCBP*, p. 204.

7   'Stanzas', 'Written 14 May 1837 at Roe Head', *SHCBP*, p. 58.

8   'The trees by the casement are moistened with dew' (*c.* May 1837), *SHCBP*, pp. 205—6; 'He could not sleep! — the couch of war' (*c.* May 1837), *SHCBP*, pp. 206—7; '"O! let me be alone" he said' (*c.* January 1838), *SHCBP*, pp. 223—5, and 'Long, long ago — before the weight of pain' (*c.* 1838), *SHCBP*, pp. 220—1.

9   Copy Book of Poems (PML). Another transcript of this poem exists in the hand of Charlotte's husband, the Rev. A. B. Nicholls (B).

10 Charlotte to Ellen Nussey, 5 May 1838: *SHLL*, vol. 1, p. 165.

11 *Ibid.*, p. 266.

12   Edinburgh, 1811 (BPM: B42); inscribed on the fly-leaf 'Presented to Miss Brontë with the love & best wishes of a Sincere Friend. Heald's House, May 23 d 1838.'

13   Unpublished manuscript, beginning 'Amen! Such was the sound given in a short shout which closed the evening Service at Ebenezer-Chapel' (BPM: B114).

14   F. H. Grundy, *Pictures of the Past,* p. 76: Grundy, who knew Branwell from 1841, says that his habit of taking opium began after his failure at Bradford.

15   There is evidence in the manuscript that Charlotte never intended the first scene to be more than a fragment. At the bottom of p. 2 she concluded the interview between Charles Townshend and Louisa Vernon after the service, when Charles declines an invitation to supper. Charlotte then changed her mind and, in even smaller script than usual, squeezed an alternative version on to the page: Charles finally yields to Louisa's entreaty and enters her house.

16   See Branwell's unpublished manuscript, 15 December 1837, included in the 'Percy' fragments (BPM: B149(6)).

17   In the manuscript (BPM: B114) the word 'chaussure' has been rather pretentiously inserted above the cancelled word 'pumps': at an early stage in her writing Charlotte felt the temptation to use a French word irrespective of its appropriateness.

18   Winifred Gérin, ed., *Five Novelettes,* p. 110.

19   Unpublished manuscript (BPM: B98(6)).

20   Unpublished manuscript, *Stancliffe's Hotel* (BPM: B114).

21   Compare Charlotte's description of a child's reaction to her sister's corpse here and Branwell's similar incident in his poem known as 'Caroline' (*SHCBP,* pp. 321—2): both were probably written in the same year and may contain biographical details, as has been pointed out by Winifred Gérin in the case of 'Caroline' (*Branwell Brontë,* p. 12). The name 'Harriet' occurs in both descriptions.

22   Unpublished poems, 'Deep the Cirhala flows' and 'The rumour of invaders through all Zamorna ran' (BPM: B114).

23   Unpublished manuscript, 'My Compliments to the weather' (BPM: B98(6)).

24   *Mina Laury,* Winifred Gérin, ed., *Five Novelettes,* p. 137.

25   Unpublished manuscript, *Stancliffe's Hotel* (BPM: B114).

26   *Mina Laury,* Winifred Gérin, ed., *Five Novelettes,* p. 131.

27   *SHCBM,* vol. 2, pp. 147—8.

28   Winifred Gérin, ed., *Five Novelettes,* pp. 263—9.

29   *Caroline Vernon, ibid.,* p. 332.

30   *Henry Hastings, ibid.,* p. 178.

31   Unpublished manuscript, *Stancliffe's Hotel* (BPM: B114).

32   Compare Charlotte's earliest description of factory pollution in the unpublished manuscript *The Adventure's of Mon Edouard de Crack* (HCL: MS. Lowell I(3)).

33   Unpublished manuscript, *Stancliffe's Hotel* (BPM: B114); compare

Elizabeth Longford's account of 'Peterloo' in *Wellington: Pillar of State,* pp. 59—61.

34 Elizabeth Longford, *Wellington: Pillar of State,* p. 61: parallels for this incident can also be found in the reform riots of 1831, especially those in Bristol which Elizabeth Longford refers to as 'the worst catastrophe since the Gordon Riots of 1780' (p. 271).

35 Winifred Gérin, ed., *Five Novelettes,* p. 244; 'Pendleton' is derived from 'Pendle Hill' and 'Boulshill' from 'Boulsworth Hill', both in the Pennine Range just west of Haworth. Colne is the name of a town across the Pennines from Haworth.

36 'All this day I have been in a dream', *SHCBM,* vol. 2, pp. 255—6: 'scribes' altered to 'scrubs' from the manuscript (BPM: B98(8)).

37 Unpublished manuscript, *Stancliffe's Hotel* (BPM: B114).

CHAPTER 24:
WILLIAM PERCY AND ELIZABETH HASTINGS

1 *SHCBM,* vol. 2, p. 373.

2 See unpublished manuscript by Branwell, included among the 'Percy' fragments, 30 December 1837 (BPM: B149(7)).

3 *SHCBM,* vol. 2, p. 227 (facsimile only): the following details of Augusta's life are derived from Branwell's manuscript known as the *History of Angria VIII* (20—31 August 1836), which is probably part of *The Life of feild Marshal the Right Honourable Alexander Percy,* now untraceable.

4 'Harriet I' (27 August 1837) *SHCBP,* pp. 328—35, and 'Harriet II' (14 May 1838), *SHCBP,* pp. 342—52.

5 Unpublished manuscript, *Ashworth, c.*December 1840—March 1841 (HCL: Widener Collection); a later manuscript related to the Angrian Saga.

6 *SHCBM,* vol. 2, pp. 353—4.

7 Unpublished manuscript, *Ashworth* (HCL: Widener Collection).

8 From Charlotte's poem 'Beneath Fidena's Minister', included in *The Duke of Zamorna: SHCBM,* vol. 2, pp. 370—71.

9 *SHCBM,* vol. 2, p. 357: compare Charlotte's poem 'Review at Gazemba' (7 July 1838), *SHCBM,* vol. 2, pp. 345—7.

10 *Ibid.,* p. 359.

11 *Ibid.,* p. 361.

12 *Ibid.,* p. 375.

13 *Ibid.,* p. 390.

14 *SHLL,* vol. 1, p. 170: there is no definite evidence of any surviving manuscripts, poetry or prose, written by Charlotte between 21 July 1838 and 24 February 1839. However, it is possible that the untitled and undated fragment, beginning 'But it is not in Society that the real character is revealed' (BPM: B113(7)), was written late in 1838.

15 These same events, however, are related in Branwell's unpublished

fragment (4 February 1839) included among the manuscripts known as *Love and Warfare* (PML).

16 *SHCBM,* vol. 2, p. 390.
17 Miss West, in Charlotte's unpublished manuscript fragment, 'But it is not in Society that the real character is revealed (BPM: B113(7)).
18 Winifred Gérin, ed., *Five Novelettes,* pp. 208—9: an obvious self-portrait.
19 Undated and untitled frament beginning 'But it is not in Society that the real character is revealed' (BPM: B113(7)). The significance of this manuscript has been overlooked in previous discussions of *Henry Hastings.*
20 Winifred Gérin, ed., *Five Novelettes,* p. 220; compare Lucy Snowe: 'I had feelings: passive as I lived, little as I spoke, cold as I looked, when I thought of past days, I *could* feel', yet 'in catalepsy and a dead trance, I studiously held the quick of my nature', *Villette,* vol. 1, p. 134.
21 Winifred Gérin, ed., *Five Novelettes,* p. 223; Miss West, like Elizabeth (and Charlotte, if we can judge from her letters), prides herself on her knowledge of human nature. It is interesting to compare this incident with Charlotte's record of her own uncharacteristic fit of temper, Mrs Gaskell, *The Life of Charlotte Brontë,* vol. 1, p. 235.
22 Winifred Gérin, ed., *Five Novelettes,* p. 244; compare 'I have some qualities which make me very miserable, some feelings that you can have no participation in, that few, very few people in the world can at all understand', Charlotte to Ellen Nussey, *c.* 1836, *SHLL,* vol. 1, p. 141.
23 Winifred Gérin, ed., *Five Novelettes,* p. 247.
24 *Ibid.,* p. 256.
25 Unpublished manuscript, 'But it is not in Society that the real character is revealed' (BPM: B113(7)).
26 *SHLL,* vol. 1, p. 241.
27 *Villette,* vol. 1, p. 134.
28 Winifred Gérin, ed., *Five Novelettes,* p. 211.
29 Mrs Gaskell, *The Life of Charlotte Brontë,* vol. 1, p. 216.
30 Winifred Gérin, ed., *Five Novelettes,* p. 243.
31 *SHLL,* vol. 1, p. 173.
32 Winifred Gérin, ed., *Five Novelettes,* p. 202.
33 *Ibid.,* pp. 201—3.
34 *Ibid.,* p. 242.
35 28 May 1836: manuscript fragment by Branwell, known as the *History of Angria V, SHCBM,* vol. 2, pp. 180—5 (part facsimile).
36 Winifred Gérin, *Branwell Brontë,* pp. 109—11: this information cannot be substantiated by biographical fact. Little evidence survives of Branwell's trip to London, even the date is uncertain. Biographers have relied on Branwell's juvenilia for explanations of the event; but although there are possible parallels, the heavy reliance on them seems unjustified.
37 Letter from Branwell at Haworth to J. H. Thompson, Bradford, 17 May 1839 (Winifred Gérin, *Branwell Brontë,* p. 147.)

38 Unpublished manuscript by Branwell, *The Life of Warner Howard Warner:* (BPM: B152(1)).

39 Unpublished and untitled fragment by Branwell, 25 April 1838 (location unknown; formerly in the possession of Mrs C. B. Branwell); transcript lent by Professor Ian Jack.

40 Unpublished manuscripts by Branwell (BPM: B149(1—7)).

41 *SHCBM,* vol. 2, p. 321.

42 *Ibid.,* p. 340.

43 Three unpublished *Percy* fragments by Branwell: 20 October 1837; undated; and 15 December 1837 (BPM: B149(1—7)).

44 A group of five unpublished prose fragments by Branwell (PML).

45 *c.*1845 (Collection of Harry B. Smith, New York): privately printed for J. A. Symington, 1924.

46 Unpublished fragment by Branwell, 15 December 1838, included in *Love and Warfare* (PML); and Winifred Gérin ed., *Five Novelettes,* p. 259. Compare a similar scene in the early juvenilia in which Zenobia is again studying Zamorna's Angrian maps in *High Life In Verdopolis, SHCBM,* vol. 1, p. 336 (facsimile only).

CHAPTER 25: FAREWELL TO ANGRIA

1   Winifred Gérin, ed., *Five Novelettes,* p. 278.

2   *Ibid.,* p. 277.

3   *SHLL,* vol. 1, p. 180.

4   'I used to think I should like to be in the stir of grand folks' society but I have had enough of it — it is dreary work to look on and listen', *ibid.,* p. 178.

5   Winifred Gérin, ed., *Five Novelettes,* p. 282.

6   *Ibid.,* p. 285.

7   *SHLL,* vol. 1, p. 176; and Winifred Gérin, ed., *Five Novelettes,* p. 288.

8   Winifred Gérin, ed., *Five Novelettes,* p. 280.

9   Winifred Gérin, ed., *Five Novelettes,* p. 114.

10 *SHCBM,* vol. 2, p. 369.

11 Winifred Gérin, ed., *Five Novelettes,* pp. 351—2.

12 *Henry Hastings, ibid.,* p. 254.

13 Fannie Ratchford, *The Brontës' Web of Childhood,* p. 148.

14 See Charlotte's Preface to the second edition of *Jane Eyre,* p. xxx.

15 Winifred Gérin, ed., *Five Novelettes,* pp. 309 and 353: compare Byron's motto 'Trust Byron!', *Letters and Journals of Lord Byron: with Notices of his Life,* By Thomas Moore (Paris: 1837), p. 5.

16 Winifred Gérin, ed., *Five Novelettes,* pp. 353—4.

17 *A Brace of Characters* (30 October 1834), *SHCBM,* vol. 2, p. 53 (facsimile only).

18 Winifred Gérin, ed., *Five Novelettes,* p. 363.

19 *The Duke of Zamorna, SHCBM,* vol. 2, p. 369.

20 Winifred Gérin, ed., *Five Novelettes,* p. 296.

21 *Ibid.,* p. 311.

22 See Winifred Gérin, introduction to *Caroline Vernon* in *Five Novelettes,* p. 274: a similar discrimination led Charlotte to write an alternative version to Zamorna's letter to Caroline in ch. 4 of Part II.

23 Winifred Gérin, ed., *Five Novelettes,* p. 319.

24 *SHLL,* vol. 1, p. 155.

25 *Ibid.,* p. 157.

26 *Ibid.,* p. 156.

27 *SHCBM,* vol. 2, pp. 403—4: this untitled manuscript, known by its first line 'I have now written a great many books', appears to be Charlotte's last explicit reference to her imaginative world and has therefore been called her 'Farewell to Angria'.

28 Namely, an untitled manuscript known as Ashworth, *c.*1840/1841 (HCL: Widener) and four fragments related to it (PML).

29 *SHCBM,* vol. 2, p. 404.

30 'Preface' to *The Professor.*

CHAPTER 26: ASHWORTH AND ANGRIA

1 See Fran Carlock Stephens, 'Hartley Coleridge and the Brontës', *TLS,* 14 May 1970, p. 544. My dating of this letter is based on the postmark 'De. 10' and the findings of C. W. Hatfield (see note 3 below).

2 Four prose manuscripts referred to by their first lines:
   i) 'Alexander Percy esq^{re} was a man much known about the country' (includes material later incorporated into *Ashworth,* chs. 1 and 3).
   ii) 'Miss Percy was a pupil in Mrs Turner's Seminary at Kensington' (includes material incorporated into *Ashworth,* ch. 2).
   iii) 'Miss Percy and Miss Thornton being both now settled in Yorkshire': pp. 1—6 only (a probable early draft of *Ashworth,* ch. 4, which no longer exists). The remainder of this manuscript (pp. 7—12), together with a further fragment previously thought to be a separate manuscript ('Leeds and the clothiers of Bradford'), constitutes the end of ch. 2 and all of ch. 3 of the HCL *Ashworth* manuscript (which includes ch. 1 and the beginning of ch. 2 only).
   iv) 'hand over the heart & seemed to look into the marble face for life' (possibly an early draft of a later part of Ashworth which no longer exists).

   The first two fragments and part of the third were published in *BST* (1940) 10:50:15—24.
   The close relationship between the PML fragments and the HCL manuscript ('Ashworth and Son') as first noted by Melodie Monahan in her scholarly edition of *Ashworth,* to which I am indebted for my knowledge of the final *Ashworth* manuscript: Ph.D. dissertation for the University of Rochester, 1976 — referred to in the following notes as *Monahan.*

3 Between 6 May 1840 and 10 December 1840: C. W. Hatfield has pointed out that the stamps on the wrapper in which Hartley Coleridge returned Charlotte's manuscript were issued between 6 May 1840 and 9

February 1841 (*BST*(1940) 10:50:15). Since Charlotte wrote a draft letter on the reverse of this wrapper and sent the final version of her letter to Hartley Coleridge on 10 December 1840, he must have returned her manuscript before this date.

4 My dating of the final *Ashworth* manuscript is much later than that of earlier scholars. It is based on the fact that although the original 'Ashworth' drafts of a Percy/West story (in PML) were probably written in December 1839/January 1840 (based on internal evidence and the fact that they are unlikely to have been written until *Caroline Vernon* was completed), the letter Charlotte sent to Hartley Coleridge in December 1840 refers to the same Percy/West story and not the later Ashworth/West story. Thus the change of name from Percy to Ashworth (and Thornton to De Capell) must post-date Charlotte's letter to Hartley Coleridge. This later dating is supported by the opening of Ashworth; Charlotte had only just completed *Caroline Vernon* in December 1839 and is unlikely to have written the following first sentence of *Ashworth* a month or so later: 'Long disuse of a pen that was once frequently handled makes me feel as if my hand had lost some of its cunning.' Moreover, the fact that both *Ashworth* and her letter to Hartley Coleridge include references to Richardson, and in particular to Sir Charles Grandison, may indicate that they were written about the same time: that is, late 1840/early 1841.

5 Letter to Hartley Coleridge, 10 December 1841: *TLS,* 14 May 1970, p.544.

6 Unpublished manuscript (PML: see the third item under note 2 above). Following the end of ch. 3, Charlotte has written the following notes in the manuscript:

School-Scene
Introduction to Yorkshire
Gillwood, Ripley Towers — De Capell-Hall
Miss Thornton & Miss Percy were

This appears to be a plan: a summary of chs. 2 and 3 of *Ashworth* and a possible intention for ch. 4. Based on the final phrase which repeats the beginning of an earlier draft (see note 2 above), Dr Monahan includes the early draft (altering the names Percy and Thornton to Ashworth and De Capell) as ch. 4 of her edition of Ashworth. The story is still obviously incomplete and she notes that further fragments of *Ashworth* may still exist.

7 *Monahan,* p. 124.

8 *Ibid.,* p. 127.

9 *Ibid.,* p. 133.

10 A picture by the Verdopolitan artist William Etty, showing the tutorship of S'Death, 'the hoary mentor' of young Percy, is referred to in *SHCBM,* vol. 2, p. 64 (facsimile only).

11 Untitled fragment by Branwell, *ibid.,* p. 227 (facsimile only). The name Wharton also appears briefly in *Jane Eyre,* p. 578.

12 Unpublished manuscript by Branwell (BPM: B141).
13 Winifred Gérin ed. *Five Novelettes,* p. 273.
14 *Monahan,* p. 42.
15 *Ibid.,* p. 157.
16 *Ibid.,* p. 158.
17 *Ibid.,* pp. 145—6; cf. this early use of the image with its recurrence in *Jane Eyre* (for example, pp. 307, 395 and 422).
18 *Ibid.,* pp. 158—9.
19 *Ibid.,* pp. 163—4; compare Charlotte's recent experience of 'haughty' treatment by Mrs Sidgwick: *SHLL,* vol. 1, pp. 177—9.
20 *Ibid.,* p. 145.
21 *Monahan,* p. 172;
    cf. 'For the roar of the battle, like thunder, had flown,
    And red on Assaye the heaped carnage was lying'
    (Composed and sent to Wellington by Lt. J. E. Alexander, 1829): this is a reference to the bloody victory of Assaye (1803) won by Wellington in India, where he had an aide-de-camp called General West (Elizabeth Longford, *Wellington: The Years of the Sword,* p. 92). Details from the Duke of Wellington's life can still be detected in Charlotte's later writing: see Herbert Rosengarten's Cambridge Ph.D. dissertation (1974), *Charlotte Brontë's "Shirley": an edition,* p. 48, n.303.
22 *Monahan,* p. 177.
23 *Ibid.,* p. 186.
24 *Ibid.,* p. 193.

CHAPTER 27: BRANWELL'S INFLUENCE

1 Unpublished manuscript dated 30 December 1837 (BPM: B149(7)): the original is difficult to read and I am indebted to a transcript by C. W. Hatfield (BPM). This is one of 7 prose fragments referred to as 'Percy' which were inappropriately renamed 'The History of Angria X' by the editors of the Shakespeare Head Brontë but never included in their edition (see *SHCBM,* vol. 2, p. 342).
2 The note comparing Charlotte's description of a 'Gytrash' in the Clarendon Edition of *Jane Eyre* (p. 590) with that of Branwell in an unfinished story (mentioned in Winifred Gérin's *Branwell Brontë*) does not identify the source of Branwell's description, which is the above 'Percy' fragment (BPM: B149(7)).
3 Unsigned review in the *Daily News,* 3 February 1853 (Miriam Allott, *The Brontës: The Critical Heritage,* pp. 172—3).
4 *Daily News,* April 1855 (Miriam Allott, *The Brontës: The Critical Heritage,* p. 303).

CHAPTER 28: THE SEARCH AFTER LOVE

1 Unpublished manuscript (BPM: B80(9)).
2 Unpublished manuscript (HCL: MS. Lowell I(3)).

3   Unpublished manuscript, *Four Years Ago* (location untraced: see Hatfield transcript in BPM).
4   Unpublished and undated manuscript (BPM: B91(1)), written on the reverse of *The African Queen's Lament*, 12 February 1833.
5   Unpublished manuscript (BPM: B91 (1)).
6   Referring to Marion Hume: *High Life In Verdopolis, SHCBM*, vol. 2, p. 346 (facsimile only).
7   *High Life In Verdopolis, ibid.*, p. 345 (facsimile only).
8   *Henry Hastings*, Winifred Gérin, ed., *Five Novelettes*, p. 254; compare *Othello*, V: 2, 345.
9   *Mina Laury*, Winifred Gérin, ed., *Five Novelettes*, p. 131.
10 *Caroline Vernon, ibid.*, p. 352.
11 *Ibid.*, p. 364.
12 See Inga-Stina Ewbank, *Their Proper Sphere: A Study of the Brontë Sisters as Early-Victorian Female Novelists* (London: 1966), p. 27.
13 Unpublished manuscript, 'All this day I have been in a dream' (BPM: B98(8)).
14 Unpublished manuscript, 'Well here I am at Roe-Head' (PML).
15 Unpublished manuscript, 'But it is not in Society . . .' (BPM: B113(7)).
16 Unpublished manuscript, 'All this day I have been in a dream' (BPM: B98(8)).
17 *Henry Hastings*, Winifred Gérin, ed., *Five Novelettes*, p. 220.
18 *SHLL*, vol. 1, p. 178.
19 *Monahan*, p. 167.
20 On the reverse of Charlotte's 'Farewell to Angria', *c.* late 1839 (BPM: B125), the following notes occur: 'Boy-destroyer/Mr Squeers/Dotheboys-Hall Greta-Bridge/Yorkshire/Favoured by Chas Dickens Esqre'. It is interesting to compare this reference to the tyrannical figure posing as an educationalist in *Nicholas Nickleby* with Mr Brocklehurst. Charlotte's early response to the cruelty often inflicted on homeless children may have been influenced by Dickens. Certainly, this reference shows that Charlotte read *Nicholas Nickleby* as soon as it appeared in monthly numbers in 1838—39).

CHAPTER 29: TWO RIVAL BROTHERS

1   Unpublished manuscript, *A Day Abroad* (HL: HM2577).
2   *Monahan*, pp. 176—8.
3   *SHCBM*, vol. 1, p. 327 (facsimile only).
4   *The Duke of Zamorna, ibid*, vol. 2, p. 386. The brothers also meet in Zamorna in *Stancliffe's Hotel*, but William cuts his brother's pompous speech short and walks on: unpublished manuscript (BPM: B114).
5   *Monahan*, p. 129.
6   Catherine II, Empress of Russia (1762—96) married the grand duke Peter who was mentally and physically subnormal. Her dislike for her son, Paul, lay in his resemblance to his father in appearance and character (noted in *Monahan*, p. 140).

7 *Monahan,* p. 156; compare *Jane Eyre,* pp. 174—5, and *Villette,* vol. 1, p. 228. Charlotte's image of the sea or river of life is common to both the juvenilia and the novels, as is the idea of 'diving' into someone's character or into the 'waves' of thought:

> Look into thought and say what does thou see
> Dive, be not fearful how dark the waves flow
> Sink through the surge and bring pearls up to me
> Deeper aye deeper, the fairest lie low.

This unpublished poem (BPM: B98(7) was written at Roe Head, so presumably these 'pearls' represent Charlotte's Angrian dream-world. Pearls are symbols of purity in the juvenilia and are particularly associated with Marian Hume: see the poem 'The pearl within the shell concealed', which is included in *Visits in Verreopolis*, vol. 1, *SHCBP,* p. 128. In *Villette,* Lucy Snowe prizes human affection 'as if it were a solid pearl' (vol. 1, p. 43).

8 For example, see 'Stanzas On The Fate of Henry Percy', *SHCBP,* pp. 162—71. For references to Timothy Steaton (or Steighton as the name was originally spelt in the juvenilia) see especially *Passing Events,* Winifred Gérin, ed., *Five Novelettes,* p. 51, and Branwell's manuscript *The Wool is Rising, SHCBM,* vol. 1, p. 412 (facsimile only).

9 My attention was drawn to the opening of *The Professor* in a lecture by and later discussion with Mr George Watson.

10 *SHLL,* vol. 3, p. 206.

11 *Ibid.,* vol. 2, p. 161.

12 14 December 1847: *SHLL,* vol. 2, p. 162.

13 Although I have studied the original manuscript, I am indebted to Joseph R. Geer's transcription of *John Henry,* submitted as part of his dissertation for an A.B. at Princeton University, 24 March 1965: *The Artist at Work: A Critical Study of Charlotte Brontë's Manuscript, 'John Henry'* (see also a summary of this thesis in *BST*(1966) 15:76: 20—7. Joseph Geer shows that *John Henry* is both a recasting of *The Professor* and an early draft for *Shirley*; but he fails to recognize that John Henry is the same manuscript as *The Moores,* which has long been known as a forerunner of *Shirley* and which was published in *'Jane Eyre', to which is added 'The Moores'* (London, 1902), Appendix. Comparison between John Geer's transcription, the original manuscript, and the latter publication soon showed that *John Henry* and *The Moores* were the same manuscript and not two of the three known early drafts of *Shirley,* as previously thought. This has been confirmed by Dr Herbert Rosengarten in the Clarendon Edition of *Shirley,* pp. xiii—xiv.

14 Manuscript p. 4 (PUL: Taylor Collection).

15 Renamed 'Steele' in ch. 3 of *John Henry.*

16 In the early part of William Moore's letter he refers to Mr Calvert and Dr Greatorix as Mr Seacombe and Dr McShane, underlying even more overtly their affinities with the Crimsworths' Seacombe relations in *The Professor.*

17 *'Jane Eyre', to which is added 'The Moores',* p. 539.
18 *SHLL,* vol. 2, p. 161.
19 Unpublished manuscript (BPM: B109).
20 Three early drafts in pencil of the beginning of an unfinished story relating to Willie Ellin:
    1) 'I will not deny that I took a pleasure in studying the character of Mrs Widdop' May 1853 (HCL: MS.Eng. 35.4).
    2) 'In other countries and in distant times — it is possible', 22 June 1853 (HCL: MS Eng 35.4).
    3) '"Stop" — said the expectant victim earnestly', *c.* June 1853 (BPM: B111).
    All three fragments were published in *BST* (1936) 9:46:3—22.
21 Lord Charles Wellesley is also whipped by his elder brother, the Marquis of Douro: see for example, *The Green Dwarf,* Fannie E. Ratchford and William Clyde DeVane, *Legends of Angria,* p. 7.
22 Mrs Gaskell, *The Life of Charlotte Brontë,* vol. 2, p. 53.

CHAPTER 30: THE AUTHORIAL VOICE

1 Mrs Gaskell states that Charlotte occasionally used the pseudonym 'Charles Thunder' in letters to her friends, using 'her Christian name, and the meaning of her Greek surname', *The Life of Charlotte Brontë,* vol. 1, p. 220. C. W. Hatfield could not recall any extant letters by Charlotte which were signed 'Charles Thunder' (*BST* (1940) 10:50:16); and nowhere in her surviving juvenilia does Charlotte use this name.
2 *Strange Events* (in *Young Men's Magazine*), 29 August 1830, *SHCBM,* vol. 1, p. 19.
3 Between August 1841 — July 1842, Branwell published six poems in the *Halifax Guardian* (Winifred Gérin, *Branwell Brontë,* p. 186).
4 *SHLL,* vol. 1, p. 155.
5 *Ibid.,* p. 157.
6 Unpublished manuscript (BPM: B114).
7 Charlotte quotes from *Night Thoughts* in *The Poetaster,* vol. 2, *Studies in Romanticism* 20 (Winter 1981), p. 494. Mr Brontë's copy survives in the BPM (526).
8 Unpublished manuscript, 'Song' (BPM: 12).
9 Winifred Gérin, ed., *Five Novelettes,* p. 184.
10 Preface to *Corner Dishes,* unpublished manuscript (HL: HM 2577).
11 See p. 105 for a discussion of Charlotte's early fascination with the theatre. Compare also *Villette,* vol. 1, p. 176.
12 Unpublished manuscript (BL: Add. MS. 34255).
13 *SHCBM,* vol. 2, p. 284.
14 Unpublished manuscript (HCL: MS. Lowell I(3)).
15 Tom Winnifrith, *The Brontës and Their Background,* p. 225, n. 43.
16 George Edwin MacLean, ed., *The Spell: An Extravaganza,* p. 143.
17 *SHCBM,* vol. 2, p. 284.

18   Branwell is known to have owned a copy of *Childe Harold's Pilgrimage* (Paris, 1827), which he bought in Liverpool on 30 May 1835 (BPM: 114).
19   Probably derived from the *Arabian Nights' Entertainments,* this is the most common narrative form in Charlotte's early stories.
20   Unpublished manuscript, 'Now as I have a little bit of time' (PML).
21   Unpublished manuscript, *Stancliffe's Hotel* (BPM: B114).
22   *The Professor,* p. 166.

CHAPTER 31: A VISUAL IMAGINATION

1   'Reminiscences of Charlotte Brontë', *BST* (1899) 2:10:68.
2   Mrs Gaskell, *The Life of Charlotte Brontë*, vol. 1, p. 152.
3   2 September 1829: *SHLL,* vol. 1, p. 82.
4   Winifred Gérin, ed., *Five Novelettes,* p. 42; Winifred Gérin was the first to note Charlotte's use of Gilpin's 'Cross of Rivaulx' (*Charlotte Brontë,* p. 118) but it is not obvious that she was aware of Charlotte's actual copy of the picture which survives only as a photograph in the BPM (Symmington Collection).
5   William Finden's 'Lausanne', 'Geneva', 'Maid of Saragoza' and 'Lady Jersey' (BPM).
6   Martin's 'Deluge', for example, is compared to a wild scene in *The Search after Happiness*, Winifred Gérin, *Charlotte Brontë,* p. 44.
7   *Ibid.,* p. 45.
8   *My Angria and the Angrians, SHCBM,* vol. 2, p. 25.
9   Mrs Gaskell, *The Life of Charlotte Brontë,* vol. 1, p. 96: the original page which included this title no longer exists, but the undated list of thirteen painters is preserved in the BPM: B80(13).
10 Untitled fragmentary manuscript, beginning '"Well Etty" said I,' 5 December 1834, *SHCBM,* vol. 2, p. 64 (facsimile only). William Etty (1787—1849) was a Yorkshire artist who became a member of the Royal Academy in 1829.
11 See for example the following unpublished manuscripts in *Blackwood's Young Men's Magazine: Revi[e]w of the painting of the Spirit of Cawdor ravine,* 21 August 1829 (BPM: S.G.95) and *Review of The Cheif Geni in Council,* 9 December 1829 (BL: Ashley MS. 157).
12 *The Swiss Artist* (*BST* (1919) 5:29:267-270) and *The Swiss Artist Continued,* unpublished manuscript (BL: Ashley MS. 157), a serial in the two issues of *Blackwood's Young Men's Magazine* for December 1829. See also *Conversations* (in *Young Men's Magazine*), 1 September 1830, *The Bookman* (December 1825), pp. 155—6.
13 See *The Duke of Zamorna, SHCBM,* vol. 2, p. 388.
14 Unpublished manuscript, *Review of the Cheif Geni in Council* (BL: Ashley MS.157); compare *Villette,* vol. 1, p. 209.
15 Unpublished manuscript (HCL: Lowell autograph).
16 Unpublished manuscript (BPM: B84).
17 George Edwin MacLean, ed. *The Spell: An Extravaganza,* pp. 105—6.

18 *The Professor,* p. 53: 'Three — nay four — pictures line the four-walled cell where are stored for me the records of the past.'

19 *Jane Eyre,* p. 140.

20 *High Life In Verdopolis, SHCBM,* vol. 1, p. 344 (facsimile only).

21 Winifred Gérin, ed., *Five Novelettes,* p. 362.

22 Unpublished manuscript, *Visits in Verreopolis,* vol. 1 (manuscript untraced: transcript lent to the author by Professor Ian Jack).

23 Compare also the sinister red room at Gateshead. Charlotte's early sensitivity to rich colours is noticeable in her descriptions of Genii Palaces and the sumptuous homes of the Duke of Zamorna.

24 Ian Jack shows how Charlotte's close observation of character was fostered by her interest in physiognomy and phrenology, in 'Physiognomy, Phrenology and Characterisation in the Novels of Charlotte Brontë,' *BST* (1970) 15:80:377—91.

25 *'Jane Eyre', to which is added 'The Moores',* p. 543.

26 Unpublished manuscript, *High Life In Verdopolis, SHCBM,* vol. 1, p. 337 (facsimile only).

27 *Jane Eyre,* pp. 160 and 166.

28 Unpublished manuscript, *Stancliffe's Hotel* (BPM: B114).

29 Winifred Gérin, ed., *Five Novelettes,* p. 200.

30 *SHLL,* vol. 3, p. 147.

31 Unpublished manuscript (HCL: Lowell autograph).

32 *The Return of Zamorna, SHCBM,* vol. 2, pp. 285—7.

33 Clement Shorter and C. W. Hatfield, eds., *The Twelve Adventurers and Other Stories,* p. 51: an early instance of the frost/ice and fire/sun images as correlatives for personal feeling. Polar skies and cold landscapes become particularly associated with the theme of isolation and loneliness in the novels. Characters assume an elemental significance: St John Rivers is like 'an iceberg' (*Jane Eyre,* p. 568), Jane is associated with fire (*Jane Eyre,* p. 489), and Charlotte was eager that Lucy Snowe's surname should be indicative of cold (*SHLL,* vol. 4, 18).

34 Unpublished manuscript, 'Now as I have a little bit of time' (PML).

35 *The Professor,* pp. 54 and 188.

36 J. Lempriere, *Bibliotheca Classica; or, A Classical Dictionary, containing A Full Account of All the Proper Names mentioned in Ancient Authors* (London, 1797), a gift to Mr Brontë from a Cambridge pupil (BPM: 212). Several pages contain the obvious scribblings of young children.

37 See ch. 1, pp. 23—4.

38 'Death of Darius Codomannus', *SHCBP,* pp. 154—62.

39 *A Day Abroad, SHCBM,* vol. 1, p. 371 (facsimile only).

40 A. Edward Newton, ed., *Derby Day and Other Adventures,* pp. 348, 360 and 370.

41 See especially *High Life In Verdopolis, SHCBM,* vol. 1, p. 340 (facsimile only) and George Edwin MacLean, ed., *The Spell: An Extravaganza,* p. 102.

42 *A Peep Into A Picture Book, SHCBM,* vol. 1, p. 361.

43 *SHCBM,* vol. 2, p. 69 (facsimile only).

44 Ellen Nussey, 'Reminiscences of Charlotte Brontë', *BST* (1899) 2:10:70.
45 T. A. J. Burnett, ed., *The Search After Happiness,* pp. 33—4; compare for example the Book of the Revelation, 21: 10—21.
46 Unpublished manuscript, *Leisure Hours,* 29 June 1830 (BPM: B83).
47 See discussion of *Tales of the Islanders,* p. 50.
48 See especially *A Day Abroad, Passing Events, The Return of Zamorna, Julia* and *Stancliffe's Hotel.*
49 *Speech of His Grace The Duke of Zamorna, SHCBM,* vol. 1, p. 480 (facsimile only).
50 Unpublished manuscript, 'St. John in the Island of Patmos', 30 August 1832 (original manuscript untraced; transcription by Rev. A. B. Nicholls in B).
51 'Long since as I remember well' (SUNY). See also Charlotte's poem 'Lament for the Martyr who dies for his faith', *SHCBP,* p. 178, for a similar reference to St Stephen.
52 *A Peep Into A Picture Book, SHCBM,* vol. 1, p. 360.
53 *From the Verdopolitan Intelligencer, SHCBM,* vol. 2, p. 96 (facsimile only).
54 *SHCBM,* vol. 2, p. 96 (facsimile only); an obvious allusion to Bunyan. Compare also the pervasive image in *Jane Eyre* of life as a journey towards that country 'from whose bourn No traveller returns'; and William Crimsworth's pilgrimage through life in *The Professor.*
55 Unpublished manuscript, 'Well here I am at Roe Head' (PML).
56 *TLS,* 14 May 1970, p. 544.
57 Unpublished manuscript, 'My Compliments to the weather' (BPM: B98(6)).
58 *The Duke of Zamorna, SHCBM,* vol. 2, p. 349.
59 *SHCBP,* p. 202.
60 Unpublished manuscript, 'Well here I am at Roe Head' (PML).

CONCLUSION

1 *SHLL,* vol. 3, pp. 23 and 37.
2 Fannie Ratchford states that 'Shirley herself is the continuation of an Angrian beauty, named Jane Moore, who represented Emily Brontë' (PMLA, 1928, vol. 43.I, p. 500). There are some similarities between Shirley and Jane Moore, such as their wealth, patriotism, handsome features and glossy curls (attributes common to almost every Angrian heroine) and certain incidents in their behaviour which Fannie Ratchford aptly identifies in *The Brontës' Web of Childhood,* pp. 218—20.
3 'I have now written a great many books', *SHCBM,* vol. 2, p. 404.
4 *BST* (1940) 10:50:16; early draft of Charlotte's letter to Hartley Coleridge written on the inside of the wrapper in which her story was returned (PML).
5 *BST* (1924) 6:34:231—2.

6   See M. H. Spielman, 'An early essay by Charlotte Brontë', *BST* (1924)
    6:34:237.
7   Enid Duthie, *The Foreign Vision of Charlotte Brontë,* p. 60.
8   Preface to *The Professor.*
9   Mrs Gaskell, *The Life of Charlotte Brontë,* vol. 2, p. 53.

Select Bibliography

EDITIONS OF CHARLOTTE BRONTË'S WORKS
USED IN THIS STUDY

Alexander, Christine, ed., *Something about Arthur.* Austin: Humanities Research Center, University of Texas at Austin, 1981

Bellour, Raymond, ed., *Charlotte Brontë: Patrick Branwell Brontë* (an edition of 10 juvenile works translated into French). Paris: J. J. Pauvert, 1972

Bentley, Phyllis, ed., *The Professor, Tales from Angria, Emma: A Fragment.* London: Collins, 1954

Burnett, T. A. J., ed., *The Search After Hapiness: A Tale by Charlotte Brontë.* London: Harvill Press, 1969

Gérin, Winifred, ed., *Five Novelettes.* London: Folio Press, 1971

Holtz, William, ed., *Two Tales by Charlotte Brontë: 'The Secret' & 'Lily Hart'.* University of Missouri Press, 1977

Jack, Jane, and Smith, Margaret, eds., *Jane Eyre.* Oxford: Clarendon, 1969

MacLean, George Edwin, ed., *Lament befitting these 'Times of Night'.* Reprinted from *The Cornhill Magazine,* August 1916. London: Smith, Elder, 1916

MacLean, George Edwin, ed., *The Spell: An Extravaganza.* Oxford: Oxford University Press, 1931

Monahan, Melodie, ed., *Ashworth: An Unfinished Novel by Charlotte Brontë.* Ph.D. dissertation for the University of Rochester, 1976

Monahan, Melodie, ed., 'Charlotte Brontë's *The Poetaster:* Text and Notes'. *Studies in Romanticism,* 20 (Winter 1981), pp. 475—96

Newton, A. Edward, ed., *Derby Day and Other Adventures* [includes the only edition of 'A Leaf from an Unopened Volume']. Boston: Little, Brown, 1934

Nicoll, W. Robertson, ed., *'Jane Eyre' to which is added 'The Moores'.* London: Hodder and Stoughton, 1902

The Professor (The Shakespeare Head Brontë). Oxford: Basil Blackwell, 1931

Ratchford, Fannie E., and DeVane, William Clyde, eds., *Legends of Angria: Compiled from The Early Writings of Charlotte Brontë.* New Haven: Yale University Press, 1933

Rosengarten, Herbert, ed., *Charlotte Brontë's 'Shirley': An Edition,* 4 vols. Ph.D. dissertation for the University of Cambridge, 1974

Rosengarten, Herbert, and Smith, Margaret, eds., *Shirley.* Oxford: Clarendon, 1979

Shorter, Clement, ed., *The Brontës: Life and Letters,* 2 vols. London: Hodder and Stoughton, 1908

Shorter, Clement, ed., *The Violet: A Poem written at the Age of Fourteen.* London: privately printed by Clement Shorter, 1916

Shorter, Clement, ed., *Voltaire's 'Henriade': Book I Translated from the French.* London: privately printed by Clement Shorter, 1917

Shorter, Clement, ed., *The Four Wishes: A Fairy Tale.* London: privately printed by Clement Shorter, 1918

Shorter, Clement, ed., *Latest Gleanings: Being A Series of Unpublished Poems Selected from Her Early Manuscripts.* London: privately printed by Clement Shorter, 1918

Shorter, Clement, ed., *Napoleon and The Spectre: A Ghost Story.* London: privately printed by Clement Shorter, 1919

Shorter, Clement, and Hatfield, C. W., eds., *The Complete Poems of Charlotte Brontë.* London: Hodder and Stoughton, 1923

Shorter, Clement, and Hatfield, C. W., eds., *The Twelve Adventurers and Other Stories.* London: Hodder and Stoughton, 1925

Spielmann, M. H., ed., *An Early Essay of Charlotte Brontë* [On Millevoye's 'La Chute des feuilles'. In French with corrections by C. Heger]. Reprinted from *BST,* 1924. Bradford, 1924

Villette (The Shakespeare Head Brontë), 2 vols. Oxford: Basil Blackwell, 1931

Wise, Thomas James, ed., *The Adventures of Ernest Alembert: A Fairy Tale.* London: printed for private circulation, 1896

Wise, Thomas James, ed., *Richard Coeur de Lion and Blondel: A Poem.* London: printed for private circulation, 1912

Wise, Thomas James, ed., *Saul and Other Poems.* London: printed for private circulation, 1913

Wise, Thomas James, ed., *The Orphans and Other Poems.* London: printed for private circulation, 1917

Wise, Thomas James, ed., *The Red Cross Knight and Other Poems.* London: printed for private circulation, 1917

Wise, Thomas James, ed., *The Swiss Emigrant's Return and Other Poems.* London: printed for private circulation, 1917

Wise, Thomas James, ed., *Darius Codomannus: A Poem.* London: printed for private circulation, 1920

Wise, Thomas James, and Symington, John Alexander, eds., *The Brontës: Their Lives, Friendships and Correspondence* (The Shakespeare Head Brontë), 4 vols. Oxford: Basil Blackwell, 1932

Wise, Thomas James, and Symington, John Alexander, eds., *The Poems of Charlotte Brontë and Patrick Branwell Brontë* (The Shakespeare Head Brontë). Oxford: Basil Blackwell, 1934

Wise, Thomas James, and Symington, John Alexander, eds., *The Miscellaneous and Unpublished Writings of Charlotte and Patrick Branwell Brontë* (The Shakespeare Head Brontë), 2 vols.: 1 (1936) and 2 (1938). Oxford: Basil Blackwell

The many publications of individual juvenile manuscripts in *BST* and in *The Bookman* are referred to in the notes.

OTHER WORKS CONSULTED IN THIS STUDY

Allott, Miriam, *The Brontës: The Critical Heritage.* London: Routledge & Kegan Paul, 1974

Arabian Nights' Entertainments: Consisting of One Thousand and One Stories Told by The Sultaness of the Indies. Translated into French from the Arabian MSS. by M. Galland of the Royal Academy and now rendered into English from the last Paris Edition. A New Edition, Corrected [by R. Gough], 4 vols. London: Longman, 1798

Benson, E. F., *Charlotte Brontë.* London: Longmans, Green & Co., 1932

Bentley, Phyllis, *The Brontës.* London: Home & Van Thal, 1947

Blackwood's Edinburgh Magazine, 1820—1840: articles referred to from this magazine are listed in detail in the relevant footnotes

Blom, Margaret Howard, *Charlotte Brontë.* London: George Prior and Boston: Twayne, 1977

Brontë, Emily, *The Complete Poems of Emily Jane Brontë,* ed. C. W. Hatfield. New York: Columbia University Press, 1941

Brontë Emily, *Wuthering Heights,* ed. Hilda Marsden and Ian Jack. Oxford: Clarendon, 1976

Brontë, Patrick, *Brontëana: The Rev. Patrick Brontë's Collected Works,* ed. J. Horsfall Turner. Bingley: printed for the editor, 1898

Brontë, Patrick Branwell, *And the Weary are at Rest.* London: privately printed for J. A. Symington, 1924

Brontë Society Transactions, 1895—1982. Keighley: Keighley Printers

Burkhart, Charles, *Charlotte Brontë: A Psychosexual Study of her Novels.* London: Victor Gollancz, 1973

Byron. *Letters and Journals of Lord Byron: with Notices of His Life,* ed. Thomas Moore. Paris: A. and W. Galignani, 1837

Byron, *Byron: Poetical Works,* ed. Frederick Page (1904); 3rd. ed. 'corrected' by John Jump. Oxford: Oxford University Press, 1970.

Cecil, Lord David, *Early Victorian Novelists: Essays in revaluation.* London: Constable, 1934

Chadwick, Mrs Ellis H., *In the Footsteps of The Brontës.* London: Pitman, 1914

Chapple, J. A. V., and Pollard, Arthur, eds., *The Letters of Mrs Gaskell.* Manchester University Press, 1966

Christian, Mildred G., 'A Census of Brontë Manuscripts in the United States'. *The Trollopian,* II (1947—8) and III (1948)

Christian, Mildred G., 'The Brontës', in *Victorian Fiction: A Guide to Research,* ed. Lionel Stevenson. Cambridge, Mass.: Harvard University Press, 1964

Cook, Davidson, 'Brontë Manuscripts in the Law Collection' in *The Bookman,* November, 1925, pp. 100—4

Craik, W. A., *The Brontë Novels.* London: Methuen, 1968

Croxall, Samuel., *The Fables of Aesop; with Instructive Applications.* Halifax: Milner and Sowerby, 1857

De Quincey, Thomas, *The Confessions of an English Opium-Eater.* London: Dent, 1907

Du Fresnoy, Abbé Lenglet, *Geography for Youth,* 'Translated from the French', 14th ed. Dublin: P. Wogan, 1795

Duthie, Enid L., *The Foreign Vision of Charlotte Brontë.* London: Macmillan, 1975

Ewbank, Inga-Stina, *Their Proper Sphere: A Study of the Brontë Sisters as Early-Victorian Female Novelists.* London: Edward Arnold, 1966

Friendships Offering 1829, pp. 143—213. [Includes 'Castle Campbell', by Delta; 'The Will', by Leitch Ritchie; and 'The Minstrel Boy', by The Ettrick Shepherd.]

Gaskell, E. C., *The Life of Charlotte Brontë,* 3rd ed., 'revised and corrected', 2 vols. London: Smith, Elder, 1857

Geer, Joseph R., *The Artist at Work: A Critical Study of Charlotte Brontë's Manuscript, 'John Henry'.* A.B. dissertation for Princeton University, 1965

Gérin, Winifred, *Anne Brontë: A Biography.* London: Allen Lane, 1959

Gérin, Winifred, *Branwell Brontë: A Biography.* London: Hutchinson, 1961

Gérin, Winifred, *Charlotte Brontë: The Evolution of Genius.* Oxford: Clarendon, 1967

Gérin, Winifred, *Anne Brontë: A Biography.* London: Allen Lane, 1959

Gérin, Winifred, *The Brontës: I. The Formative Years* (British Council Pamphlet: 'Writers and their Work'). London: Longman, 1973

Gérin, Winifred, *The Brontës: II. The Creative Work* (British Council Pamphlet: 'Writers and their Work'). London: Longman, 1974

Goldsmith, Rev. J., *A Grammar of General Geography. For the use of Schools and Young Persons,* 'Corrected and Modernised'. London: Longman, 1825

Grundy, F. H., *Pictures of the Past: memories of men I have met, and places I have seen.* London: Griffen & Farrar, 1879

Hatfield, C. W., 'The Early Manuscripts of Charlotte Brontë: A Bibliography' in *BST,* vol. 6: parts 32 (1922), pp. 97—111; 33 (1923) pp. 153—65 and 34 (1924) pp. 220—35.

Hatfield, C. W., ed., *Catalogue of the Bonnell Collection in the Brontë Parsonage Museum Haworth.* Haworth: The Brontë Society, 1932; rpt. 1968 with the permission of The Brontë Society for Dawson and Sons, London

Hinkley, Laura L., *The Brontës: Charlotte and Emily.* London: Hammond, 1947

Horsfall Turner, J., ed., *Brontëana: The Rev. Patrick Brontë's Collected Works.* Bingley: 1898

Jack, Ian, *English Literature 1815—1832* (Oxford History of English Literature). Oxford: Clarendon, 1963

Jack, Ian, 'Physiognomy, Phrenology and Characterization in the Novels of Charlotte Brontë.' *BST,* volume 15: part 80 (1970), pp. 377—91

Kingsland, William G., 'A Leaf from An Unopened Volume.' *Poet-Lore,* vol 9, spring, 1897, pp. 169—81

Kingsland, William G., 'Early Romances of Charlotte Brontë: II. — 'The Green Dwarf'.' *Poet-Lore,* vol. 9, autumn, 1897, pp. 479—97

Lane, Margaret, *The Brontë Story: A Reconsideration of Mrs Gaskell's 'Life of Charlotte Brontë'.* London: William Heinemann, 1953

Leyland, F. A., *The Brontë Family: With Special Reference to Patrick Branwell Brontë.* 2 vols. London: Hurst and Blackett, 1886

Lock, John, and Dixon, W. T., *A Man of Sorrow: The Life, Letters and Times of the Rev. Patrick Brontë 1777—1861.* London: Nelson, 1965

Lockhart, J. G., *The Life of Sir Walter Scott.* London: Dent, 1906

Longford, Elizabeth, *Wellington: The Years of the Sword.* London: Weidenfeld & Nicolson, 1969

Longford, Elizabeth, *Wellington: Pillar of State.* London: Weidenfeld & Nicolson, 1972

Maurier, Daphne du, *The Infernal World of Branwell Brontë.* London: Victor Gollancz, 1960

Morell, Sir Charles [pseudonym of James Ridley], *The Tales of the Genii: Translated from the Persian,* 2 vols. London: printed for J. Booker, etc., 1820

Nussey, Ellen, 'Reminiscences of Charlotte Brontë.' *Scribner's Monthly,* May, 1871; rpt. *BST,* volume 2, part 10 (1899), pp. 58—83

Oliphant, Mrs, *Annals of a Publishing House: William Blackwood and his sons; their magazine and friends.* 2 vols. Edinburgh: W. Blackwood & Sons, 1897

Peters, Margot, *Unquiet Soul: A Biography of Charlotte Brontë.* London: Hodder and Stoughton, 1975

Pinion, F. B., *A Brontë Companion: Literary Assessment, Background, and Reference.* London: Macmillan, 1975

Quertermous, Harry Maxwell, *The Byronic Hero in the Writings of the Brontës.* Ph.D. dissertation for the University of Texas, 1960

Ratchford, Fannie E, 'Charlotte Brontë's Angrian Cycle of Stories.' *PMLA,* vol. 43. I, 1928, pp. 494—501

Ratchford, Fannie E, 'The Brontës' Web of Dreams.' *Yale Review,* 1931, pp. 139—57.

Ratchford, Fannie Elizabeth, *The Brontës' Web of Childhood.* New York: Columbia University Press, 1941

Ratchford, Fannie E, *Gondal's Queen: A Novel in Verse by Emily Jane Brontë.* Austin: University of Texas Press, 1955

Rosengarten, Herbert J., 'Charlotte Brontë's *Shirley* and the *Leeds Mercury*'. *SEL,* 16, no. 4, autumn, 1976, pp. 593—600

Rowse, A. L., *The English Past: Evocations of Persons and Places.* London: Macmillan, 1951

Russell, J. C., *General Atlas of Modern Geography.* London: Baldwin & Cradock, n.d. (*c.* 1830)

Schwartz, Roberta Christine, *The Search After Happiness: A Study of Charlotte Brontë's Fiction,* Ph.D. dissertation for Wayne State University, Michigan, 1968

Scott, Sir Walter, *The Lay of The Last Minstrel,* A Poem, 5th ed. London: Longman, 1806

Scott, Sir Walter, *The Vision of Don Roderick; A Poem* (1811). Bound with *Rokeby; A Poem* (1813). Edinburgh: John Ballantyne

Scott, Sir Walter, *Tales of My Landlord, collected and arranged by Jedediah Cleishbotham* [pseudonym of Sir Walter Scott], 4 vols. Edinburgh: William Blackwood, 1816

Scott, Sir Walter, *Ivanhoe* (1819). London: Dent, 1906

Scott, Sir Walter, *Kenilworth* (1821). London: Dent, 1906

Scott, Sir Walter, *Life of Napoleon Buonaparte, Emperor of the French . . . By the author of 'Waverley', Etc.* Edinburgh: William Blackwood, Longman, Rees, etc., 1827

Scott, Sir Walter, *Tales of a Grandfather: Being the History of Scotland from the Earliest Period to the Close of the Rebellion 1745—46.* London: Adam and Charles Black, 1898

Scruton, William, *Thornton and the Brontës.* Bradford: John Dale & Co., 1898

Shapiro, Arnold. *A Study in the Development of Art and Ideas In Charlotte Brontë's Fiction.* Ph.D. dissertation for Indiana University, 1965

Shorter, Clement K., *Charlotte Brontë and Her Circle.* London: Hodder and Stoughton, 1896

Sinclair, May, *The Three Brontës.* London: Hutchinson, 1912

Southam, B. C., *Jane Austen's Literary Manuscripts: A study of the novelist's development through the surviving papers.* Oxford: Oxford University Press, 1964

Southey, Robert, *Life of Nelson.* London: Dent, 1960

Stephens, Fran Carlock, 'Hartley Coleridge and the Brontës,' *TLS,* 14 May 1970, p. 544

Stevens, Joan, ed., *Mary Taylor Friend of Charlotte Brontë: Letters from New Zealand and Elsewhere.* Auckland: Oxford University Press, 1972

Swift, Jonathan, *Gulliver's Travels & Other Writings,* ed. L. A. Landa. Oxford: Oxford University Press, 1976

Tillotson, Kathleen, *Novels of the Eighteen-Forties.* Oxford: Clarendon, 1954

Tocquot, Mr, *A New and Easy Guide to the Pronunciation and Spelling of the French Language.* London: printed for the Author, 1806

Wemyss Reid, T., *Charlotte Brontë: A Monograph.* London: Macmillan and Co., 1877

Wheeler, Michael, 'Literary and Biblical Allusions in *The Professor.' BST,* volume 17, part 86 (1976), pp. 46—57

Winnifrith, Tom, *The Brontës and Their Background: Romance and Reality.* London: Macmillan, 1973

Wise, Thomas James, *A Bibliography of the Writings in Prose and Verse of the Members of The Brontë Family.* London: printed for private circulation, 1917

Wise, Thomas James, *A Brontë Library: A Catalogue of Printed Books, Manuscripts and Autograph Letters By the Members of the Brontë Family.* London: printed for private circulation, 1929

Wharey, James Blanten, ed., *The Pilgrim's Progress,* 2nd ed., revised by R. Sharrock. Oxford: Clarendon, 1960

Wroot, Herbert E., *Persons and Places: Sources of Charlotte Brontë's Novels.* Shipley: publication of the Brontë Society, 1935

Index

Abernethy, Mr, 43
'About a week since I got a letter from Branwell', 143, 279 n.3, 282 n.15
'About 9 months after my arrival at the GT', 266 n.13
Ackroyd, Tabbitha, 20, 22, 42
Ad[d]ress To The Angrians, 124, 132–3, 255
Adrian, Fort, 159, 186
Adrianopolis (capital of Angria): building of, 123–4; landmarks in, 127; defeat and occupation of, 147–8; less popular since war, 177; compared to Martin's paintings, 235; other refs, 92, 132, 160, 162, 174, 185, 186, 279 n.8
An Adventure in Ireland, 69, 252
The Adventures of Ernenst Alembert, 69–70, 76, 266 n.1
The Adventure's of Mon Edouard de Crack, 58–9, 213–14, 232, 253, 259 n.5, 284 n.32
Aeschylus, 22, 24
Aesop's Fables, 26, 40, 264 n.3
The African Queen's Lament, 87, 101, 254, 273 n.3, 291 n.4
Albion (Marquis of Douro), see Wellesley, Arthur
Albion and Marina, 55–6, 71–2, 75, 81, 185, 232, 253
Alembert, Ernenst, 69–70, 239
Alford, Dr Henry, 112; source, 275 n.4

Allen, Miss, see Vernon, Louisa
'All this day I have been in a dream', 143, 256, 279 n.9, 13, 283 n.2, 285 n.36, 291 n.13, 16
Almeida, Lord, see Wellesley, Arthur Julius
Alnwick, 142, 151–8 passim, 163, 166, 177, 206, 239, 278 n.25
An American Tale, 252
Anectdotes of the duke of Wellington, 24, 252
Angria (province of Angria), 123, 125, 148, 178, 187
Angria, City of, 125, 147, 175
Angria, Kingdom of: opposition to establishment of, 85, 101, 147; formation of, 113–14, 122–6, 164, 212; source of, 240–1; society of, 116, 123–4, 127, 129, 167, 175, (comics) 117, (artists) 120; future destruction planned, 120–1, 240; symbol of sun of, 123, 126, 239–40; Charlotte's early attitude to, 124, 212; geography of, 124–6, 144, 177–9, 193, (towns) 147; country estates in, 173, 178; warlike nature of, 126, see also battles; internal strife in, 132–5; enemies of, 132, 278 n.25, see also Ashantee tribes; opening of parliament in, 133; war inside Angria, 146–8; expelled from Verdopolitan Union and occupied, 147–53; fights back, 155;

peace in, 157, 158; other refs, 106, 131, 134, 139, 149, 156, 157, 166, 174, 176, 189, 206

Angrian Legend, 139–99; summary of, 2; formation of, 122–35; central theme, 131, 135; conscience versus, 139–42, 144, 228–30, 246; powerful effect of, 142, 156–7, 169–70, 243; poems related to, 170; Charlotte's innovation in, 175; hinders Charlotte's writing, 182, 208–9, 245–6; farewell to, 199–200; significance of climate and sun in, 239–40; other refs, 22, 145, 161, 171, 195, 207, 210, 211, 292 n.7; *see also* Angria *and* battles

Anvale, 147

Arabian Nights' Entertainments, 18, 30, 52, 81, 106, 241, 272 n.10, 294 n.19

Arbor, Captain, 95

Arbuthnot, Mrs Charles, 47, 261 n.58, 281 n.30

Ardrah, Arthur Parry, Marquis of, 85, 132, 133, 147–53 *passim,* 159, 189, 247, 248, 270–1 n.15, 278 n.25

Ardsley, town of, 155, 157, 175

Arthuriana, 86, 103–7, 108, 110, 111, 251, 261 n.51, 266 n.10, 274 n.17

Arundel (province of Angria), 124, 125, 126, 153, 180

Arundel, Earl of, *see* Lofty Viscount Frederick

Ascension Isle, 151, 155

Ashantee tribes (or Negroes): country of, 19, 34; war against, 29, 31, 101, 102, 132, 135, 174, 278 n.24; compared to Jews, 273 n.3; threat to Angria by, 135, 190–1, 277 n.14; occupy Adrianopolis, 147

Ashworth, Mr Alexander, 204–7, 221

Ashworth, Brother, *see* Percy, Alexander

Ashworth, Edward, 206

Ashworth, Miss Mary, 204, 206–7, 208

Ashworth, Mrs Mary (née Wharton), 205–6, 289 n.11

Ashworth, William, 206

Audubon, John James, 22

Babel, Tower of, 18, 235

Babylon, 18, 116, 124, 235, 273 n.3

Badey (Badey or Badhri), *see* Hume Badey, Dr. Alexander

battles, in juvenilia: the Twelves against the Ashantees, (Marathon and Pass of Thermopylae) 22, (Rosendale Hill) 91, (Coomassie) 101; the Great Insurrection, (Fidena) 109; War of Encroachment, (Velino) 127; First Angrian War: 'Campaign of the Calabar', (Dongola and Loango) 160, 277 n.14, 278 n.17, 25, 279 n.1; Second Angrian War, (Grantley, Westbeach, Ludlow, Anvale) 147, (Edwardston) 151, (Ardsley) 155, 157; 'Campaign of the West', (Leyden) 158, 161. (Westwood) 158, (Evesham) 159, 170 *see also* Brontë, Branwell

Beauchamp, Eugene, 58

Beck, Madame, 215

Bellingham, James, 67, 74, 80

Bentinck, Lord, 43

Bewick, Thomas, 22

Bibliotheca Classica, 240, 295 n.36

Bible, The: as a source of inspiration and imagery, 18, 50, 115, 240–3, 262 n.11, 268 n.28, 273 n.3; Northangerland's speech and, 195; quotations with phrases from, 47, 88, 188, 197, 203, 216

Black Bull Hotel, Haworth, 135

Blackwood's Magazine, 18, 28, 30, 36, 68, 101, 227, 262 n.13, 275 n.4; *The Noctes Ambrosianae,* 20

Blackwood's Young Men's Magazine, see Young Men's Magazine

'blue-stocking' in juvenilia, 24, 61, 116

Boas, Mr, 224

Boaster (Our Fellows' Play), 40

Bonaparte, Napoleon, *see* Napoleon

Boswell, James, *Life of Johnson,* 22

Boulshill, 178, 285 n.35

Boulsworth, 126

A Brace of Characters: described, 274 n.13, 275 n.12; other references, 18 (quoted only), 119, 255, 278 n.23, 287 n.17

Bradford: Charlotte's juvenile view of, 19; Branwell's experience at, 173, 188, 189, 192, 284 n.14; in *Ashworth,* 209

Brandon, Dr Charles, 144

Brannii (or Brany), Chief Genius, 30, 32, 35, 84, 85, 96, 99; becomes S'death, 86

Branwell, Elizabeth (Charlotte's aunt): character and care of Brontë children, 11—12; religion of, 18; magazine subscriptions of, 14, 21; political attitude of, 48; portrait in juvenilia of, 51; Charlotte taught French by, 67; financial support of Branwell by, 188

Branwell's Blackwood's Magazine, see *Young Men's Magazine*

Bravey (or Bravi), William, 34, 92

Bravey's Inn (or Bravey's Hotel): meeting place for the Young Men and literati, 68, 92, 106; Rotunda in, 95, 106; Elysium in, 162, 164; echoes in later writing, 209

The Bridal, 80—3, 87, 89, 93, 103, 254, 258 n.3, 272 n.10, 15

Brock, Lieutenant, 60

Brocklehurst, Mr, 218, 291 n.20

Brontë, Anne: role in Glass Town Saga, 27—8, (little evidence of) 1, 28, (discontented with) 28, 63, 72; Charlotte's early writing for, 11, 32; Gondal Saga, 1, 2, 85, 163, 264 n.6, 270 n.13, 282 n.23; as Anne Wiggins, 17; Chief Genius Annii, 30, 32, 84, 99; lisp of, 261 n.3; and Our Fellows' Play, 40; and The Islanders' Play, 42—3, 63, 275 n.4; at School, 175; as governess, 192

Brontë, Branwell:
pseudonyms, 104, 124, 133, 149, 157, 160—1, 189, 247, 248, 249;
nature and quantity of manuscripts by, 6, 146;
as leader of the Young Men's Play, 1, 27, 28, 227;
as leader of Our Fellows' Play, 40—1;
and the Islanders' Play, 42—3, 46, 63;
initiator of the 'Young Men Tongue', 35;
initiator of the Young Men's Magazine, 36—7, 211, 227;
initiator of plots based on war, politics and commerce, 2, 22, 32, 34, 41, 79—80, 110, 133, 135, 145—7, 150, 153, 157, 242, 278 n.24;
favourite theme of, 102;

creator of Mary Percy, 111;
fascination for geographical detail, 33, 124—5;
preference for poetry, 64—5, 211;
serious attitude to writing, 65;
French interests of, 21, 62, 64, 67, 85, 110, 198, 211;
enthusiasm for music and boxing, 16—17, 128—9;
participation in politics by, 135;
as a painter, 188—9, 234;
illustrations by, 84, 100, 152, 194 (description only) 95;
abortive journey to London to enter the Royal Academy Schools, 135, 189, 279 n.8, 286 n.36;
Charles Wentworth, alter ego of, 189;
as favoured only son, 28, 227;
drinking and opium habits of, 161, 173, 189, 284 n.14;
later writing of, 189—91, 210—11;
first of the Brontë children to appear in print, 227;
and *Blackwoods,* 20, 227;
satirized by Charlotte, 16—17, 37, 51, 64—6, 128—9, 160—1, 118—19;
manuscripts of,
And the Weary are at Rest, 190;
Battell Book, 262, n.8;
Branwell's Blackwood's Magazine, 19 (quoted only), 30—1, 35, 36—7, 41, 42, 95 (referred to only), 213, 260 n.34, 262 n.8, 9, 35, 263—4 n.1;
Caractacus. A Dramatic Poem, 65, 267 n.6;
'Caroline', 284 n.21;
A Collection of Poems by Young Soult the Rhymer, 37 (quoted only), 64;
'Dirge of the Genii', 38;
'Harriet I', 285 n.4;
'Harriet II', 285 n.4;
An Historical Narrative of the 'War of Encroachment' (or *'Agression'*), 110, 274 n.19, 25, 275 n.12, 276 n.2;
The History of Angria I, 278 n.21, 25;
The History of Angria II, 147;

Brontë, Branwell *(continued)*:
The History of Angria IV, 280
   n.13;
The History of Angria V, 283
   n.7, 286 n.35;
The History of Angria VI, 280
   n.16;
The History of Angria VII, 280
   n.16;
The History of Angria VIII, 280
   n.16, 22; 281 n.26; 282 n.20,
   285 n.3;
The History of Angria IX, 155;
   280 n.23, 281 n.29, 34;
*History of the Rebellion In My
   Fellows,* 40—1, 262 n.8;
The History Of The Young Men,
   28, 33, 74, 95, 124, 261 n.3,
   262 n.7, 13, 263 n.16, 10, 268
   n.30;
'An Hour's Musings', 273 n.10;
Laussane: A Dramatic Poem, 65,
   67, 260 n.40;
Letters From An Englishman, 35,
   67, 74, 79, 80, 83, 92, 96,
   101, 106, 108, 110, 124, 127,
   128, 266 n.5, 16, 269 n.15,
   16, 270 n.3, 4, 10, 15;
The Liar Unmasked, 65;
*The Life of feild Marshal the
   Right Honourable Alexander
   Percy,* 113, 282 n.20, 285 n.3;
*The Life of Warner Howard Warner,
   Esq.,* 189, 282 n.21, 287 n.38;
Love and Warfare, 190, 191,
   285—6 n.15, 287 n.46;
The Monthly Intelligencer,
   84—5, 91, 106;
A Narrative of the First War, 277
   n.14, 280 n.16;
'Ode on the Celebration of the
   Great African Games', 84, 99;
Percy or *The History of Angria
   X,* 190, 284 n.16, 285 n.2,
   287 n.43, 290 n.1, 2;
The Pirate, 85, 92, 101, 271
   n.19, 272 n.5;
The Politics of Verdopolis, 85,
   102, 105, 110, 111, 112, 127,
   148, 195, 206, 273 n.7, 275
   n.10;
'Queen Mary's Grave', 281 n.26;

Real Life in Verdopolis, 104, 273
   n.9, 3, 276 n.22;
The Revenge A Tragedy, 65, 260
   n.40, 267 n.6;
The Rising of the Angrians, 279
   n.4, 280 n.10;
'Shine on us, God of Afric, shine',
   126;
'Sound the loud Trumpet o'er
   Afric's bright sea', 126;
Verdopolis and the Verdopolitans,
   113, 277 n.14, 278 n.25, 279
   n.1;
'Welcome heroes, to the War!',
   126;
The Wool Is Rising, 127, 206,
   219, 220, 271 n.15, 276 n.16,
   31, 292 n.8;
see also Brannii, Chief Genius;
   Brontë, Charlotte, collaboration
   with Branwell
Brontë, Charlotte:
education, formal, of, (at home) 16,
   18, (Clergy Daughters' School)
   28, 262 n.15, (at Roe Head)
   72—4, (in Brussels) 67, 204,
   216, 244;
as governess, 192, 204, 206, *see
   also* Roe Head;
adolescent religious crisis of, 141,
   144, 164, 225, *see also* 'Roe Head
   Journal';
urge to improve herself, 87—88;
influence of Mr Brontë on, 12—24,
   215, 234;
Irish or 'Western' influence on, 19,
   69, 167, 175;
influence of the Duke of Wellington
   on, 24—5, 46—50, 53, 118, 209,
   265 n.9, 13, 15, 16, 290 n.21;
French influence on the writing of,
   21, 66—7, 80, 105, 115, 132,
   151, 162, 187, 190, 197, 198,
   213, 284 n.17, *see also* Paris *and*
   Frenchy Land;
love of theatre, 105, 231;
interest in politics, 20, 24, 35,
   46—50, 61, 131, 134—5, 187;
fascination with the supernatural,
   (Biblical source) 18, (Irish source)
   19, (in juvenilia) 24, 30, 55, 57,

Brontë, Charlotte *(continued)*:
    68—9, 71—2 (ignis fatuus) 207,
    (gytrash) 211, (second sight) 117,
    223;
    sensitivity to natural landscape and
      climate, 16, 238—40;
    interest in physiognomy, 100, 144,
      238, 295 n.24;
    early artistic influences on, 16, 21,
      82, 87, 93, 171, 177, 234—8,
      282—3 n.3, (painters whose
      works Charlotte wished to see)
      236;
    illustrations by, ii, 11—13, 60, 73,
      82, 94, 99, 109, 126, 154, 168,
      234—6, 239;
    critiques of engravings by, 237;
    visual imagination of, 234—43;
    sensitivity to colours, 295 n.23;
    early literary influences, 13—24, 82,
      88, 108, 141, 177, 197, 198,
      229—30, 231, 240; *see also*
      Byron; Scott; *and other authors*
      under separate entries;
    sense of humour in the writing of,
      16—18, 51, 61, 64, 66, 92, 128,
      150—1, 161, 171, 177, 182,
      196—7, 232, 241;
    attitude to the woman writer,
      198—9, 203, 227—8;
    guilt about her 'world below', 139,
      169, 227—30, 246;
    pseudonyms of, 225, 227, 293 n.1,
      (Lord Charles Wellesley) 2, 7, 38,
      58, 61, 62, 68, 88, 97, (Captain
      Tree) 39, 57, 62, 96, 97,
      (Marquis of Douro) 58, 62,
      (Charles Townshend) 149, (in her
      novels) 227, 246;
    collaboration with Branwell, 6,
      (close co-operation) 63—4,
      67—8, 74, 79, 96, 110—11, 122,
      131—5, 155, 160, 181, (rivalry
      and discord) 35—7, 65, 83—4,
      146—7, 149, 156—7, 158, 189,
      211, (nature of partnership
      changes) 161, 183, 192; *see also*
      'UT' *and Young Men's Magazine;*
    Branwell's influence on, 66—7,
      106, 146—7, 190, 210—12;
    attitude to Branwell's writing, 37,
      65—6;

    early stories of,
      bibliography of, 256—7;
      basic plot which fascinated
        Charlotte, 2, 213;
      as Chief Genius Tallii, 30, 32, 37,
        85, 99;
      as Charlotte Wiggins, 17;
      little interest in the Young Men's
        Play or Our Fellows', 35, 41;
      leader of the Islanders' Play, 43;
      see also juvenilia; manuscripts; *and*
        separate manuscript entries
    poems of,
      'Again I find myself alone and
        ever', 280 n.8;
      'Beneath Fidena's Minister' 285
        n.8;
      'The Bridal', 271 n.1;
      'But once again, but once again',
        279 n.4;
      'Captain Flower's Last [?Novel]',
        110, 274 n.23;
      'The cloud of recent death is past
        away', 271 n.1;
      'Death of Darius Codomannus',
        240, 295 n.38;
      'Deep the Cirhala flows', 170, 282
        n.10, 284 n.22;
      'Eamala is a gurt bellaring bull',
        95;
      'He could not sleep! — the couch
        of war', 283 n.8;
      'Henriade', 66—7, 268 n.15;
      'Holy St Cyprian! thy waters
        stray', 167;
      'Hurrah for the Gemini!', 127;
      'Justine', 214;
      'Lament for the Martyr who dies
        for his faith', 296 n.51;
      'Lines by one who was tired of
        dullness . . .', 263 n.7;
      'Lines on seeing the portrait of
        — —', 265 n.8;
      'Lines spoken by a lawyer . . .',
        263 n.6;
      'Lines written beside a fountain in
        the grounds of York Villa',
        108;
      'Long, long ago — before the
        weight of pain', 283 n.8;

Brontë, Charlotte *(continued):*

'Long since as I remember well',
  279 n.3, 280 n.21, 296 n.51;
'Look into thought', 292 n.7;
'Matin', 265 n.8;
'The moon dawned slow in the
  dusky gloaming', 236;
'A National Ode for the
  Angrians', 276 n.11;
'Of College I am tired', 54;
'O Hyle thy waves are like
  Babylon's streams', 259 n.20,
  273 n.3;
'"O! let me be alone" he said', 283
  n.8, 8;
'O There is a land which the sun
  loves to lighten', 270 n.21;
'O when shall our brave land be
  free', 38;
'Parting', 283 n.1;
'The pearl within the shell
  concealed', 292 n.7;
'The Red Cross Knight', 106;
'Review at Gazemba', 285 n.9;
'The rumour of invaders through
  all Zamorna ran', 284 n.22;
'Saul', 259 n.20;
'A single word — a magic spring',
  170;
'Song', 293 n.8;
'Stanzas', 283 n.7;
'Stanzas On The Fate Of Henry
  Percy', 107, 111, 282 n.26,
  292 n.8;
'St. John in the Island of Patmos',
  259 n.20, 271 n.1, 296 n.50;
'The Town besieged', 171, 282
  n.10;
'The trees by the casement are
  moistened with dew', 283 n.8;
'The trumpet hath sounded', 74,
  84, 269 n.6;
'Turn not now for comfort here',
  280 n.6;
'Verses by Lord Charles
  Wellesley', 265 n.4;
'The Violet', 22 (quoted only),
  266 n.11;
'The Vision', 65, 267 n.10;
'We wove a web in childhood',
  140, 169, 255, 282 n.24;
'When thou sleepest', 283 n.6;
'The Wounded Stag', 259 n.20;

'Written upon the occasion of the
  dinner given to the literati of
  the Glass Town', 57;
'Zamorna's Exile', (Canto I) 151,
  (Canto II) 155;
post-Angrian prose manuscripts of,
  Ashworth, 203—9, 210, 218,
    220, 221, 244, 245, 257, 271
    n.10, 285 n.5, 7, 288 n.2, 28,
    289 n.4;
  John Henry or *The Moores,*
    222—4, 292 n.13, 15, 295
    n.25;
  Preface (to *The Professor*): 'I had
    the pleasure of knowing M^r
    Crimsworth very well', 223—4;
  'Willie Ellin' fragments, 293 n.20;
  Scheme of a Mag[azine] Tale,
    245;
  Emma, 3, 216;
novels of,
  The Professor: (as a reaction to
    the juvenilia) 199, 233,
    244—6; (prototype of the
    narrator William Crimsworth)
    174, 226, 229, 237, 238;
    (recasting of) 221—4, 292
    n.13, 16; (two rival brothers in)
    206, 221; (further links with
    the juvenilia) 68, 215—16,
    239, 275 n.17, 295 n.33, 296
    n.54; (other references) 1, 3,
    200, 288 n.30, 292 n.9, 294
    n.22, 295 n.18, 35, 297 n.8;
  Jane Eyre: (as a major departure
    from the juvenilia) 226, 245,
    246; (imagery of juvenilia
    similar to) 186, 280—1 n.24,
    290 n.17, 292 n.7, 295 n.23,
    33, 296 n.54; (echoes of
    juvenile characters in), 18, 184,
    209, 215, 216, 218, 238, 243,
    244, 259 n.21, 283 n.6, 289
    n.11; (two brothers theme in)
    222; (structure of *Caroline
    Vernon* compared to) 211;
    (further links with the
    juvenilia) 22, 68, 186, 196,
    237—8; (other references) 223,
    287 n.14, 295 n.19;
  Shirley: (structure of *Henry
    Hastings* compared to) 211;

Brontë, Charlotte *(continued)*:
  (two rival brothers in) 223;
  (narration of) 225; (precedents
  for satire on clergy in) 232, see
  also *juvenilia,* religion in; (early
  drafts of) 223—4, 292 n.13;
  (further links with the
  juvenilia) 68, 83, 161, 209,
  216, 244, 260 n.38, 296 n.2;
  Villette: (links with the juvenilia)
  68, 187, 215, 216, 218, 223,
  230, 286 n.20, 292 n.7, 293
  n.11, 295 n.33; (other
  references) 224, 286 n.27;
Brontë, Elizabeth, 20, 25, 29, 261 n.60
Brontë, Emily: role in Glass Town Saga,
  (little evidence of), 1, 28, (discontented
  with) 28, 63, 72, 211; Gondal Saga, 1,
  2, 85, 163, 264 n.6; as Jane Wiggins,
  17; and school, 28, 135; Chief Genius
  Emmii, 30, 84, 99; and the Young
  Men's Play, 27—8; and Our Fellows'
  Play, 40; and the Islanders' Play,
  42—3, 47, 63; *Wuthering Heights,*
  283 n.6; other refs, 92, 244, 278
  n.18, 282 n.23
Brontë family:
  childhood play of, 25, 261 n.60;
  portrait by Branwell of, 84; name of,
  260 n.27; interest in Nelson, 109;
  disruption in, 135; love of art, 234;
  partnership of four Brontë children,
  (development of the Glass Town Saga
  shows) 1, 28, 40—1, 62; (emotional
  security of) 12, 187; (dissolution of),
  43, 63, 72—6, 85, 211; (Charlotte and
  Emily) 47; (Emily and Anne) 68, 84,
  85; (possible later collaboration) 163;
  see also Genii, Chief; Brontë,
  Charlotte, collaboration with Branwell
Brontë, Mrs Maria, 11, 14—16, 25
Brontë, Maria, 20, 25, 29, 259 n.4, 261
  n.60
Brontë, Revd, Patrick: visit from Mrs
  Gaskell, 3; widower, 11; early
  description of, 12; writing by, 13;
  character, interests and influence as
  father, 12—24, 215, 234; liberal view
  of education, 16, 18; Irish background
  of, 19; purchase of toy soldiers by, 27;
  interest in politics, 48, 135; Branwell
  taught classics by, 37, 67, 99; library
  membership of, 61; illness of, 69;

books of, 18—21, 82, 229, 295 n.36;
  memories of Luddite Riots, 83;
  supported Branwell's career, 189;
  sermon on Eruption of Bog, 259 n.4
Brontë Parsonage Museum, Haworth:
  preservation of manuscripts in, x; 4,
  19
Brougham, Henry, Lord, 134
Brunswick, Frederick, Duke of York and
  First King of The Twelves, 7, 31, 32,
  34, 91, 93
Brushwood Hall, 103, 104—5, 108,
  254, 266 n.12
Brushwood Hall, 104—5
Bud, Captain John (pseudonym of
  Branwell): 'greatest prose writer', 29,
  88, 247; works by, 29, 65, 81, 162,
  247; friend of Lord Charles Wellesley,
  61, 70, 97; rival of Captain Tree, 249;
  other refs, 95
Bud, Sergeant, 37, 61, 66, 95, 247
Bull, John, 43
Bunyan, *Pilgrim's Progress,* 19; allusions
  to, 18, 283 n.4, 296 n.54
Burghersh, Lord (relative of Duke of
  Wellington), 118
Burns, Helen, 218
'But it is not in Society that the real
  character is revealed', 217 n.15, 285
  n.14, 286 n.17, 19, 25
Byron, George Gordon, Lord: influence
  on Charlotte of, 2, 83, 118—19, 151,
  234—5; influence on Branwell of, 21;
  heroines' worship of, 21, 112, 197;
  Charlotte recommends reading, 22, 88;
  Mr Brontë's books on, 82; Zamorna as
  Byronic hero, 117-18, 155, 196, 229;
  life as a source, 119, 196, 215, 287
  n.15; Moore's *Life of Byron,* 82, 196;
  Childe Harold's Pilgrimage, 21, 232,
  237—8, 294 n.18; *Manfred,* 21; *Cain,*
  21, 22, 188; *The Destruction of
  Sennacherib,* 75; *English Bards and
  Scotch Reviewers,* 106; *The Corsair,*
  272 n.5; *Hebrew Melodies,* 273 n.3;
  other refs, 178, 208
Byron, Harriet (heroine of Richardson's
  Sir Charles Grandison), 245

Calabar (province of Angria), 123, 125

Calabar, River, 124, 125, 147, 148, 170, 177; 'Campaign of the Calabar', 135, 160, 277 n.14

Calais, 183

Calvert (or Seacombe), Mr, 222, 292 n.16

Cam[p]bell Castle, 237, 238—9, 253, 266 n.1, 268 n.23

Campbell, Thomas, 22

Caroline Vernon: detailed discussion of, 192—8; structure in, 211, 212, 245; Byron's influence on, 21, 229; romantic infatuation in, 168, 199; Zamorna's infidelity in, 177; other refs, 203, 204, 206, 233, 238 (quoted only), 256, 284 n.29, 288 n.22, 289 n.4, 291 n.10

Cartwright, Mr (owner of Rawfolds Mill, Liversedge), 83

Cartwright, John, 91

Castlereagh, Harriet, 120, 247

Castlereagh, Lord (Earl of Stuartville): political associate of Wellington, 24, 265 n.15; satirised in early juvenilia, 24, 50; reappears in later juvenilia, 55; friend of Zamorna, 122, 147, 247; Lord Lieutenant of Zamorna province, 125, 133; other refs, 157, 173, 176

Catalogue of my Books, 29, 232, 253, 264 n.2, 266 n.1

Catherine II, Empress of Russia: as possible source, 221, 291 n.6

Caucasus Mountains, 19, 52

Caversham Colonel George Frederick, Baron of, 88, 89, 190, 205, 271 n.10

Caversham, Lord, 181

Characters of the Celebrated Men of the Present Time, 39, 66, 68, 252, 266 n.9, 270 n.2; 59 (quoted only)

Chantry, Sir Henry, 120

Charles X, source in The Islanders' Play, 49

Charlesworth, Lady Emily, 97, 99, 249

Chateaubriand, François René, Vicomte de, *Travels in Greece and the Holy Land,* 21

Cheeky, Alexander, 34

Chenille, Monsieur, 162

Cirhala Plains, 157

Cirhala River, 158, 159, 282 n.10

Clairmont, Claire, 196

Clarence Wood, 159

Clarissa, 21, 245

Cleopatra, 184; as source, 23

Clown (Our Fellows' Play), 40

Coleridge, Hartley, 203, 204, 243, 245, 288, n.1, 3, 289 n.4, 5, 296 n.4

Coleridge, Samuel Taylor, 260 n.39

Colne-moss, 178, 285 n.35

Conversations, 72, 252—3, 266 n.7, 15, 267 n.3, 11, 294 n.12

Coomassie, as source, 19; Battle of, 101; Mountains of, 190

Cooper, Sir Astley, 43, 46—7

Corner Dishes, 232, 251, 293 n.10

Cowan Bridge, 28, 261 n.60, 262 n.15

Cowley, Lord (brother of Duke of Wellington), 118

Cowper, William, 260 n.39

Crack, Edouard de, 58, 213—4

Crackey, 34

Crashey (Crashie or Crashi), Butter, 34, 80, 88, 92, 106

Crimsworth, Edward, 221, 222, 224

Crimsworth, William: descendent of William Percy and William Ashworth, 174, 221—2, 238; recast as William Moore and Willie Ellin, 222—4; anti-romanticism of, 229; antagonism with brother, 206; as narrator, 226, 233, 237; sober destiny determined by juvenilia, 199; further links with juvenilia, 216, 239, 296 n.54

Dahomey, Plains of, 54

Damriel, 30

Danash, 81, 93, 272 n.10

Dance, *see* Vernon, Louisa *and* Vernon, Lord George

Daniels, Thaddeus, 205

Darius Codomannus, 240

A Day Abroad: Warner family gathering in, 117, 127, 128; enthusiasm for Angria in, 123; comedy in, 128—9; Branwell's enthusiasm for boxing in, 128—9, 276 n.26; other refs, 132, 162, 255, 271 n.10, 291 n.1, 295 n.39

A Day at Parry's Palace, 63, 211, 253

De Capell, Mr, 204, 208—9

De Capell, Miss Amelia, 207, 208, 209, 218, 223

De Capell-Hall, 289 n.6

De Capell, John, 220

De Capell, Thornton, 220
De Lisle, Frederick or Sir Edward, 247;
    friend of Zamorna, 59, 120; portrait
    painter in juvenilia, 72, 150, 240;
    source for, 266 n.10
De Quincey, Thomas, 173
A Description of London (1824), 19
*Description of the Duke of Ws small
    palace situated on the Banks of the
    Indirce,* 252, 266 n.3
De Walden Hall, 223
Dewsbury Moor, 169, 171, 283 n.3
Dickens, Charles, *Nicholas Nickleby,*
    291 n.20
Dongola, City of, 125, 277 n.14
Douro (province of Angria), 125
Douro, City of, 125
Douro, Marquis of, *see* Wellesley, Arthur
Douro Villa, 104, 149, 237
Dovelike, Mrs Laura, 51
Doverham, 183
Driver, Mr, 134
Dryden, John, 22
Duke of Z & E Percy, 129, 133, 186,
    255, 276 n.30
The Duke of Zamorna, 180—3; early life
    of Zamorna in, 163; early life of Percy
    in, 206, 210; narrators of, 175, 199,
    221, 226; events in, 175, 190;
    William Percy's attitude to marriage
    in, 184; other refs, 211, 220, 224,
    256, 271 n.10, 273 n.6, 285 n.8, 287
    n.19, 291 n.4, 294 n.13, 296 n.58
Dundee, George (or Sir John Martin),
    59, 235; source for, 266 n.10

Ebenezer Chapel, Verdopolis, 171
Ebon, 69
Eden Cottage, 196
Edwardston, City of, 126, 151, 175
Edwardston Hall, 173, 178
Eldon, John Scott, Lord, 50, 265 n.15
Ellen, George Frederic, 189, 190
Ellin, Mr, 216
Ellin, Edward, 224
Ellin Hall, 224
Ellin, Willie, 218, 224
Ellrington Hall, 117, 129, 157
Ellrington, Lady Paulina Louisada
    (mother of Zenobia), 7
Ellrington, Lady Zenobia: source for,
    23—4, 240; dress of, 238; 'blue-
    stocking', 61, 108, 123, 191, 287

n.46; rival for Marquis of Douro's
    love, 61, 71, 81, 117; marriage to
    Rogue (Alexander Percy), 92, 102,
    104, 149, 162; separation from
    husband, 155; reunion with husband,
    166; in middle-age, 195; patronises
    Ellen Grenville, 215; other refs, 7, 95,
    120, 121
Ellrington, Lord *see* Percy, Alexander
Ellrington, Lord Henry (father of
    Zenobia), 7
Ellrington, Surena, 156
Elm Grove Villa, 110, 130, 277 n.35
Elysium, 162
Emanuel, Paul, 216
Enara, General Henri Fernando di, 125,
    147, 153, 157, 159, 166, 174, 247
The Enfant, 36, 41, 213, 252
Ennerdale, 155
Eton College, 53, 54, 91
Etrei (province of Angria), 125, 191
Etty, Sir William, 120, 121, 236, 248,
    289 n.10, 294 n.10
Etty, Zorayda, 121
Euripides, 22
Evelina, 21
'Every-body knows how fond Arthur is of
    patronizing rising talent', 106, 254,
    261 n.51, 274 n.16, 18, 277 n.5
Evesham, 158, 159, 163, 170, 171,
    175, 190
*Extracted from the last number of the
    Northern Review,* 255, 277 n.13,
    18 (quoted only)
An Extraordinary Dream, 68, 253
Eyre, Jane: male narrator of juvenilia
    compared to, 226; parallels in
    juvenilia, 216, 218, 237, 238, 243,
    283 n.6, 295 n.33; a source of
    Rochester's cry to, 18; Tabbitha
    Ackroyd like nurse to, 22; Elizabeth
    Hastings as prototype for, 184, 186,
    209, 218;

Faction Du Mange, 20
Fairbourne, Marian, 207, 209
Fala Plains, 157
Farewell to Angria, see 'I have now
    written a great many books'
Fennell, Revd John (Charlotte's uncle),
    48, 234
Fezan, 19
Fidena, City of, 80, 181

Fidena, Duke of, *see* Sneachie, John
  Augustus
Fielding, Henry, 231
Figgs, Mr Sudbury, 17
Finden, William, 82, 126, 168, 234,
  237, 270 n.7
Finic, 93, 119, 272 n.9
'Fitzarthur' *see* Wellesley, Ernest Edward
Fitzgerald, Lord Edward, 196
Fitzgerald, William Vesey, *see* Vesy
Fitzgibbon, Matilda, 216, 218
Flanigan, Maurice, 117, 128
Flower, Captain Sir John, Viscount
  Richton (pseudonym of Branwell),
  247; works by, 67, 104, 133, 155,
  156, 273 n.3, 274 n.23, 276 n.16,
  282 n.21; Branwell's pseudonym, 104,
  149, 156, 189; exposes arrogance of
  those in high society, 104, 124;
  describes Adrianopolis, 124;
  misgivings about future of Angria,
  132; early patron of Henry Hastings,
  158; machinations against Hastings,
  158, 160; ref to, 129
Flute (or Steele), Tim, 222
Fogharty, 48
'The following strange occurrence',
  253, 266 n.1, 268 n.22
The Foundling: discussion of, 91—6;
  Captain Tree's spite in narration of,
  97; a last appearance of the Genii in,
  86; Charlotte's pseudonym in, 271
  n.8; other refs, 85, 108, 177, 254,
  272 n.14, 275 n.17
Four Years Ago: manuscript of, 158,
  282 n.19; discussions of, 161—4;
  other refs, 165, 181, 211, 256,
  276 n.21, 291 n.3
Foxley, Miss, 107, 218
A Fragment: 'Overcome with that
  delightful sensation of lassitude',
  74—5, 254, 270 n.1
A Fragment August the 7 1829: 'One
  Cold dreary night . . . ', 252, 265 n.3,
  275 n.9
Fragment August the 8 1829: 'On the
  third day . . .', 252, 261 n.57
Franceville, Marquise de, 184
Fraser's Magazine, 21
Freeling, Mr, 104
Freetown, 150, 163, 282 n.24

A Frenchmans Journal, 67, 253, 267 n.3
Frenchy Land (or France), 32, 33;
  Edouard de Crack in, 58, 213; *Young
  Men's Magazine* sold in, 62; Napoleon,
  founder of, 64; a Republican retreat
  for enemies of Angria, 190, 198; other
  refs, 153, 155, 183; *see also* Paris
A Fresh Arrival, 106—7, 127, 254,
  259 n.8
Friendship's Offering, 21, 237
From the Verdopolitan Intelligencer,
  133, 255, 270 n.15, 275 n.5,
  278 n.27, 296 n.53

Gaaldine, 85
Gambia, 19
Gambia, River, 75, 150
Game Keeper, 55
Gaskell, Mrs Elizabeth: first to recognize
  Charlotte's juvenilia as her literary
  apprenticeship, 3—4; incorrect view of
  Revd Brontë, 12; rearrangement of
  manuscripts for publication, 264 n.1;
  information on the Brontës from *The
  Life of Charlotte Brontë* by, 12, 234,
  238, 246; historical evidence derived
  from *The Life* by, 83, 112;
  correspondence between Mary Taylor
  and, 87, 144
Gateshead, 295 n.23
Gazemba, City of, 125, 174, 182
Gazemba, Fort, 153
Genii, Chief: evolution of, 30, 32, 69,
  211; destruction of Glass Town and,
  76, 84—6; Biblical source of, 18, 241;
  Branwell's dislike of, 37—8; tyranny
  and powers of, 31, 34, 38, 80, 214,
  242; The Islanders' Play and, 46, 51;
  fusion of Little King and Queens with,
  53; changing interests of, 63; final
  appearances of, 86, 93, 96, 99; as
  expletive, 135; palaces of, 18, 31, 241,
  295 n.23
George IV, 47, 49, (as Prince George in
  Tales of the Islanders), 48
Gibbon, Edward, *The History of the
  Decline and Fall of the Roman
  Empire,* 23
Gifford, John, 95, 99, 106
Gifford, William, 106
Gillwood Hall, 204, 289 n.6

Gilpin, William, 234—5, 282—3 n.3, 294 n.4

Girnington Hall, 128, 160, 173, 175, 178, 185, 193

Glass Town ('The Great Glass Town'): sources, 18, 19, 30; building of, 29, 31, 32; centre of Confederation, 32—3; early newspapers of, 37; descriptions of, 54, 55, 58—9, 67, 97—99; illustration by Charlotte of, 94; change of name, 59; society of, 59, 60—1, 181; robbery in library of, 60—1; model for other towns, 62; authors in, 57, 232; other references, 54, 214; *see also* Verdopolis

Glass Town Confederacy: formation and map of, 32—3; scenery of, 56; magazine circulation in, 62; The Great Insurrection in, 79—80, 81, 83, 109; War of Encroachment in, (against Ashantees) 101, 113, (against French) 108, 113, 132; other refs, 63, 85, 88, 134, 150, 271n.15

Glass Town Saga: summary of development in, 1—2; sources of, 19, 22, 24; establishment of, 25—6; fusion of early 'plays' into, 53—6; temporary abandonment of, 72—6, 269 n.6; subservient role of Emily and Anne in, 63, 84; source for Gondal, 85; the last of the early saga, 96, 211; early saga recalled, 95, 97—101, 161—4, 181—2, 205—6, 210; change of direction in, 111—13; planned well in advance, 120—1; reality of, 225—6, 243; other refs, 81, 120, 131, 132, 143, 150, 153, 163, 199, 207, 213, 245; *see also* juvenilia; battles

Goethe, Johann Wolfgang von, 65

Goldsmith, Oliver, 22

Gondal Saga, 1, 2, 28, 47, 85, 163, 262 n.14, 264 n.6, 270 n.13, 282 n.23

Gordon (province of Verdopolitan Federation), 123, 129

Gordon, Captain Julian (or George Charles), 162, 196, 205, 249

Gordon, Lady Helen Victorine, Baroness, 7, 119, 143, 153, 215

A Grammar of General Geography, by Goldsmith, 19, 28, 262 n.13

Grandison, Sir Charles, 245

Grantley, 147

Grant's Coffee House, Verdopolis, 173

Grassmere, 177

Grassmere Manor, 118, 142, 214

Gravey (or Gravi), Edward, 27, 34, 92, 126, 275 n.4

Greatorix (or McShane), Mr, 222, 292 n.16

The Green Dwarf, 86, 95, 97—101, 103, 104, 254, 271 n.19, 272 n.1, 293 n.21

Greenwood, Mr, 17

Grenville, Ellen, 116—17, 120, 215, 238, 247

Grenville, General, 95, 116, 117, 247

Greville, Lady Charlotte, 281 n.30

Greville, Lady Georgina, 155

Grey, Catherine, 157

Grey, Charles, Earl, 116, 134

Grey, George Turner, 157, 175

Guadima, River, 54, 124, 126, 150

Guelph, Frederick, *see* Brunswick, Frederick

Gulliver's Travels, by Swift, 52; Lord Charles Wellesley's experience compared to that of Lemuel Gulliver, 226

Gytrash, 211, 290 n.2

Haidée, 82

Halford, Sir Henry, 47; character in juvenilia, 43, 46, 275 n.4

Hall, Ellen, 207, 208, 209, 218

Hall of Justice, Glass Town, 31

Hallows Hall, 189

Hamilton, Sir Edwin, 105, 120

Hampshire, 205, 207

Hanghimself, Monsieur, 213

Harborough, James, 129

Hardinge, Sir Henry, 50

Harlaw, Marquis of, *see* Ross, Edward Tut

Hart, Lily, Marchioness of Fidena, 7, 106, 108—10, 115, 130

Hartford, General Edward, Lord, 247; friend of Zamorna, 147; Mina Laury and, 153, 165, 280 n.20; rejected by Mina and duel with Zamorna, 166—7, 170, 174; machinations against Henry Hastings, 160—1, 184, 188; Jane Moore's pursuit of, 176, 183; other ref. 175

Hartford Hall, 166, 178

Hasleden, Mr, 91

Hastings, Elizabeth: discussion of, 184—8; model for later heroines, 168, 209, 218; autobiographical source of, 178, 199, 208, 217; provides refuge for brother, 190; sensitivity and superior understanding of, 207, 238; self-control of, 196, 216, 242—3; Charlotte's emotional commitment to, 246; other refs, 226, 247

Hastings, Captain Henry: 'Poet of Angria', 126, 127; supersedes Flower as Branwell's narrator of Angrian events, 133, 135, 147, 148, 149, 157, 277 n.14; character of, 160—1; dissolute career of, 174, 158, 183—4, (as Wilson) 188, 189—91; close association with Branwell of, 135, 160—1, 188—9, 210; Elizabeth Hastings and, 185, 188; other refs 247, 248, 278 n.25

Hawkscliffe: forests of, 124, 126; scene at, (in *Passing Events*) 149, (in 'Roe Head Journal') 157; 'The Cross of Rivaulx', home of Mina Laury at, 166, 178, 248; Hawkscliffe-House, 193; Caroline Vernon's childhood near, 195, 197

Haworth: used in stories, 11, 47, 187, 193, 285 n.35; as Howard, 17, 178; importance for Charlotte's writing, 73, 139, 142, 156, 171, 243; elections in, 134—5; *see also* Yorkshire

Hay Man (Our Fellows' Play), 40

Heatons of Ponden House, 21

Heger, Monsieur, 245

Helen of Troy, 184

Helstone, Mr, 209

Henriade, La, by Voltaire: Charlotte's translation of, 21, 66—7; Charlotte's copy of, 267 n.14

Henry VIII, 22

Henry Hastings: discussion of, 183—91; Hastings in, 158; Branwell as Hastings in, 161; domestic comedy in, 177, 229; Haworth landscape in, 178, 211; Elizabeth Hastings in, 178, 216; structure of, 197, 211, 212; narrator's perversity in, 231; realism in, 233; other references, 192, 256, 271 n.10, 284 n.30, 287 n.12, 291 n.8, 17

Herodotus, 24, 61

High Life In Verdopolis: discussion of, 115—18; Marquis of Douro in, 89, 112, 120; Mina Laury in, 89, 119, 153, 167; Thornton in, 127; 'Fitzarthur' in, 119, 153; Mary Percy, heroine of, 176; landscape in, 177; the self-conscious narrator in, 231, 232; shows Charlotte's uncertainty about Angria, 212; other refs, 110, 206, 255, 272 n.3, 274 n.13, 276 n.15, 277 n.2, 287 n.46, 291 n.6,7, 295 n.20, 26,41

Hill, Lord Arthur, 265 n.9

Hill, Sir George (character in the juvenilia), 47, 55, 150

Hill, General Sir Roland, 47

The History of the Year, 25—7, 40, 42, 251, 260 n.29, 262 n.15

Hoffmann, Ernst Theodor Amadeus, 20

Holme, Paulina, 216, 218

Homer, 22, 23, 65

Horse Guards, 19; in juvenilia, 49, 59

Houssain, Prince, 106

Howard, 17, 178

Howard, John, 128, 129

Howard Moors, 178

Hume, Elizabeth, 71

Hume, Marian, Duchess of Douro: source of, 25; childhood sweetheart of the Marquis of Douro, 56; rival of Zenobia Ellrington, 61, 71, 81; a fairy-tale heroine, 71—2, 81—3, 238, 292 n.7; courtship and marriage of, 80—3, 90; son of, 106, 112, 119, 121; forsaken by Douro, 74—5, 215; victimized by Lord Ellrington, 107, 163; death of, 111—12, 115; Charlotte's fascination for the dead Marian, 113; other references, 7, 52, 65, 95, 104, 108, 118, 149, 162, 227, 230, 291 n.6

Hume, Dr John Robert, 46, 71

Hume Badey, Dr Alexander (or Sir A. Hume, Duke of Badhi), 7, 35, (source) 46, 55, (source of his dissection of corpses) 61, 67, 68, 107

Hunsden, Yorke, 224

Hunter, (Our Fellows' Play), 40

'I have now written a great many books', 203, 204, 244, 257, 288 n.27, 291 n.20, 296 n.3

'I'm just going to write because I cannot help it', 143, 154, 256, 281 n.31
Inghams of Blakewell Hall, Mirfield, 192
Ingleside, 186, 196, 216
An Interesting Passage in the Lives of Some eminent men of the Present time, 60—1, 80, 253, 267 n.9, 272 n.9
Invincible, 31, 34
Ireland: birthplace of Mr Brontë, 13; early manuscripts taken by Mr Nicholls to, 4; Brontë interest in politics of, 48, 50, 134; source of the 'western' part of the Glass Town Confederacy, 175; Irish or 'Western' characters, 167, 175; early stories set in, 69, 237
Islanders' Play, 25, 26, 28, 32, 42—52, 275 n.4; amalgamation with Young Men's Play, 53—6
Isphahan, 19

Jersey, Lady, 82, 281 n.30
Jibbel Kumri, *see* Mountains of the Moon
Johnson, Samuel, *Lives of the Poets,* 22; *Rasselas,* 54
Jonson, Ben, 65; *Poetaster,* 230
Jordon, Lord (or Sheik Abdulla Medina), 7, 125, 147, 158, 161, 181, 248, (source) 280 n.7
Jordon Villa, 181
Journal of a Frenchman, see A Frenchmans Journal
Joynes, Revd., 190
Julia, discussion of, 158—61; structure of, 171, 211; Methodism satirized in, 171; William Percy's omnipresence in, 174—5; Caroline Vernon first meets Zamorna in, 195; other refs, 163, 170, 176, 256, 283 n.3
juvenilia:
    summary of development of the saga, 1—2;
    complexity of detail in, 1, 2, 121, 245;
    diagrams of relationships of principal characters, 7;
    list of other principal characters, 247—9;
    constant refinement of characters in, 102;

the term 'juvenilie', 1;
need for work on, 5;
spelling of names in, 270 n.11, 272 n.6, 275 n.4;
sources of, 12—26, 113, 225, 234—5, 240—3, 261 n.60;
violence and coarseness in, 96, 213, *see also* battles;
amalgam of precocity and naïvety in, 226;
earliest description of Industrial Yorkshire in, 58—9, *see also* Yorkshire;
references to painting in, 187, 199, 209, 234—9;
political allegory in, 47—50;
religious reference in, 18, 50, 69, 222, 241—3, (as a source of comedy) 17, 150—1, 171, 232, 241, (clergy satirized) 128, 161, (Methodism satirized) 149, 150—1, 171, 206, 232, (assumed absence of) 5, 258 n.6, 259 n.14, (conscience about Angria) 139—42, 144, 228—30, 246;
favourite themes in: the abandoned child, 213—16, 218, 223, (sources) 215, 221, 291 n.20; the position of governess, 139—45, 184—7, 207—9, 213, 216—18; two rival brothers, 219—224, (source) 24—5, (Wellesley) 97, 119, 219—20, 293 n.21, (Sneachie) 220, (Percy) 174, 183, 219, 220, (Ashworth) 206, 221, (Crimsworth) 206, 221—2, (Rochester) 222, (Moore) 222, (Ellin) 224; romantic love, 21, 71—2, 74—5, 80—1, 83, 85, 89—90, 108, 166—8, 196, 211—12, 216; 'East' versus 'West', 175;
autobiography in, 142, 143, 173, 183, 186—9, 193, 198, 199, 208, 215, 216—18, 238, 286 n.18, 21, 22, *see also* 'Roe Head Journal';
realism in, 176—9, 192—4, 199, 211, 216, 239, (lack of) 211, 220, (first attempt at a realistic novel) 203—9, 210—11, 221, 244;

juvenilia *(continued)*:
    anti-romanticism in, 61, 66, 72,
        185, 196, 229—30;
    Charlotte's technique in, 5, (lack
        of concern with plot) 117, 149,
        158—9, 182, 210—11, 212, 245,
        (concern with character) 117, 149,
        158, 159, 161, 216, (use of
        imagination) 140—5, 158, 243,
        (male narrator) 225—33, 243,
        (poetic method) 141, 170—1,
        (typical method of early stories)
        51—2, (typical early description)
        54, (epistolary style) 180, 221—2,
        232, (drama) 61, (variety of genre
        in magazines) 62, (poor spelling
        and punctuation) 19—20, 260
        n.29, (early prescription for a
        novel) 232—3, (self-conscious
        author) 231—2, (improvement
        in structure of stories) 165, 197,
        211, 245; (critical attitude
        towards writing) 192, 199,
        216, 244—6;
    relationship of juvenilia to later
        writing, 6, 201—46, *see also*
        Brontë, Charlotte, novels of;
    see also manuscripts; Brontë,
        Branwell; Brontë family; Glass
        Town Saga; Angrian Legend

Kashna, King of the Ashantees, 92
Kashna, 19
Kay-Shuttleworth, Sir James, 3
Keelder, Shirley, 216, 244, 296 n.2
The Keep of the Bridge, 69, 252
Keighley: toy soldiers purchased from,
    29; nearest stationers in, 36;
    newspapers collected from, 20
Keighley Mechanics' Institute library,
    20—1, 23, 61
King, Major John, 190—1
King, Robert, *see* S'Death
King Boy, 147
King Jack, 147
Kirkham Lodge, 175
Kirkwall, Charles, 175

Ladies' Magazine, 20
LaLande, Madame, 155
Lamb, Lady Caroline, 196, 281 n.30
Lancy, Alexander De, 54, 55
Last Will And Testament Of Florence

Marian Wellesley, 111—12, 115, 255
A Late Occurrence, 92, 108, 118, 186,
    255, 272 n.2, 276 n.17
Laury, Justine, 214
Laury, Mina, 248; adolescent love of
    Marquis of Douro and, 89—90; as
    Zamorna's devoted mistress, 153,
    165—8, 215, 216; Hartford's
    unrequited love of, 165—7, 247, 280
    n.20; as guardian of Zamorna's sons at
    Grassmere Manor, 118, 119, 214; as
    mistress of the Cross of Rivaulx, 178;
    as the 'Maid of Saragoza', 168, 237;
    mother of, 214; other refs, 108, 198,
    229; see also *Mina Laury*
Laury, Ned, 61, 67, 88, 89, 108, 214,
    248
Laussane, Comte de, 67
A Leaf from an Unopened Volume:
    future of Angria planned in, 113,
    120—1, 146, 240; first description of
    Angria in, 122; Finic described in, 272
    n.9; other refs, 191, 255, 261 n.47,
    273 n.6, 274 n.1
Le Brun, 59, (source) 266 n.10
Leeds Intelligencer, 13, 20
Leeds Mercury, 13, 20, 47
Leisure Hours, 253, 241
Leopold, Prince (in *Tales of the
    Islanders*), 47
A Letter from lord Charles-Wellesley,
    253
*Letter to the right honourable Arthur
    Marquis of Ardrah,* 133, 241, 255
Leyden, 158, 161
Liffey Castle, 253, 237
Lily Hart, 92, 108—10, 254, 274 n.13,
    14
Lister, Miss, 140
list of painters whose works I wish to see,
    236
Little King and Queens, 46, 48, 50, 51,
    53
Lismore, 186
Lockhart, John Gibson, 43
Lockhart, Johnny, 43; transposed into
    The Islanders' Play, 43, 48
Lofty, Viscount Frederick, Earl of
    Arundel: Zamorna's friend and
    general, 122, 147, 157; marriage to
    Edith Sneachi, 127; other refs, 7, 125,
    166, 173, 248

Lofty, Lord Macara, 248; anti-hero of *The Tragedy and The Essay,* 105; discredited suitor of Ellen Grenville, 117, 238; member of Northangerland's Provisional Government in Verdopolis, 153; Louisa Vernon's *affaire* with, 159; Charles Townshend and, 159; opium addiction of, 171—3, other refs, 7, 188, 190

London: significance to Charlotte of, 116, 205; Branwell's experience of, 189, 286 n.36; featured in *Ashworth,* 204, 205, 208, 220

Longinus, 23

Lonsdale, Mr, 184

Lonsdale, Mary, 184

Ludlow, 147

Lyon, Emma (Lady Hamilton), 108, 109

Macqueen, James, 190

Macshane, Arthur, 205

MacTerrorglen, Sir Jehu (or Jeremiah Simpson), 147, 151, 155, 159, 181, 190, 205, 249

Magne, Richard, *see* Young Man Naughty

Maimoune, 30, 93, 272 n.10

Manchester, as used in the juvenilia, 178, 206

manuscripts, early: difficulty of transcription, size and script of, x, 3; as basis for study of Charlotte's apprenticeship, 1; natural division into three periods of, 2; nature and history of, 3—4; previous work on, 4—5; chronological list of, 250—7; origins of, 25—6; earliest surviving, 11—12; handmade booklets, 11, 36, 103; problems of authorship, 38—9, 95—6; dating based on time of composition, 173, 198, 269 n.3; interrelationship of, 107—8; 'Roe Head' manuscripts, 143; fragmentary nature of Branwell's, 6, 146; nature of later, 158; Angrian poetry, 170—1; *see also* juvenilia; Young Men's Magazine; Brontë, Branwell, Emily, Anne; *separate titles of Charlotte's manuscripts*

Marina, *see* Hume, Marian

Martin, John, 234, 294 n.6

Martineau, Harriet, 197, 212

Massena, General, 147, (source) 280 n.7

Massinger Hall, 187, 188, 190

Mearius, 65

Medina, Sheik Abdulla, *see* Jordon, Lord

Melbourne, Lord, 134

Mermaid, 107

Methodism: satirized in the juvenilia, 149, 150—1, 171, 206, 241; methodist book-keeper of juvenilia reappears in later writing, 222

Methodist Magazine, 14

Military Conversations, 38, 252

Milton, John, 13, 18, 22, 88, 118, 132

Mina Laury, discussion of, 165—8; structural unity of, 171, 211, 245; realism in, 207; romantic love in, 212; other refs, 174, 176, 256, 282 n.1, 284 n.24, 26

Mirza, 52

Mithras, 240

Monkey, 32, 34

Monkey's Land (or Isle), 33, 95, 104, 132, 160, 163

Montmorency (or Montmorenci), Hector Matthias (or Daniel), 248; grotesque grandee of early Verdopolis, 95; infamous early associate of Percy, 162, 181; enemy of Zamorna, 150, 190; member of Northangerland's Provisional Government in Verdopolis, 153; reappearance in later manuscript of, 205; other references, 121, 189, 196, 275 n.4, 278 n.25

Montmorency, Julia, 121, 248

Moore, George, 175

Moore, Harriet, 175

Moore, Jane, 248; the introduction of, 171, 175, 184; discussion of, 175—6; as an insensitive Angrian beauty, 184, 238; Mary Percy's jealousy of, 177; echoes in later manuscripts of, 209, 223, 244, 296 n.2; other references, 183, 188, 247

Moore, John Henry, 222

Moore, Louis, 223

Moore, Robert, 223

Moore, Thomas, 196; *Life of Byron,* 22, 82, 270 n.7; *Life of Sheridan,* 22

Moore, William Calvert, 222, 238, 292 n.16

Moral Sketches, by Hannah More, 18

Morena, John, Duke of, 134
Mornington, 142, 167
Mountains of the Moon (or Jibbel
    Kumri), 19, 57
Mulready, Dennis, 69
Murat, Joachim, 132
Murray, General, 55, 150, (source) 265
    n.6
My Angria and the Angrians: discussed
    in, 123–4, 126–30; satire on
    Branwell in, 17 (quotation only);
    Howard identified as Haworth in, 178;
    cynicism of narrator in, 241;
    Adrianopolis described in, 294 n.8;
    other references, 92, 133, 174, 176,
    255, 275 n.16, 277 n.32, 278 n.26
'My Compliments to the weather', 143,
    175, 256, 281 n.7, 284 n.23, 296
    n.57
Napoleon Bonaparte, 27, 132, 266 n.10,
    280 n.7; transposed into the juvenilia,
    32, 55, 99, 213, (as Branwell's chief
    man) 27, 64, 85, 151, (as Caroline
    Vernon's hero) 196, 197
Naughty (or Naughten), Richard, *see*
    Young Man Naughty
Nelson, Duke of Bronté, 109
Nicholls, Revd Arthur Bell (husband of
    Charlotte Brontë), 3, 4, 223, 283 n.9
Niger River, 19, 30; border between
    Angria and the old Glass Town
    Confederacy, 135, 150
Nineveh, 116
North, Christopher, 43
Northangerland (province of Angria),
    113, 123, 125
Northangerland, Earl of, *see* Percy,
    Alexander
Northangerland House, 124
'Now as I have a little bit of time', 143,
    256, 281 n.3, 294 n.20, 295 n.34
Nussey, Ellen: Charlotte recommends
    books to, 22, 88; reminiscences of, 24,
    85, 234, 241; Charlotte stays with, 87,
    183, 198; Charlotte writes to, 112,
    116, 134, 135, 286 n.22; confessional
    letters to, 139, 144–5, 171; other
    references, 208, 283 n.1, 3, 10
Nussey, Revd Henry, 187–8

O'Callaghan Castle, 69
O'Connell, Daniel, 50, 116

O'Connor, Arthur, 117, 128, 161–2,
    181, 205, 248
O'Connor, Harriet, 101, 181–2, 205,
    248
O'Donell, Henry, 54, 55
Old Man Cockney, 55
Old Rogue, *see* Percy, Edward Snr.
Olympia, River, 124, 126, 129, 177
Olympian Hills, 150, 155, 157, 178
Olympian Valley, 178
O'More, Lady Honor, 162
'The origin of the Islanders', 42, 44, 251,
    264 n.1
'The origin of the O'Deans', 40, 42, 251
O'Shaugnesy, 48
Ossian, Poems of, by James MacPherson,
    19
Our Fellows' Play, 2, 25, 26, 40–1, 79
Ovid, 230

Pakenham, Lady Catherine, *see*
    Wellington, Kitty Pakenham, Duchess
    of,
Palace School, 43, 275 n.4
Palladio, Andrea, 124
Pamela, 22, 245
Paris: as juvenile source, 19; Brontës'
    attitude to, 21; Charlotte's ambition to
    visit, 67; capital of Frenchy Land in
    the Glass Town Saga, 55, 58, 62, 67,
    213; retreat of revolutionaries in the
    Angrian Legend, 162, 183, 190;
    Caroline Vernon's education in, 195,
    197–8
Park, Mungo, 20
Parry, Arthur, *see* Ardrah, Marquis of
Parry, Captain Sir William Edward, 20,
    28; as Emily's chief man in The
    Young Men's Play, 248, 28, 30, 34;
    King of Parry's Land, 32, 62, 63, 80,
    85, 270–1 n.15; supports his son
    Ardrah against Zamorna, 150, 278
    n.25
Parry's Land (or Parrisland), 32–3, 47,
    (description of) 63, 157, 158
Passing Events: discussion of, 149–52;
    as evidence of Branwell's influence,
    146, 212; Louisa Vernon in, 159;
    Mina Laury in, 166; Methodism
    satirized in, 171; Mary Percy as
    mother in, 176; Caroline Vernon first
    introduced in, 195; lack of structure

in, 211; visual description in, 234;
other refs, 256, 292 n.8
Pauline Louisada, *see* Ellrington, Lady
Paulina Louisada
Peel, Sir Robert, 47, 48, 116, 134, 265
n.15, 17; transposed into the juvenilia,
50, 51, 55
A Peep Into A Picture Book: Marian
Hume's death explained in, 112, 275
n.2; structure of, 117; Zamorna
described in, 118, 277 n.3, 295 n.42;
Fidena described in, 127, 296 n.52;
other references, 96, 255
Pelham, Sir Robert Weaver, 112
Pendlebrow, 126
Pendleton, 178, 187, 285 n.35
Peninsular Wars, 20, 24, 47, 49, 113,
266, n.10, 280 n.7
Pequene, City of, 125
Percy, Miss, *see* Ashworth, Miss
Percy, Alexander (alias Rogue; later Lord
Ellrington and Duke of
(Northangerland):
    summary of role in juvenilia of, 2;
    Branwell's creation of 'Rogue', 17,
        80, 91;
    first appearance in Charlotte's
        manuscripts of, 81, 83;
    relationship of Zamorna and, 2,
        131—3, 135, 162—4, 182;
    leader of rebellions, 8, 109;
    alter-ego of, 86;
    early career of, 97, 99—102,
        104—5, 162—4, 181—2;
    marriages of, 101—2, 181—2, 248;
    dual personality of, 99—100;
    atheism of, 241;
    becomes Lord Ellrington, 92;
    becomes Earl of Northangerland,
        113, 125;
    victimisation of Marian Hume by,
        107, 108;
    aversion to male offspring, 102,
        107, 121, 127, 129, 182, 214,
        221, 248;
    relationship with his daughters,
        111, 154—5, 197;
    Zenobia and, 92, 149, 166;
    Louisa Vernon and, 159—60;
    political role of, 110 (as Prime
        Minister of Angria) 131—3,
        (subverts Verdopolis as 'Brother

Ashworth') 150—1, 278 n.25,
    (takes control of Verdopolis and
    declares a Republic) 151, 153,
    (defeat and exile of) 155, 157,
    160, 176, 189, 279 n.8;
    associates of, 162, 205, 248—9,
    271 n.10, 289 n.10;
    as a comic character in old age, 171,
    182, 195;
    prototype for Ashworth, 204—5;
    illustrations of, 100, 154, 194;
    other refs, 7, 72, 121, 122
Percy, Alexander (of West Riding of
Yorkshire), *see* Ashworth, Alexander
Percy, Edward: discussion of, 129, 219;
    early career of, 107, 129—30, 183,
    220; marriage of Maria Sneachi and,
    127, 129; antagonism towards his
    brother William, 174, 183;
    relationship with Zamorna, 129, 176,
    219; Angrian Minister for Trade, 174;
    prototype for later characters, 206,
    219, 221—4; other refs, 7, 101, 173,
    177
Percy, Edward Snr. ('Old Rogue'), 7, 80,
    181, 270 n.2
Percy, Lady Helen, 7
Percy, Henry, 7, 101, 107, 111, 163,
    182
Percy, Hermione Marcella, 121
Percy, Lady Maria Henrietta (née
    Wharton), 7, 101—2, 107, 182,
    205—6
Percy, Mary Henrietta, Duchess of
    Zamorna and Queen of Angria:
    introduction of, 111; appearance and
    character of, frontispiece, 112—14,
    119, 176—7, 207, (in middle-age)
    195; as Queen of Angria, 113, 123,
    148, 174, 185, 207; as future
    Empress, 120—1; as pawn in the
    relationship between her father and her
    husband, 2, 133, 135, 149, 152; dying
    at Alnwick, 151, 153, (on her death
    bed) 154, 155, 156, 163, 239; reunion
    with Zamorna, 157; concern for
    Northangerland, 160; Zamorna's
    neglect of, 165, 170, 176—7, 215,
    229; as mother, 176—7, 215; as
    prototype for Mary Ashworth, 206—7;
    other refs, 7, 102, 118, 126, 131, 153,
    182, 183, 279 n.8

Percy, Colonel Sir William: early career
      of, 129–30, 220; physical appearance
      and character of, 174, 206, 217, 238;
      army career of, 174, 183–4; as
      narrator, 175, 176, 180, 183, 226;
      relationship with his brother Edward,
      174, 183, 291 n.4; friendship with
      Charles Townshend, 174–5, 180,
      221; attempted seduction of Elizabeth
      Hastings by, 184–6; pursuit of Henry
      Hastings by, 188, 190; prototype for
      later characters, 206, 219, 221–4;
      other references, 7, 101, 277 n.35
Percy Hall, 101, 113, 142, 181, 205
Persia: characters study language of, 24,
      106, 108; used in juvenilia, 106, 243;
      Angria compared to, 240;
      Zoroastrianism as an Angrian source,
      243
Philomel, 58
Philosophers' Island, 92, 107, 143, 265
Pigtail, 41, 58, 67, 92
The Poetaster: inspirational poetry
      ridiculed in, 61, 267 n.12; Branwell's
      poetry mocked in, 65–6; Marquis of
      Douro and Marian Hume in, 72, 230;
      source of, 230, 260 n.36; Finic
      appears in, 272 n.9
Plato, 23
Polignac, Prince Jules de, 49
Polignes, Prince, 48, (source) 49
Ponden House, 21
Pope, Alexander, 22, 37, 65
Porteous, Dr, 127
The Post Office, 103–4, 108, 272 n.3,
      273 n.2
Pretty-foot, Monsieur, 62
Price, Mr, 105, 273 n.8

Quarterly Review, 106
Quashia Quamina, 248; early career,
      101, 214; a constant threat to Angria
      as leader of the Ashantees, 120, 132,
      133, 277 n.14; Angria invaded by,
      147–8; retreat of, 190–1; savage
      murder of 'Fitzarthur' by, 153; lust for
      Mary Percy of, 148; pursuit of
      Caroline Vernon by, 195, 197;
      planned extermination of, 120–1

'rare apes', see 'Rare lads'

'Rare lads', 62, 88, 89, 95, 248, 278
      n.25
Ratchford, Fannie Elizabeth: valuable
      pioneering work of, 4; confirmation of
      information on Branwell by, 6;
      disagreement on abandonment of Glass
      Town Saga with, 75–6, 269 n.6; on
      Shirley, Jane Moore and Emily Brontë,
      296 n.2
Ratten, 47
Reed, Mrs, 215, 218
Repton, Humphrey, 237
The Return of Zamorna, discussion of,
      156–7; Charlotte assets her
      independence from Branwell in, 211,
      212; Methodism satirized in, 171;
      structure of, 211, 231; joint narrators
      of, 175; other refs, 159, 170, 175,
      256, 281 n.1, 295 n.32
Reuter, Mademoiselle Zoraide, 215
Review of the causes of the late War, 252
Review of The Cheif Geni in Council,
      252, 294 n.11, 14
*Revi[e]w of the painting of the Spirit of
      Cawdor Ravine,* 252, 294 n.11
Rhymer, Henry, *see* Young Soult
Richardson, Samuel: influence of, 232,
      245, 289 n.4; Charlotte's need to avoid
      'Richardsonian multiplication', 245;
      Pamela, 22, 245; *Clarissa,* 21, 245; *Sir
      Charles Grandison,* 245; Harriet
      Byron, 245
Richton, Viscount, *see* Flower, Captain
      Sir John
Ripley Towers, 289 n.6
Rivaulx, Cross of, 166, 178, 234–5,
      (source) 282 n.3
Rivers, St John, 243, 295 n.33
Robinson, William, 188
Rochester, Mr, 18, 216, 222, 238, 244,
      259 n.21, 283 n.6
Roe Head, Miss Wooler's school: effect
      on Glass Town Saga of Charlotte's
      boarding at, 72–6; her superior
      knowledge at, 18, 241; conscientious
      pupil at, 73, 87; her experience
      widened by, 83, 89; she leaves, 79; her
      experience as a teacher at, 135,
      139–45, 178–9, 216–17, 242; her
      writing suffers at, 2, 73, 139, 169,
      175; concern for and comfort in the
      Angrian saga at, 157, 161, 212; move

to Dewsbury moor, 169, 283 n.3
Charlotte leaves for good, 171;
experiences transposed into later
writing, 208; other refs, 67, 187, 225,
292 n.7
'Roe Head Journal': discussion of,
139—45; Charlotte's frustration with
Branwell shown in, 147; she imagines
the effects of Mary Percy's death,
153—4; Angrian Peace described in,
157; Mary Percy's concern for
Northangerland in, 160; Jane Moore
introduced in, 175, 176;
autobiographical descriptions echoed in
juvenilia, 173, 178—9; plight of the
lonely governess revealed in, 169,
216—17; Charlotte's guilt about her
'world below' shown in, 228; her
visual imagination revealed in, 243;
manuscripts quoted and described
from, 148, 158, 169; other refs, 231,
246, 279 n.3
Rogue, Alexander, *see* Percy, Alexander
Roland, 206
Romalla, 126
A Romantic Tale, 29, 30—2, 55, 58,
251
Rome, ancient, 116
Rosa, Salvator, 237
Rosendale, Lord, *see* Sneachie, John
Augustus Jnr.
Rosier, Eugene, 132, 159, 248
Roslyn, Lady Flora, 116
Ross, Edward Tut, Marquis of Harlaw,
248, 271 n.15
Ross, Captain John, 20, 28; as Anne's
chief man in The Young Men's Play,
248, 28, 30, 32, 34, 62, 85; close
friend of Parry, 63; supports Parry's
son Ardrah against Zamorna, 150
Rossestown (or Ross's Town), 190
Rosslyn, James St Clair Erskine, Lord,
265 n.15, 273 n.4; transposed into
juvenilia, 50
Ross's Land (or Rossesland), 32, 157,
158, 176, 190
Roswal, 157
Rotunda, *see* Bravey's Inn
Rousseau, Jean-Jacques, 107
Rover, 151, 153, 156
Royal Academy, London, 135
Rundell, Mr, 88

Sadler, Michael, 43
Sahara Desert, 57
Sai-Too-Too, King of the Ashantees,
101, 92, 248
Saldanah Park, Adrianopolis, 127
Saragoza, The Maid of, 168, 237
Saunderson, Mr, 158, 281 n.8
Scar Chapel, Ingleside, 186
Scar House, 196, 216
A scene in my Inn, 252
Scene On The Great Bridge, 252
Scotland, references in juvenilia to, 75,
85, 119
Scott, Sir Walter: Brontë children's
access to, 21; Charlotte recommends
poetry and fiction of, 22; Emily's chief
man in the Islanders' Play, 43;
Charlotte influenced by, 83, 97,
180—1, 222, 232; allusions to, 18,
208, 260 n.39; *Hebrew Melodies,* 273
n.3; *History of the Emperor Napoleon,*
24; *Kenilworth,* 88; *The Pirate,* 272
n.5; *Tales of My Landlord,* 180—1;
The Vision of Don Roderick, 171
The Scrap Book, 251
S'Death (or King), Robert Patrick, 17,
86, 132, 151, 181, 205, 221, 248,
271 n.19, 289 n.10
The Search after Happiness, 54—5, 213,
241, 252, 294, n.6
Seaton, City of, 125
The Secret: discussion of, 107—8;
dating of, 274 n.14; suffering of
Marian Hume in, 111; Julia and
Edward Sydney quarrel in, 115;
Edward Percy first introduced in, 219;
other refs, 110, 128, 182, 215, 254,
272 n.3, 274 n.18, 282 n.26
Segovia, Augusta (or Maria) di, 7, 101,
113, 121, 181, 182, 205, 248, 285
n.3
Selden House, 176, 182
Senegal, 19
Senegambia, *see* Wellington's Land
Seringapatan, 50, 51, 55, (source) 265
n.16
Seymour, Earl, 118
Seymour, Mr, 109
Seymour, Cecilia, 130, 174
Shakespeare: First Folio in Ponden House,
21; allusions to, 22, 65, 68, 89, 117;
Charlotte recommends, 22, 88;

Hamlet, 22; *Henry VIII,* 22; *Julius Caesar,* 22; *Macbeth,* 22; *A Midsummer Night's Dream,* 22; *Othello,* 22, 291 n.8; *Richard III,* 22
Shelley, Percy Bysshe, 197, 260 n.39
Shelley, Lady, 281
Siddons, Mrs, 105
Sidgwicks of Stonegappe, 192, 193, 206, 208, 217–18, 290 n.19
Silence, 253, 267 n.3, 274 n.12
The Silver Cup A Tale, 252
Simpson, Jeremiah, *see* MacTerrorglen, Sir Jehu
Sinclair, Dr, 182
'Sir it is well known that the Geni', 38 (quoted in full), 252
Skeleton, 92
Smith, George, 3, 221, 224
Smith, Samuel, 104
Sneachie, Alexander, King of Sneachiesland (or Sneaky's Land): replaces Napoleon as Branwell's chief man in The Young Men's Play, 32–3, 34, 64; rebellion in kingdom of, 80; persuaded to accept his son Fidena's wife, 110; disowns his son Thornton, 127–8; supports Zamorna in war against Angria, 150; close friend of Wellington, 150, 281 n.8; echo in *Ashworth* of, 209; other refs, 7, 158, 276 n.20
Sneachie, Edith, Princess Royal of Sneachiesland, 7, 110, 116, 127
Sneachie, (or Sneachi), John Augustus, Duke of Fidena: character of, 220, 242–3; helps quell the rebellion in Sneaky's Land, 80; clandestine marriage to Lily Hart, 108–10; son of, 106, 110, 121; trusted friend of Marian Hume, 111–12; Zamorna and, 121, 122, 132; as leader of the Constitutionalists and Prime Minister of the Verdopolitan Union, 134; forced to resign, 278 n.25; supports Zamorna in war, 150, 153, 155; reorganizes Verdopolis, 158, 189; prototype, (for John De Capell in *Ashworth*) 220; (for St John Rivers) 242–3; other refs, 7, 127, 128, 271 n.15, 275 n.4
Sneachie, John Augustus Jnr., Marquis of Rosendale, 7, 106, 121, 274 n.13

Sneachie, Lady Maria, 7, 110, 116, 117, 127, 129, 160, 276 n.31
Sneachie, Thornton Wilkin, *see* Thornton, General
Sneak, Jerry, 88–9
Sneaky (also Sneachi or Sneachie), *see* Sneachie, Alexander
Sneaky's Land (or Sneachiesland), 32–3, 181, 190, 214; rebellion in, 80, 109
Snowe, Lucy, 187, 216, 230, 286 n.20, 292 n.7, 295 n.33
Sofala, 119, 272 n.9
Something about Arthur, discussion of, 88–90; manuscript of, 103, 271 n.11; mill attack in, 83; violent scenes in, 96; first hints of the Marquis of Douro's degenerating character in, 104; Douro's 'first love' in, 167; role of the narrator in, 226, 228–9, 230; other references, 85, 97, 108, 254
Sophocles, 22
Soult, Alexander (or Alphonse), Marquis of Marseilles, Duke of Dalmatia, *see* Young Soult
Southey, Robert, 22, 198–9, 203, 216, 227–8, 260 n.39; *Life of Nelson,* 22, 108
Speech of His Grace The Duke of Zamorna, 133, 255, 296 n.49
The Spell: discussion of, 118–20; building of Adrianopolis in, 123; fascination for Douro in, 196; Marquis of Douro's son dies in, 90; cause of Marian Hume's death reported in, 112; friendship of Douro and Edward Percy in, 129, 219; antagonism between Edward and William Percy in, 130; William Percy's marriage in, 130, 174; use of letters in, 180, 232; Repton-like descriptions in, 237; other refs, 220, 255, 272 n.9
Staël, Madame de, 23–4, 92
Stancliffe's Hotel: discussion of, 171–8; antagonism of William and Edward Percy in, 291 n.4; dispersal of mob by cavalry in, 206; realism in, 207; structure of, 211; narrator of, 226; anti-romanticism of, 229; 'Deep the Cirhala flows', 282 n.10; other refs, 180, 256, 284 n.20, 25, 31, 33, 285 n.37, 294 n.21, 295 n.28
Stancliffe's Hotel, 173, 174, 176

Stanhope, Dr, 127

Stanley, Edward, 116

St Clair, Earl, 97, 99, 101, 102, 134, 181, 247, 249, (source) 273 n.4

Steaton (or Steighton), Timothy, 129, 130, 221, 222, 292 n.8

Steighton, Captain, 107

Stephen, St, 242

St Helena, 19

St Michael's Cathedral, Verdopolis, 112, 123

Stonegappe, 192, 193, 217

Strafford, Lord, *see* Sydney Edward

Strange Events, 68, 253, 293 n.2

Strathelleraye, Duke of, *see* Wellington, Duke of

Strathelleraye, *see* Strathfieldsaye

Strathfieldsaye, 48, 50, 51, 55, (source) 265 n.13

Stuartville, 176

Stuartville Park, 173

Stumps, 32, 34, 59, 80

Stump's Land (or Isle), 33, 95, 104, 132, 133

Summerfield House, 173

The Swiss Artist, 252, 268 n.18, 294 n.12

Switzerland, 19

Sydenham Hills, 124, 126, 157, 178, 193

Sydney, Edward, Prince of York and, later, Lord Strafford, 7, 91−2, 93, 94, 95, 108, 115, 127, 153, 177

Sydney, Lady Julia, *see* Wellesley, Lady Julia

Tabby, *see* Ackroyd, Tabbitha

Tales of Flood and Field, by Malcolm, 24

Tales of the Genii, by Sir Charles Morell, 18, 241

Tales of the Islanders: discussion of, 42−52, 264 n.1, 2; link with Our Fellows' Play, 41; link with Young Men's Play, 55; evidence of Brontë partnership in, 62−3; caricature of Branwell in, 66; Duke of Wellington in, 24, 68, 209; adolescent love of Douro in, 92; early use of letters in, 24, 180; early interest in plot in, 211; two brothers in, 219; religious themes in, 241; other refs, 58, 72, 95, 250, 252−3, 259 n.11, 15, 261 n.52, 264

n.4, 5, 265 n.7, 9, 11, 14, 2, 266 n.1

Talleyrand, Prince de, 85

Tallii or (Taley), Chief Genius, 30, 32, 37, 85, 99

Tasso, Torquato, 22

Taylor, Mary: emigration to New Zealand, 30; evidence of Charlotte's school days from, 73, 75, 87, 144; Charlotte confides in, 74, 87, 208; Charlotte's visits to and from, 139, 183; Charlotte borrows French books from father of, 198

The Tea Party, 107, 108, 162, 254

Thackeray, William Makepeace, 197, 231

Theatre Royal, London, 105

'There was once a little girl and her name was Ane': discussion of, 11−12, 32; dating of, 258 n.1; other reference, 251

Thomson, James, 22

Thompson, J. H., 286 n.37

Thornton, 11, 13, 127

Thornton, Miss, *see* De Capell, Miss Amelia

Thornton Sneachie, General Wilkin (or Wilson): character of, 220; Yorkshire-like dialect of, 176; mysterious family past and early career of, 107, 127−8, 162, 214; friend and general of Zamorna, 122, 147, 157, 159; Lord Lieutenant of Calabar province, 125; marries Julia Wellesley, 160, 272 n.4; prototype for later character, 209, 220; other references, 7, 173, 175, 184

Thornton Hotel, 122, 128

Thunderbolt, 88

Thurstons of Darkwell Manor, 210−11

Tower of All Nations, 18, 31, 67, 93, 226, 235

Townshend, Charles (pseudonym of Charlotte): successor to Lord Charles Wellesley, 149; description of, 173−5; as cynical narrator, 149, 192, 225, 228−9, 231, 246; favourite subject of, 157, 161; narrative method of, 156, 158−9, 160, 171−6, 180; weariness of 'heroics', 182−3, 199; relationship with William Percy, 174−5, 180; attitude to elder brother Zamorna, 150, 159, 220, 229; links with later writing, 220−2, 226, 229;

other refs, 165, 188, 284 n.15; *see also* Wellesley, Lord Charles

Tracky, 34

The Tragedy and The Essay, 105, 254

Tree, Sergeant, 60, 62, 249

Tree, Captain (pseudonym of Charlotte), 249; as an early Glass Town author, 39, 57–8, 81, 96, 115, 225, 232, 270 n.2; antagonism between literary rival Lord Charles Wellesley and, 61, 101, 266 n.15; shoots Marquis of Douro, 89; other refs, 60, 62

Trill, 58

Tringia, 58

Trinity Cathedral, Adrianopolis, 127

A True Story, 252

Turner, Mrs, 204

'Twelves': possible source of, 18; origins as toy soldiers, 27; the original 'Young Men', founders of Glass Town, 31, 34, 84, 91, 92, 101; Wellesley replaces York as leader of, 32; Maimoune, protector of, 93

Two Romantic Tales, 250

United Service Journal, 24

Upperwood House, Rawdon, 204

'UT', poems signed as, 38–9

Verdopolis: Glass Town replaced by, 59; original name of, 59; description of, 93–5, 177; rebellion in, 79–80; society of, 83, 95, 105–6, 115–16, 117; Olympic Games, 84, 270 n.10, 99; Horse Race in, 88; Rotunda in, 162; Methodism in, 151, 171; exodus to Adrianopolis from, 123–4; newspapers in, 132, 133; opening of Parliament, 133, 134, 151; political strife in, 133–4, 149, 278 n.25; becomes a Republic, 150–1, 159; Angria threatened by, 147; recaptured by Constitutional troops, 155, 157–8; Charlotte's visions at Roe Head of, 144; London and, 189, 205; other refs, 81, 113, 127, 132, 166, 173, 176, 187, 190, 205, 231, 283 n.7

Verdopolitan Union (successor to the Glass Town Confederacy): creation of Angria upsets political organisation of, 134; Fidena as Prime Minister of, 134; Angria expelled from, 147; Ardrah

replaces Fidena as Prime Minister of, 278 n.25; civil war in, 150, 249; landscape of, 177; Branwell's manuscript discusses history of, 162; geographical references to, 183, 186

Vernon, Caroline, 7; 1st appearance of, 160; education and seduction of, 195–8, 214, 216; narrative presentation of, 226–7, 238

Vernon (or Dance), Lord George, 7

Vernon (or Dance), Louisa (née Allen and formerly Marchioness of Wellesley): mistress of Alexander Percy, 101, 150, 155, 159–60; character of, 195, 215; *affaire* with Macara Lofty, 159, 171–3; with her daughter Caroline, 160, 215; mocked by Charles Townshend, 229; reappears in *Ashworth,* 205; other refs, 7, 116, 284 n.15

Verreopolis, *see* Verdopolis

Vesey (William Vesey Fitzgerald), 50, 265 n.15

Victorine, Lady Helen, *see* Gordon, Lady Helen Victorine

Virgil, 22–3, 65; *Aeneid,* 22; *The Works of Virgil,* 22–3

The Vision, 254

Vision Island, 43, 46, 55

A Visit to the Duke of Wellington's small palace situated on the Banks of the Indirce, 252, 266 n.3

Visits in Verreopolis: scandalmongering of Lord Charles Wellesley in, 61, 81; Young Soult mocked in, 64; Douro's romance with Marian Hume in, 61, 72; other references, 254, 266 n.8, 18, 260 n.41, 261 n.51, 268 n.21, 29, 292 n.7, 295 n.22

Vittoria, Princess, 32, 48, 262 n.14, 15

Waiting Boy, 27, 32

Walker, Amelia, 208, family of, 183

Wansbeck, 143

Warner, Charles, 128, 129

Warner, Revd Henry, 117, 127

Warner, Rufus, 69

Warner, Warner Howard, 249; Calvinism of, 18, 149; gift of second sight, 117, 156, 214–15, 259 n.21; resemblance to Peel, 55, 116; physical appearance of, 238; courtship and marriage of, 116—17, 247; as powerful family head, 128; friend and general of Zamorna, 122, 157, 176; critical of Zamorna, 149, 166, 174; authority on Angria, 123; Lord Lieutenant of Angria province, 125; finds Zamorna's dying son and vows vengeance, 153, 155; reorganizes affairs of state after the Angrian War, 158; as Prime Minister of Angria, 174, 191; quarrels with Elizabeth Hastings, 185; Branwell's manuscript about the life of, 163, 189; other references, 118, 151, 160, 166, 173, 193, 214, 268 n.27

Warner Hall, Angria, 173, 178

Warner Hills, 147, 151, 153, 178

Warner Hotel, Verdopolis, 117

Waterloo, 266 n.10

Waterloo Palace, 56, 63, 64, 88, 91, 105

Wellesley, Marchioness of, *see* Vernon, Louisa

Wellesley, Arthur, Marquis of Douro, Duke of Zamorna, King of Angria

and the future Emperor Adrian (pseudonym of Charlotte): source of, 24—5, 113, 240—1; supersedes Wellington as the focus of Charlotte's writing, 2, 46, 72, 89;

early pseudonym of Charlotte, 38, 58, 62, 115, 228;

antagonism between Lord Charles Wellesley and, 97, 119, 219, 293 n.21;

superior talents of, 59, 68, 75, 81, 105, 107;

as patron of the arts, 59, 105, 120;

degenerating character of, 104, 111, 149, 150, 214;

Byronic character of, 112, 117—18, 119—20, 151, 155, 162, 196, 214;

marriages and *affaires* of, 7, 119, 143, 186, 214—15, 272 n.9; (and Marian Hume) 71—2, 80—1, 106—7, 112, 215, 230; (and Mina Laury) 89—90, 118, 164—8, 215; (and Mary Percy) 112, 135, 149, 152, 156, 157, 165, 176—7, 215, 239; (and Caroline Vernon) 160, 195—8;

ambiguous relationship between Alexander Percy and, 2, 102, 121, 131—5, 151—2, 162—4, 176, 182, 195, 198, 278 n.25;

relationship of, (and Young Soult) 64, 106, (and Zenobia) 71, 117, (and Fidena) 108, 110, 132, 243, (and Quashia) 148, 248, (and Thornton) 127, 162, (and Warner) 116, (and Edward Percy) 129, 219, (and Hartford) 166;

becomes Duke of Zamorna, 113;

future as Emperor Adrian planned, 120, 240;

becomes King of Angria, 122—3, (sun image) 239—41;

Angrian politics and, 132—5, (defeated in war) 147—51, (exiled) 151, (returns) 156—7, (unpopular in Angria) 176;

attempted assassinations of, 121, 190;

Charlotte's fascination for, 2, 140, 142, 165, 246;

change in Charlotte's attitude to, 171, 182, 193, 194, 229;

Charlotte's moral attitude to, 215, 228;

echoes in later writing of, 209, 243;

illustrations of, 60, 152

Wellesley, Arthur Jnr., 7, 177

Wellesley, Arthur Julius, Lord Almeida: source of name Almeida, 24; birth of, 106—7; nursed by Mina Laury, 90, 119; death of, 90, 112, 214; other references, 7, 121

Wellesley, Lord Charles Albert Florian (pseudonym of Charlotte): first mentioned in juvenilia, 46; supersedes Captain Tree as prose writer, 58; source of, 24; 'UT' and, 38; pets of, 58; disposition of, 59, 68; love of scandal, 59—61; as narrator, 68, 103—4, 122, 174—5, 220, 225—6, 246; as cynical narrator, 61, 72, 228—9, 230, 240; antagonistic commentator on his brother Marquis of Douro, 119—20, 215, 219—20, 228, 230; under guardianship of Thornton, 122, 128; becomes Charles Townshend, 2, 149; other references, 7, 35, 62, 247; *see also* Townshend,

Charles; *and, for his role in various stories, see separate manuscript titles*
Wellesley, Edward Howard, 7
Wellesley, Elizabeth (wife of Gerald), 7
Wellesley, Ernest Edward 'Fitzarthur', Baron Gordon, 7, 18, 119, 153, 214, 275 n.12
Wellesley, Victor Frederick Percy, Marquis of Arno, 7; as Prince Adrian Percy, 121
Wellesley, Revd Dr Gerald (Primate of Wellington's Land), 7, 118, 186; source, 118, 186
Wellesley, Julia: marriage and relationship of Edward Sydney and, 91—2, 108, 127; as Verdopolitan belle, 95, 120; marries Thornton, 127, 160, 162, 175, 272 n.4; characters teased by, 128, 160; echoes in later writing of, 209; other refs, 7, 75, 115, 159
Wellesley, Julius Warner di Enara, Earl of Saldanha, 7; as Alexander Ravenswood, 121
Wellesley, Lucy, 7, 186
Wellesley, Maria (or Irene), 7, 177
Wellesley, Richard, Marquis of, 7, 118, 160, 229
Wellesley, Lady Richard, 7
Wellesley, Rosamund, 7, 186, 196, 215, 216
Wellesley House, 116, 117, 177, 231
'"Well Etty" said I', 255, 294 n.10
'Well here I am at Roe-Head', 143, 255, 280 n.9, 291 n.14, 296 n.55, 60
Wellington, Arthur Wellesley, 1st Duke of: source for Charlotte's characters, 24—5, 53, 71, 113, 116, 118, 134, 155, 167, 177, 186, 280 n.7, 281 n.30; Mr Brontë's enthusiasm for, 24; transposed into the juvenilia as Charlotte's chief man, 24, 53, (in the Young Men's Play) 27—8, 30—2, 34, (in the Islanders' Play) 43, 46—52, (in the Glass Town Saga) 67, 68, 71, 80, 92—3, 102, (in the Angrian Legend) 130, 150, 158; role of *deus ex machina* in the early saga, 89, 107; role as protector of children, 101, 214; retainers of, 88; friends and associates of, 247—9, 281 n.8; gradually replaced by his sons, 2, 46, 59, 72;

superseded as a source by Byron, 118; source for later writing, 209, 290 n.21; other refs, 7
Wellington, Kitty Pakenham, Duchess of, 71; transposed into the juvenilia, 7, 108, 150, 167, 182
Wellington's Land (Wellingtonsland or Senegambia): Charlotte's favourite kingdom of the Glass Town Confederacy, 32—3, 142; English landscape of, 56, 112; Irish or 'Western' associations of, 167; Wellington's Glass Town in, 62, 110; Douro and Mina Laury meet in, 89; Alexander Percy's married life in, 101; Mary Percy's early life in, 112—3, 206; echoes in later writings, 205—6; other refs, 81, 107, 150, 162, 182, 186
Wentworth, Charles, 189, 283 n.7
Westbeach, 147
Wesleyan Chapel, Slugg Street, Verdopolis, 151
West, Miss: discussion of, 184—5; insight into human nature, 238, 286 n.21; prototype of Elizabeth Hastings, 184, 216; autobiographical source of, 186—7, 217; echoes in later writing of, 207, 218; narrative presentation of, 226—7; other ref., 286 n.17
West, General, 203, 204, 208—9, 245, 290 n.21
West, Arthur Ripley, 205, 209
Westall, Richard, 171
Westwood, 158
Wharton, Lord George, 206
Wharton, Maria Henrietta, *see* Percy, Lady Maria Henrietta
Wharton, Miss Mary, *see* Ashworth, Mrs Mary
White, Gilbert, 22
Wiggins, Patrick Benjamin, 117; Branwell satirized as, 16—17, 128—9, 276 n.28
Wilcox, Miss, 216
Wilson's Creek, 190
Wise, Thomas James, 4, 95, 96
Wolfe, Charles, *Remains,* 22
Wooler, Miss, 18, 83, 139, 169, 171, 208
Wordsworth, William, 13, 16, 22, 88, 260 n.39

Wuthering Heights, see Brontë, Emily
Wynne, Alicia, 223, 238

York, Duke of, *see* Brunswick, Frederick
York, Prince Edward of, *see* Sydney, Edward
Yorke, Hiram, 209
Yorkshire: transposed into Charlotte's writing, 58—9, 193, 195, 204; Yorkshiremen-like characters, 58—9, 63, 129, 193, 206, 207, 209; industrial descriptions, 58, 129, 177, 284 n.32; in Branwell's later writing, 211; in the early writing of Emily and Anne, 63; Mr Brontë's livings in, 13; Charlotte's reaction to climate of, 240; emigration from, 30; Yorkshire painters in juvenilia, 236; other refs, (Luddite Riots, Liversedge) 83, (Birstall) 87, 134, (Huddersfield) 144, 179, (Hopton, Calder River) 179, (Mirfield) 183, 192, (Leeds) 188, 209, (Skipton) 192, (Swarcliffe) 193, (Bradford) 209, (Rievaulx Abbey) 282—3 n.3; *see also* Yorkshire Dialect; Roe Head; Haworth
Yorkshire dialect, 35, 127, 193, 209
York Villa, 162
Young, Edward, *Night Thoughts on Life, Death and Immortality,* 229, 260 n.39
Young Man Naughty (Richard Naughten Mange), 61, 62, 67, 150, 153, 248, 278 n.25
Young Men's Magazine: source of, 20; manuscripts of, 267 n.1; script of, 74; *Branwell's Blackwood's Magazine,* 35, 36—7, 94, 213, 260 n.28, 34; *Blackwood's Young Men's Magazine,* 35, 36, 37—9, 47, 48, 268 n.18; *Young Men's Magazine,* 58, 62—8, 106, 229, 266 n.7, 15, 267 n.2, 3, 268 n.17, 269 n.4, 293 n.2; echoes in later writing, 209; art reviews in, 236, 294 n.11, 12; other refs, 92, 250—1

Young Men's Play: origins of, 25, 26; development of, 27—39; amalgamation with the Islanders' Play into the Glass Town Saga, 2, 53—6, 57, 59; tone of writing in, 96; other refs, 52, 64; see also *Young Men's Magazine* and 'Young Men Tongue'
'Young Men Tongue', 34—5, 41, 68, 95, 96, 132
Young Murat, 64
Young Napoleon, 64
Young Ney, 64
Young Soult, 'The Rhymer' (Branwell's pseudonym), 249; source of, 266 n.10; Branwell's association with, 65, 70, 85; Marquis of Douro's friendship with, 59, 64, 68, 106; Lord Charles Wellesley's (Charlotte's) ridicule of, 61, 64, 66; becomes Alphonse Soult, Marquis of Marseilles, Angrian Ambassador to Verdopolis, 106; future Duke of Dalmatia, 120; other refs, 36, 115, 132

Zamorna (province of Angria), 113, 125, 126, 128, 133, 147, 173
Zamorna, City of: capital of Zamorna Province, 125; enemy occupation of, 151, 153; succeeds Adrianopolis as centre of Angrian society, 177, ('Rose of Zamorna') 223; industrial and commercial centre, 174, 177, 180; landscape surrounding, 178—9; events in, 128, 133, 183; riot against Zamorna suppressed in, 176—8, 206; Elm Grove Villa in, 730; Stancliffe's Hotel in, 173; home of Elizabeth Hastings, 185, 187; other refs, 166, 291 n.4
Zamorna Palace, 127, 148, 160, 279 n.8
Zenobia, *see* Ellrington, Lady Zenobia
Zoilus, 65
Zorayda, 93; *see also* Etty, Zorayda
Zoroastrianism, 240

Haworth Church